I0866319

Beyond Suffering

Contemporary Chinese Studies

This series, a joint initiative of UBC Press and the UBC Institute of Asian Research, Centre for Chinese Research, seeks to make available the best scholarly work on contemporary China. Volumes cover a wide range of subjects related to China, Taiwan, and the overseas Chinese world.

Glen Peterson, *The Power of Words: Literacy and Revolution in South China, 1949-95*
Wing Chung Ng, *The Chinese in Vancouver, 1945-80: The Pursuit of Identity and Power*
Yijiang Ding, *Chinese Democracy after Tiananmen*
Diana Lary and Stephen MacKinnon, eds., *Scars of War: The Impact of Warfare on Modern China*
Eliza W.Y. Lee, ed., *Gender and Change in Hong Kong: Globalization, Postcolonialism, and Chinese Patriarchy*
Christopher A. Reed, *Gutenberg in Shanghai: Chinese Print Capitalism, 1876-1937*
James A. Flath, *The Cult of Happiness: Nianhua, Art, and History in Rural North China*
Erika E.S. Evasdottir, *Obedient Autonomy: Chinese Intellectuals and the Achievement of Orderly Life*
Hsiao-ting Lin, *Tibet and Nationalist China's Frontier: Intrigues and Ethnopolitics, 1928-49*
Xiaoping Cong, *Teachers' Schools and the Making of the Modern Chinese Nation-State, 1897-1937*
Diana Lary, ed., *The Chinese State at the Borders*
Norman Smith, *Resisting Manchukuo: Chinese Women Writers and the Japanese Occupation*
Hasan H. Karrar, *The New Silk Road Diplomacy: China's Central Asian Foreign Policy since the Cold War*
Richard King, ed., *Art in Turmoil: The Chinese Cultural Revolution, 1966-76*
Blaine R. Chiasson, *Administering the Colonizer: Manchuria's Russians under Chinese Rule, 1918-29*
Emily M. Hill, *Smokeless Sugar: The Death of a Provincial Bureaucrat and the Construction of China's National Economy*
Kimberley Ens Manning and Felix Wemheuer, eds., *Eating Bitterness: New Perspectives on China's Great Leap Forward and Famine*
Helen M. Schneider, *Keeping the Nation's House: Domestic Management and the Making of Modern China*

Beyond Suffering: Recounting War in Modern China

Edited by James Flath and Norman Smith

UBCPress · Vancouver · Toronto

21 20 19 18 17 16 15 14 13 12 11   5 4 3 2 1

Printed in Canada on FSC-certified ancient-forest-free paper (100% post-consumer recycled) that is processed chlorine- and acid-free.

Library and Archives Canada Cataloguing in Publication

Beyond suffering: recounting war in modern China / edited by James Flath and Norman Smith.

(Contemporary Chinese studies, 1206-9523/1925-0177)
Includes bibliographical references and index.
ISBN 978-0-7748-1955-8 (bound); 978-0-7748-1956-5 (pbk.)

1. China – History, Military – 20th century. 2. War and society – China – History – 20th century. 3. China – History, Military – 19th century. 4. War and society – China – History – 19th century. I. Flath, James A. (James Alexander). II. Smith, Norman (Norman Dennis). III. Series: Contemporary Chinese studies

e-book ISBNs: 978-0-7748-1957-2 (PDF); 978-0-7748-1958-9 (epub)

Canada

UBC Press gratefully acknowledges the financial support for our publishing program of the Government of Canada (through the Canada Book Fund), the Canada Council for the Arts, and the British Columbia Arts Council.

This book has been published with the help of a grant from the Canadian Federation for the Humanities and Social Sciences, through the Aid to Scholarly Publications Program, using funds provided by the Social Sciences and Humanities Research Council of Canada, and with the help of the K.D. Srivastava fund.

Printed and bound in Canada by Friesens
Set in Helvetica Condensed and Minion by Artegraphica Design Co. Ltd.
Copy editor: Robert Lewis
Proofreader: Kate Spezowka
Cartographer: Eric Leinberger

UBC Press
The University of British Columbia
2029 West Mall
Vancouver, BC V6T 1Z2
www.ubcpress.ca

For Diana

Contents

Tables and Figures

Tables

Figures

Preface: Lisbon, Xuzhou, Auschwitz: Suffering as History

Timothy Brook

St. Paul's Hospital in the city of Gui'de was the site of an incongruous celebration on New Year's Day 1939. Gui'de (now Shangqiu) sits on the flatlands of Henan, south of the Yellow River. The first major city to the east is Xuzhou, where, for the first five months of 1938, Chinese forces had fought to resist the Japanese invasion. As long as the battling forces focused on Xuzhou, Gui'de lay far enough away to escape the turmoil. But when the Chinese defence of Xuzhou collapsed on 14 May 1938, the region was plunged into what Diana Lary has called "a ghastly limbo."[1] Gui'de was one of the innumerable places to suffer the consequences.

The invaders arrived in Gui'de two weeks after the fall of Xuzhou. For the next three months, they sealed the city and stripped it of its assets.[2] The one institution they could not dispossess was St. Paul's Hospital, which medical missionaries from the Anglican Church of Canada had founded in 1912. Like foreign residents elsewhere in the territories that came under Japanese occupation, the Canadians remained at their post as the Japanese advanced, demarcating the hospital as a safety zone. Over 3,000 local people, most of them women, took refuge there. They suffered, but as survivors, not victims. St. Paul's had to close its refugee camp at the end of the summer, but it continued to function as the one hospital to which Chinese felt they could safely turn for medical help.

As 1938 came to an end, the situation in Gui'de was still grim. Dr. H.H. Gilbert, the director of the hospital as well as the chair of the Kweiteh [Gui'de] Area Relief Committee, reported back to Canada that few Christians were in the mood to celebrate Christmas: "How could you expect the people to throw themselves whole-heartedly into celebrations when their country had been lost to an enemy invader, they themselves enslaved in the reaches of a military ogre, and their fellow countrymen in other parts of the land fighting and dying and suffering in defence of their homeland!" Despite all that they had suffered, people converged on the hospital from all over the city and the surrounding countryside on New Year's Day 1939 to present the Anglican missionaries with memorials of gratitude for the work the hospital staff had done to ease their suffering. Some of these memorials were carved into wood and others written on silk, but five were incised into stone steles two metres tall. Two of the stones were presented by delegations from the North Suburb – one of them from the

Muslims of the North Suburb – and the other three were donated by elders of the villages to the north, west, and east of the hospital. One was marked with the crest of the Henan Diocese of the Anglican Church, and another carried a Union Jack and a Red Cross flag painted in colour. The steles were erected at the entrance leading from the forecourt into the hospital so that all who came to the hospital would know what the missionaries had done. "Our Chinese friends," Gilbert wrote home, "tell us that these stones will last for about 800 years."[3]

Gilbert's Chinese friends were mistaken. They could not have guessed that these memorials would be removed after the Communist state was established in 1949. Once foreign missionaries were excoriated as agents of foreign imperialism, their story – in which the people's redemption came from hospital staff who were not Chinese, much less Communists – was the wrong story to tell. Shangqiu Number One Municipal People's Hospital, as St. Paul's is known today, acknowledges its founding by Canadian missionaries, but nothing further is said or known.[4] The hospital has been absorbed into an official discourse that is now modernist rather than anti-imperialist. The building of the modern state, not the compassion of fellow human beings nor the rescue of Chinese from Japanese, is the storyline now.

Suffering is a universal condition, bound as we all are to the dazzlingly brief experience that is the life of one person. But one does not have to be Buddhist to recognize birth and death as the wellspring of suffering. Suffering comes in many intermediate guises as well. There is the suffering that arises from living in a natural world made unstable by physical forces – flood and earthquake, for example. There is social suffering, which is produced by the norms and practices that constitute societies and which may range from discrimination to poverty to racism.[5] There is the political suffering that states impose, from policing to disenfranchisement to torture. And there is wartime suffering, the subject of this volume. For soldiers, wartime suffering means combat injury and death in the first instance but also fear and anxiety, brutalization and dehumanization, and extraction from the routines that constitute normal life. To civilians, war brings everything the people of Gui'de had to go through, from the "collateral damage" of armed combat to the broader impact of conflict on food, shelter, and security.

Most readers of this book will have no personal experience of wartime suffering. The reports we see in the media are of war waged elsewhere – in Iraq, in Afghanistan, in the Congo. For us, war is never fought close to home. And just as it is kept at a distance in space, so too do we think of the suffering of war as separated from us in time – archaic, almost atavistic. When we do not locate grand suffering elsewhere, we assign it to the past, to a time when the technical and moral breakthroughs we associate with modernity did yet work their magic. Desperate poverty, social degradation, mass starvation, and total war are for most of us scenes in the theatre of another age. They are offences to what we understand as modernity. The promise of the modern is to provide governmental institutions, legal guarantees, and technical capacities that were unavailable in earlier times to remove the conditions that produce suffering. Modernity is supposed to banish all suffering, almost to transcend the physical limits of life itself.

None of these promises is true, of course, least of all the promise to end war. What modernity has actually done is to enhance the human cost of warfare, increase the scale and frequency at which armed aggression is committed, and move it elsewhere. Modern warfare mocks modernity's false claim that it has come to benefit humankind. It also mocks modernity's erasure of the theologies of suffering that have consoled the victims of state power for centuries. Except for the more virulent strains of the Near Eastern monotheisms of Christianity and Islam that survive in parts of the United States and the Middle East, most people in the world today do not believe that suffering will be corrected or rewarded in an afterlife. We rely instead on the illusory protections of modernity itself. Keeping suffering carefully elsewhere and in the past relieves most of us of the need to come to terms with the brutality of the modern condition.

Not so the people of Gui'de in 1938. Modernity for those living in the penumbra of Xuzhou meant having to deal with soldiers bearing modern arms and arriving on modern trucks and modern railways to impose the modern dream of economic imperialism. What modernity brought them was the suffering of total war.

Reflecting on the experience of evil, moral philosopher Susan Neiman has identified two poles of suffering. One she calls "Lisbon," the other "Auschwitz." Lisbon stands for the purely arbitrary catastrophe of the great earthquake on 1 November 1755, which flattened the city of Lisbon, followed by a tsunami and fires in which a third of its population of 275,000 lost their lives. The deaths of 90,000 happened because of a shift of tectonic plates and had no human author, no human intent. Auschwitz, the site of the notorious death camp that the Nazi regime operated between 1940 and 1945 to exterminate Jews and other undesirables, names suffering in the absence of natural causes, suffering that is produced by human intent alone.[6] Lisbon victims have no one to blame for their suffering. Human agents can make suffering of the Lisbon type worse – officials who siphon relief funds into their own pockets rather than succour the starving, or builders who fail to meet safe construction minima in order to enrich themselves (as in the great Sichuan earthquake of May 2008, after which it was discovered that corrupt contractors had pocketed some of their budget intended for metal reinforcing rods for school roofs) – but their effects are at the margin. The suffering at Auschwitz belongs to an entirely different category. There is no ambiguity about blame. The guards, the prison authorities, and their superiors may have constructed a logic that permitted them to commit evil and insulated their consciences from moral reflection, but their acts were undertaken with the intent to cause suffering and death. Without that intent, there would have been no suffering. The causation was entirely intentional and entirely direct.

What happened in the Xuzhou region in 1938 lies at neither of these poles. I propose it here as a third type of suffering, closer to Auschwitz than to Lisbon yet entailing very different consequences for historical memory – more a third corner of a triangle of suffering than a point midway between the other two. Like Auschwitz, Xuzhou was the product of war and impossible without war. The Japanese attack on this region midway between the Yangzi Valley and the Yellow River flood plain had clear military objectives. These included linking the two separate Japanese invasions at Shanghai and Beijing and driving back the Chinese army from the eastern zones of the country, and in this sense the attack was part of what "normally" happens in war. But the scale of civilian suffering far exceeded what could be deemed militarily necessary for the Japanese army to advance. In this sense, Xuzhou had something of Auschwitz about it, for the scale of suffering it produced signalled an intent far exceeding military necessity. Some Japanese commanders believed that it was vital to their campaign to impress on the Chinese people the peril of resistance if their occupation of China was to succeed, and so there may have been at least a conscious unwillingness to diminish civilian suffering and perhaps even the intention to ensure that civilians suffered on a significant scale. The intent was not extermination, as it was at Auschwitz, but the Japanese army's indifference to personal suffering conveyed an impression of something beyond "collateral damage."

Xuzhou is further distinguished by what followed: the Chinese decision to breach the dike holding back the Yellow River farther west at Huayuankou. The military logic at the time was that, Xuzhou having fallen, the Japanese army had to be stopped at all costs, if only temporarily, in order to give Chinese troops a breathing space to regroup and reorganize. Xuzhou was not submerged, as it sat at a location that the flood waters could not reach, nor was Gui'de, as it happens, but vast tracts of farmland in the regions west and south of these cities were submerged. The vast inundation was not Lisbon, for it was human agency, not nature itself, that provoked this violent natural disruption. But the effects were masked, even excused, by the necessities of war. Most who died were unaware that nature was not to blame. Indeed, the first reports – concocted by Chinese military propaganda – were that the Japanese, not the Chinese army, had bombed the dike as a form of environmental warfare. Once this camouflage was abandoned, the Chinese leadership reverted to the argument that any measure was justified to slow the Japanese advance. The number who died, loosely estimated now at half a million, exceeded the toll in Lisbon (estimated at 90,000), as one would expect when comparing a modest eighteenth-century city with a large twentieth-century farming region, but the two events were roughly equivalent in terms of the percentage of people whose lives, if they preserved them, were disrupted. Besides those who died downriver from the breach, half a million were left homeless and many more were forced into flight.[7]

The breaching of the dike and the defeat at Xuzhou are normally treated as separate events in the history of the war, the one certainly following the other but not intimately linked. If we put them together as two sides of the same coin of suffering that civilians had to pay not just for the Japanese invasion but for the Chinese defence as well, Xuzhou emerges even more distinctively as a type of suffering that is neither Auschwitz nor Lisbon. It becomes a third case, in which there is neither a clear author to take the blame, nor no author at all, but several authors among whom blame cannot so readily be distributed.

Diana Lary, whose work on wartime suffering inaugurated scholarly inquiry into the problem and inspired the conference at which the essays in this volume were first presented, has been careful not to use her research on Chinese suffering during the Japanese invasion, at Xuzhou and elsewhere, as an occasion for apportioning blame. Her focus has been on those who suffered rather than on those who caused suffering.[8] In the rush to assign blame or, worse perhaps, in the rush to fold all that suffering into a narrative of sacrifice for the nation that prevailed in the end, there is a danger that the burden of the war for those who actually experienced it will be diminished or forgotten. Many at the time may have conceived of their suffering in national terms, yet their suffering preceded the narratives attached to it. Their suffering therefore deserves to be recorded separately from the tales it is used to tell if their experience is to survive as an episode in the history of the powerless, not just as a stand-in for someone else's (or something else's) triumph.

Diana Lary has also observed, however, that cataloguing suffering does not necessarily lead toward historical analysis. In the case of the Japanese invasion, it seems paradoxically to have had the opposite effect, to block an approach to what she has called "a larger meaning." As she and her co-editor of *The Scars of War,* Stephen MacKinnon, have noted, reciting the atrocities of the period can quickly leave the historian feeling "caught within a mesh of vague generalities about the banality of evil, the cruelty of the Japanese, and the horror of war. We are somewhere between windy generalization and deep despair about the human condition. It seems so difficult to say anything meaningful about suffering that it is easier to ignore it or push it aside.[9]

What are we to do with this deficit of meaning? The medical anthropologist Paul Farmer, who has dealt with suffering firsthand as the co-director of the Clinique Bon Saveur in rural Haiti, suggests that suffering evades meaning by virtue of a kind of existential gap. We may be able to achieve consensus on what constitutes suffering, yet the suffering of others has a lesser degree of reality than the suffering of ourselves.[10] When this is not the case, as particularly for Auschwitz, it is because the event is remembered by a group whose identity is constructed at least in part on the conviction that the victims of suffering are "us." The suffering that real people experienced then is transmuted into something that has meaning now; in the case of Auschwitz, this meaning derives from what it signifies to be Jewish or gypsy, or even simply human, in the present. This is how we tend to deal with the difficulty that Lary and MacKinnon have noted about suffering, which is that it is "hard to ennoble except through transcendent narrative."[11] Ennoblement may be essential for commemoration to take place, but there is always the danger that the sufferings of others are exploited to push forward agendas to which they themselves might have been hostile and that have little connection with how they coped with their actual experience. The ennobled people and the transcendent nation come after the fact.

When the people of Gui'de gathered on New Year's Day to honour those who protected them in a time of great suffering, they ennobled nations that were not their own. The nations represented in the commemorative inscriptions they presented to the staff of St. Paul's Hospital were Great Britain, and indirectly Canada (which did not yet have a flag independent of the British Empire), and Switzerland (the Red Cross flag in reverse). One could argue that these were signs that had to be used because the Chinese nation could not speak in its own name under military occupation. Property marked with such talismans was beyond the reach of the Japanese. Only by calling on the names of third-party nations such as these, which the Japanese had not yet been able to declare illegal (this would happen in December 1941), could the Chinese stand up to the invader.

Decoding the signs on the steles to obtain this sort of nationalist interpretation may capture some of the sentiment in the air in 1939, but it pretends to know better than the people of Gui'de how they suffered and why they chose to thank the Canadians. If I am arguing for the existential validity of suffering, I do not wish to imply that the Chinese military should not have done everything in their power to resist, nor deny that the Japanese army should not have been there in the first place. My point is that neither assertion is sufficient to give meaning to the experience of the millions of ordinary people who found themselves caught between two states locked in deadly combat. Simply by surviving, the people of Gui'de did indeed keep their nation alive and resist its being swallowed into the Japanese empire. Additionally, this suffering may have strengthened their attachment to the Chinese nation that emerged after the war.[12] Ennoblement may have helped some to make sense of their suffering and provided their descendants with a way to make sense of their legacy. But ennoblement is not a tool for historical analysis. Historians need to be aware of the national valences that attach to suffering, as these animate mentalities of suffering and produce powerful effects. But we also need to incorporate what those who suffered understood of their own experience at the time, lest the retrospective imperatives of national commemoration take us further from the real causes of suffering, in many of which the nation is closely implicated, then as now.

Equally important for acknowledging suffering as history is to ask not just what causes suffering but also what suffering causes. Those who suffer do not simply suffer and do nothing. They act, both to survive at the time and to respond afterward to their traumas. They also leave traces of their suffering, which later generations may revive and re-enact through narratives of transferred victimization, thereby provoking further cycles of action. The capacity of suffering to come back and produce other effects may therefore be the strongest argument in favour of writing suffering into history. As Lary and MacKinnon suggest at the end of their introduction to *The Scars of War*, wartime suffering may eventually help to explain the violence of the postwar decades, from the virulent settling of scores in the early 1950s right down to the Cultural Revolution. The capacity of suffering to have delayed effects reminds us of the importance of integrating suffering into our accounts of the past, lest we fail not just to see the subjectivities driving people's actions but also to detect the consequences to which these subjectivities may have led.

Lisbon is where the 1755 earthquake is remembered; its memory extends no further. A massive statue of then prime minister Sebastião de Melo, later Marquis of Pombal, who built today's Lisbon on the ruins of the old, recalls 1755 but as a history of reconstruction rather than of suffering. This suffering, having no author, has become distant and abstract. Auschwitz has spawned a far larger and more inclusive memory, in part because it lies in the recent past and concerns all who are disturbed by war and atrocity, in part because it has been appropriated by a Zionist political identity, but most of all because it has an author who can be blamed and an intent that cannot be denied.

Xuzhou is now largely forgotten except by professional historians and by some who live in the region. Largely forgotten too is the internationalism that moved foreigners to stay behind in the cities and towns, like Gui'de, that came under attack and to do something to relieve the suffering of ordinary people in a time of war.[13] Xuzhou has a complicated history that cannot be untangled neatly in any one party's favour or mobilized to any one party's discredit. It is a more complicated case than either Lisbon or Auschwitz, and its memory is more difficult to organize and use. But if we forget Xuzhou, we forget what the violence of war does and what civilians can be made to suffer in the name of warring states. Only by recognizing suffering as history's proper subject, not just its byproduct, as Diana Lary has done, can we begin to understand what happens in places such as this.

Notes

1 Diana Lary, "A Ravaged Place: The Devastation of the Xuzhou Region, 1938," in *The Scars of War*, ed. Diana Lary and Stephen MacKinnon (Vancouver: UBC Press, 2001), 106.

2 Bernard T.L. Tseng, "State of the Church in the Diocese of Honan, China, during and after the War" (received 14 December 1946), Anglican Church of Canada Archives: Missionary Society of the Church of Canada, Leonard A. Dixon Files, China Files, Box 79.

3 H.H. Gilbert, "Annual Report" (1 December 1938 to 30 November 1939), Anglican Church of Canada Archives: Missionary Society of the Church of Canada, Leonard A. Dixon Files, China Files, Box 77.

4 See the brief overview at http://www.sqsyy.com/yyjj.asp, the website of the Shangqiu Number One Municipal People's Hospital.

5 On social suffering, see Arthur Kleinman, Veena Das, and Margaret Lock, eds., *Social Suffering* (Berkeley: University of California Press, 1997).

6 Susan Neiman, *Evil in Modern Thought: An Alternative History of Philosophy* (Princeton, NJ: Princeton University Press, 2002).

7 Diana Lary, "Drowned Earth: The Strategic Breaching of the Yellow River Dyke, 1938," *War in History* 8, 2 (April 2001): 206.

8 For example, in the introduction to *The Scars of War*, she and her co-editor Stephen MacKinnon innovatively position Chinese suffering during the Japanese occupation in the context not of Japanese brutality but of the century of violence preceding the Japanese occupation. They note that blame should be assigned in cases of specific acts of violence but not generalized in such a way that deeper explanations are avoided. See Diana Lary and Stephen MacKinnon, "Introduction," in *The Scars of War*, ed. Diana Lary and Stephen MacKinnon (Vancouver: UBC Press, 2001), 6-8.

9 Ibid., 14. The evasiveness of "suffering" as a historical topic is underscored by its absence from the index of *The Scars of War*.

10 Paul Farmer, "On Suffering and Structural Violence: The View from Below," in *Social Suffering*, ed. Arthur Kleinman, Veena Das, and Margaret Lock (Berkeley: University of California Press, 1997), 261.

11 Lary and MacKinnon, "Introduction," 14.

12 As the anthropologist of Tamil society E. Valentine Daniel has noted, those who suffer by virtue of their national identity tend to identify the nation as their refuge and to align

their individual suffering with the suffering of the nation. Daniel also makes the interesting argument that the recursion to national identity is an "aestheticizing impulse" in that it promises "to bring forth order out of disorder, mold form from that in which form is absent." E. Valentine Daniel, "Suffering Nation and Alienation," in *Social Suffering,* ed. Arthur Kleinman, Veena Das, and Margaret Lock (Berkeley: University of California Press, 1997), 309-11.

13 The effect of relief on the commemoration or narration of calamity is a topic that would benefit from further reflection. As Diana Lary notes in her conclusion to "Drowned Earth," 207, the failure of most Chinese civilians to receive relief during or after the Japanese occupation has made their suffering even less accessible to us now.

Beyond Suffering

Introduction

James Flath and Norman Smith

In the spring of 2009 Chinese audiences lined up in record numbers for two new films on the 1937 Nanjing Massacre and engaged in widespread debate over their merits. Florian Gallenberger's *John Rabe* and in particular Lu Chuan's *City of Life and Death (Nanjing! Nanjing!)* were deemed remarkable for their realistic accounts of the massacre and bold portrayals of both Chinese victims and their Japanese victimizers as something beyond the stock heroes and villains who have dominated media representations, including films, in the past. But as one blogger wrote, beyond stirring deep emotions, *City of Life and Death* still failed to engage the underlying historical problems:

> *City of Life and Death* is practically a science fiction movie. Don't get me wrong, I'm not saying that the Nanjing Massacre was imagined ... But we're in need of a "truth" that is not just a Yes or No answer. We also need a Why and a How, a Who and a When, and only then will we be able to ground our reflections and discussions in the truth, only then will the judgments and conclusions we reach have real value and meaning. We want history to be a mirror, but when history is unclear, what can it reflect?[1]

Leaving aside philosophical debates over "truth" and the uses of history, historians should at least be able to agree with this film critic on the need to recount more fully the complex nature of the chaos and suffering of war, as well as the forms of memory that it inspires.

And there is much to remember. China's "modern history" is recognized as having begun with the Opium War of 1839-42 and as progressing through the Second Opium War of 1856-60, the Taiping, Nian, and Muslim rebellions during the 1850-60s, the Sino-French War of 1884, the Sino-Japanese War of 1894-95, the Boxer Uprising of 1900, the 1911 Revolution, and the many conflicts falling under the "warlord era" of the 1920s. Most traumatic of all was the Anti-Japanese War (War of Resistance) of 1937-45, which was presaged by the Japanese occupation of China's Northeast in 1931 and followed by the Civil War of 1945-49 and its antecedent Cross-Strait Crisis.[2] As Diana Lary and Stephen MacKinnon suggest, "If looked at cumulatively as a cycle of officially sanctioned violence that began in the mid-nineteenth century, Chinese experience with the arbitrary violence and destruction of war has no European parallel."[3] And yet compared to our knowledge of the European context, our knowledge regarding the toll of that violence and its continuing influence on Chinese society still presents us with innumerable unanswered questions.

What we do know about Chinese conflict and suffering is largely informed by the frameworks of social, political, and cultural history. Joseph Esherick's pioneering study *The Origins of the Boxer Uprising* (1988), for example, treats the Boxer conflict primarily as a problem of ecology, economy, popular culture, and sectarianism. Edward McCord's *Power of the Gun* (1993) and Arthur Waldron's *From War to Nationalism* (2003) provide more complete sketches of the operational side of Chinese militarism during the 1920s, but their works are also grounded in questions of politics and ideology. Studies of the Anti-Japanese War, from Edgar Snow's *Red Star over China* (1937) to J.H. Boyle's *China and Japan at War, 1937-1945: The Politics of Collaboration* (1972) and Parks Coble's *Facing Japan: Chinese Politics and Japanese Imperialism, 1931-1937* (1991), largely bypass logistical and operational questions to emphasize the Communist Party-Guomindang (CCP-GMD) struggle for supremacy. The end of the Cold War has resulted in national and international political realignments throughout East Asia, and with those realignments priorities have begun to shift to the politically sensitive subject of memory, especially as it relates to Japanese war responsibility and the Nanjing Massacre. Notable scholarly works include collected volumes by Joshua Fogel, ed., *The Nanjing Massacre in History and Historiography* (2000) and Bob Tadashi Wakabayashi, ed., *The Nanking Atrocity, 1937-38: Complicating the Picture* (2007) as well as Sheila Miyoshi Jager and Rana Mitter's *Ruptured Histories: War, Memory, and the Post-Cold War in Asia* (2007).[4]

The benefit of this past scholarship is that we have grown to understand warfare in China as being a socially, culturally, and politically integrated phenomenon. At the same time, however, we are left with a less than complete understanding of militarism – which is problematic since, as Hans van de Ven indicates, if we fail to understand battles and wars, we will inevitably fail to understand the history on which they weigh so heavily.[5] A great deal of work remains to be done on this particular front, but since those remarks were published in 1996 we have begun to see a gradual turn toward the much neglected problem of militarism, warfare, and the suffering that it produces. In particular, *Scars of War: The Impact of Warfare on Modern China* (2001), edited by Diana Lary and Steven MacKinnon, set an example by exposing warfare in China as raw and unfiltered experience.

Given that wartime violence occurs amid the most chaotic of circumstances and leaves only the barest of documentary traces, we have to accept that we may never achieve definitive accounts of either events or victims. In this volume, contributors address incidents pertaining to the Boxer Uprising, the Warlord Era, the Anti-Japanese War, and the Cross-Strait Crisis, yet every incident brought to light implicitly suggests countless others in need of further analysis. Such is the knowledge of China's military history that major incidents, pivotal campaigns, and even entire wars remain only vaguely outlined. On a more human scale, we may never fully know something as basic as how many people died in the conflicts that have come to define the latter years of the Qing Dynasty and the first half of the twentieth century, much less know all of their stories. But if we are to gain a deeper understanding of how China has been affected by both war-inflicted suffering and memory, we have to provide some account, however fragmentary, of those who experienced or inflicted that suffering and whose legacies inspired earlier generations of remembrance as well as present-day commemoration. As Vera Schwarcz writes in her study of grief in China, "In order to fathom the hearts of strangers in pain, we must accept the fractured vision (and versions) of those who have known social suffering first hand. Fragments of experience must suffice in place of encompassing theories about the nature of pain."[6] Many of the hardships described in this volume have scarcely registered against the chaotic backdrop of modern Chinese history, but as Schwarcz suggests, it is precisely incidents like the massacres at Blagovoschensk and Xiaogan or the trials faced by Jiangxi Number One Children's Home and Lingnan University discussed in this volume that bring us closer to understanding the larger problem of war and suffering in modern China.

With contributions ranging in topic from late-imperial military theory to massacres, refugees, social-reform movements, monuments, and memory, the current volume inherits the social, political, and memorial stances that have defined earlier scholarship while also extending further recognition to the experience of war, the suffering of it, and the ways that it is remembered. The first section, "Society at War," examines ways that militarization and war structure and destabilize society. Next, in the section on "Institutional Engagement," we turn to political, cultural, and military institutions and their relationships to war and suffering. The final section, "Memory and Representation," examines the creation of cultural representation and memory through various media, monuments, and social controls. Collectively, the chapters underline the complexity of recounting war and memories of it.

Society at War

Norman Smith, Bernard Hung-kay Luk, Chang Jui-te, and Michael Szonyi demonstrate how militarization and war acted to structure and destabilize society, with varying ramifications for individuals. The increasing social presence of the military is reflected in how people lived their lives, the ways that they represented their lives and contemporary society, and how they subsequently remembered them. This section especially focuses on life in occupied or wartime Manchukuo, Hong Kong, Chongqing, and Jinmen.

Norman Smith's "Writing and Remembering the Battle against Opiates in Manchukuo" documents a state-led campaign in Manchukuo, in which colonial administrators tried to mobilize writers in support of a battle against drug consumption to control public opinion and thereby dissociate the regime from the opiate addiction, war, and death with which it had come to be identified, both domestically and abroad. Writers were encouraged to use "social realism" to depict a cohesive, constructive society, yet the result was a legacy of dark, pessimistic literature that underscored the regime's failings. The backdrop to the propaganda war was an ongoing struggle to increase the working capacity of labourers and to free up resources (including opium) for the war that ravaged Asia. Ultimately, these efforts were no more successful than the movement to paint the regime in a positive light as Manchukuo authorities attempted to gain the co-operation of writers whose work undermined the very regime that they were employed to promote.

In "War, Schools, China, Hong Kong: 1937-1949," Bernard Hung-kay Luk demonstrates how school administration, teachers, and students in war-torn Hong Kong engaged in a struggle for survival by uprooting and shifting locations as they tried to stay one step ahead of the war. Mobilization for them became part of daily life. Instruction in language, history, art, and music became exercises in patriotism as school authorities and students organized extracurricular activities to raise funds or produce material for the war effort. The schools became essential elements of the wartime environment, participating in a wide range of wartime activities. Luk provides insight into how the war forced the schools to mobilize and adapt to the war even as it tore them apart. When forced out of school, individuals were faced with diminishing choices. The most resourceful were able to find new schools or join other organizations such as the CCP or the GMD. The less resourceful faced bleaker choices: some children found themselves consigned to orphanages; others simply became refugees. In this we have a reminder that suffering grows out of the disintegration of social mechanisms meant to sustain communities, leaving the individual dangerously exposed to disorder.

Such disorder informs Chang Jui-te's chapter, "Bombs Don't Discriminate? Class, Gender, and Ethnicity in the Air-Raid Shelter Experiences of the Wartime Chongqing Population." In this study of the Japanese bombardment of Chongqing, Chang contradicts the perception that mobilization can cause a society to pull together against a common enemy and shatters the illusion of wartime solidarity by illustrating the many ways that the act of mobilization exacerbated already existing social divisions. Chang demonstrates how the "solidarity" argument oversimplifies the historical realities of contemporary Chongqing by downplaying its inherent complexity. In some respects, the intensive bombardments reinforced a sense of togetherness among the population, but Chang questions the integrity of this solidarity, revealing that the impact of the bombardments was not uniform among different social classes and that vulnerability to bomb attacks differed between social classes and identities. GMD efforts to structure a cohesive defence were undermined by the instability of war and pre-existing socio-economic divisions.

Michael Szonyi's chapter, "Militarization and Jinmen (Quemoy) Society, 1949-1992," provides an important reminder that lives are not put on hold by warfare, that day-to-day existence is not divided from global political processes, and that wars do not end when bombs stop falling. Szonyi argues that society is influenced not only by war but also by militarization, defined by Cynthia Enloe as "the step-by-step process by which something becomes controlled by, dependent on, or derives its value from the military as an institution or militaristic criteria."[7] Szonyi makes clear that such a definition has great relevance to the citizens of Jinmen, who, for decades, experienced a "state of exception," a suspension of the legal order. That "state of exception," or "state of emergency," became a way of life as militarization spread throughout society. As one informant noted, the goal was to mobilize the population into "combat villages" for the purpose of making "every person a combat fighter; every village a combat fort." The long-term effects of this militarization were thorough, influencing everything from hygiene and sex to agricultural production. Militarization became linked to the production of modern life and the modern state and in turn was paralleled by movements on the Mainland in the People's Republic of China to co-ordinate and galvanize populations there.

Institutional Engagement

At one level, political, military, social, and cultural institutions have the potential to provide continuity, mediate between opposing forces, relieve suffering, and minimize chaos. Conversely, the failure of those institutions amid chaotic conditions exposes society to the elements and leaves people to suffer and inflict suffering with no recourse to formal sanctuary. But as Victor Zatsepine, Edward McCord, Colin Green, and Colette Plum argue in their respective chapters, institutions do not passively stand or fall on the sidelines of conflict. Geopolitical processes create, manipulate, or attack institutions, using them and the people they represent as pawns in larger power struggles. In that sense, chaos and suffering can also serve a particularly brutal institutional logic.

In "The Blagoveshchensk Massacre of 1900: The Sino-Russian War and Global Imperialism," Victor Zatsepine shows that despite a lengthy period of peaceful relations between Russia and Qing China, the two sides had developed no mechanism through which they could even discuss the possibility of evacuating Chinese and Manchu residents from Blagoveshchensk before the humanitarian crisis rapidly escalated. In contemporary Manchuria, there were no institutions standing between the military and society, nothing whatsoever to protect Qing citizens or to provide humanitarian aid. Zatsepine illustrates how, beyond merely taking advantage of the lack of institutional infrastructure, Russian authorities deliberately sowed chaos along the frontier, using violence as a means to alter the balance of power in their favour. As General K.N. Gribskii pronounced, this was to ensure that "the name of the Amur Cossack will thunder through all of Manchuria and strike terror among the Chinese population" in preparation for the Russian occupation of Manchuria later that summer.[8] In the final section of this volume, Blaine Chiasson demonstrates how a reinvigorated Chinese regional administration later turned this relationship around, but in the short term Russia was able to create the perception that the Qing Dynasty was incapable of managing its affairs. In a poignant example, Zatsepine notes that although Qing authorities were not even in a position to fish the victims out of the river, Russian steamers continued to ply the Amur, and their passengers continued to be served breakfast on time. Russia's comparative institutional advantage had the effect of shifting Sino-Russian relations from co-operation to Russian military dominance.

In "Victims and Victimizers: Warlord Soldiers and Mutinies in Republican China," Edward McCord shows that institutions were only marginally better developed in 1920s Hunan. The failure of military institutions, banks, chambers of commerce, and even the district yamen, hampered by a dysfunctional tax system, meant that none were capable of meeting the basic salary needs of the military rank and file. Recognizing this, mutinous soldiers targeted the most visible financial institutions but turned on the public after failing to obtain satisfactory restitution. For the soldiers, this was presumably an effort to claim outstanding pay rather than to change the nature of those institutions, but that was not the case with their commander, Wang Zhanyuan, who sought to use the resulting chaos to manipulate regional financial and political institutions to his own benefit. Even someone as belligerent as Wang understood the need to control the violence and placate the public, although his strategy for doing so never developed beyond assigning scapegoats and finally gunning down the soldiers behind the mutinies. In making victims of the victimizers, Wang perpetuated the cycle of violence that would eventually force him from power.

Colin Green's study of GMD military reforms, "Turning Bad Iron into Polished Steel: Whampoa and the Rehabilitation of the Chinese Soldier," reveals that Chiang Kai-shek understood better than Wang Zhanyuan that breaking the cycle of violence could begin with reform of military institutions. But Chiang's response went beyond technical institutional reforms to encompass what Alexander Woodside in this volume refers to as "culturalist" controls that were needed to support institutional changes. We may charitably suggest that the GMD did not deliberately sow chaos as the means to bringing about military reform, but Chiang used the constant threat of violence to promote the citizen-soldier as a "missionary" of the New Life Movement, to forge new models of citizens through the conversion of untrained and undisciplined soldiers that had become the norm, and ultimately, to extend those ideals to the rest of society. Unfortunately, the reforms, although initially quite successful, failed to produce lasting effects and could not prevent the degeneration of the military or of society at large. As Chang Jui-te's chapter reveals, even though the residue of that ethic still survived in the GMD's wartime capital, Chongqing, it quickly evaporated once the bombs started to fall. Chiang's culturalist reforms proved no match for the Japanese military.

One does not normally think of soldiers and orphans as being comrades in arms, but Colette Plum's chapter, "Orphans in the Family: Family Reform and Children's Citizenship during the Anti-Japanese War, 1937-1945," demonstrates that just as the GMD sought the creation of model citizens through military training, so too did it establish orphanages as an institution that, by facilitating the creation of a new form of citizenry, was to go beyond merely stabilizing children's lives. The orphanages were obviously intended as a benevolent enterprise to relieve suffering, but Plum shows that the GMD also used orphanages, in conjunction with the greater chaos of the Japanese invasion, to bring about institutional change. As in the above examples, institutional change proved in large part to be a response to the failure of other institutions. In this case, the GMD was responding to perceived failures of the family. For the GMD, not only was the war creating problems, but the old family system also impeded "the creation of healthy and productive citizens." The GMD was not just trying to create model orphans or model orphanages but was also trying to create a new citizenry in which orphans could play up the idea of the GMD as a "national parent" by becoming model "children of the *mínzu*." But whereas some saw the orphanages as an opportunity to take advantage of a failed family, others saw the failure of the family as something that would create only further instability, laying bare the contradictions and failures of the GMD's family policy.

Memory and Representation

It is often assumed that memory is lodged in the past and begins where experience leaves off. But as Alexander Woodside, Blaine Chiasson, James Flath, and Diana Lary write, memory is perpetually active, persistently involved in experience, and constantly evolving new personal, community, and increasingly global dimensions.

In his study of late imperial military policies, "Controlling Soldiers: The Memory Scars of Late Imperial China," Alexander Woodside addresses "the problem of controlling or governing soldiers," which was not simply construed as an institutional problem but also framed as a failure of memory to retain all of the examples of moral degradation of the past through which society had been reduced to chaos and made to suffer. For Confucian scholars, many of whom were also veterans of bloody military campaigns, there was a compelling need to control the military through the influences of Confucian humanism – the best examples and counterexamples of which could be found in the past. But Woodside argues that memory was not just a recollection of the past, or the use of the past to exhort the present, but also a fundamental aspect of the debate over the "formation and preservation of human moral character itself."

In "Chinese Savages and Chinese Saints: Russians and Chinese Remember and Forget the Boxer Uprising in 1920s China," Blaine Chiasson points out that memory can also be a condition of political and social situations, demonstrated by the icon of the 220 Holy Martyrs of the Boxer Rebellion, which memorializes the victims through emphasis on their Orthodox and Chinese identities rather than their Russianness. Chiasson also examines the hybrid nature of the life of Harbin's mayor, Ma Zhongjun, to show how colonial legacies have been treated in a postcolonial context. The diametrically opposed memories of Chinese and Russians regarding the Blagoveshchensk Massacre, also outlined in this volume by Zatsepine, show that there is no common memory and that memory becomes especially complicated in a multi-ethnic, multicultural, and multipolitical region such as Manchuria. However, not only is unified memory impossible, but it is also not even desirable because of the inherent risks of imposing that memory on a diversified ethnic community; particularly painful memories, as Chiasson points out, risk "rending a fragile society or accommodation asunder."

If changeable memories can be drawn on to support diverse political factions, the mutable identity of historical monuments, James Flath argues in "Setting Moon and Rising Nationalism: Lugou Bridge as Monument and Memory," can also be bent to the will of their managerial authorities. Beginning deep in China's imperial past as a symbol of culture and continuity, Lugou (Marco Polo) Bridge witnessed in 1937 what many consider to be the first battle of the Anti-Japanese War, and consequently the bridge emerged as a symbol of Chinese resistance and nationalism. Although its reputation went into decline during the era of Mao Zedong, with the restoration of Sino-Japanese diplomacy in the late 1970s, the bridge began to represent a much more complex set of issues extending far beyond its historical role. Flath argues that Lugou Bridge acquired its political potency through its authoritative lineage, which conditions but does not prevent appropriation by new generations of political and cultural authorities. Like fragments of memory, the fragmentary material past becomes embedded in the modern and expanded historical site and thereby supports new interpretations, new memories, and new histories.

In this volume's concluding chapter, "War and Remembering: Memories of China at War," Diana Lary calls our attention to the "vast and almost numbing" scale of suffering that lies at the heart of memories and representations of China's turbulent twentieth century. Memory depends on its locus: it may emerge as a political creation, it may be altered through the transformative role of an evolving media, and it may vary from one region to another, not to mention from one family and individual to another. Adding to this complexity are the subjects of memory – death, abuse, separation, and loss, as well as rebirth and survival. Memory is also conflicted, as demonstrated by Jerome Ch'en's memories of his wartime education, the benefits of which were qualified by loss. Memory born of suffering is inherently unstable, constantly reforming in shifting patterns of understanding as it builds up and tears down the foundations of individual psyches, local communities, and nation-states.

Conclusion

So what of those who, why, when, and where questions that opened this introduction? Having answered at least a few of them in this volume, are we any nearer to understanding the roots, the experiences, and the remembrance of suffering; does the "mirror of history" reflect any more clearly for our efforts? A modest respondent might suggest that we have only introduced further convolutions to the problem, but in doing so we would only be driving suffering and remembrance back into the shadows. As historians, we have to accept that most of the details revealing individual suffering will forever remain beyond our grasp. We can only imagine, for example, the terror that gripped the Chinese residents of Blagoveshchensk as Russian Cossacks forced them toward the Amur River on 17 July 1900 or the panic that erupted in the ranks of Wang Zhanyuan's mutinous soldiers on 10 June 1921 when they stepped from their train expecting to be served a complimentary breakfast only to find themselves standing on their own execution ground. But if this volume achieves anything, it connects suffering to larger geopolitical processes and reveals that chaos is neither happenstance nor temporary. To the contrary, chaos is all too frequently planned and manipulated by the powers that make war their business and perpetuated by societies unable to break the cycle of violence. Even memory can be destructive, although as Diana Lary reminds us, it is also a means of coming to terms with one's community, one's family, and oneself. There may be no definitive moment when all of the questions are answered and memories resolved, but as Lu Xun observed in the conclusion to his short story "My Old Home" (1921), history and memory do offer a way forward: "Hope cannot be said to exist" writes the author, "nor can it be said not to exist. It is just like roads across the earth. For actually the earth had no roads to begin with, but when many men pass one way, a road is made."[9]

Notes

1 jix/Douban, 8 May 2009, translated at http://www.danwei.org/film/john_rabe_nanjing_city_life_death.php#readmore.

2 One could go on to mention the Korean War, the hardships of the Mao era, various border wars in the 1960s and 1970s, and the countless "mass incidents" that continue to threaten Chinese social stability down to the present, although these lie outside the scope of this volume.

3 Diana Lary and Stephen MacKinnon, eds., *Scars of War: The Impact of Warfare on Modern China* (Vancouver: UBC Press, 2001), 6.

4 See also Lee Ching Kwan and Guobin Yang, eds., *Re-envisioning the Chinese Revolution: The Politics and Poetics of Collective Memories in Reform China* (Washington, DC: Woodrow Wilson Center, 2007); T. Fujitani, Geoffrey M. White, and Lisa Yoneyama, eds., *Perilous Memories: The Asia-Pacific War(s)* (Durham, NC: Duke University Press, 2001); Marc Gallicchio, ed., *The Unpredictability of the Past: Memories of the Asia-Pacific War in U.S.-East Asian Relations* (Durham, NC: Duke University Press, 2007); Li Feifei, Robert Sabella, and David Liu, eds., *Nanking 1937: Memory and Healing* (Armonk, NY: M.E. Sharpe, 2002); Vera Schwarcz, *Bridge across Broken Time: Chinese and Jewish Cultural Memory* (New Haven, CT: Yale University Press, 1998); Takashi Yoshida, *The Making of the "Rape of Nanking": History and Memory in Japan, China, and the United States* (Oxford: Oxford University Press, 2006).

5 Hans van de Ven, "War in the Making of Modern China," *Modern Asian Studies* 30, 4 (1996): 755.

6 Vera Schwarcz, "The Pane of Sorrow: Public Uses of Personal Grief in Modern China," *Daedalus* 125, 1 (1996): 119.

7 Cynthia Enloe, *Maneuvers: The International Politics of Militarizing Women's Lives* (Berkeley: University of California Press, 2000), 291.

8 General K.N. Gribskii, quoted in George Alexander Lensen, *The Russo-Chinese War* (Tallahassee, FL: Diplomatic Press, 1967), 108.

9 Lu Xun, "My Old Home," in *Selected Stories of Lu Xun,* trans. Yang Hsien-yi and Gladys Yang (Peking: Foreign Languages Press, 1972), 63-64.

Part 1: Society at War

1

Writing and Remembering the Battle against Opiates in Manchukuo

Norman Smith

Opium and war are foundational to narratives of modern Chinese history, the start of which is dated to the Opium War (1839-42). This chapter examines the status of opium in the wartime culture of China's Northeast, namely the Japanese colony of Manchukuo (1932-45), a century after China's first drug-fuelled battles with Britain. The colony has been remembered, if at all, as a militaristic, oppressive, narco-state. At the same time, Manchukuo also fostered Chinese and Japanese anti-opium activists whose critiques helped to generate the negativity with which the period has been remembered. Yet, for decades, their work has been absent from popular memory and historical study. In this volume, Colette Plum argues that during the War of Resistance (1937-45) orphans were ascribed new significances. So, too, were opium and its users. Foreign occupation and war branded both with a negativity that for decades consigned them to a solely humiliating past. Also in this volume, Diana Lary suggests that for survivors of the war, "the closing-down of memory was a way to erase pain – and with the silence, a tacit recognition that the memories themselves were of pain, not of glory or triumph" (p. 263). In the Northeast, opium and those connected to it were twinned with occupation and war as signposts of a past worthy only of forgetting or grave censure.

This chapter outlines the history of opium in the Northeast from the late Qing Dynasty (1644-1912) through the occupation and the height of the Sacred War (1941-45). Attention is focused on Manchukuo's opium industry and cultural production to demonstrate how war influenced policies and practices in both arenas. In the early 1940s opium and culture were monitored by officials aspiring to regime legitimization, but despite laws against recreational opium consumption and the production of culture that critiqued Manchukuo, depictions of opium and its users grew in prominence and spawned narratives more critical than might be expected of cultural production within a colonial state at war. Official campaigns against opium spurred social critiques that supported the anti-opium movement while demonizing contemporary society. Writers such as Lan Ling (1919-2003) and Mei Niang (b. 1920) depicted opium, poverty, and patriarchy as constituent elements of "women's difficulty" *(funü de kunan)*.[1] Wang Qiuying (1914-97) and Ye Li (1902-86) linked opium use with social decline and a Chinese abrogation of civic duty. Such narratives produced a negativity that ultimately cast into doubt the motives of the movement's proponents, demonstrating how a battle against drugs within a larger war context complicates efforts to reconcile the past and memories of it.

Opium was introduced to the Northeast during the Kangxi era (1662-1723), cultivated starting around 1860, and first taxed in 1885.[2] John Jennings has argued that in the "frontier" region, opium played a role "similar to that of gold in the settlement of California,"[3] drawing immigrants to engage in regional development. Opium became a requirement of polite society that was offered to guests like tobacco and tea.[4] It also had important medicinal uses, especially as a painkiller.[5] Despite restrictions on opium, by the end of the Qing Dynasty in 1912, it was one of the region's top agricultural products. The warlord regime of Zhang Zuolin, which eventually succeeded the Qing in the Northeast, half-heartedly extended existing restrictions, but the lucrative industry proved resilient in a vast region with a relatively dispersed population, limited state resources, and officials with disparate priorities. Farmers began to cultivate opium exclusively. Researchers strove to increase levels of morphia in poppies and to bolster production of morphine for export to Japan in order to reduce reliance on German sources. Opium spread, becoming cheaper and more potent.

In the 1920s opium was a mainstay of the Zhang regime. Ronald Suleski has detailed how "opium was used as a money-grab as Zhang tried to pay for pretensions to rule all of China."[6] Zhang moved to control the opium market and to reap its profits. Opium Monopoly Offices opened in the regional centre of Fengtian (present-day Shenyang) and increased rapidly in number along counties bordering railways owned by Japan's South Manchurian Railway (SMR) conglomerate. Opium revenues were forwarded to Zhang in Beijing and invested in his army. In 1928, after Zhang's murder by the Japanese military, control over the region fell to his son Zhang Xueliang, who in 1929 reasserted an opium regulatory framework to dovetail with Republican law, to no avail. Two years later, Zhang's rule was ended by Japanese invasion while he was undergoing rehabilitation in Beijing for his own longstanding use of opium.

Supporters of the Japanese invasion cited widespread opium addiction as a justification for the occupation. In October 1932 SMR researchers estimated that "roughly 5 percent of Manchukuo's total population of 30 million were opium and narcotic addicts – 1.5 million people (nearly ten times the peak number of registered opium addicts on Taiwan)."[7] Officials subsequently argued that the Japanese army had to intervene to save the indigenous population: "With the Manchu and Mongol races opium-smoking is, so to speak, a historically hereditary disease," which was exacerbated by inhumane Han Chinese warlord rule.[8] The extent to which the population suffered from the "historically hereditary disease," however, has recently been challenged by Jiao Runming's calculation of a 1931 population of 30,000 addicts, or 0.1 percent of the population.[9] Regardless of how much opium was actually consumed, Manchukuo publications consistently condemned the decadence of the previous Zhang regimes, decrying "the whole body of public servants [who], in fact, seemed to be devotees of Morpheus."[10] Officials and reformers labelled opium the "arch-enemy of mankind,"[11] an insidious remnant of Western imperialism. They advocated restricted cultivation and an end to imports as key elements of Japan's "civilizing mission." In November 1932 the Opium Law was promulgated to gradually lessen and eventually eradicate recreational opium use.[12] According to the Opium Law, permits for smoking opium would be granted by the Manchukuo Monopoly only to adult, non-Japanese addicts who sought rehabilitation. Recreational opium use was to be discouraged, but until it was eradicated the state would control and profit from it. Chronic underfunding of Japan's imperial project, as demonstrated in studies by Michael Barnhart and Alan Baumler, made the sale of opium an appealing and lucrative source of revenue for Japan's colonial regimes and those who sought to profit from them;[13] Manchukuo's Kangde emperor (r. 1934-45), Henry Aisin-Gioro Puyi (1906-67), claimed in his autobiography that one-sixth of Manchukuo state revenue was derived from opium.[14]

The Monopoly's launch in 1933 lent further credence to longstanding critiques of opium use. For decades, articles condemning opiates had appeared regularly in leading Japanese-owned, Chinese-language newspapers, such as Fengtian's *Shengjing shibao (Shengjing Times)*. Under the new regulatory framework, they became even more frequent; representative examples include "Mafei zhi hai" ("The Harm of Morphine"), "Yinzhe de xin" ("An Addict's Letter"), and "Jin yan lun" ("Discussion of the Smoking Prohibition").[15] The state's highly publicized anti-opium platform encouraged cultural production that violated Manchukuo's publication laws, which forbade overly critical work.[16] Increasingly strict cultural policies, designed to encourage the "special, independent characteristics of Manchukuo literature" *(Manzhou wenxue de duli tese)*,[17] contributed to an exodus of young Chinese writers, including Xiao Jun (1908-88), who left the colony. Before Xiao departed, in the short story "Zhuxin" ("Candlewick"), he cited "the rustling sounds of opium being smoked" as a characteristic of Harbin.[18] Emulating Lu Xun, Xiao aspired to heighten public consciousness through his writing. He depicted Harbin as "a hell on earth" *(diyu de renjian)*, a description echoed by other writers.[19] Western observers joined in critiques of Manchukuo's opium industry, claiming it as evidence of the genocidal nature of Japanese rule in an attempt to overturn narratives of Western oppression and to recuperate American and British participation in the trade. In 1934, for example, in "Japan Builds a New Colony," famed journalist Edgar Snow, who later detailed Communist activities in *Red Star over China*, recounted his impressions of Manchukuo for the American publication *Saturday Evening Post*. Snow blamed the Japanese for turning "once delightful" Harbin into "a place of living death."[20]

The Manchukuo Monopoly and the Opium Law were decried by local and foreign critics who argued that they were manipulated for Japanese benefit – that is, "to destroy independent competitors, not opium use."[21] Kathryn Meyer has detailed how the Kempeitai (military police) and Special Service Section (army intelligence) took control of the manufacture of heroin and morphine, driving out remaining European firms; private heroin manufacturers who survived came to terms with the army. For many Japanese and their allies, dealing in opium was lucrative.[22] Nitan'osa Otozō, for example, rose from obscurity to reign as a regional opium king.[23] Yamauchi Saburō founded the South Manchuria Pharmaceutical Company, through which donations to the Japanese imperial army were made in exchange for military decorations; Yamauchi even claimed that Fujita Osamu, who built his fortune in the drug trade, had financed the establishment of Manchukuo.[24] Furumi Tadayuki, once assistant director-general for administrative affairs in Manchukuo, argued that the colony was "an immense installation created by a top secret fund of the Guandong Army," which provided "colossal profits which became the financial source for Japan's military schemes."[25] Under Japanese rule, the port of Dalian was credited with the highest annual consumption rates of morphine and cocaine in the world.[26] Perhaps the most visible manifestation of the Monopoly's failings, however, was the "ash heap of Mukden [present-day Shenyang],"[27] an unceremonious dumping ground for dead and dying Chinese addicts outside the city's West Gate. The blatant failure of the Monopoly to achieve its professed ambitions cast suspicion on the entire industry, a condition exacerbated by the state's colonial nature and the outbreak of war.

On 1 July 1937, just days before the War of Resistance began, laws regarding cultural production were tightened, and changes to the Opium Law followed. Seven major newspapers closed, as their publishers were daunted by the threat of increasing bureaucratic oversight.[28] Revisions to the Opium Law, implemented in response to the war and rising criticism, placed the industry even more firmly under Japanese dominion. The expansion of hostilities across much of China necessitated increased supplies of opium for medical uses, at least, thus launching further calls to reduce domestic consumption in Manchukuo. In December 1937 the State Retail Sale System was established, with the aim of ending opium use in ten years. Officials again vigorously declared support for the eradication of opium, denying accusations that the state benefited from its sale. The director of Manchukuo's General Affairs Board, Hoshino Naoki, argued that his government recognized that the financial losses associated with opium addiction outweighed the benefits.[29] Officials responded to critics by claiming that annual profits were less than 10 million yuan, an insignificant figure, they contended, because annual opium consumption was estimated at 180 million yuan and "was costing yet another 150 million yuan per year in lost labor productivity and in added policing and administrative burdens."[30] They suggested that the eradication of opium addiction could free up to 300 million yuan annually for vital industrial development, a priority they vigorously pursued.

As the war continued, criticism of recreational opium use grew exponentially. The director of the Monopoly, Lo Cheng-pang, argued that the administration aimed for "the eventual eradication of the noxious habit permeating the whole of society."[31] Whether Lo's aim was to justify the existence of the Monopoly by arguing that the "whole of society" was permeated by opium or to discredit six years of Monopoly operations, the effect was the same – Manchukuo was yet again depicted as a drug haven. Even harsher criticism emanated from outside the colony, beyond the reach of censors and officials. In *Bushido: The Anatomy of Terror,* Alexandre Pernikoff argued that the Japanese sought the region's "moral destruction" by disseminating free or artificially cheap narcotics among peasants (including "trial offers" for property owners and "junior doses" that were cheaper than bread for children), promoting cheap prostitution, and breaking up families.[32] Pernikoff suggested that such tactics were "more subtle and more effective" than jail, torture, or murder.[33] In Pernikoff's view, "Manchuria was being slowly poisoned to death, while the Japanese army reaped huge financial benefits."[34] In *Secret Agent of Japan: A Handbook to Japanese Imperialism,* Amleto Vespa, a self-described fascist who claimed he had previously been pressured by the Japanese to work undercover for them, delivered a similarly damning portrait of Manchukuo. Vespa contended that in Harbin "one cannot find a street where there are no opium-smoking dens or narcotic shops."[35] Thus, by arguing that the numbers of dens and shops far exceeded contemporary estimates of approximately seventy opium shops in Harbin, Vespa and Pernikoff echoed earlier descriptions by Xiao Jun, Edgar Snow, and Lo Cheng-pang in *Shengjing shibao,* a newspaper frequently critical of the Monopoly.[36]

Vespa's denunciation of Japanese rule in Manchukuo was at least partly in response to race-based rhetoric, as illustrated in his citation of a "Japanese Military Command" booklet as evidence that the Japanese sought to "poison the whole world": "The use of narcotics is unworthy of a superior race like the Japanese. Only inferior races, races that are decadent like the Chinese, the Europeans, and the East Indians, are addicted to the use of narcotics. This is why they are destined to become our servants and eventually disappear."[37] This racial rhetoric, whether the source is authentic or not, parallels official assertions in the *Manchukuo Yearbook* that Manchus and Mongols shared a "historically hereditary disease" of opium-smoking. Vespa continued to condemn the Japanese as harshly as Japanese officials attacked Western imperialists and Han Chinese warlords. Such race-based views of addiction were not uncommon. Nakamura Kōjirō, for example, argued that the Japanese may not have been susceptible to opium but that they were vulnerable to alcohol addiction and should avoid excessive consumption of alcohol, which he identified as a tool of Western imperialism that had been deployed to destroy Native communities in Canada and Hawaii.[38] These race-based views of addiction reflect beliefs built into the foundations of the Greater East Asia Co-Prosperity Sphere, which was conceived in the wake of Western imperialism, social Darwinism, and eugenics and which proved ruinously divisive to Japan's "civilizing" project.

The oppressive Manchukuo environment forced writers to face difficulties that alternately enhanced and hindered their independence: financial compensation was woefully inadequate, and they risked losing even their pitiful incomes if they ran afoul of censors. In October 1939, in the journal *Nihon Hyōron (Japan Debate),* a writer using the pen name M.G.M. suggested that a viable literary world had failed to materialize because intellectuals could not rely on writing to earn an income.[39] Arguing that surveillance of the Chinese-language literary world was overly intrusive, M.G.M. stressed that local literature was doomed to inconsequence unless writers were provided with more freedom and money. This dire evaluation failed to account for idealistic writers who pursued literary careers regardless of the poor pay and risks. Additionally, Japanese intellectuals such as Kobayashi Hideo, Abe Tomoji, and Kishida Kunio encouraged writers to "describe reality" *(miaoxie zhenshi)* and to "expose reality" *(baolu zhenshi),* with particular emphasis on economic hardship, social disorder, and the low status of women. Chinese writers pursued aims similar to those of their Japanese counterparts, with left-wing Japanese writer Shinichi Yamaguchi approvingly noting that "realism seem[ed] to predominate among the main literary trends" in Manchukuo literature.[40]

The work of two Chinese writers, Lan Ling and Mei Niang, is representative of contemporary social realism and opium narratives. In Lan Ling's 1940 poem "Xiao xiang de chuxi" ("New Year in a Small Alley"),[41] a starving widow makes a last-ditch effort at prostitution on New Year's Eve to earn money to feed her starving baby, but her only potential client is a "morphine ghost."[42] His addiction, combined with her poverty and distress, undermines her frantic effort to raise money. The woman collapses, presumably to die in the freezing snow with her "virtue" intact, as a "good wife, wise mother" *(xianqi liangmu)* ought, thus leaving her child alone in a dark, freezing apartment.[43] At the end of the poem, as firecrackers explode around her, she slips out of consciousness. Lan's portrait of a desperate widow dying amid New Year's celebrations highlights a compounding of women's subjugation by opium addiction in Manchukuo.

The cost of addiction is poignantly detailed in Mei Niang's second volume of collected works, published in 1940: *Di'er dai (The Second Generation)*.[44] The short story "Zhui" ("The Chase") links addiction and patriarchy in the life of an "opium prostitute" *(yan ji)*.[45] A young girl, Guihua, starts working at an opium den after her father dies in order to support her drug-addicted mother and brother, who also drinks heavily. As the only member of the family who is not incapacitated by addiction, she earns money by employing the one skill that her mother taught her: how to prepare an opium pipe. Through her work, Guihua becomes addicted to opium at the cost of her youthful beauty, her ability to earn a living, and her dignity.[46] On New Year's Eve, as she joyfully anticipates telling her mother about a new rich client, her brother returns home and demands her wages. When Guihua refuses, he berates her and storms out. Traumatized, Guihua turns to the mirror and sees "a monkey-shaped face in the mirror, with two cheeks dead-red and lips painted blood-purple."[47] Transfixed with horror at her unrecognizable appearance, Guihua's eyes fill with tears, which summon memories of her father's funeral. In a swell of self-consciousness, she comprehends the family burden that has cost her "virgin's body and heart."[48] Her brother's outburst, which has destroyed her celebratory mood, finally makes her cognizant of the "life-killing addiction" *(yaoming de yanyin)* that has taken such a toll on her.[49]

Guihua's life is brought to ruin by addiction and subjugation in a business that was regularly condemned by Manchukuo officialdom. Both women in "Zhui" are victimized by men, and Guihua is further oppressed by her mother's addiction. Guihua's free-spending father has left the family with inadequate savings and no means of support. Her brother's character is reflected by his appearance: he has a skinny green-white face, dishevelled hair, rotting teeth, and the odour of a dog. Neither man has a positive influence on Guihua's life, and "Zhui" climaxes as Guihua returns to the brothel, where she is fired. Her male boss verbally abuses her in front of co-workers, cheats her out of her wages, and pummels her, tossing her like garbage into the alley. When she lifts her bloodied face from the curb, her wretched fate is played out in front of her as a dog feasts on the flesh of a cat before tossing its skeleton aside. Beaten, starving, penniless, and craving a fix, Guihua peers out from the alley to see her brother "walking past accompanied by a young simple girl. Her elder brother's face looked as if he'd just caught a fish."[50] With Guihua's use expended, both her brother and her boss turn to new, "young simple" girls to prey on. In "Zhui" the female characters are utterly consumed by men and life-killing addiction.

Also in *Di'er dai,* Mei Niang links familial decline with opium and Manchukuo in "Zuihou de qiuzhenzhe" ("The Last Patient").[51] This short story depicts a young family's visit to a health clinic. The woman ostensibly seeks treatment for anaemia, but it is really the couple's opium addiction for which they seek relief. The doctor suspects from the woman's "pale grey" face that she is addicted to opium.[52] Dishevelled, dirty, and constantly yawning, they appear incapable of caring for themselves or their baby, who is filthy from neglect. Devoid of social and parental skills, the couple bickers over who really abuses opium and what type of "medicine" they are seeking; they both refuse the doctor's proffered needle as too costly, but the implication is that they are seeking a drug to share later.[53] The man convinces the doctor to prescribe laudanum, an opium-based liquid.[54] As the pathetic couple shuffles out of the clinic, having achieved their goal, a light glints across the national-flag badge on the man's cap, thus linking their condition with the colonial state.

Lan Ling and Mei Niang depicted opium and addiction as inherently subjugating, vivid manifestations of women's disempowerment in Manchukuo. As in official rhetoric, Lan and Mei condemned the use of opium, yet they linked it with what they identified as Manchukuo's patriarchal foundations. Their work thus supported Manchukuo's opium regulations while subverting cultural policies by not representing Manchukuo as a "paradise land" *(le tu).* In February 1941, in response to such critical literature, officials launched the Ba bu *(The Eight Abstentions),* which provided sanctions ranging from censorship to imprisonment for dark, pessimistic writing that officials argued denigrated Manchukuo and Japan.[55] The Eight Abstentions reflect the type of work being produced ten years after the establishment of Manchukuo. Officials soon supplemented them with the Gangyao yiwen zhidao *(Summary of Guidelines to Art and Literature),* dictating the adoption of Japanese literary traditions and professional organizations as models for Manchukuo's literary world.[56] Media chief Muto Tomio stressed that in order for the "arts to fulfil the national system's needs, we still need to focus on the organization of professionals."[57] On 27 July 1941 Manzhou wenyijia xiehui (Manchukuo Writers and Artists Concordia) was established to mobilize writers to "assist in the promotion of the Greater East Asia Sacred War."[58] Manchukuo's writers responded in a humbled manner. Gu Ding pronounced the Summary of Guidelines the "most significant matter" of the year.[59] Wang Qiuying mourned the "need to sweep away descriptions of the dark side."[60] Over the following months, Muto published even more missives condemning "the very troublesome matter" of dark literature.[61]

The dangers of opium were further publicized via medical literature and in advertisements for government policies and institutions that in the early 1940s adopted militaristic overtones. In an illustrated ad for the prohibition of opium and morphine from *Shengjing shibao,* the body of a uniformed man slices through the word opium (see Figure 1.1).[62] Behind him, marching celebrants wave a Manchukuo flag and a banner proclaiming "National Refusal" *(guomin jujue),* explicitly linking the refutation of opium with patriotism, national duty, and the masses. Ads such as this were featured regularly, underlining the earnest position of anti-opium activists, who advocated reform, the self-interest of those who sought to legitimize the Japanese invasion to "save" the local population, and efforts to improve domestic and international perceptions of the regime.

Ads also advocated rehabilitation in Kangsheng yuan (Healthy Life Institutes). This example, from the capital Xinjing's state-run Chinese-language newspaper *Datong bao (Great Unity Herald),* exemplifies the official stance on rehabilitation (see Figure 1.2).[63] A woman holds a banner that beseeches: "Give up opium and morphine." She towers over a number of faceless bodies that raise their arms upward. The caption on the right side reads: "Opium dens guide you into hell, Healthy Life Institutes lead you into paradise." Drawing on propaganda portraying Manchukuo as a "paradise land," Healthy Life Institutes were meant to symbolize the state's benevolence through rehabilitation. The female figure, standing tall and proud above the masses, melds the nurturing nature of rehabilitation with the ideal of the "good wife, wise mother," through which officials sought to modernize women of the region.[64] But active rehabilitation of Manchukuo's addicts, regardless of their numbers, was well beyond available resources.

In the early 1940s, Manchukuo officials acknowledged that the anti-opium movement was failing, stating that the "number of addicts is roughly estimated at one million, although no thorough surveys have as yet been made."[65] Officials conceded that resource allocation was insufficient to implement policy and, further, that addicts were reluctant to voluntarily register out of fear of taxes, compulsory labour, or other punishment.[66] Wartime demands for increased labour and industrial production led to condemnation of "opium fiends" as immoral, physically weak, and ruinous to the labour pool. In the journal *Contemporary Manchuria* it was estimated that only 2 to 3 percent of addicts (no distinctions were made between occasional, regular, or heavy users; all users were labelled "addicts") could withstand labour, an intolerable statistic for officials engaged in war.[67] Anti-addict narratives in official publications underlined state priorities: recreational opium use was to be eradicated in service of war demands rather than for the sake of users and their families.

Discussion of opium eradication inevitably extended to the relative merits of rehabilitation techniques. Journals such as *Jiankang Manzhou (Healthy*

FIGURE 1.1 Prohibition of Opium and Morphine. *Source: Shengjing shibao (Shengjing Times),* 3 October 1941, 5.

Manchukuo) frequently outlined the most up-to-date programs, often with reference to international scientific discoveries. In "Yaowuxue shiyezhong de yapian" ("Opium from a Pharmaceutical Perspective"), Zhang Guochen (a professor at Xinjing's Medical University) sought to raise awareness about the psychological and economic tolls of opium addiction and about the difficulties of rehabilitation. Zhang outlined the dangers of what he described as the widely held belief

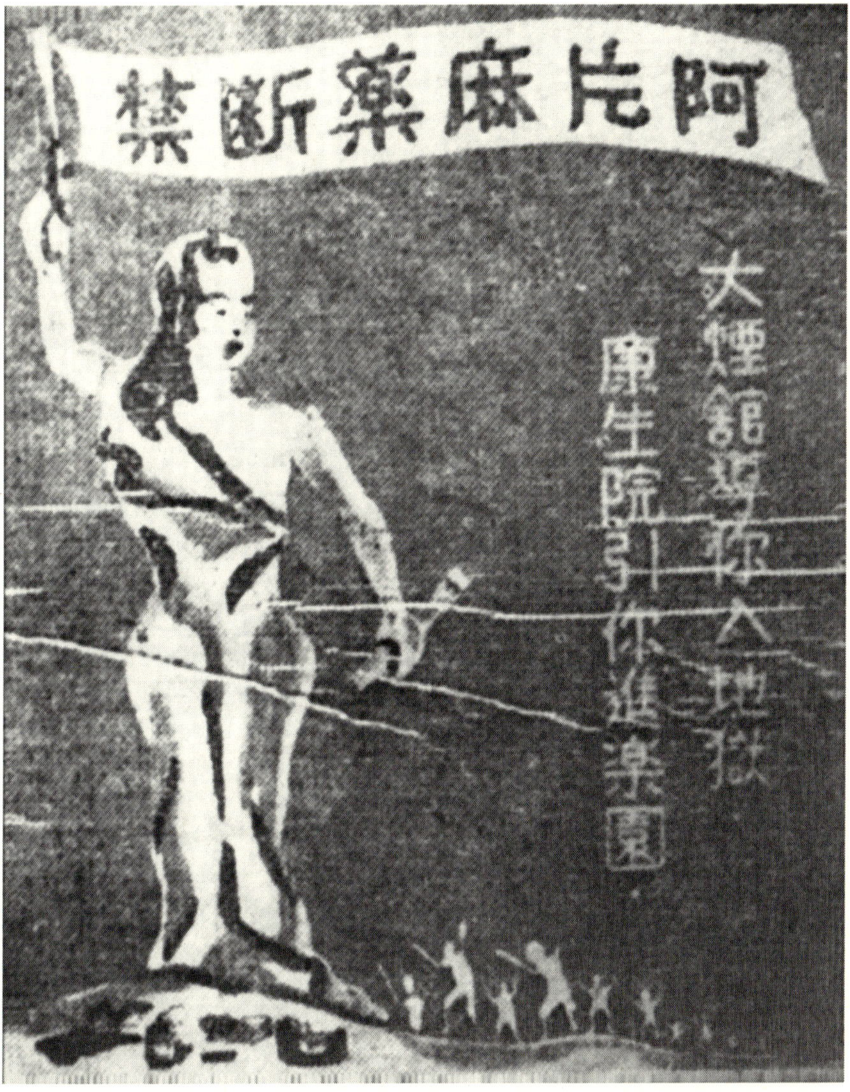

FIGURE 1.2 "Healthy Life Institutes Lead You into Paradise." *Source: Datong bao (Great Unity Herald),* 6 December 1941, 4.

that opium was simply a recreational product.[68] In "Yapian" ("Opium"), Zhang Jiyou (director of Manchukuo's People's Welfare Department) detailed successes in Germany (Manchukuo's wartime ally) with three types of withdrawal – immediate, short-term (eight to ten days), and more gradual (two to three weeks), providing analysis of potential benefits and drawbacks of the various procedures.[69] In Manchukuo a wide range of rehabilitation treatments existed, from withdrawal and harm reduction to forced labour; "the period of accommodation for each addict [was ideally] 50 days."[70] Even in positive contexts, however, rehabilitation is controversial: sudden withdrawal or forced labour can result in physical damage or death, and harm reduction raises cries of addiction-enabling. But in a colonial, wartime environment, in which officials openly discussed the need for industrial development and framed opium use and control in race-based terms, rehabilitation, no matter what the process, was deeply suspect.

Rehabilitation efforts were undermined by the diversion of resources to war demands, the quelling of domestic unrest, and economic development. Officials conceded that rehabilitation programs at the forty-six Healthy Life Institutes were "far from satisfactory in point of scale and equipment."[71] Forty-six ill-equipped, overcrowded institutions could not serve a population of addicts in the tens or hundreds of thousands. Individuals were thus forced to seek cures at home with a growing range of products aimed at consumers, to receive treatment in hospitals or health clinics, or to risk jail or death. To make matters worse, rehabilitation was elusive: according to state statistics, seven of ten attempts ended with a relapse.[72] Reformers thus faced the unenviable task of applying inadequate funding to controversial treatments that had limited success. Insufficient resources and war demands hampered reform efforts in Manchukuo, as elsewhere in Japan's empire and in the Republic of China. Across Asia in the early 1940s the fight against opium was a difficult proposition in terms of resources, official commitment, and public awareness.

In 1941 Wang Qiuying underlined the importance of battling opium in the novel *He liu de diceng (The Bottom of the River)* by representing opium as a causal factor of the Japanese invasion.[73] The novel is set in 1930s Fengtian and criticizes the elite for a "dissipated bourgeois lifestyle" at a time of national crisis.[74] Their profligate lives are contrasted with those of the poverty-stricken, virtuous country folk, who pine for the long-lost Qing Dynasty; rural life is a world apart, yet it is also vulnerable to devastation by the occupying forces. Wang extols rural society, thus reflecting the official promotion of "rural values" noted by Prasenjit Duara,[75] yet Wang is critical of both the brutality of the occupation and the privileged Chinese who did not prevent it. The novel recounts the male protagonist Lin Mengji's move from the countryside to attend university in Fengtian. Lin ignores his parents' warning to avoid their urban relatives and is "contaminated" by them.[76] Ultimately, he fails in his studies. Further, his involvement in Changshi hui (Common Sense Society), a group of youths dedicated to consciousness-raising among the masses, is ended by the invasion.

Wang blames Japanese occupation on a Chinese dereliction of duty that has its genesis in the elite's opium addiction. The wealthy shirk their responsibilities and are negative examples for their children, who become wastrels. The "yellow and skinny" matriarch is most ravaged by opium addiction.[77] During the invasion, on "a night of terror in history" *(lishi shang de yi ge kongbu zhi ye),* she toys with her pipe, and the servants hurry about flustered, without a trace of the patriarch.[78] The invasion encounters no resistance and exacerbates youth's "intoxication" *(mizui)* with petty affairs.[79] Lin's cousins don't smoke opium but spend their lives gambling, eating in expensive restaurants, and pursuing love affairs. Lin, unable to focus on his studies, returns home defeated. At the conclusion of *He liu de diceng,* Lin revisits Fengtian to find his uncle dead and his lonely aunt cradling her opium pipe. With the servants discharged, the family scattered, and the region under foreign occupation, the full price of their intoxication is realized.

In 1942 the costs of opium intoxication were the subject of the popular song *Jie yan ge (Quit Smoking Song),* sung by Li Xianglan (Japanese name, Yoshiko Yamaguchi, b. 1920), the most famous entertainer from Manchukuo. In it, Li decries the "truly terrifying" cost of opium, which turns one's "life blood to mud."[80] *Jie yan ge* was the theme song of the Japanese-produced, Chinese-language movie *Wanshi liufang (Eternity),* which dramatizes the Opium War. The film and song were produced in Japanese-occupied Shanghai and were intended to incite anti-opium, anti-Western sentiments. Instead, they underline a central contradiction in Japanese colonial culture: through support for government's anti-opium policies, cultural producers undermined Japan's "civilizing" mission by explicitly linking opium with Chinese subjugation. *Jie yan ge* was heralded across China, in territories held by the Communists, Nationalists, and the Japanese, and is symbolic of the wartime border-crossing of Chinese-language cultural production that still awaits further critical scholarly attention. In Manchukuo, sympathetic Japanese encouraged the production of such contentious work even at the height of war. In April 1943 Kitamura Kenjiro argued that if Manchukuo writers followed the dictates of colonial officials and

> depart from emotion and bury their heads in constructive [pro-state commentary], what kind of condition is that? Isn't this tragic? Writers should have the intention to write on the constructive side, but they must be allowed mainly to write on the side of emotions. Only with this kind of rich foundation can Manchukuo literature finally have a hundred flowers bloom.[81]

Although Kitamura argued that writers "should have the intention" of writing constructively, he stressed their need to express their emotions. Thus, despite onerous wartime surveillance, anti-opium narratives continued to circulate in East Asia.

In the final years of the occupation, colonial officials, harried by war demands and ambiguous Chinese cultural production, adopted a decidedly martial tone in their policies. On 4 January 1944 the Manchukuo Literary Association initiated use of the slogan "wielding pens as swords" *(yi bi dai jian)* to steel the hearts and minds of Manchukuo subjects for an intensified war effort.[82] By September the ponderous regulatory framework and paper shortages led to amalgamation of the largest journals into *Xin Manzhou (New Manchukuo),* which held a writing contest on the theme of "Dadongya shengzhan yu women de juewu" ("The Greater East Asia Sacred War and Our Consciousness"). Organizers hoped for an outpouring of patriotism, but they received more in-depth depiction of the Chinese suffering of economic deprivation and adversity.

It was in this atmosphere that Wang Qiuying published his short story "Lou xiang" ("Vulgar Alley"), which examines life in a suburb that the narrator describes as a "festering finger."[83] The poverty-stricken community revolves around an opium den owned by the "greedy ruffian" Gao, who uses his profits to make loans to neighbours at usurious interest rates.[84] Even though none of the residents appear addicted to opium, they are all "trampled on in the evil environment" fostered by Gao's business.[85] Their misgivings regarding the Manchukuo Monopoly are expressed through debate regarding whether Gao's lucrative business is licensed. Negativity toward the state is accentuated by the neighbours' apprehension over Gao's business and the eviction to labour camps of all residents without "regular" employment, a threat to almost all of the Chinese. Their misery is relieved only by occasional drinking binges, which on one occasion provide the backdrop for the ironic deployment of two Manchukuo wartime slogans, "Dedicated Service to the National Economy" *(jingji baoguo)* and "Exterminate Dark Behaviour" *(pumie anxing).*[86] The dedicated service to the national economy that lies at the centre of the "festering finger" is the operation of an opium den, which fuels the dark behaviour that "suffocates to death" *(dusi)* its Chinese inhabitants.[87]

In "Lou xiang," Wang links the opium industry with degeneracy. Opium dealer Gao is greedy and lascivious, his son is an inveterate gambler, and his daughter is "loose."[88] Gao forces an aging entertainer to become his mistress in order to pay off her debts; she resigns herself to being "played with" by men.[89] Gao's son exposes himself, urinates in public, and screams obscenities at young women. The only positive act attributed to the family is performed by the daughter, who gives a student some money to save his sick friend. But she steals the money from her father and gives it to the student only to pressure him to have sex with her. "Lou xiang" climaxes as Gao is stabbed to death by a poor worker who mourns the love of his life, the aging entertainer. In a final insult, Gao's fatal stab wounds are compared to his daughter's "big gaping mouth."[90] At the end of "Lou xiang," the aggrieved worker stands stoically beside the dead Gao. Neighbours gather around but are reluctant to summon the authorities because to them justice has seemingly, and unexpectedly, been served. With a violence that befitted his life, Gao dies for the betterment of a community ravaged by a lack of morality, indicting the opium industry and those who profit from it.

In 1944 as well, Ye Li's "San ren" ("Three People") was published in a volume of his collected works titled *Hua zhong (Flower Tomb)*. In "San ren" sex worker Ye Fen narrates her tragic life to a man whom she eventually discovers was her primary-school teacher, Liu Linggen.[91] Following a night of drinking, Liu passes out in an unlicensed brothel in the company of his former student. When he regains consciousness, Ye recounts to him how her mother, who resented being married to a poor teacher, began entertaining men and smoking opium. In short order, her mother spent her days with "opium addicts" *(yan ke)* and "morphine ghosts" *(mafei gui)*.[92] Ye reveals how her father divorced her mother after she burgled the family home for money to buy morphine. Ye and her mother then lived with a woman who sold Ye to the brothel in order to support their morphine habits. Ye is depicted as a victim of "patriarchal society" *(zongfa shehui)* who suffered from subjugation as a young woman.[93] Unable to comprehend the addiction that tore her family apart, Ye asks Liu, "in the past, wasn't Lin Zexu's refusal of narcotics ... entirely for the nation, for the people, for our later generations? But the people don't know their sad history."[94] Ye links the fate of the nation and its people with the forgotten "sad history" of China's engagement with narcotics, the famous anti-opium Qing official Lin, and the Opium War. Moved by his former student's predicament and her reminder of China's sad history, Liu resolves to save himself and rescue Ye from her "evil environment."[95]

The work of Wang and Ye exemplifies the negative opium narratives encouraged by officials even in the final months of Manchukuo. In their writings, opium is associated with social decline, foreign aggression, and the "sad history" of modern China. They depict the elite indulging in opium as a diversion or selling it for profit even as more altruistic behaviour was demanded to save the nation and its people. The lower classes are shown to be trebly oppressed by addiction, local Chinese elites, and the burden of an immoral society. These stories bolster official condemnation of opium use, yet although Manchukuo officials emphasized the economic ramifications of addiction, these writers cautioned of moral decline and its toll. Opium is shown to intoxicate the Chinese, alienating them from a state that appeared incapable of assuaging their suffering. This alienation is marked in these men's writings by sexist stereotypes, which depict women as reliant on, or undermining, the men who are often depicted as their "saviours." Their gendered stance is markedly different from that adopted by Lan Ling and Mei Niang, who even more forcefully condemned patriarchal society and its ramifications for women.

Throughout the war, anti-opium reformers and anti-Japanese activists condemned "the Japanese [for] turning Manchuria into the world's chief narcotic supply base,"[96] branding this image into individual and collective memories of the regime. Manchukuo officials had staked claims to legitimacy via a "civilizing" project that included eradicating opium use and rehabilitating addicts. But their policies turned against them, as officially sanctioned condemnation of opium across media accentuated the Monopoly's failings and, by extension, those of the Manchukuo regime. Since the state claimed control over the opium industry, the industry's apparent flourishing reflected negatively on the regime. Ironically, the collapse of Manchukuo in 1945 is argued to have increased opium distribution in the region as the regulatory framework disappeared, stock from the defunct Monopoly issued into the markets,[97] and farmers sought a high-value crop with which to sustain themselves during the Civil War of 1945-49. It was Communist Party (CCP) victories through the late 1940s that ultimately forced an end to recreational opium use. What successive regimes had professed to seek for decades, and the Sacred War had failed to secure, was achieved under early socialist rule. Zhou Yongming has described how popularly supported, strict enforcement policies melded with the end of war to legitimize CCP rule in a manner that had long evaded previous regimes.[98] Opium's reign was ended.

Opium had flourished in the Northeast. Once a mainstay of the regional economy, it had enticed Han migration that enabled rulers of China to claim the Manchu homelands for their own, pre-empting Japanese and Russian (or Soviet) territorial ambitions. It provided a leisurely diversion with which to combat the rigours of life in the frontier region and served important medical purposes. Opium was even said to have left its mark in the local dialect, as harvests signalled the start of autumn, the "smoke season" *(yan ji)*.[99] In the early 1920s opium was a major element of the Northeast's robust economy, which was the envy of other parts of China. Opium produced revenue for economic and military development; it helped to fund Zhang Zuolin's national aspirations in China and later those of the Japanese military across Asia. Following the Japanese invasion, however, the dangers of opium dominated official rhetoric and popular culture despite opium's role in Japanese expansionism.

The inability of Manchukuo officials to actualize their own widely publicized eradication policies undercut the state's legitimacy. Under Japanese occupation, opium industries expanded, producing cheaper and more potent supplies that filled tax coffers and lined the pockets of the occupiers, their allies, and others who sought financial gain. But although opium could bring wealth and prestige to those who controlled the industry, the regulatory framework around it enabled, criminalized, stigmatized or killed users, disheartened anti-opium reformers, and stirred race-based prejudices. Manchukuo's Opium Law was undermined by Japanese dealers and their Korean and Chinese partners, who experienced few real restrictions in the production and distribution of opium. The Janus-faced Monopoly robbed the state of goodwill that might have pertained from other facets of its modernization agenda, all of which was tainted by ever-increasing militarization and racist oppression. Rehabilitation programs failed to win popular support because even the most well-intentioned reforms were defeated not only by officials who wearied of consigning resources to an endeavour that didn't directly contribute to their own enrichment, economic development, or the war but also by their low success rates. The failings of the Monopoly gave the impression that it was no more than a façade for Japanese drug dealing, making the regime appear not only ruthlessly parasitic but also impotent to effect the social change cited by officials as the reason for the occupation and war.

Opium attained a prominent position in Manchukuo's Chinese-language culture through social realism as Chinese writers sought to raise mass consciousness; recreational opium use was an attractive target and an ideal vehicle for political commentary, regardless of one's personal stance on opium use. The opium narratives outlined in this study bolstered Manchukuo's anti-opium program and heightened awareness of the dangers of drugs to the exclusion of any positive reference to their recreational use. Literature was deployed to promote state regulation of opium, yet it also enabled critical reflection on the nature of Manchukuo rule. Since the Japanese were officially prohibited from using opium, Chinese criticism of opium addiction was not perceived by officials to be critical of the Japanese per se but rather of Chinese weakness and wilful disobedience to the law, discourses officialdom also promoted. Chinese writers decried elite indulgence in, or profit from, opium while the lower classes groaned under the weight of colonization, war, patriarchy, poverty, and addiction.

In Manchukuo's Chinese-language media, little sympathy was extended to addicts, or "ghosts," a term that accentuated the "half-death" nature of depictions of opium addiction. Opium may once have been considered a requirement of polite society, but occupation and war had spawned regulatory frameworks and an environment that spelled an end to presumptions of culture. In the opium narratives outlined above, a critical disjuncture attests to contemporary gender constructs. Both men and women condemned opium addiction for its destructive nature, but men tended more explicitly to link this destruction with society or the nation, whereas women associated it with the family and, especially, its patriarchal foundations. These opium narratives not only underline Confucian maxims that consigned women to the domestic sphere but also reflect deep-seated anxieties over the health, status, and self-identities of the Chinese in Manchukuo – not the economic or industrial obsessions that came to dominate official rhetoric.

The Chinese writers discussed in this chapter echoed the Manchukuo regime's anti-opium agenda because it appealed to them as well as to many colonial officials, who treated opium and popular culture with a similar disdain: they acknowledged that both required supervision, and laws were drafted to control them, but Manchukuo officialdom never mustered the willpower, resources, or legitimacy necessary to bring either fully to heel. As war spread across Asia, Japan's empire grew ever more reliant on the eradication of recreational opium use to increase industrial and military capacity even as it depended on the revenues generated by opium sales. Ultimately, anti-opium narratives worked to the state's disadvantage; claims in 1944 that the number of addicts in the colony had reached a daunting 1.2 million[100] did little to instill confidence in the regime. Not only was the handful of Kangsheng yuan (Healthy Life Institutes) numerically inadequate, but postwar memoirs also tend to depict the institutes as little more than drug-distribution centres or labour camps. Such accounts argue that addicts who entered rehabilitation lost their lives, causing locals to mock the centres as Kengsheng yuan (Cheating Life Institutes).[101] The failings of state-sponsored rehabilitation programs led Chinese to ridicule the Shengkang yuan (Raising Resistance Institutes).[102] The "resistance" that such centres inspired is suggested by the summary execution of directors of Healthy Life Institutes by enraged locals on liberation in 1945.[103] Unsuccessful rehabilitation programs in a racist militarized environment, which historian Yamamuro Shin'ichi has termed an "Auschwitz state,"[104] cemented anti-Manchukuo feeling and contributed to postoccupation memories of this sentiment.

In Manchukuo, writers' support for official drug policies enabled the production of a Japanese-sponsored, Chinese-language literature that did not simply parrot official policy but rather added fuel to the fire of anti-Manchukuo narratives and forged a legacy that consistently reinforced negative memories of the regime. Although the Japanese escape explicit criticism, dark portraits of opium addiction and subjugation are implicitly critical of their rule. Despite its military might, the Manchukuo regime proved unable to fully silence its critics or to curtail the opium industry; in fact, certain forms of criticism were encouraged. The condemnation of opium and, by extension, imperialist subjugation proved as damaging to the Japanese as such narratives had to the British. Yet since the collapse of Japan's empire, the battle against opium in Manchukuo has been forgotten. Major studies by Zhou Yongming and Alan Baumler examine twentieth-century antidrug campaigns in China with no reference to activities in Japanese-held territories. Japanese rule in China's Northeast has been utterly excoriated in popular memory and in scholarly study for wartime atrocities, including drug trafficking. But those Chinese and Japanese who battled opium have to date been excluded from historical narratives, even though their work lay at the heart of domestically produced anti-opium, anti-Manchukuo discourses.[105] In this volume, Bernard Hung-kay Luk outlines how disruptions caused by war and Japanese occupation altered the education of Chinese in Hong Kong, impacting both personal lives and careers. In Mainland China, for decades after the collapse of Manchukuo, those who had attained high-profile careers during the colonial era, like the writers Mei Niang and Wang Qiuying, had their personal lives and careers devastated, as they were hounded as traitors for their career achievements under Japanese occupation, regardless of the critical nature of their work. With regime change and the shifting of historical narratives, those whose work battled opium use were consumed by the condemning memories that they had played no small part in creating.

Acknowledgment

An earlier version of this chapter was published as "Opiate Addiction and the Entanglements of Imperialism and Patriarchy in Manchukuo, 1932-45," *Social History of Alcohol and Drugs* 20 (2005): 66-104.

Notes

1 Mei Niang, "Wo de qingshao nian shiqi: 1920-1938" [My childhood: 1920-1938], in *Xunzhao Mei Niang* [Searching for Mei Niang], ed. Zhang Quan (Beijing: Mingjing chubanshe, 1998), 127. All translations of quotations from non-English sources are mine.

2 *Contemporary Manchuria* 3, 1 (1939): 25-26.

3 John M. Jennings, *The Opium Empire: Japanese Imperialism and Drug Trafficking in Asia, 1895-1945* (London: Praeger, 1997), 78.

4 Opium culture is discussed in Zheng Yangwen, *The Social Life of Opium* (Cambridge, UK: Cambridge University Press, 2006).

5 Zhang Guochen, "Yaowuxue shiyezhong de yapian" [Opium from a pharmaceutical perspective], *Jiankang Manzhou* [Healthy Manchukuo], April 1941, 6.

6 Ronald Suleski, *Civil Government in Warlord China: Tradition, Modernization, and Manchuria* (New York: Peter Lang, 2002), 207.

7 Jennings, *Opium Empire,* 83.

8 *Manchoukuo Yearbook: 1941,* 731.

9 Jiao Runming, *Jindai Dongbei shehui zhu wenti yanjiu* [Research on Various Questions in Modern Northeast Society] (Beijing: Zhongguo shehui kexue chubanshe, 2004), 283.

10 *Manchoukuo Yearbook: 1941,* 728.

11 Ibid.

12 See *Contemporary Manchuria* 3, 1 (1939): 38-44.

13 Michael A. Barnhart, *Japan Prepares for Total War: The Search for Economic Security, 1919-41* (Ithaca, NY: Cornell University Press, 1987); Alan Baumler, *The Chinese and Opium under the Republic: Worse Than Floods and Wild Beasts* (New York: State University of New York Press, 2007).

14 Cited in Timothy Brook and Bob Tadashi Wakabayashi, "Introduction: Opium's History in China," in *Opium Regimes: China, Britain, and Japan, 1839-1952,* ed. Timothy Brook and Bob Tadashi Wakabayashi (Berkeley: University of California Press, 2000), 17. The emperor's assertion must be suspect because of the context within which he wrote his autobiography and the extent of his personal knowledge of the Manchukuo state's financial operations.

15 "Mafei zhi hai" [The harm of morphine], *Shengjing shibao* [Shengjing Times], 30 December 1933, 4; Ah Ling, "Yinzhe de xin" [An addict's letter], and Yue Ai, "Jin yan lun" [Discussion of the smoking prohibition], *Shengjing shibao* [Shengjing Times], 3 October 1941, 5.

16 Jie Xueshi, "Ri Wei shiqi de wenhua tongzhi zhengce" [State policies of cultural domination during the Japanese occupation], in *Dongbei lunxian shiqi wenxue guoji xueshu yantaohui lunwenji* [Collection of Papers from the International Symposium on Literature of the Enemy-Occupied Northeast], ed. Feng Weiqun, Wang Jianzhong, Li Chunyan, and Li Shuquan (Shenyang: Shenyang chubanshe, 1992), 190-91.

17 Qian Liqun, ed., *Zhongguo lunxianqu wenxue daxi: Shiliao juan* [Compendium of the Literature of China's Enemy-Occupied Territories: Volume of Historical Data] (Nanling, Guangxi: Guangxi jiaoyu chubanshe, 2000), vol. 11, 9.

18 Published under the pen name San Lang, "Zhuxin" [Candlewick], in *Bashe* [Trek], ed. San Lang and Qiao Yin (Harbin: Wuri huakan yinshuashe, 1933), reprinted in *Zhuxin ji* [Candlewick Collection], ed. Liang Shanding (Shenyang: Chunfeng wenyi chubanshe, 1989), 18.

19 Ibid., 12.

20 Edgar Snow, "Japan Builds a New Colony," *Saturday Evening Post,* 24 February 1934, 81.

21 Kathryn Meyer, "Japan and the World Narcotics Traffic," in *Consuming Habits: Drugs in History and Anthropology,* ed. Jordan Goodman, Paul E. Lovejoy, and Andrew Sherratt (London: Routledge: 1995), 197.

22 Ibid., 187.

23 Ibid.

24 Ibid., 194, 197.

25 Yamamuro Shin'ichi, Joshua Fogel, ed., *Manchuria under Japanese Dominion* (Philadelphia: University of Pennsylvania Press, 2006), 231.

26 Motohiro Kobayashi, "Drug Operations by Resident Japanese in Tianjin," trans. Bob Tadashi Wakabayashi, in *Opium Regimes: China, Britain, and Japan, 1839-1952,* ed. Timothy Brook and Bob Tadashi Wakabayashi (Berkeley: University of California Press, 2000), 154.

27 Jennings, *Opium Empire,* 85.

28 Xu Naixiang and Huang Wanhua, *Zhongguo kangzhan shiqi lunxianqu wenxue shi* [History of the Literature of the Enemy-Occupied Territories during China's War of Resistance] (Fuzhou: Fujian jiaoyu chubanshe, 1995), 1.

29 Losses cited included lost work hours, reduced levels of workers' skills, and land lost to opium that could be used to grow food, to mine, and so on. Jennings, *Opium Empire,* 87.

30 *Contemporary Manchuria* 3, 1 (1939): 36. Jennings, *Opium Empire,* 87, argues that 1938-39 opium revenues were approximately 30 million yuan.

31 Lo Cheng-Pang, "The Fight against Opium," *Pan Pacific* 3, 4 (1939): 71.

32 Alexandre Pernikoff, *Bushido: The Anatomy of Terror* (New York: Liveright, 1943), 105.

33 Ibid., 173.

34 Ibid., 106.

35 "Shops" could be just a hole in the wall: heroin addicts could knock at a door, whereupon a "small peep-hole opens, through which he thrusts his bare arm and hand with 20 cents

in it. The owner of the joint takes the money and gives the victim a shot in the arm." Amleto Vespa, *Secret Agent of Japan: A Handbook to Japanese Imperialism* (London: Victor Gollancz, 1938), 96-97.

36 Hua Jiangrong, "Yan lou suohua: Ge lingmaisuo nü zhaodai sumiao" [Trivial talk about opium dens: Sketches of monopoly hostesses], *Shengjing shibao* [Shengjing Times], 10 April 1936, 7.

37 Vespa, *Secret Agent of Japan,* 101. This text is also cited in Mark Gayn, *Journey from the East* (New York: Alfred A. Knopf, 1944), 418.

38 Nakamura Kōjirō, "Kessenka no sake to tabako" [Drinking and smoking under the condition of total war], *Manshūkōron* [Popular Debates in Manchukuo] (March 1945): 58-61.

39 Kazeta Eiki, "Wei Manzhouguo wenyi zhangye de fazhan" [The development of bogus Manchukuo's literary rules and regulations], in *Dongbei lunxian shiqi wenxue guoji xueshu yantaohui lunwenji* [Collection of Papers from the International Symposium on Literature of the Enemy-Occupied Northeast], ed. Feng Weiqun, Wang Jianzhong, Li Chunyan, and Li Shuquan (Shenyang: Shenyang chubanshe, 1992), 160.

40 Shinichi Yamaguchi, "Contemporary Literature in Manchuria," in *Concordia and Culture in Manchoukuo,* ed. Manchuria Daily News (Xinjing: Manchuria Daily News, 20 July 1938), 27.

41 Lan Ling, "Xiao xiang de chuxi" [New year in a small alley], *Xin shige* [New Poetry] 1 (1940), reprinted in *Dongbei xiandai wenxue daxi, 1919-49: Shige juan* [Compendium of Modern North-Eastern Literature, 1919-49: Volume of Poetry], ed. Zhang Yumao, vol. 12, 808-11 (Shenyang: Shenyang chubanshe, 1996). For details on Lan's life, see Norman Smith, "Writing Chinese Women in Japanese-Occupied Manchuria: The Legacy of Lan Ling," *Women, Reading, Writing* 2, 3 (Winter 2008): 13-17.

42 Lan, "Xiao xiang de chuxi," 810.

43 For details on the "good wife, wise mother" construct in Manchukuo, see Norman Smith, *Resisting Manchukuo: Chinese Women Writers and the Japanese Occupation* (Vancouver: UBC Press, 2007).

44 For further details on Mei Niang, see Norman Smith, "'Only Women Can Change This World into Heaven': Mei Niang, Male Chauvinist Society, and the Japanese Cultural Agenda in North China, 1939-41," *Modern Asian Studies* 40, 1 (February 2006): 81-107.

45 Mei Niang, "Zhui" [The Chase], in *Di'er dai* [The Second Generation] (Xinjing: Wencong han xinghui, 1940).

46 Ibid., 136.

47 Ibid., 135.

48 Ibid., 136.

49 Ibid.

50 Ibid., 144.

51 "Patient" is a compound of two characters, *qiu* (to seek) and *zhen* (needle). The couple, however, is not seeking a needle but rather drugs that they can more easily share. Mei Niang, "Zuihou de qiuzhenzhe" [The last patient], in *Di'er dai.*

52 Ibid., 88.

53 Ibid., 89.

54 Ibid.

55 The Eight Abstentions are reproduced in Yu Lei, "Ziliao" [Data], *Dongbei wenxue yanjiu shiliao* [Historical Research Materials of North-Eastern Literature] 6 (1987): 181.

56 The Summary of Guidelines is reproduced in ibid., 174-78.

57 Kazeta, "Wei Manzhouguo wenyi zhangye de fazhan," 164.

58 Ibid., 165.

59 Xu and Huang, *Zhongguo kangzhan shiqi lunxianqu wenxue shi,* 267.
60 Ibid., 269.
61 Ibid., 266.
62 *Shengjing shibao* [Shengjing Times], 3 October 1941, 5.
63 *Datong bao* [Great Unity Herald], 6 December 1941, 4.
64 For details, see Smith, *Resisting Manchukuo,* 30-40.
65 *Manchoukuo Yearbook: 1941,* 722.
66 Ibid.
67 *Contemporary Manchuria* 3, 1 (1939): 20; *Manchoukuo Yearbook: 1941,* 727, 730.
68 Zhang, "Yaowuxue shiyezhong de yapian," 8-12.
69 Zhang Jiyou, "Yapian" [Opium], *Jiankang Manzhou* [Healthy Manchukuo], March 1939, 12.
70 Lo, "Fight against Opium," 72.
71 *Manchoukuo Yearbook: 1941,* 722. In 1939, 46 institutes (each with a capacity of 2,672 patients) were established, with a planned 156 more to be constructed before 1942, yet in 1942 there were still only 46 institutes; see *Contemporary Manchuria* 3, 1 (1939): 33-36. Based on US government statistics, Jennings, *Opium Empire,* 101, argues that 189 treatment centres were established.
72 *Manchoukuo Yearbook: 1941,* 725.
73 This novel was originally published under the pen name Qiu Ying, *He liu de diceng* [The bottom of the river] (Dalian: Shiye yanghang chubanbu faxing, 1941), reprinted in *Zhongguo xiandai wenxue buyi shuxi* [Addendum of Modern Chinese Literature Series], ed. Kong Fanjin, vol. 5 (Jinan, Shandong: Mingtian chubanshe, 1990).
74 Ibid., 834.
75 Prasenjit Duara, *Sovereignty and Authenticity* (Oxford: Rowman and Littlefield, 2003).
76 Qiu, *He liu de diceng,* 742.
77 Ibid., 721.
78 Ibid., 811.
79 Ibid., 805.
80 This song is also known as the *Get off Opium Song,* words by Li Juanqing, music by Liang Leyin; see *Li Xianglan Collection* (Taipei: Zhonghua Records, 1999).
81 Kazeta, "Wei Manzhouguo wenyi zhangye de fazhan," 169.
82 Xu and Huang, *Zhongguo kangzhan shiqi lunxianqu wenxue shi,* 267.
83 Wang Qiuying, "Lou xiang" [Vulgar alley], *Chuangzuo liancong* [Creative Crowd] 2 (1944), reprinted in *Zhuxin ji* [Candlewick Collection], ed. Liang Shanding (Shenyang: Chunfeng wenyi chubanshe, 1989), 111.
84 Ibid., 116.
85 Ibid., 119.
86 Ibid., 112.
87 Ibid., 131.
88 Ibid., 127.
89 Ibid., 120.
90 Ibid., 141.
91 This story was written in 1939 and published in 1944. Ye Li, "San ren" [Three people], in *Hua zhong* [Flower Tomb] (Xinjing: Zhushi huishe dadi tushu gongsi, 1944), reprinted in *Zhuxin ji* [Candlewick Collection], ed. Liang Shanding (Shenyang: Chunfeng wenyi chubanshe, 1989).
92 Ibid., 261.
93 Ibid., 264.

94 Ibid., 261.

95 Ibid., 263.

96 Pernikoff, *Bushido,* 104.

97 See Lu Shouxin, "Ha'erbin de yapian yandu" [Harbin's poisonous opium smoke], in *Wei Man wenhua: Wei Man shiliao congshu* [Bogus Manchukuo Culture: Collection of Historical Materials on Bogus Manchukuo], ed. Sun Bang (Changchun: Jilin renmin chubanshe, 1993), vol. 7, 446.

98 Zhou Yongming, *Anti-Drug Crusades in Twentieth Century China: Nationalism, History, and State Building* (Oxford: Rowman and Littlefield, 1999).

99 Yang Chaohui and An Linhai, "Wei Man shiqi de Rehe yapian" [Rehe opium during the bogus Manchukuo period], in *Wei Man wenhua: Wei Man shiliao congshu* [Bogus Manchukuo Culture: Collection of Historical Materials on Bogus Manchukuo], ed. Sun Bang (Changchun: Jilin renmin chubanshe, 1993), vol. 7, 425.

100 Wang Guiqin, "Wei Man shiqi de 'yapian duanjin' zhengce" [The bogus Manchukuo 'opium prohibition' policy], in *Dongbei jingji lüeduo* [Northeast Economic Exploitation], ed. Sun Bang (Beijing: Zhonghua shu ju, 1991), 707.

101 Wang Xianwei, "Jin yan zhengce de qipian xing" [The fraudulent nature of the smoking prohibition], in *Dongbei jingji lüeduo* [Northeast Economic Exploitation], ed. Sun Bang (Beijing: Zhonghua shu ju, 1991), 711.

102 Mou Jianping, "Wei Man de dupin zhengce" [The narcotic policies of bogus Manchukuo], in *Dongbei jingji lüeduo* [Northeast Economic Exploitation], ed. Sun Bang (Beijing: Zhonghua shu ju, 1991), 723.

103 Han Yu, "Zong du zhengce xia de Benxi" [Benxi village under the narcotics policies], in *Wei Man wenhua: Wei Man shiliao congshu* [Bogus Manchukuo Culture: Collection of Historical Materials on Bogus Manchukuo], ed. Sun Bang (Changchun: Jilin renmin chubanshe, 1993), vol. 7, 449.

104 Yamamuro Shin'ichi, ed., *Manchuria under Japanese Dominion,* 4.

105 Baumler, for example, in *The Chinese and Opium under the Republic,* outlines four major anti-opium movements in China without reference to efforts made in occupied territories.

2
War, Schools, China, Hong Kong: 1937-49

Bernard Hung-kay Luk

> *The Anti-Japanese War produced a change in collective consciousness among many Chinese ... The Chinese responded to the violence of war with a spirit of resistance – a patriotic pride in the survivor community.*
>
> – Diana Lary and Stephen MacKinnon, *Scars of War*, 10

Preamble: War and Suffering Remembered

In September 2005 the Bel Canto Chorus of Hong Kong gave a performance of songs from the War of Resistance era in the City Hall to mark the sixtieth anniversary of the victory over the Japanese invaders.[1] The organizers had wanted to hold the event on 18 September in order to commemorate the Shenyang Incident of 1931, but as that day happened to coincide with the Mid-Autumn Festival, a traditional family celebration that takes precedence over most other activities, they had to settle for an alternative date. Singing such wartime classics as *On the Sungari River, Defend the Yellow River, 800 Brave Men,* and *March of the Volunteers,* the singers of the chorus were too young to have lived through the tumult of the invasion. But many in the audience were old enough to have had direct personal experience of the war and the suffering, and they had indeed learned many of the songs during their school days. The resonance between the performers and the full house brought the history of the war to life for the younger generations who were there. And the mindful observer may also note that the repertoire of the evening, comprising songs of Nationalist as well as Communist provenance, still could be performed publicly only by a chorus based in Hong Kong.

Schools and Social Divisions in Hong Kong before the Second World War

This chapter attempts to outline the vicissitudes of schools, teachers, and students in Hong Kong during the twelve years of the Japanese invasion and Chinese resistance, followed by the Civil War of 1945-49 between the Chinese Nationalist and Communist forces. Although the general outline of the history of the wars is well known and the impact of the wars on subsequent Chinese politics has been the subject of important studies – most notably *Scars of War,* the volume of scholarly essays initiated and edited by Diana Lary and Stephen

MacKinnon – little has been written with a focus on the war and its effects on education in Hong Kong and its south China hinterland. In fact, the war years have been left blank in most histories of education in Hong Kong. This chapter aims to fill in some of that gap.[2]

Hong Kong before the Second World War did not have an integrated school system of its own. Rather, separate school streams co-existed, reflecting the broad divisions in Hong Kong society. Although all suffered when Hong Kong fell under Japanese occupation, the various streams of schools fared differently depending largely on their economic and cultural backgrounds and their social networks.

Prewar opportunities for education were very uneven. Most of the children (especially girls) either did not attend or attended only for a short time.[3] The streaming was the product of the particular colonial milieu of the time. There was a small handful of segregated schools for British children, but most missionary and government schools enrolled a mix of Chinese, Indian, Eurasian, and European pupils. Racial streaming affected only a tiny proportion of pupils. For the Chinese inhabitants who constituted over 95 percent of the population, much more important was the streaming of Chinese pupils by curriculum, which was a matter of parental choice.

Hong Kong as a Chinese society partook of many of the conflicts between the "conservative" and the "modern," the "traditional" and the "westernized," the "right" and the "left," that rocked China throughout the early twentieth century. In colonial Hong Kong – culturally contiguous but politically separate from Mainland China – a wide spectrum of Chinese opinions and options was openly manifest. Hence three streams of schools for Hong Kong Chinese pupils co-existed in the 1920s and 1930s, each stressing a different set of knowledge and values and each catering to a different clientele. These were the Anglo-Chinese schools, the modern Chinese schools, and the traditional *sishu*. A parent could send sons to one stream and daughters to another or a favourite son to one stream and the rest of the children to another as part of a broader strategy for the future of the family. By and large, the poorer classes could afford only to send their children (usually just the sons) to the cheaper sishu, whereas the two modern streams were available for the better-off.

Not only did the three streams teach differently, but they were also funded and sponsored differently. Teaching mainly in English a curriculum derived largely from British Empire sources, with Chinese as one of the subjects, most of the Anglo-Chinese schools were sponsored by Christian missionaries from Western countries, although a handful of them were directly run by the Education Department of the colonial government. All of these schools were funded out of the public purse – with grant-in-aid for the missionary schools and a government budget line for the government schools, which enabled them to charge school fees that did not recover full costs – even if they were still prohibitively expensive for most families. They also operated in large purpose-designed buildings they owned, with all of the facilities expected of a modern school. These schools either equipped their students for English-speaking or bilingual careers in commerce or government service in Hong Kong or prepared them to attend Hong Kong University. Thus they were considered elite institutions.

The sishu at the other extreme taught traditional lessons based on Classical Chinese texts, without using any modern equipment, to small groups of pupils in nonformal settings that were often just the living quarters of the teacher within some crude tenement. The curriculum was traditional and highly flexible; most of the pupils did not attend for more than a few years, which was as long as their parents could afford the modest fees. These small schools run by individual literati, which actually enrolled the large majority of Hong Kong pupils before the Second World War, did not receive any public funding and were completely dependent on the fees paid by the parents or by school sponsors such as guilds, charities, and native-place associations. Although a few of the sishu enjoyed prestige and affluence by catering to the demand of wealthy families for a prep-school education before their children advanced to either of the two modern streams, most sishu barely managed to survive precariously with the support of a few dozen impoverished parents in the neighbourhood who could not afford anything more highly priced. The courses, like those in the sishu of earlier times, were of only a few years' duration and did not lead to any careers; a few of the pupils might have been able to continue their education in either of the two modern streams.

The modern Chinese schools, situated between the two extremes, were run by modern-minded Chinese educators following basically a curriculum devised by the Chinese Ministry of Education (in Beijing, Nanjing, or Chongqing, depending on the period). Many of them were connected with the Chinese Protestant churches, notably the Church of Christ in China, the Presbyterian Church, or the Baptist Church. Some others were led by members of gentry families prominent in the government or military of Guangdong. A few were started by women from wealthy Hong Kong or Canton families who created worthwhile careers for themselves outside the home. Since they were financed entirely from tuition, these schools were typically housed in rented mansions located in precincts populated by the Chinese middle classes, and they charged fees considerably higher than those of the government-supported Anglo-Chinese schools to maintain the modern equipment and staff they needed. They prepared their students for careers in the modern sector in China or in Hong

Kong, which demanded somewhat less English than did those jobs employing students from the Anglo-Chinese schools; some of the students also aimed to attend university on the Mainland.

When war came, the pattern of a school's funding and sponsorship largely determined its fate and that of its students and staff. But it should be pointed out here that before the Second World War all three school streams in Hong Kong were linked to Mainland China in many ways. As an entrepot dependent for its livelihood on the China trade, Hong Kong could not afford to be cut off from the Mainland, and its elites were never educated to be ignorant about China. All schools expected of their students a certain attainment in Chinese studies. All of them used textbooks published in China; even many books adopted for English language and literature in the missionary schools were produced by the Commercial Press in Shanghai. Many pupils from both of the modern streams went on to attend universities or to take up careers on the Mainland. And many of the modern Chinese schools had dual registration, both with the Education Department in Hong Kong and with the authorities in Nanjing and in Canton. Indeed, some of them operated branches on either side of the border, particularly in the Pearl River Delta cultural region defined by the tri-cities of Canton, Hong Kong, and Macau. Last but not least, a large majority of the Hong Kong population had been born in the Pearl River Delta or elsewhere in Guangdong and still had strong family, social, education, and economic ties there, and there was no government-imposed restriction of movement across the border prior to the 1950s. Before the Second World War, Hong Kong education can perhaps be best described as half in and half out of the education scene of modern China. How a school fared during the war depended to a large extent on the strength and durability of its ties with the hinterland in south China.

From 7/7 to the Fall of Canton: The Impact on Hong Kong

> *China's real nightmare was to come when she had to deal with soldiers who not only had license to treat civilians as they liked, but were also efficient at doing so – the soldiers of Imperial Japan.*
>
> Diana Lary, *Warlord Soldiers*, 106

The Japanese invasion of China started with the Shenyang Incident of 18 September 1931, which resulted in the takeover of Manchuria by the Japanese Kwantung Army. But it was the Marco Polo Bridge Incident outside Beijing on 7 July 1937 (the 7/7 Incident) that marked the beginning of the full-scale War of Resistance. For the first year, the hostilities were concentrated in north and central China, although there were also numerous destructive episodes of bombing of Canton by Japanese warplanes. However, the Japanese army landed at Daya Bay, east of Hong Kong, on 12 October 1938 for the onslaught of Canton – which had not been anticipated by the Guangdong provincial forces under the command of General Yu Hanmou. This brought full-scale war to south China. Unprepared, the Chinese forces were not able to stop or delay the enemy. Canton fell within a week of the landing, and the provincial government moved to Qujiang (Shaoguan) in the mountainous region in the north of the province. The occupation of Canton and the larger towns of southern Guangdong lasted for the duration of the war, with all of the dire consequences for the civilian population and their schools in the region of the Pearl River Delta.[4]

The 7/7 Incident had two major impacts on Hong Kong: economic boom and population explosion. The Japanese takeover of Beijing and Tianjin, and the subsequent onslaughts of Shanghai and Nanjing, redirected the focus of China's external trade away from its northern and eastern ports and toward Hong Kong. With the fall of Shanghai and Nanjing, Hong Kong also became the major remaining port on the China coast for the import of war materiel. The long-demanded linkage at Canton between the Kowloon-Canton Railway and the Canton-Hankou Railway was finally allowed to be made. Land and river transport between Hong Kong and its hinterland was improved and strengthened, and trade rapidly exceeded pre-Depression levels. At the same time, local manufacturing of light consumer goods, which had a long history and enjoyed a small boost from the Depression-era Commonwealth Preference Tariffs, now picked up and expanded. By 1941 nearly one-quarter of Hong Kong's workforce was engaged in manufacturing industries.[5]

Meanwhile, Hong Kong played its traditional role as a safe haven for people fleeing turmoil in Mainland China – a role first begun in the 1850s during the Taiping Rebellion. The census of 1931 had recorded a population of 864,000. The census of 1941 was not held on account of the unsettled conditions, but the Air Raid Precaution Service of the Hong Kong government made an unofficial survey that estimated the population at more than 1.6 million.[6] Most of the doubling of the population took place between 1937 and 1941 – indeed, between the fall of Canton in late 1938 and the Battle of Hong Kong barely three years later. The refugees came from many parts of China, not just the south; and they came in many shapes and sizes. Some, like the 10,000 housed in the Hong Kong government's refugee camps (and supplied with soybean drink donated by the fledgling Vitasoy company), were destitute.[7] Some were wealthy families who brought with them part of their businesses and a good deal of cash. Some were the cultural elites and trendsetters for the arts, publishing, and political opinion from Beijing, Nanjing, and Shanghai, who collectively created the glittering ephemera of Hong Kong as the temporary cultural capital of China.[8] But the majority were poor men, women, and children running ahead of the enemy, packing themselves into squalid tenement buildings, or just sleeping on the streets, finding whatever jobs they could in the nascent factories, and eking out a mere survival in this receptive but uncomforting urban strangeness.

The Refugees from the Mainland and Their Schools in Hong Kong

> *Insecurity is intangible, hard to measure. It is felt, not assessed statistically.*
>
> – Diana Lary, *Warlord Soldiers*, 110

The *Hong Kong Administrative Report* on 1936 recorded a school enrolment of 79,679.[9] The *Report* on 1937 counted 86,993, noting a "marked influx of both Chinese and Europeans to the more secure confines of the Colony, accompanied by a sharp rise in the attendance figures of educational institutions."[10] The *Report* on 1938 again noted that "the continued unsettled conditions in China caused by the Sino-Japanese conflict were again responsible for an influx of both Chinese and Europeans, and there was a sharp rise in the attendance figures of educational institutions ... [This reached] the record figure of 104,134."[11] By 1939, covered in the last available *Report* before Hong Kong fell to the Japanese army, the enrolment was 118,193.[12]

Those enrolled in schools were still very much a minority of the school-age population. The total enrolment increased about 48 percent between 1936 and 1939, falling behind the doubling of the overall population. Although the children of most of the refugees probably were not in school most of the time and although many of the better-off newcomers enrolled their children in pre-existing local Hong Kong schools, some of the latter in fact brought their schools with them – from kindergartens to universities.

It has been noted above that during the decade before the war, a number of schools had branches operating both on the Mainland and in Hong Kong. One of the better-known among these was Pui Ching (Peizheng), a primary and middle school associated with the Baptist Church of Guangdong-Guangxi, which had its main campus in the suburbs of Canton. In 1934 the leaders of the school accepted the invitation of a group of Hong Kong businessmen who were also members of the church to set up a branch there. They were able to obtain a large piece of land from the Hong Kong government and considerable funding support from their church. The Hong Kong branch was fully functioning by the time the war began. When Canton was bombed, the Pui Ching school there first moved out of town, then to Macau. After Canton fell, the campus there was taken over by the invaders, and Hong Kong and Macau, where many of the wealthy families of its pupils were seeking refuge, became the main campuses of the school.[13]

Other Canton schools might not have had a branch campus in Hong Kong, but when war came to Canton, they packed up whatever they could and moved to the safe haven of the British colony in order not to submit to the invaders and perhaps also to follow their clientele.[14] It is not possible from available sources to estimate what proportion of schools in Canton and other Guangdong towns moved to Hong Kong, but most schools that did move seem to have been ones of the modern Chinese type, especially modern schools connected with Chinese Protestant churches, if only because they had the ways and means to do so. The majority of the sishu, lacking any material or social resources other than the individual teachers themselves, probably just folded. And even if some of them did move to Hong Kong, they have left no records.

Prominent examples of the schools that moved to Hong Kong were Pui To (Peidao), a Baptist girls' school,[15] and Zhenguang (True Light), a Presbyterian girls' school.[16] The most eminent of these schools-in-exile was of course Lingnan University. As soon as the Japanese army landed at Daya Bay, President W.L. Lee (Li Yinglin) of the university travelled from Canton to Hong Kong to organize for a move. He was able to negotiate a time-share arrangement with the vice-chancellor of Hong Kong University (HKU), Professor Duncan Sloss. Lingnan classes would be held in HKU classrooms in the evenings, and Lingnan staff and students were given access to HKU libraries. President Lee was also able to rent a farm in the New Territories as the temporary campus for the School of Agriculture. Within a few weeks, Lingnan resumed most of its academic activities in Hong Kong – except for the Medical School, which moved to the International Settlement in Shanghai.[17] (President Lee signed over the title of the vast and beautiful campus of Lingnan at Kangle, in what was then a suburb of Canton, to the American missionary board, represented by his American colleagues, who were to hold it safe against the Japanese invaders. The American and Canadian Protestant missionaries of the university, together with the French Catholic bishop of Canton, turned the campus into an asylum for several thousand Cantonese civilians displaced by the war, until the North Americans were themselves evicted and interned by the Japanese occupation after Pearl Harbor.)[18]

Shortly before its hurried departure from Canton, Lingnan had played host to several hundred refugee students of Beida, Tsinghua, and Nankai who were on their way from Changsha to Kunming (where they would join the newly amalgamated Xinan Lianda [Southwest United University]), as well as more than two thousand nursing students training for the war effort.[19] Now the tables were turned. Such was the vicissitude of wartime education. Lingnan was able to become the grateful recipient of the hospitality of HKU because the two institutions had shared years of amiable collaboration, their leaders were well acquainted with one another, and their student bodies came from the same social strata of Hong Kong, the Pearl River Delta, and southeast Asia. Two other private universities from Canton that fled to Hong Kong, Guangzhou Daxue and Guomin Daxue, were not so well endowed or connected and had to make do in the rented premises of middle schools or tenement units in poorer parts of Kowloon and the New Territories.[20]

It must not be assumed that when a school went into exile, its staff and student body remained intact. In fact, the human composition of a school on the move was very fluid, as each person might have different reasons to stay put, to move with the school, or to go elsewhere. Although few details are extant for all of the schools that fled Canton for Hong Kong or other destinations, one may note that even with Lingnan's safe and smooth transfer to the HKU campus, there were still considerable drops and additions. Before it went into exile, Lingnan had over 800 students at its Kangle campus, including perhaps 300 associate students who were refugees from northern universities. Some 520 reassembled at HKU to finish the semester, many of whom might have come from Hong Kong families. The following semester the enrolment was 460 students, old and new. As the university moved again, the enrolment fluctuated.[21]

Competing for space with all of the people and organizations that moved into Hong Kong during these early years of the war was an expensive proposition, but a number of schools and even some individual educators were able to secure enough support to do so satisfactorily.[22] One example was Dr. K.W. Hung (Hong Gaohuang), a former professor of education at Lingnan University and a school principal in Canton. He came to Hong Kong in 1937 to help Pui Ying (Peiying), another Canton Protestant school, set up its branch. Seeing that there was still considerable unmet demand for quality schooling, he decided to establish a new school of his own in 1938. Renting a large mansion in the Causeway Bay district on Hong Kong Island, Ling Ying (Lingying) School opened that autumn – on the eve of the Japanese march on Canton – with some 500 students in primary and junior-middle grades. By the last semester before the Battle of Hong Kong (autumn term, 1941), Ling Ying had 1,453 students in all grades from kindergarten to senior middle, thirty-eight classes total. It also proudly owned 23,000 volumes in its library and full sets of scientific equipment in its laboratory – all of which was paid for out of the tuition fees and donations received since 1938.[23]

On the opposite end of the socio-economic scale, many thousands of refugee children did not have the means to attend any school, let alone an expensive one. Some of those who had no families were taken in by orphanages established on the initiatives of Chinese government officials or local Hong Kong philanthropists. They were given some vocational training and, on attaining employment age, were to be repatriated to the Mainland.[24] From available sources, it is not possible to estimate how many children were raised in these orphanages, but there is nothing to indicate that there were more than a few thousand. There were also some two thousand children attending classes in the refugee camps set up by the Hong Kong government in the New Territories, according to the *Hong Kong Administrative Report* on 1939, but no details are available.[25]

For the street urchins who were not orphans, there were efforts made by a group of Chinese political leaders sojourning in Hong Kong to make available some free schooling for them.[26] Between 1939 and 1941 there were decrees issued by the various Chinese government authorities to China-registered schools in Hong Kong to set up evening free schools for refugee children.[27] The local students of a number of Hong Kong-based secondary schools, including missionary schools and colonial government schools, also volunteered their time and effort to teach evening classes for free in order to help children of poor families, whether they were locals or refugees. An example was the evening free school organized by the King's College students' society of the class that would have sat the Hong Kong School Certificate Examinations (the Grade 11 graduation examination) in the summer of 1942. (King's College was, and still is, a prestigious government-run Anglo-Chinese secondary school.) Members of the class organized themselves into the Xingwu she (I Awake Society). Between 1939 and the Battle of Hong Kong in December 1941, these teenagers taught literacy skills during the evening to some two dozen street children in the neighbourhood of their school in the West Point district of Hong Kong Island.[28] Because such volunteer services, although probably quite numerous, were spontaneous, uncoordinated, and unregistered, it is not possible to estimate the scale of the overall provisions.

Leaving Hong Kong

Shortly after they had found their foothold in Hong Kong, the refugee schools from Canton were instructed by the Guangdong provincial government to move again.[29] They were told it was their patriotic duty to follow the provincial government to northern Guangdong and not to hide away under colonial protection in Hong Kong and Macau. When these schools did not respond to the call, they were threatened with deregistration.[30] When the pressure became too strong to resist, they reluctantly made plans to leave Hong Kong in stages and head for northern Guangdong, where the provincial government had relocated in the mountainous region bordering Guangdong, Hunan, and Jiangxi. By the time Hong Kong itself fell to the Japanese, the Canton-based schools that still remained in Hong Kong also had no alternative but to leave. However, many of the students, especially the younger ones, would stay with their families in Hong Kong. The older ones would choose to move with their schools, to stay in Hong Kong or Macau, or to go elsewhere in Mainland China for school or work. Some opted to go to war, joining the Nationalists or the Communists.

Hong Kong Responses to the War

> *If looked at cumulatively as a cycle of officially sanctioned violence that began in the mid-nineteenth century, Chinese experience with the arbitrary violence and destruction of war has no European parallel.*
>
> – Diana Lary and Stephen MacKinnon, *Scars of War*, 6

Officially, the United Kingdom was neutral in the War of Resistance until the start of the Pacific War on 8 December 1941. As a British colony, Hong Kong was also officially neutral, and the colonial government maintained a correct line to the extent of censoring local Chinese newspapers for "anti-Japanese propaganda." Unofficially, however, there was a great deal of sympathy for China, not only among the 95 percent of the population who were Chinese but also among many expatriates. The Catholic bishop Henry Valtorta, for example, an Italian cleric of the Pontifical Institute of Foreign Missionaries of Milan (PIME), whose own country's Fascist government was invading Abyssinia, issued two pastoral letters in 1937, first in August and then in December, exhorting his faithful to support the Chinese war effort with prayer, donations, and other legal means.[31] The British principal of King's College, a civil servant of the colonial government, not only did not censor the singing of War of Resistance songs in his school but even arranged for the famous Wuhan Chorus to perform its popular patriotic repertoire in the school hall during one of its several fundraising tours to the colony, much to the arousal of the students.[32]

In the schools, many organized activities took place to support the Chinese war effort. Patriotic mobilization was infused into language, history, art, music, and other lessons by teachers. Donations were collected by school authorities or student volunteers; fundraising concerts and drama performances were given. Winter clothing and bandages were sewn in girls' schools for Chinese soldiers on the front.[33] Some of this was prompted by the Chinese national or Guangdong governments through the schools that they registered, and the rest was initiated by local Hong Kong groups such as charitable organizations or churches. The proceeds were collected and offered to the Chinese Red Cross or various arms of the Chinese government. Patriotic fervour remained high, but it did not necessarily touch everyone. There is evidence that some students in schools or universities were not impressionable, although not unaware of the tragic events that were taking place to the north.[34]

Meanwhile, local newspapers represented the entire spectrum of Chinese opinion on the war: from Nationalist to Communist to collaborationist. And a School of Journalism was established in Hong Kong by left-wing writers to provide a six-month course to train young people to be reporters for the front or behind enemy lines, to educate the masses, and to "expose the lies of the traitors" (i.e., the collaborationists).[35]

The large influx of people and institutions from war-torn China into Hong Kong (and into the foreign concessions in the treaty ports up the coast) testified to the belief, common among both British and Chinese in Hong Kong, that the Western-controlled territories would be safe from Japanese attack and that Japan would never dare arouse the ire of the white imperialists. This faith remained strong despite the fact that by the summer of 1940, France had fallen to Nazi Germany and Britain was fully preoccupied with the fight for its own survival.

In 1938, with the gathering of the storm clouds, the Hong Kong government set up a committee to look into air-raid precautions.[36] An office was established, and guidelines were drawn up.[37] By early 1941 school principals throughout Hong Kong were given instructions on what to do in case Hong Kong was bombed.[38] Air-raid drills were instituted, and air-raid-shelter wardens were trained to direct the civilian population to the shelters. Some of the wardens were senior secondary students in the government schools.[39] But the sense of security continued, and the Hong Kong government's decree in the summer of 1941 to repatriate European (i.e., white British) women and children was met with almost universal resentment – by Europeans for being unnecessary and by Chinese, Indians, and Eurasians for being discriminatory. The reinforcement of the British garrison with Canadian troops in November only added to the false sense of security. The coming of the assault on 8 December 1941 was a rude shock.

Hong Kong under Japanese Occupation

> *The agonies and uncertainties of being a refugee for the long term traumatized a generation to the point that survival by any means became their principal goal in life.*
>
> – Diana Lary and Stephen MacKinnon, *Scars of War*, 13

For many people in Hong Kong, the first inkling that war had broken out occured when they witnessed the bombing of Kai Tak airfield early one morning, which completely destroyed the very limited British capacity for air defence. The siege that followed was short and sharp, but the Chinese population was not mobilized in any way by the government for what it saw as a colonial struggle between Britain and Japan. Nevertheless, civilians also suffered a great deal, as they were caught in the crossfire and subject to the disorder and pillaging in the wake of fighting.

The eighth of December 1941 started as a normal school day, but as soon as the students arrived at school, they were told that all classes had been suspended indefinitely and that they should go home as quickly as possible. Some school buildings were requisitioned by the British military for use as hospitals or other facilities.[40] Other schools came under Japanese artillery fire because of their exposed positions close to military targets. A number of schools quickly dismissed the staff with whatever severance pay they could muster on short notice, while also offering them the option to stay with the school if they so wished. Schools with staff and/or students who had come from outside Hong Kong and who had stayed in residence on school premises hurriedly stocked up on food.[41] Those who had escaped to Hong Kong from the Mainland just a few years before had the benefit of experience. By the time the British surrendered on Christmas Day, the ones who knew that they would be targets for coercion or reprisal, such as President W.L. Lee of Lingnan University and other educators closely associated with the Chinese resistance, also had to make plans for hiding and escape – from the Japanese and especially from the collaborationists.[42]

Under the Japanese occupation, the schools remained closed while the new colonial masters made their efforts to root out the legacies of the old. All British and Allied teachers were put away in internment camps. The teaching of English would be replaced with the teaching of Japanese, and schools would be allowed to reopen on condition that the Japanese language and Japanese culture would be made part of the curriculum. So new textbooks had to be prepared, and teachers had to be retrained for the purpose. Short residential courses were provided by the military government for a few hundred teachers who applied and were selected for them. It was not until mid-May 1942 that twelve schools reopened. These were joined by another nine shortly afterward.[43]

In 1941 the population of Hong Kong was estimated at 1.6 million. When Japan surrendered in August 1945, it was estimated at about one-third that number. Hong Kong lost about 23,000 people per month during the three years and eight months of the Japanese occupation through voluntary repatriation to Mainland China (encouraged by Japanese policy), deportation to forced labour on Hainan Island, and death from violence, disease, or starvation. The economy was depleted along with the population, as Hong Kong lost the trade that was its raison d'etre before the war. No wonder, then, that school enrollment also dropped precipitously, from some 120,000 in 1941 to about 4,000 in 1945.[44]

Although all schools suffered, treatment by the occupation power was differentiated. Schools formerly run by British or Allied officials or missionaries were not allowed to resume; only private Chinese schools and those run by missionaries from neutral or Axis countries could do so. A handful of Catholic schools led by Italian, French, or Irish missionaries or protected by the Italian Bishop Valtorta were allowed to function, as long as they added the Japanese language to the curriculum. But Protestant schools could not do so because of their British, American, or Chongqing connections. Among Chinese schools unconnected with any foreign interests or Chinese government, a few were permitted, or coerced, to reopen. Among the latter was Master Lo Sheung-fu's (Lu Xiangfu) sishu, one of the most prestigious of its kind before the war and headed by one of the last remaining graduates of the Qing imperial examinations. After operating reluctantly for about a year, it closed permanently in 1943.[45] Most of the sishu simply disappeared from the scene, never to recover even after the war.

The majority of the schools did not reopen under the occupation. Many of their premises were broken into and pillaged. There is some evidence that the Japanese army took good care of libraries and their stocks. The only part of HKU that remained intact throughout the occupation was the library, and at least one school had its entire library holdings carted away by Japanese troops to be kept at HKU.[46] By 1944, when the supply of food and fuel became desperate, many disused school buildings were pillaged for the furniture and other wooden parts that could be chopped up for firewood. This included the roof of the main hall of HKU. By the end of the war, much work was needed to make the school buildings adequate for use again.[47]

Hong Kong Refugees on the Mainland

> *All Chinese had detailed maps of danger, constantly updated through rumour. They knew not to travel alone, to keep away from places where soldiers concentrated.*
>
> – Diana Lary, *Warlord Soldiers*, 107

There is no systematic account of the almost 1 million people (some two-thirds of the population) who left Hong Kong during the Japanese occupation. Many longtime residents or southern refugees undoubtedly returned to Canton or the Pearl River Delta towns and villages from which they or their parents had come to Hong Kong. The better-off northern refugees might have returned to Shanghai, Beijing, Tianjin, or other major cities from which they had escaped a few years before, or they may have gone into "Free China." The more politically inclined would choose to go to Chongqing or Yan'an. There were also many teachers and students who left Hong Kong for the Mainland, where they remained in Guangdong and pursued their particular goals.

The preferred routes for many people going into the Mainland from occupied Hong Kong was to travel by sea to the French-leased territory of Guangzhouwan (Zhanjiang) in western Guangdong, which was under the Vichy umbrella, and from there to continue overland to Wuzhou or Guilin in Guangxi or to northern Guangdong.[48] This would completely bypass Japanese lines, although banditry was still a concern. Alternatively, one could take the ferry to Macao and from there go into the Pearl River Delta, parts of which were also under Japanese occupation, or one could take local craft from the eastern New Territories to sail for Huizhou on the coast just to the northeast of Hong Kong. Either route would be more direct but also riskier.[49] The Hong Kong–Guangzhouwan–Guilin–Qujiang route required two to three weeks. That was the route followed by a number of schools that migrated around the time of the Japanese takeover of Hong Kong.

Circuitous as the way to Qujiang was, it was not the last leg of the journey. The schools, teachers, and students who heeded the call of the Guangdong government to move to Free China did not enjoy the effective protection of that government. Over the next four years, many of them had to flee again, from the threat of famine or more often from yet another Japanese incursion. The case of Ling Ying school has been recorded by its principal in fullest details. Founded in Hong Kong in 1938 (and registered in both Hong Kong and Guangdong), it moved some 300 kilometres to Meixian in north-eastern Guangdong in January 1942 after the fall of Hong Kong. In May 1943, when famine struck Meixian, it moved again, to Guilin in Guangxi, some 600 kilometres to the west as the bird flies. Barely a year later, when the Japanese army occupied western Hunan and threatened Guilin, it moved downriver, back toward Guangdong, stopping a few weeks in each location until it arrived outside Qujiang, about 350 kilometres east of Guilin, by the end of 1944, only to run again a few months later when Qujiang itself fell to the Japanese. Then it went back to eastern Guangdong, via a few stops, and was back in Meixian when news of the Japanese surrender came. From there, it moved to the coast, about 100 kilometres away, and held classes in Shantou for two months while waiting for passage to Hong Kong. Over four years, it was located in eight different places, always just ahead of calamity, using whatever means of transportation – often unreliable and hazardous – that happened to be available. In each location, usually chosen because of some personal or institutional tie, the school enrolled a fluctuating group of students – some who had followed it from Hong Kong and many more who were recruited locally and lost to the school when it had to move again.[50] Other Hong Kong schools, such as Pui Ching, Pui To, and True Light, although somewhat less itinerant, also shared the insecurity and tribulations of Ling Ying.[51] The same can be said of Lingnan University and its affiliated primary and middle schools, which moved to northern Guangdong just before and just after the Japanese takeover of Hong Kong. The story of wartime Lingnan is well recorded in many memoirs of staff and students, as well as in the poetry of Professor Sin Yuk-ching (Xian Yuqing), one of the best Classical-style poets of her generation, who published *Liuli Bai Yong (A Hundred Poems of Peregrination)* soon after her return to the Kangle campus in Canton in 1945.[52] The repeated flights of these schools testified to the resilience, faith, commitment, and dedication of the teachers and principals, as well as to the wide and unfailing network of support of the Chinese Protestant churches, which sustained their efforts with donations, with recruitment drives, and in other ways.

Most of the sources extant on the wartime experiences of schools relate to the Protestant ones that had branches on both sides of the border before the war and had establishments that remained strong in Hong Kong after 1949, allowing the memories to survive. There is a dearth of information on the wartime experiences of private Chinese schools that were Hong Kong-based before the occupation – modern ones or sishu – or on their teachers and students, as these schools either did not survive the war or, reconstituted after 1945, functioned for only a few years and then disappeared without leaving any traceable details. This is a structural bias of the sources that reflects the structural imbalance of the educational institutions themselves. The Protestant schools were more likely to be based on sizable, multilocational Chinese organizations, whereas Catholic ones in this period remained centred on foreign missionaries. As for private Chinese schools, often they had been built around the personalities of individual educators and were unsupported by any larger organization, or they had political support that did not survive the war or the Communist Revolution. In such instances, the institutional memory would be lost with the demise of the person.

Lacking any systematic collection of wartime memories, one could rely only on sporadic sources of more or less piecemeal oral history or individual memoirs. From these, one learns that many an educational career was truncated by the war. Hon Chi-fun, for example, was a top-notch student at Wah Yan College, the Jesuit secondary school in Kowloon, and stood a very good chance to attain a scholarship from HKU. But when Hong Kong fell, he sought refuge with his family in his father's ancestral town in the Pearl River Delta and survived the war years to return to Hong Kong for clerical jobs in commerce and the civil service.[53] Stanley Kwan, another promising student, was in the last year of secondary school at King's College and served as an air-raid-shelter warden during the Battle of Hong Kong. Under the occupation, he and his brothers went into Free China, where he served as an interpreter between the Chinese and American armies. After the war, he returned to Hong Kong to continue work as a translator.[54] Similar experiences were duplicated by many Hong Kong men and women. Although Hon later distinguished himself as one of Hong Kong's most famous artists and even though Kwan made his mark setting up the Hang Seng Index for the stockmarket, these achievements were realized *despite* their missed opportunities for higher education. Most young persons in Hong Kong or south China who were displaced by the Japanese invasion were not able to make up for their lost years.

There were also those who went into the Mainland and joined the resistance. The better-known examples were: some Hong Kong Chinese who had been civil servants, teachers, or students; workers for the British Army Aid Group (BAAG), an intelligence-gathering and support unit operating in occupied Hong Kong and Guangdong, which reported to the Allied forces in Guilin and Chongqing; and the East River Guerrillas, a Communist-led organization based in eastern Guangdong and fighting in occupied parts of the province and in Hong Kong. Oral-history interviews of the younger guerrillas who had attended rural schools in the New Territories on the eve of the occupation suggest that many of them probably would not have continued in school for long anyway since they had come from poor rural families.[55] Their participation in the East River Brigade took them away from their villages and from Hong Kong to various military or political careers on the Mainland after the war. At least one of these young guerrillas was able to resume his studies and in time received training in the Soviet Union to be a nuclear engineer.[56]

The Civil War

> *The long-term effects of insecurity, fear, and terror are still with us. The social distortions of war, the sense of injustice born of its haphazard cruelty ... the feeling of being abandoned ... the domination of life by fear and anxiety – all of these had long-term effects on Chinese society.*
>
> – Diana Lary, *Scars of War*, 114

On the surrender of Japan, the British colony of Hong Kong was restored, as were many of the schools in Hong Kong and in Guangdong. But peace did not prevail, for the War of Resistance was followed almost immediately by the Nationalist-Communist Civil War, which in turn was followed within a year by the Korean War. War and suffering continued to dominate China and Hong Kong. A huge influx of refugees again went into Hong Kong, bringing the population from some 600,000 at the Japanese surrender to nearly 2 million by early 1950. Many schools, teachers, and students again found themselves on the run. By the time the Korean War ended, all the Christian schools in the People's Republic of China had closed, with some surviving in their Hong Kong branches or managing to set up successor institutions in Hong Kong. Among these were Chung Chi College, established by the remnants of Lingnan and other Protestant universities under the leadership of the former president of Lingnan, Professor W.L. Lee, who in 1938 had first led Lingnan to move to Hong Kong.[57] Another group of scholars, those with a Confucian rather than a Christian orientation, under the leadership of Qian Mu and Tang Junyi, founded New Asia College in Shamshuipo, one of the poorest districts of Kowloon. Yet another group formed the amalgamation of private universities relocated from Canton, known as the United College of Hong Kong, while the Baptist Church developed Hong Kong Baptist College on the basis of the Pui Ching school, which continued to thrive in Hong Kong. In many ways, the moving of schools and scholars from 1948 through 1951 was a re-enactment of the experience of 1938 to 1941, enlarged.[58]

And this was the case not only with the moving of institutions. On a more personal level, the war – with its attendant suffering and peregrinations – left indelible marks on the people who experienced it, especially young students for whom those years were formative. One of my own teachers in primary school during the early 1950s mumbled incessantly to herself, "feiji, dapao, yuanzidan" (aeroplanes, artillery, atom bombs), until she was removed from the staff. In a more positive vein, out of their adolescent wartime experiences came the commitment to nationalism of eminent community leaders of postwar Hong Kong such as the teacher-unionist Szeto Wah (Situ Hua), the essayist and literary historian Lo Wai-luen (Lu Weiluan), and the banker-statistician Stanley Kwan (Guan Shiguang).[59] It was this collective experience, recalled after sixty years, that brought such an emotional resonance to the Bel Canto concert in 2005 – an experience of shared suffering that gave meaning and substance to the idea of an imagined community.

On the other hand, the acute insight of Diana Lary and Stephen MacKinnon that "modern Chinese society has been traumatized mentally and at times paralyzed by a pervasive fear of chaos or *luan*"[60] as a result of the long years of war could be applicable in Hong Kong no less than on the Mainland and ought to be carefully considered by historians and social scientists as one of the most salient explanations for the remarkable stability of the colonial society in the postwar decades.

Notes

1 Bel Canto Chorus, *Buqu de Zhonghua: Kangzhan Shengli Liushi Zhounian Jinian Yanchanghui* (Hong Kong: Xianggang Meisheng Hechangtuan, October 2005).

2 Two recent works that partially fill the gap are A.E. Sweeting, *Education in Hong Kong, 1941 to 2001,* pt. 1, "Occupational Hazards (And Therapy?), 1942-1945" (Hong Kong: Hong Kong University Press, 2004), esp. 81-82n2; and Zhang Huizhen and Kong Qiangsheng, *Cong Shiyiwan Dao Sanqian: Lunxianshiqi Xianggang Jiaoyu Koushu Lishi* (Hong Kong: Oxford University Press, 2005).

3 For further details, see Lu Hongji, *Cong Rongshuxia dao Diannaoqian: Xianggang Jiaoyu de Gushi* [From under the Banyan Tree to in Front of the Computer: The Story of Hong Kong Education] (Hong Kong: Step Forward Press, 2003), ch. 5.

4 He Bangtai, ed., *Guangzhou Kangzhan Jishi (Guangdong Wenshi,* vol. 48) (Guangzhou: Guangzhou Shi Zhengxie Wenshi Ziliu Weiyuanhui, with Guangdong Renmin Chubanshe, 1995), provides a broad overview of the war years in the city of Guangzhou and its immediate environs.

5 T.N. Chiu, *The Port of Hong Kong* (Hong Kong: Hong Kong University Press, 1973), 52-55.

6 Hong Kong Government, *Hong Kong Annual Report 1946* (Hong Kong: Hong Kong Government Printer, 1947), 9.

7 Cai Baoqiong, *Housheng yu Chuangye* (Hong Kong: Hong Kong Vitasoy Company, 1990), 10-13.

8 Lu Weiluan, *Xianggang de Youyu* [The Melancholy of Hong Kong] (Hong Kong: Wide Angle Press, 1985), provides the best survey of the famous men and women of letters from Mainland China seeking refuge in Hong Kong between 1937 and 1941.

9 Hong Kong Government, *Hong Kong Administrative Report 1936* (Hong Kong: Hong Kong Government Printer, 1937), Appendix O: "Report of the Director of Education for the Year 1936," 27, Table 1.

10 Hong Kong Government, *Hong Kong Administrative Report 1937* (Hong Kong: Hong Kong Government Printer, 1938), Appendix O: "Report of the Director of Education for the Year 1937," 5.

11 Hong Kong Government, *Hong Kong Administrative Report 1938* (Hong Kong: Hong Kong Government Printer, 1939), Appendix O: "Education Department, Hong Kong: Annual Report for 1938," 6.

12 Hong Kong Government, *Hong Kong Administrative Report 1939* (Hong Kong: Hong Kong Government Printer, 1940), Appendix O: "Education Department, Hong Kong: Annual Report for 1939," 1.

13 Pui Ching Middle School, *Guangzhou Peizheng Zhongxue Liushi Zhounian ji Xianggang Fenxiao Shiliu Zhounian Jinian Tekan* (Hong Kong: Pui Ching Middle School, 1949[?]), 4-7.

14 See, for example, Pui Ying Middle School, *Peiying Zhongxue Cangxiao Bai Zhounian Jinian Tekan* (Hong Kong: Pui Ying Middle School, 1979[?]), 68-69. Compare the less fortunate circumstances of Guangdong Shengli Zhongqu Linshi Zhongxue [Guangdong Provincial Interim Middle School for the Central District], set up by the provincial authorities for refugee students in borrowed premises of a Guomindang-affiliated school in Kowloon; see *Ta Kung Pao* 6, 6 (1940), reprinted in Mai Xiaoling and Fang Jun, comps., *Xianggang Zaoqi Baozhi Jiaoyu Ziliao Xuancui* (Changsha: Hunan Renmin Chubanshe, 2006), 174.

15 Pui To Girls' Middle School, *Peidao Bashi Zhounian Xiaoqing Tekan* (Hong Kong: Pui To Girls' Middle School, 1968), 25-37.

16 Liang Jialing, *Jing E Le Yu Wo Zhenguang* (Hong Kong: True Light Middle Schools, 2002), 85-86.

17 Li Ruiming, *Lingnan Daxue* [Lingnan University] (Hong Kong: Lingnan [Daxue] Choumu Fazhan Weiyuanhui, 1997), 101, 103-4. News about the move of Lingnan to Hong Kong and the agreement with HKU were reported by *Ta Kung Pao* 11, 7 (1938), reprinted in Mai and Fang, comps., *Xianggang Zaoqi Baozhi,* 197-98; and by *Sing Tao Jih Pao* 8, 16-21 (1940), reprinted in Mai and Fang, comps., *Xianggang Zaoqi Baozhi,* 207-8. Activities of Lingnan students at HKU provided inspiration for Eileen Chang's short story *Se, Jie,* now made into the award-winning film *Lust, Caution* by director Ang Lee.

18 Li, *Lingnan Daxue,* 102.

19 Ibid., 101; Pu Xuefeng, "Zi Gang Zhi Dian," in *Xuefu Jiwen: Guoli Xinan Lianhe Daxue* (Taipei: Nanjing Chuban Youxian Gongsi, 1981), 88-89.

20 *Sing Tao Jih Pao* 8, 16-21 (1940), reprinted in Mai and Fang, comps., *Xianggang Zaoqi Baozhi,* 209-10.

21 Ibid. Among all the exiled institutions, Ling Ying School has made available the most detailed record of enrolment through its repeated peregrinations:

1938	September	Hong Kong	535 pupils
1939	February	Hong Kong	715 pupils
1939	September	Hong Kong	907 pupils
1940	February	Hong Kong	1,050 pupils
1940	September	Hong Kong	1,085 pupils
1941	February	Hong Kong	1,233 pupils
1941	September	Hong Kong	1,453 pupils
1942	September	Meixian	108 pupils
1943	February	Meixian	96 pupils
1943	June	(departed) Meixian	20+ pupils
1943	August	Guilin	545 pupils
1944	February	Guilin	527 pupils
1944	June	(departed) Guilin	50+ pupils
1944	September	Pingle	215 pupils
1944	October	Zhaoping	80+ pupils
1945	April	Dapu	12 pupils
1945	August	Meixian	95 pupils
1945	September	Meixian	75 pupils
1945	October	Shantou	58 pupils
1946	February	Hong Kong	1,076 pupils
1946	September	Hong Kong	1,342 pupils
1947	February	Hong Kong	1,574 pupils

See *Lingying Zhongxue Shi Zhounian Jinian Tekan* (Hong Kong: Ling Ying College, 1948), 107-23.

22 Su Mianhuan, *Peiying Shihua* (Hong Kong: Peiying Shihua Bianji Weiyuanhui, 1999), 398-99. See also Pui To Girls' Middle School, *Peidao Bashi Zhounian,* 25.

23 *Lingying Zhongxue Shi Zhounian,* English section, 1-4.

24 *Sing Tao Wan Pao* 3, 19 (1939); *Kung Shang Jih Pao* 3, 20 (1939); *Ta Kung Pao* 10, 8 (1939); *Sing Tao Wan Pao* 5, 14 (1940); *Sing Tao Jih Pao* 6, 30 (1940). The above are reprinted in Mai and Fang, comps., *Xianggang Zaoqi Baozhi,* 92-101.

25 Hong Kong Government, *Hong Kong Administrative Report 1939,* O-7.

26 *Sing Tao Wan Pao* 3, 12 (1939), reprinted in Mai and Fang, comps., *Xianggang Zaoqi Baozhi,* 4.

27 *Sing Tao Jih Pao* 4, 14 (1939), and 11, 30 (1939), reprinted in Mai and Fang, comps., *Xianggang Zaoqi Baozhi,* 5-6.

28 Guan Shiguang, *Qishi Nian Lai Jia Guo: Yige Lao-Xianggang de Huiyi,* Hong Kong Life Stories No. 2 (Toronto: Joint Centre for Asia Pacific Studies, 1999), 30.

29 *Ta Kung Pao* 7, 24 (1940), and *Sing Tao Jih Pao* 4, 28 (1941), reprinted in Mai and Fang, comps., *Xianggang Zaoqi Baozhi,* 7-8; *Sing Tao Jih Pao* 8, 16-21 (1940), reprinted in Mai and Fang, comps., *Xianggang Zaoqi Baozhi,* 207-10.

30 Su, *Peiying Shihua,* 406.

31 Sergio Ticozzi, PIME, ed., *Historical Documents of the Hong Kong Catholic Church* (Hong Kong: Hong Kong Catholic Diocesan Archives, 1997), 156-59.

32 Guan, *Qishi Nian,* 29-30.

33 See, for example, Pui To Girls' Middle School, *Peidao Bashi Zhounian,* 34; Pui Ching Middle School, *Guangzhou Peizheng Zhongxue Liushi Zhounian,* 28; Liang, *Jing E Le Yu Wo Zhenguang,* 86; Yeung Chung College, *Yangzhong Zhongxue Shiwu Zhounian Jinian Tekan* (Hong Kong: Yeung Chung College, 1939), 2; Lai Chak School, *Lize Zuanxi Jinian Tekan, 1929-1989* (Hong Kong: Lai Chak School, 1989), 40; and Guan, *Qishi Nian,* 29. Meifang School, *Xianggang Sili Meifang Nuzi Zhongxuexiao Zuijin Wunian Gaikuang* (Hong Kong: Meifang School, 1933), 5, shows that such patriotic activities in support of Chinese war efforts went back to the Manchurian crisis in 1931.

34 See, for example, Brian Yu, *Arches of the Years,* Hong Kong Life Stories No. 1 (Toronto: Joint Centre for Asia Pacific Studies, 1999), 61-64.

35 *Sing Tao Jih Pao* 4, 25 (1939), reprinted in Mai and Fang, comps., *Xianggang Zaoqi Baozhi,* 199-200; *Sing Tao Jih Pao* 10, 9 (1939), reprinted in Mai and Fang, comps., *Xianggang Zaoqi Baozhi,* 204-5. All translations of quotations from non-English sources are mine.

36 Hong Kong Government, *Hong Kong Administrative Report 1938,* Appendix P: "Report on Air Raid Precaution for 1938," item 1, 1-3.

37 Hong Kong Government, *Hong Kong Administration Report 1939,* Appendix P: "General Statement on A.R.P. during the period 1st January 1939 to 31st December 1939," item 1, 1-6.

38 *Ta Kung Pao* 2, 3 (1939), reprinted in Mai and Fang, comps., *Xianggang Zaoqi Baozhi,* 4. See also *Nanhua Ribao* 11, 24 (1941), reprinted in Mai and Fang, comps., *Xianggang Zaoqi Baozhi,* 13.

39 Guan, *Qishi Nian,* 35-37.

40 La Salle College had been requisitioned by the Hong Kong government since 1939 to use as an internment camp for nationals of the Axis powers. See Peter Chiu and Cecilia Fung, eds., *La Salle College: 70th Anniversary, 1932-2002* (Hong Kong: La Salle College), 37.

41 See, for example, Su, *Peiying Shihua,* 403.

42 Li, *Lingnan Daxue,* 105.

43 Sweeting, *Education in Hong Kong,* 83-87; *Nanhua Ribao* 5, 5 (1942), 5, 11 (1942), and 8, 11 (1944), reprinted in Mai and Fang, comps., *Xianggang Zaoqi Baozhi,* 13-14; *Sing Tao Jih Pao* 3, 10 (1942), and *Nanhua Ribao* 5, 19 (1942), reprinted in Mai and Fang, comps., *Xianggang Zaoqi Baozhi,* 121-22.

44 Sweeting, *Education in Hong Kong,* 82-83.

45 Ibid., 83-87, 90. Wah Yan College, a Catholic secondary school run by Jesuit fathers from neutral Ireland, was allowed to reopen in 1942; see Kowloon Wah Yan College Old Students' Association, *Wushiliu-hao de Xingguang: Jiulong Huaren Shuyuan Cangxiao Bashi*

Zhounian Jiniance (Hong Kong: Kowloon Wah Yan College Old Students' Association, 2004), 42. Similarly, Sacred Heart, a Catholic girls' school run by the Canossian Sisters from Axis Italy, was also allowed to reopen in 1942; see Sacred Heart Canossian College, *Jianuosa Shengxin Shuyuan Cangxiao 125-nian Jinian Tekan* (Hong Kong: Sacred Heart Canossian College, 1985), 13. On the other hand, Lai Chak, a private Chinese middle school, was closed by the Japanese occupation; see Lai Chak School, *Lize Zuanxi*, 40-44. Maryknoll Convent School, run by the Maryknoll Sisters from the United States, with a large campus in suburban Kowloon Tong, was commandeered by the Japanese army as a military hospital; see Aloysius Lee, ed., *Maryknoll Convent School, 1925-2000* (Hong Kong: Maryknoll Convent School, 2001[?]), 30.

46 Su, *Peiying Shihua*, 404; *Wah Kiu Yat Po* 9, 23 (1945), reprinted in Mai and Fang, comps., *Xianggang Zaoqi Baozhi*, 211-12. Charles Boxer, a well-known historian and bibliophile and a major in the British army, was a prisoner of war during the Japanese occupation. His precious collection of rare early-edition European books printed in Asia was removed by the Japanese military from Hong Kong to Japan and kept safe for the duration of the war. After the Japanese surrender, Boxer was able to track it down and recover it intact with the help of Sir George Sansom. Professor Charles Boxer, personal conversation with author, 1975.

47 See, for example, Pui Ching Middle School, *Guangzhou Peizheng Zhongxue Liushi Zhounian*, 5.

48 See, for example, Yu, *Arches of the Years*, 74-75; Guan, *Qishi Nian*, 43.

49 *Lingying Zhongxue Shi Zhounian*, 111.

50 Ibid., 111-16.

51 Pui Ching Middle School, *Guangzhou Peizheng Zhongxue Liushi Zhounian*, 29-30; Su, *Peiying Shihua*, 404-26; Pui To Girls' Middle School, *Peidao Bashi Zhounian*, 27-28; Liang, *Jing E Le Yu Wo Zhenguang*, 87-90.

52 Li, *Lingnan Daxue*, 105-13, 181-94; *Chaoshe Chunqiu: Biye Lixiao Sanshiwu Zhounian Jinian Tekan, 1947-1982* (Hong Kong: N.p., 1982), 30-33; Xian Yuqing, *Liuli Bai Yong*, Langganguang Congzhu Series, no. 4 (Guangzhou: Langganguang Congzhu, 1947). Her wartime itinerary is traced in Zhuang Fuwu, "Xian Yuqing Xiansheng Nianbiao," appended to Foshan Daxue Foshan Wenshi Yanjiushi and Guangdong Wenshiguang, comps., *Xian Yuqing Wenji* (Guangzhou: Zhongshan Daxue Chubanshe, 1995), 866-82. However, these 100 poems of exile are not included in this volume of her collected works.

53 Oral-history interviews by author, Toronto, November 1999, published in *Zhimindi de Xiandai Yishu: Han Zhixun Qianxi Zishu (Modern Art in a Colony: Narrated by Hon Chi-fun at the Millennium)*, Hong Kong Life Stories Series, no. 5 (Toronto and Hong Kong: York Centre for Asian Research and Hong Kong Institute of Education, 2008).

54 Guan, *Qishi Nian*, 42-45, 49-53.

55 Zhang and Kong, *Cong Shiyiwan Dao Sanqian*.

56 Oral-history interviews by author, Shenzhen, August 2002, as part of the Oral History Project of the Centre of Asian Studies, Hong Kong University.

57 Li, *Lingnan Daxue*, 121, 125-26. See also *Xinya Jiaoyu* (Hong Kong: New Asia Research Institute, 1981), 43-54; and H. Rudin, "A Meeting of East and West in 1953," in *New Asia College: The Chinese University of Hong Kong*, 28-43 (Hong Kong: New Asia College, 1979).

58 The Baptist Church member most instrumental in reopening the Pui Ching school in Hong Kong, and the subsequent establishment of the Baptist College (now Hong Kong Baptist University) was Lam Tse-fung (Lin Zifeng), ably assisted by his son Lam See-chai (Lin Siqi), who later, as David S.C. Lam, Lieutenant-Governor of British Columbia.

59 See, for example, Guan, *Qishi Nian,* ch. 5, on the evolution of Stanley Kwan's national and political identity before, during, and after the war.
60 Diana Lary and Stephen MacKinnon, eds., *Scars of War* (Vancouver: UBC Press, 2001), 12.

Bibliography

School Histories

* Unless otherwise indicated, the publisher is the school.

Chiao-tung. 學府紀聞: 國立交通大學． 台北： 南京出版有限公司, 1981.

Fujen. 學府紀聞: 私立輔仁大學. 台北: 南京出版有限公司, 1982.

Fung, Vincent, ed. *From Devotion to Plurality: A Full History of St. Paul's College, 1851-2001.* Hong Kong: St. Paul's College Alumni Association, 2001.

La Salle College, Peter Chiu, and Cecilia Fung, eds. *La Salle College: 70th Anniversary, 1932-2002.* Hong Kong, 2002[?].

Lai Chak 50. 麗澤中學金禧紀念特刊, *1929-79*. Hong Kong, 1979.

Lai Chak 60. 麗澤中學鑽禧紀念特刊, *1929-89*. Hong Kong, 1989.

Ling Ying. 嶺英中學十周年紀念特刊. Hong Kong, 1948.

Lingnan 60. 香港嶺南中學六十週年校慶特刊, *1922-82*. Hong Kong, 1982.

Lingnan 80. 嶺南教育在港八十週年. Hong Kong, 2002.

Maryknoll, Aloysius Lee, ed. *Maryknoll Convent School, 1925-2000.* Hong Kong, 2000.

Mui Fong. 香港私立梅芳女子中學最近五年概況. Hong Kong, 1933.

Munsang. 民生書院六十週年紀念特刊. Hong Kong, 1986.

Nanfang. 香港南方學院師生紀念手冊. Hong Kong: 第二屆學生自治會編印, 1949.

New Asia. 新亞教育. 香港、新亞研究所編輯出版, 1981.

Pui Ching 60. 廣州培正中學六十週年暨香港分校十六週年紀念特刊. Hong Kong, 1949.

Pui Ching 65. 培正中學六十五周年紀念特刊. Hong Kong, 1954.

Pui Ching 70. 培正中學創校七十周年紀念, *1889-1959*. Hong Kong, 1959.

Pui Ching 75. 培正中學創校七十五周年紀念, *1889-1964*. Hong Kong, 1964.

Pui To 10. 香港培道女子中學十周年紀念特刊. Hong Kong, 1955.

Pui To 75. 培道女子中學創校七十五周年紀念特刊. Hong Kong, 1963.

Pui To 80. 香港培道中學八十周年紀念特刊. Hong Kong, 1968.

Pui Ying 100. 培英中學創校百周年紀念特刊. Hong Kong, 1979.

Pui Ying 1999. 蘇棉煥《培英史話. 香港: 培英史話編輯委員會, 1999.

Queen's, Gwenneth, and John Stokes. *Queen's College: Its History, 1862-1987.* Hong Kong: Queen's College Old Boys' Association, 1987.

Rudin, H. "A Meeting of East and West in 1953." In *New Asia College, CUHK*. Hong Kong: New Asia College, 1979.

Sacred Heart. 嘉諾撒聖心書院創校百廿五年紀念特刊. Hong Kong, 1985.

St. Clare's Girls' School. *St. Clare's Girls' School Diamond Jubilee, 1927-87.* Hong Kong, 1987.

Sung Lan. 香港崇蘭中學創校六十三周年特刊: 蘭院春風. 香港: 香港崇蘭中學校友會編輯出版, 1986.

True Light 1942 (劉心慈). 真光光榮簡史. 1942. Reprint, Hong Kong, 1972.

True Light 2002 (梁家麟). 真光校史. 香港、九龍: 香港真光中學校董會, 2002.

Wah Yan (九龍華仁書院舊生會編). 五十六號的星光: 九龍華仁書院創校八十周年紀念冊. 香港: 星島出版有限公司, 2004.

Xian (冼玉清). 流離百詠. 廣州: 琅玕館叢書, 1946.

Yenching. 學府紀聞: 私立燕京大學. 台北: 南京出版有限公司, 1982.

Yeung Chung. 養中女子中學十五週年紀念特刊. Hong Kong, 1939.

Ying Wa College. 英華書院一百七十周年紀念特刊. Hong Kong, 1988.

Ying Wa Girls' School (陳念賢、文蘭芳). 百年樹人萬載恩 [Ying Wa Girls' School: The blessed years, 1900-2000]. Hong Kong, 2001.

3

Bombs Don't Discriminate? Class, Gender, and Ethnicity in the Air-Raid-Shelter Experiences of the Wartime Chongqing Population

Chang Jui-te

The Nationalist government announced the relocation of its capital to Chongqing in November 1937 in a move to sustain its efforts in the protracted War of Resistance against Japan. As Chongqing emerged as the political, economic, military, and cultural centre of wartime China, it consequently became a key military target for the Japanese forces. The Japanese carried out prolonged bombings on Chongqing for five consecutive years from 18 February 1938 to 23 August 1943. During the entire period, there were about 9,000 bombing sorties; 20,000 bombs were dropped, killing or injuring nearly 30,000 people and destroying 20,000 buildings, not to mention that countless properties were either lost or damaged. In this regard, the bombardment of Chongqing turned out to be one of the most tumultuous episodes in the history of the Second World War for its long duration and the loss of lives and properties on a massive scale.[1]

The conventional view in the scholarship is that the prolonged Japanese bombardments and the common experience of evacuation were crucial factors that strengthened social solidarity among the wartime Chongqing population. This view emerged and was propagated as early as during the war. For example, the Guomindang propaganda organ *Zhongyang ribao (Central Daily)* claimed after an air raid in 1940, "China's national solidarity, one that brings together men and women through the common experience of life, death, and sufferings, has been forged and tempered by the enemy's bombs to become a will of steel."[2] In their joint wartime reminiscence, *Thunder out of China,* published in 1946 not long after the end of the war, two American journalists based in Chongqing, Theodore H. White and Annalee Jacoby, lauded the bombardments:

> The bombings were what made Chungking great and fused all the jagged groups of men and women into a single community ... All were thirsty, all were sleepless, all walked in the dust, all crouched in the caves. They began to be proud of themselves, and they began to admire those about them who were suffering the same ordeal; Chinese in Western clothes and Chinese in blue cotton gowns felt that they were the same flesh and blood.[3]

Despite some degree of truth in it, the "solidarity" argument oversimplifies the historical reality and thereby overlooks its complexity. The intensive bombardments by the Japanese forces on Chongqing did reinforce the sense of togetherness among the Chongqing population in a certain way, but questions arise as to how strong such solidarity actually was and how long it could be sustained. More important, the impact of the bombardments was hardly uniform among the different social classes, and vulnerability to bomb attacks differed between social classes and categories. This chapter seeks to unravel the relationship between social class and disparate experiences of residents of wartime Chongqing and to query the extent to which social classes and categories brought about such disparities.

High officials and social dignitaries in the upper class often built private villas in the suburbs that provided protection from the summer heat as well as from the bombings.[4] They did not have to squeeze into overcrowded public air-raid shelters with the common people, nor did they suffer from the risks posed by blocked shelter openings.[5] In those days, most of the Nationalist government's key party and governmental organizations were concentrated in the suburban districts of Shangqingsi and Zengjiayan. With their peaceful surroundings, these districts quickly filled with the villas of high party and government officials and their families, including lavish residences belonging to members of the Kuomintang Central Committee and the Executive Yuan.[6] The Xiquan (Western Spring) area of the Tongliang County near the city was another place with a high residential concentration of key political and military figures, including Bai Chongxi, Qian Dajun, and Deng Wenyi, as well as their families. Li Zhiming, who served as a lance-corporal with the Nationalist troops stationed in Xiquan, witnessed the lives of these officials, and even sixty years later his account belies his sense of admiration and envy:

> Xiquan was a microcosm of the life of the high military and political officials in the Nationalist government and their families during the War of Resistance. As I could remember, these families lived in big and beautiful houses, some of which were Western-style buildings, with maids and soldiers standing by to attend to their needs. During the weekends and holidays, lots of military vehicles drove in and out. Security was always tightened whenever huge gatherings of army generals and high government officials took place. In order to cater to the schooling needs of the children of high military and political officials, the government established a school in Xiquan that enrolled children born to high officials' families only. I used to walk around the school with Company Commander Ma Shucheng. What left me with the deepest impression was that the school built a swimming pool and employed a military officer to teach the students swimming. The high officials'

> families, be they adults or children, were dressed in neater, higher-quality clothes than those of the locals in Xiquan and exuded an air that distinguished them from the locals. I remember that I used to pass by General Bai Chongxi's residence frequently and often heard beautiful melodies from someone playing the piano in the house. Whenever I was free, I always loved to take a walk near the Bai residence.[7]

These villas were often equipped with comfortable air-raid shelters, popularly known during those days as An le dong (Shelters of Well-being and Happiness).[8] These shelters were spacious, clean, secure, and well furnished. Small electrical generators provided lighting and ventilation, and it was rumoured that some of the shelters even hosted banquets and mahjong games.[9] Because of the insufficient number of air-raid shelters in Chongqing, the Chongqing Anti-Air-Raid Command issued a ruling to these well-to-do households to allow their friends, relatives, and neighbours to make full use of extra space available in their private shelters in times of emergency and to separate the air-raid shelters from the outside with wooden fences.[10] However, the owners of the private air-raid shelters were mostly famous and powerful figures in political and business circles, a situation that made such a ruling difficult to implement in practice.[11]

By contrast, the ordinary city folks who followed the government's orders to evacuate faced a host of problems. The implementation of the policy of population evacuation by the Nationalist government was already underway in the city during the early phase of the War of Resistance, but the progress was slow since various parties paid scant attention to the policy. In 1939 the Nationalist government enforced the implementation process by ordering all organizations, schools, and shops to evacuate to Baxian, Qijiang, and other places outside of the city centre by 10 March; all anti-air-raid organizations were to arrange for necessary transportation for evacuation; and the Central Bank, the Bank of China, and the Agricultural Bank of China were to release funds for the construction of civilian housing along the Chengyu and Chuanqian highways. The Chongqing municipal government also ordered the city population to evacuate voluntarily by the 10 March deadline; otherwise, they would face compulsory evacuation from 11 March onward.

Evacuation orders impacted unevenly on the city's residents and were especially hard on the jobless, the elderly, women, children, and residents without proper residential certificates.[12] Heading the list of problems with evacuation was exorbitant transportation costs. Although the Chongqing municipal authorities implemented price controls over means of transportation such as steamships and cars by setting a uniform price for a particular transport, even this stringent measure failed to stop prices from rising sharply due to the severe shortage of supplies relative to the ever-increasing demand for transportation. For longer-range journeys, north- or south-bound transport starting from Chongqing provided by the Highway Bureau was in surprisingly short supply. Many passengers did not manage to secure transport even after waiting for ten or more days; they had to switch to less safe trucks. The truck drivers' usual practice was to load ten or more passengers on top of the goods already in the truck. This made the truck unsteady when travelling along the treacherous mountain roads, subjecting the passengers to great peril during the journey. The truck drivers were famously rude and charged the passengers fees that more than doubled the highway transport fee.[13] As for shorter-range transport such as traditional rickshaws,[14] ferry boats,[15] and sedan chairs,[16] the operators jumped at every opportunity to make a fortune out of the national crisis by jacking up the prices.

Once in the countryside, refugees continued to face health and social problems. Chongqing tended to have misty weather during the autumn and winter seasons, so the Japanese bombers intensified their attacks during spring and summer, seasons that were most prone to the spread of various epidemic diseases. This problem was exacerbated by poor hygiene, and backward medical facilities in the countryside made the residents even more vulnerable to the diseases. The conditions in the countryside hardly improved the situation, and the common folks had to grapple with deaths or near-death experiences whenever there was an outbreak of epidemics. Additionally, families that had evacuated to the countryside often had difficulties finding schools for their younger children (whereas the elder ones could be sent elsewhere to study in junior and senior high schools), so unschooled children who were kept at home became quite common among the evacuated families of the lower class.[17] After the Great Bombardments of 3 and 4 May 1939, the Ministry of Education evacuated some of its personnel to a place several kilometres away from the city called Qingmuguan and built provisional makeshift huts to settle the personnel and their families. A senior official from the ministry gave a vivid account of their life after evacuation to the countryside:

> The families had to draw drinking water from a sunken pit near the rice fields. The rice, supplied to them through official ration, was often stale and mixed with impurities. During the evenings, the old and the young in each family sat together under kerosene lamps, with the men writing their papers, the women doing their needlework, and the young revising their schoolwork, all busy with their own things. The houseflies and malaria mosquitoes disturbed days and nights, yet with no preventive means available to them, they had to bear with it. Consequently,

> I witnessed and experienced different sorts of epidemic diseases such as malaria, dysentery, and typhoid fever throughout all those years.[18]

For those who stayed in the city, air-raid shelters were of primary importance. For salaried employees, most of the public and private organizations and bodies, schools, and large factories in which they served built their own respective air-raid shelters into the surrounding mountains and hills. The entire city of Chongqing was built in mountainous terrain. Thick and solid mountain rocks were suitable for digging caves that could be sustained for a long time without collapsing. The layer of mountain rocks along the river in the Taiping Gate area, for example, could allow the digging of caves up to twenty to thirty feet high. Up one level was the Nanji Gate area, with its mountains as high as several feet. The Dongchuan Postal Administration Bureau, the Central Depository, the Central Military Commission, and the Overseas and Social Departments of the Kuomintang all built their air-raid-shelter caves in the Taiping Gate area, with the bigger ones able to accommodate as many as several thousand people and the smaller ones several hundred; the air-raid shelter cave of the Dongshan Post Office, for example, could accommodate 3,000 to 4,000 people. As the distance between the opening to the end of the cave was several hundred feet high, the cave had to be divided into upper and lower levels, with a few internal passageways and two to three exits. As for the Nanji Gate area, most of the air-raid-shelter caves belonged to the military organizations. These caves were especially towering and spacious.[19]

In general, organizations with abundant funds tended to enjoy better-equipped air-raid shelters. The best-built air-raid shelters, according to public opinion of the time, were the ones belonging to the head offices of the Bank of Communications, the Agricultural Bank, and the Sichuan Salt Industry Bank.[20] These shelters were all owned by the financial sector, and their facilities were far better than those of the public air-raid shelters. For instance, the air-raid shelter jointly built by the head offices of the Agricultural Bank and the Bank of Communications was huge, deep, and supported internally by structures made of concrete and steel. The offices and living quarters of the employees in both banks were scattered around the cave. Whenever there was an air-raid warning, the employees would immediately stop their work, put the documents and account books into boxes, and hand the boxes over to the office boys to carry into the cave. The employees would then either chat with one another in their offices or return to their living quarters to work on household chores. It was only after the sounding of the emergency alarm that the employees began to walk slowly into the cave, a manner that was in stark contrast to the sense of desperation and urgency among the common people out in the downtown area as they sought shelter from the bombs.[21]

The shelters belonging to these organizations were well furnished with comfortable seats and boasted sturdy ceilings, walls, and flooring. They were also well equipped with medical supplies, adequate lighting, and proper sanitation and ventilation facilities. The degree of comfort provided by these shelters far exceeded the actual safety needs of the employees.[22] However, there were a few exceptions. For example, when the Ministry of Education relocated to Chongqing, it had to borrow the buildings of a primary school in the suburbs for use as its temporary office. The walls of its air-raid-shelter cave were made up of soft and loose soil and were supported by structures made of wooden poles. The lighting was inadequate, and there was a total lack of ventilation. If a bomb were to fall nearby, the entire cave would collapse.[23] As for other educational institutions, state-run universities and colleges possessed shelters that were mostly firm, steady, and well equipped, but some state-run high schools and primary schools were so desperately short of funds that the students had to contribute their own money to build the shelters.[24]

The ways various organizations evacuated to the air-raid shelters were by no means uniform. Some organizations issued entry passes to employees and their families, whereas others admitted employees into the cave based on their work passes or simply allowed employees to walk in. In cases where employees were highly familiar with one another, they were simply allowed to move into the cave in whatever way they liked. The various organizations mostly dispatched some workers and office boys to set up lighting and prepare drinking water prior to the evacuation process.[25] The Nationalist government issued a ruling that during the air raids, governmental organizations had to handle urgent and important tasks inside the shelters and various meetings had to be held as normal.[26] However, if there were no urgent matters to deal with, most people either chatted with their colleagues or rested. Some organizations even allowed their employees to "play mahjong games and enjoy [themselves] in the shelter," as "there were foods prepared [for them] there and [they] hardly needed to work during the air-raids."[27]

Instead of building their own air-raid shelters, some private organizations purchased entry passes to the public air-raid shelters for their employees. For example, after the Great Bombardments of 3 and 4 May 1939, an employee in an import and export company received from his employer an entry pass that was valid for one year. The sale price of the entry pass was equivalent to two-thirds of the person's monthly salary,[28] and those in the middle-lower class could hardly afford such a price. Under the pressure of public opinion, the Chongqing

Anti-Air-Raid Command issued one order after another demanding that all organizations and households that had built their own air-raid shelters lend out whatever extra space was available to outsiders. These organizations and households were also warned not to come up with excuses to reject people from using the shelters or to manipulate opportunities to profit from the refugees.[29] However, the Anti-Air-Raid Command was not very successful in enforcing its rulings, and it was powerless to prevent the so-called Ministry of Economy Air-Raid Shelter Incident from taking place. The root cause of the incident was that the ministry saw the entry passes to its air-raid shelters as an opportunity to conduct a lucrative business. In this regard, its behaviour was hardly different from that of an ordinary businessman. As the ministry's air-raid shelter was relatively safer, there were lots of buyers. Rather than helping poor and needy refugees, the ministry exposed its ugly profiteering motive to the fullest by raising the sale price suddenly from 50 yuan all the way to 140 yuan under the excuse of an increase in prices of goods. The move caused widespread grievance and discontent among the general public, and the city's business daily, *Shangwu ribao (Commercial Daily),* led a strong attack against the incident in its editorial on 4 August 1940.[30]

The common people in the middle-lower class, especially those who had to seek their livelihoods in the downtown area, constituted a seriously disadvantaged lot. They did not have the means to evacuate to the countryside and make a living there or the means to build their own air-raid shelters. As private air-raid shelters were out of bounds to them, they had to rely on public air-raid shelters built by the government.[31]

Construction of public air-raid shelters in Chongqing started as early as after the Japanese invasion of Manchuria on 18 September 1931. The Chongqing Anti-Air-Raid Command was established in September 1937 soon after the War of Resistance broke out. In the same month, Chiang Kai-shek charged the Anti-Air-Raid Command with the responsibility of directing and assisting the people to dig and build simple anti-air-raid trenches. From the second half of 1938 onward, the Nationalist government stepped up the construction works for public air-raid-shelter caves and tunnels. In 1939 the Japanese forces started to bomb the city incessantly, but until then, "the poor did not have any air-raid shelters in which to hide."[32] It was only after the Great Bombardments that construction work for more public shelters was carried out in earnest.[33] Between 1937 and 1944 the accommodation volume of anti-air-raid facilities saw a steady rise (see Table 3.1).

Despite steady increases in the accommodation capacity of the anti-air-raid facilities over the years between 1937 and 1944, the continuous influx of refugees

Table 3.1

Population of Chongqing and the accommodation capacity of air-raid shelters, 1937-44

Year	City population	Accommodation capacity	Percentage of city population accommodated
1937	60,000	7,200	1.2
1938	62,000	33,300	5.4
1939	52,620	25,600	48.7
1940	53,320	34,690	65.1
1941	62,620	36,850	58.8
1942	78,180	42,770	54.7
1943	92,340	44,500	48.2
1944	94,600	45,000	47.6

Source: Chongqing renmin fangkong bangongshi, ed., *Chongqing Fangkong zhi* [A history of air-defence works in Chongqing] (Chongqing: Xinan shifan daxue chubanshe, 1994).

into the city ensured that the annual city population kept outnumbering the available air-raid shelter spaces. As shown in Table 3.1, even in 1940 the anti-air-raid facilities in the city could accommodate only 65.1 percent of the population. The construction of anti-air-raid shelters was seriously inadequate in terms of numbers, and the dire situation was hardly helped by the enforced occupation of shelters on a frequent basis by governmental organizations and troops for a vast array of reasons, practical or not. Even though the Air-Raid-Shelters Management Office attempted to convey to affiliated bodies of the Executive Yuan and the Central Military Commission the strong message that such enforced occupation went against the rules, these bodies were often powerless to stop the practice. The occupiers refused to move away, and the problem continued to occur, thereby reducing the available spaces where the city population could seek protection from the bombs.[34]

The allocation and usage of spaces in the public air-raid shelters by the population of Chongqing was officially determined by the number of holders of residential certificates in a particular district. This method of allocation was based on the ratio of the number of residents in the city to the accommodation capacity of the shelter caves or tunnels. Those without a residential certificate were ordered to evacuate to the countryside, as they were not permitted to use the shelters.[35] Instead of achieving an orderly evacuation of the population into the public air-raid shelters, the implementation of passes to allocate entry to the shelter caves had the opposite effect: those given prior allocation to the shelters turned bold and arrogant and refused to move promptly into the caves, whereas those not allocated crowded outside the caves in the hope of finding a loophole to sneak in. There were even capricious individuals who attempted to switch shelters, hoping to evacuate to a cave other than the one that they had been allocated. These people joined the loophole-finding crowds outside the caves. As a result, the cave entrances were often overwhelmed with crowds after the discharge of the air-raid alarms. To prevent accidents, the Air-Raid-Shelters Management Office ruled that those without shelter passes were not allowed to gather outside the shelters and that anyone found attempting to sneak in would be arrested and sent to law enforcement agencies for investigation; those people allocated a particular cave yet found occupying another were to be deprived of their original allocation.[36]

Due to inadequate government funds, overlapping of administration, and lack of administrative efficiency, the public air-raid shelters were not properly constructed, equipped, or maintained. The caves were dark and humid, and there was leaking and dripping from the top from time to time. Most shelter caves lacked ventilation facilities, and only the cave openings allowed air into the caves.[37] There were only a few public air-raid shelters with better facilities and adequate maintenance. Renowned writer Zhang Henshui (1895-1967) gave a vivid description of conditions inside the public air-raid shelters in *Renjian canjing (Human World Miseries),* a novel with wartime Chongqing as its background:

> This cave is purely a public one, with three interconnected tunnels and each tunnel illuminated by vegetable-oil lamps. The lamps were hung from a horizontal pole at the top with steel wires. Under the lamplight, two low-lying, long benches were laid out one after the other in a row on the ground. The refugees entered one by one and sat down in a manner as if they were crouching on the ground. The cave chief and his men [who served as guards] stood at the tunnel crossings and stared around incessantly. The cave had three openings, with ventilators installed at two openings and strong men among the refugees helping to turn the ventilator drives. Two men with shoulder bags containing relief medicines walked to and fro along the tunnels. At the crossings stood two barrels with covers and the wording "Nanmin yinliao, baochi qingjie" (Drinking water for refugees, please keep it clean). On seeing this, he uttered a silent whisper of regret deep in his heart. All these were so much better than the private shelters built by his organization. The voices as heard in the cave also sounded rather tiny and weak since not many people were talking.[38]

The shelter cave described by Zhang was, however, an exceptional case among the mostly poorly equipped public air-raid shelters. According to a survey conducted by the Chongqing branch of the Three People's Principle Youth Corps in June 1941, among the 240 public air-raid shelters in the city, those lacking thresholds, lighting, seats, and toilets comprised 70 to 80 percent of the total number, and those that were too dangerous to accommodate people due to blockages of mud and water comprised 10 percent. There were also more than a few *baojia* (Mutual Responsibility System) administrators who came out with all kinds of excuses to shirk their responsibilities in providing drinking water and lighting. One scholar compiled a number of statistics from the aforementioned survey on the 240 registered shelters and made these findings: only 6 shelters were equipped with lighting facilities (1 in 40); only 27 were built with thresholds and wooden fences (1 in 9); only 67 were furnished with sitting benches (1 in 4); and nearly one-quarter of the shelters suffered from dripping, leaking, flooding, poor ventilation, and deplorable filth and dirt, conditions that made it difficult for the shelters to accommodate people.[39] One Chongqing resident recalled his experience in a public air-raid shelter in the city:

> That suffocating place was overwhelmed with thousands of common folks; it was all dark around me. Lighting came to us occasionally from a kerosene lamp sitting in a slot dug in the bare cave wall. Terrifying cries were heard everywhere, and each and every cry crashed and reverberated in this narrow space, torturing one's nerves. My nostrils were quickly filled with a mixture of smells from food, urine, and minerals in the drippings from the cave walls. As I saw, before one hour was up, not much oxygen would be left in this extremely smelly hell. I felt that the fear of suffocating to death would make me crawl out of the cave with all my remaining strength, and even if the bombs were dropped everywhere outside, I simply did not care.[40]

It is little wonder that the ordinary people in Chongqing were unwilling to enter the public air-raid shelters unless they had absolutely no choice. The irregularities in the equipping and management of the shelters did not see much improvement throughout the war. This gave rise to the Great Tunnel Tragedy of 5 June 1941, in which thousands of people died from suffocation.

The Great Tunnel was the biggest public air-raid shelter in Chongqing. Its construction was begun soon after the outbreak of the war. The tunnel was nearly 4,000 metres in length, with thirteen entrances/exits and a total capacity of 10,000 heads. The construction work started in 1938 and progressed quite slowly. After the Great Bombardments of 3 and 4 May 1939, the anti-air-raid authorities, under pressure from all sides, opened early-stage sections that had been completed, but the tunnel was poorly equipped and the ventilation, lighting, firefighting, antitoxic, medical, and telecommunications facilities were extremely inadequate.[41] Whenever there was a turnout of a huge number of refugees, the air inside the tunnel would be polluted within two to three hours, and under such deplorable conditions, prolonged stays often led to death by suffocation.[42] However, as the Great Tunnel's safety standard was relatively better than that of the crude, privately dug, smaller caves, it became the main shelter for the vast majority of residents of the middle-lower class.[43]

On 5 June 1941 a prolonged bombardment drove a continuing stream of refugees into the Great Tunnel. Faced with severe overcrowding and poor ventilation, the refugees inside the tunnel panicked, breaking into a stampede that crushed and suffocated nearly 10,000 people.[44] Among the dead were labourers, factory workers, peasants, soldiers, students, teachers, and small merchants,[45] but hardly any high officials or social dignitaries were found among the casualties.[46] The tragedy caused widespread concern among the general public. Even though Japan was blamed as the ultimate culprit, public scrutiny also turned to the Nationalist government's inequitable allocation of shelter spaces and disregard for civilian safety. An editorial in the newspaper *Xin shubao (New Sichuan Daily)* pointed out directly that the comfort level of the shelters built by governmental organizations far exceeded their actual safety needs and attacked the government's negligence of the proper management of public air-raid shelters:

> The conditions in the public air-raid shelters are simply beyond description! We scarcely need mention the suffering of readers who have been to these shelters! Is this fair? Are the lives of the government officials more important than the [small] businessmen and the common folks? Apparently the more wealthy the organization, the better equipped its air-raid shelter would be. Let us ask something: where did all the money come from? Why is it that the people contributed the money and yet were treated in such inhuman ways? Even more painful is the observation that many governmental organizations occupied air-raid shelters with large accommodation capacities and yet allowed very few common people to use them. Despite their desperate and incessant pleas for mercy upon the sounding of the emergency alarm, the common folks were still denied shelter and protection. How can there be such distinctions between the rich and the poor, the public and the private, the officials and the people – heaven and the hell under the bomb attacks? This is totally beyond any human understanding![47]

The editorial issued concrete suggestions for improving the situation. One suggestion urged the clearance of spaces in shelter caves already occupied by civil-service and military organizations to admit ordinary city residents; another pointed out that all public and privately owned shelters should be opened to the common folks.[48] But none of these suggestions was accepted.

Due to the nature of their occupations, casualties among the middle-lower class were far higher during the bombings, especially among the frontline rescue workers and those whose workplaces were on the streets and in the factories. According to a survey carried out by the Chongqing Rickshaw Pullers Union in September 1939, among the 6,000 or so rickshaw pullers in the city, about 300 died from the bombings and as many as 700 to 800 were injured. There were so many casualities among rickshaw pullers because they chose not to enter the air-raid shelters for fear of losing their vehicles.[49] Based on the information in one source, the refugees housed in the air-raid-relief institutions organized by various parties in Chongqing were mostly hawkers and servants.[50] Even during the times when the bombings were most frequent, some factories, including state-run ones, were afraid of losing profits and so did not stop production.[51] Not only did certain factories fail to abide by the anti-air-raid rulings and fail to provide air-raid shelters for their own personnel, but they even prevented their personnel from seeking refuge outside the factories.[52] As a consequence, there were many casualties among the factory workers.[53] In addition, those who were in charge of law and order in Chongqing and who were watching the activities of Japanese collaborators and spies in the city, such as the military-security personnel, the police personnel, the military police, and the security-corps personnel, were also extremely vulnerable in times of bomb attacks.[54] For example, among the military police stationed in Chongqing, all personnel in the Third Battalion, which was charged with the duty of patrolling the downtown area, were forbidden to evacuate into the air-raid shelters. As a result, many military policemen died in the bombings.[55]

Great fires always followed the bombings. Among the buildings in the downtown area and suburbs, except for a few brick houses belonging to big organizations and firms, rich businessmen, and millionaires,[56] most were dilapidated and were often makeshift huts built of bamboo poles with wattle-and-daub walls and thinly thatched or tiled roofs. As the winter in Chongqing was not too cold and there was little wind, such simple makeshift buildings were adequate and could normally be used for two to three years, although as the writer Lao She (1896-1966) noted, "anyone strong enough could punch a big hole in the wall with one single blow."[57] Moreover, as the houses were built close to one another in a row, they could easily be burnt to the ground once they caught fire. During the Great Bombardments of 3 and 4 May 1939, the Japanese dropped large numbers of firebombs, and Chongqing immediately sank into a sea of fires that destroyed 90 percent of the houses.[58] According to statistics, among the Chongqing residents who died in the air raids between 1938 and 1941, only 20 percent were killed directly by bombs and shrapnel, and the remaining 80 percent were killed in fires and collapsing houses.[59]

Nowhere are the social disparities more clearly evident that in the impact of fire. During the Great Bombardments, it was noted that the brick houses of the upper class caught fire slowly, whereas the huts occupied by the middle-lower class could be totally destroyed when touched by even a single spark. Moreover, the loss suffered by someone belonging to the middle-lower class due to the destruction of huts and wooden houses by fire was often far greater than that suffered by someone from the upper class who lost a brick house.[60] Second, the deployment of fire engines was determined not by the scale of the fires but by the priority given to the protection of the residences of high officials and social dignitaries. Many of the upper-class dignitaries often made direct telephone calls to the Chongqing Anti-Air-Raid Command demanding the dispatch of fire engines. The Anti-Air-Raid Command normally sent officers to the scenes of ongoing fires with written orders from Commander Liu Chi to redeploy the fire engines and firefighters in action just for the sake of satisfying the needs of the upper-class dignitaries. By interrupting and even stopping the firefighting and rescue process, such moves by the Anti-Air-Raid Command often led to the further spread of fires, thereby causing a great deal of resentment among the firefighters.[61] Third, many houses collapsed in the fire. The Chongqing Garrison Command mobilized several thousand officers and soldiers stationed in the suburbs to put out the fires in the city. Some soldiers did not immediately rescue the victims buried in the ruins. Instead, they questioned the victims about their status. If the victims were wealthy, the soldiers would extort huge amounts of money from them and their families. It was only after the money reached their pockets through a great deal of bargaining that the soldiers began to act and rescue the victims. If the victims were not rich, the soldiers would simply ignore them.[62] Fourth, the anti-air-raid regulations strongly prohibited people from coming out before the end of the air-raid alarm. The anti-air-raid personnel were sometimes overconservative, and even when the enemy planes were long gone, they refused to end the alarm. As a result, the middle-lower-class people were unable to extinguish fires and could only watch helplessly as the fires spread.[63]

Unattached, unmarried individuals became subjects of envy after the outbreak of the War of Resistance. In times of war and chaos everywhere, the unattached were considered to be the lucky ones, as they could flee more easily from the enemy's bomb attacks without having to bear the burden of bringing along their children or elderly parents or grandparents.[64] On hearing the air-raid alarm, single men could simply move into the nearest shelter. By contrast, married women, especially those without any occupation and the means to employ servants, had to prepare foodstuffs and tea or water, bring along a bulk of luggage, and attend to children and the elderly. Zhang Henshui described in his novel *Bashan yeyu (Night Rains in Bashan)* the desperate and helpless state of women in wartime Chongqing in the process of evacuation:

> As people in the village make their way to the air-raid shelter to hide away from the enemy planes, a line is formed in the shape of a long snake. One passageway under the mountain road is only two feet wide at most. Some old women carrying sticks struggle along the way step by step, with small children supporting them. That person who seeks to catch an early place inside the shelter is not so patient. He moves his body to one side and then squeezes forward. Some middle-aged women hold babies breastfeeding at their bosom, and five to six small children hold onto the linings of their clothes. That kind of moving speed never really overtakes the older women with sticks ... With her three children and four travelling bags, Mrs. Li does not seem to be moving too smoothly. Just in front of her is a struggling Mrs. Zhen. Still in front is the wife of a petty civil servant carrying upon her shoulder a big cloth bag and in her hand a small leather suitcase with its lock damaged and tied up with ropes. Beside her are two children with heights below three feet. The children are struggling to move farther, and she is also struggling to carry her things farther. Daring not to take a rest, she moves on unsteadily with her body swaying to and fro.[65]

Women with bound feet or who were pregnant suffered even greater difficulties during evacuations, as they often tripped and fell in the midst of all the crowding and squeezing. Because of these hardships, some old women chose to remain at home rather than to seek refuge from the bombs, thereby greatly increasing their risk of becoming casualties.[66] There were also pregnant women who miscarried in the process of evacuation.[67] Unmarried teenage women might not have had so much difficulty moving about, yet they faced troubles of another kind. During the years of Japanese invasion, many parents heard about the Japanese troops' "Three Extermination Policies" of "Burn, Kill and Rob," and they became extremely anxious to marry off their daughters to prevent them from falling into Japanese hands. Many teenage women were therefore forced to leave school and marry, with some married haphazardly to middle-age strangers and even opium smokers.[68]

Women and children constituted a disadvantaged group in the process of evacuation, and they had to grapple with even more ordeals inside the air-raid shelters. To provide proper care and protection to the young and the weak, Chiang Kai-shek issued a personally written order to the mayor of Chongqing, Wu Guozhen, charging him with responsibility for installing special seats in the better-ventilated areas of the air-raid shelters for the elderly, the young, and the women. After much discussion, the Chongqing municipal government did not really put the order into practice but merely required the administrators of the various air-raid shelters to persuade refugees to give their spaces in the better-ventilated areas to the women, the young, and the elderly in times of air raids.[69] On the other hand, the Kuomintang's Chongqing branch produced a care package, called the "Reverence for Elders and Care for the Young" bag, containing medicines for the summer heat, sweets for the children, and informative pamphlets on the do's and don'ts for city residents while occupying the shelters. These items were distributed to the refugees by volunteers within the shelters. The pamphlets' contents included reminders such as "everyone should come forward and support the elderly, the young, and the sickly when they enter the air-raid shelters" or "the young, the elderly, the sickly, and pregnant women should be given priority where the seats in the shelter are concerned."[70] But the pamphlets attained limited results in encouraging the occupants to be more considerate toward the disadvantaged among them.

For young children, the conditions inside the air-raid shelters posed a serious health threat. The shelters were dark and humid, and a lengthy stay could be quite harmful to one's health, especially for children and the elderly. Mosquitoes and other insects were rampant during summer, and these often became the medium for the spread of diseases. Malaria, dysentery, pneumonia, and whooping cough were widespread.[71] Unknown numbers of children caught diseases and died.[72]

The cries of children posed another kind of problem. After staying in the shelter for a long period of time, the children would inevitably cry and weep out of fear, disorientation, and discomfort. But many people believed that the cries and weeping could draw the attention of enemy planes and turn the shelter into a target for the enemy's bombs. Consequently, the children's parents (most of whom were mothers) often became the subject of people's criticism. Unkind and sarcastic remarks were directed at them. Some would say, "You better find another place to hide tomorrow!" and others would say, "If you want to hide, just come on your own and don't bring along your children to cause us troubles!" When the enemy planes approached, some wanted the women and children to "get lost!" and even demanded that the mother strangle her weeping children with her own hands.[73] After the enemy planes dropped the bombs, the shelters often descended into chaos with people pushing and squeezing one another. The women and children were often pushed to the lower level and the able-bodied men to the upper level amidst the overwhelming crowd.[74] In the course of all this pushing and squeezing, the mothers would often prostrate themselves over their children to protect them and were themselves injured in turn.[75]

The self-sacrificing love displayed by the mothers to their children inside the air-raid shelters attracted the attention of writers and became a subject of their celebration. The following verse flowed from the pen of a poet:

> The enemy planes are dropping the bombs senselessly;
> The ground is shaking as though it is collapsing;
> The people feel like chickens and chicks within the sight of the predators in the sky,
> So anxious and helpless;
> But you don't care even a single bit of yourself;
> Fearing that the child will be snatched away from you,
> you hold him even more closely and tightly in your arms;
> The child is frightened to tears,
> wrenching the mother's heart as if it's a piece of string;
> Afraid of the scolding of people around you,
> you put your dried-up nipple into the small throats;
> Even if the nipple has become hot and painful after much sucking,
> you do not harbour any resentment whatever against the baby.
> ...
> The horrendous explosions outside the cave overturn heaven and earth;
> The dear house might be burning away at the moment;
> The dear child in your arms might close his eyes forever in the very next minute;
> You, loving and self-sacrificing mothers,
> how could you help it as drops of tears rained down one after another?[76]

In times of bombings, the impact suffered by women and children contrasted sharply with the impact on others. The most typical case was a family consisting of a husband, his wife, his concubine, and a four-month-old baby son. When the Japanese planes approached, the concubine reacted quickly by putting her son on the ground, then she asked the husband to prostrate himself over her son, and then she herself did so over the husband. The wife was asked to prostate on top, and she provided cover for all three people below. In the end, the wife was injured during the bombings, whereas the concubine, husband, and baby were all safe.[77]

Children may have been well cared for by their parents, but if their parents died during the air raids, they became a truly disadvantaged group. During the times of air raids, many wandering orphans appeared in the downtown area. Their lives and the means they sought for survival differed according to their age and physical strength: some became luggage carriers on docks, some begged for food and money door to door, some mixed with thieves, and some searched among the ruins for gold ornaments and other valuables after the bombings. In winter they surrendered themselves in huge numbers to the police stations and demanded to be sent to houses of detention and to have their wandering life put on hold. As Japanese bombings continued, the number of wandering orphans in Chongqing "rose without a limit," and most of them were able-bodied teenagers of thirteen to fourteen years old. The phenomenon attracted the attention of news media.[78]

During the years between 1938 and 1941, Nationalist China's wartime capital of Chongqing suffered from incessant and prolonged bombardments by the Japanese air forces. It was argued as early as this period that the Japanese air raids served to strengthen the social solidarity of the population in Chongqing rather than achieving its intended target of destroying China's resistance efforts. Such an argument has since been widely accepted in scholarship on wartime China. Although the argument contains some degree of truth, it overlooks the historical reality that the impact of the bombardments on the Chongqing population was by no means uniform. The present study suggests the complexity of the historical reality by examining how factors such as class and gender complicated the impact of the air raids on the Chongqing population and created wide-ranging disparities in people's wartime experiences.

First of all, the strategies and countermeasures employed by different social classes in response to the air raids were hardly adopted unanimously. High officials and social dignitaries in the upper class mostly favoured the city suburbs, where they built private villas that provided protection from both the summer heat and the bombings. Some from this upper echelon even possessed the means to construct near their homes their own exclusive air-raid shelters, which were out of bounds to outsiders. For salaried employees in the civil service and the private sector, there were basement and air-raid shelters in their office buildings to which they could rush for cover. As for the vast majority of the Chongqing population comprising the middle-lower class, they could make use only of the poorly equipped public air-raid shelters. These shelters were so badly equipped that more often than not they endangered rather than protected the lives of those seeking protection in them.

In terms of gender, the air raids in general affected women more than men. Those who were pregnant or had bound feet were more vulnerable to the attacks due to difficulty in movement. When air-raid alarms were discharged, most housewives were burdened by their children and heavy luggage while making their way to the shelters. In addition, they were often treated as pariahs by others in the shelters because of the cries of their children.

Although bombs do not discriminate, the presence of different social classes and categories generated contrasting degrees of vulnerability among the population in Chongqing in the face of heavy Japanese bombardments. Such disparities may appear insignificant in the longer term, but their impact on society at the individual level should not be ignored.

Notes

1 Major historical studies on the Japanese bombardment of Chongqing include Maeda Tetsuo, *Chongqing da hongzha* [The Great Bombing of Chongqing], trans. Li Hong and Huang Ying (Chengdu: Chengdu keji daxue chubanshe, 1990); Luo Taiqi, *Chongqing da hongzha jishi* [A Record of the Great Bombing of Chongqing] (Huhehaote: Neimenggu renmin chubanshe, 1998); Chongqingshi zhengxie xuexi ji wenshi weiyuanhui and Xinan shifan daxue Chongqing da hongzha yanjiu zhongxin, eds., *Chongqing da hongzha* [The Great Bombing of Chongqing] (Chongqing: Xinan shifan daxue chubanshe, 2002); Li Jinrong and Yang Xiao, *Fenghuo suiyue: Chongqing da hongzha* [The War Years: The Great Bombing of Chongqing] (Chongqing: Chongqing chubanshe, 2005); Zeng Xiaoyong, Peng Qiansheng, and Wang Xiaoxun, *1938-1943: Chongqing da hongzha* [1938-1943: The Great Bombing of Chongqing] (Wuhan: Hubei renmin chubanshe, 2005); Chen liwen, "Kangzhan shiqi rijun dui Chongqing de hongzha baoxing" [Japanese bombardment of Chongqing during the Anti-Japanese War], *Jindai Zhongguo* 72 (August 1989): 56-57; Pan Xun, "Kangzhan shiqi Chongqing da hongzha dui Chongqing chengshi shehui bianqian de yingxiang" [The social effects of the great bombardment in the city of Chongqing during the Anti-Japanese War], *Xinan shifan daxue xuebao* 31, 6 (November 2005): 115-18; and Sun Renzhong, "101 zuozhan jihua yu Chongqing da hongzha," *Chongqing daxue xuebao* 12, 3 (2006): 82-85.

2 *Zhongyang ribao*, 18 June 1940. All translations of quotations from non-English sources are mine.

3 Theodore H. White and Annalee Jacoby, *Thunder out of China* (New York: Sloane, 1961), 11-15.

4 He Ziquan, *Aiguo yi shusheng: Bashiwu zishu* [A Patriotic Literatus: An Account of Myself at the Age of Eighty-Five] (Shanghai: Huadong shifan daxue chubanshe, 1997), 161.

5 Qian Shiying, *Guo Gu hua piao po* [A Wandering Life as Told by Guo Gu] (Taipei: Dong da, 2003), 218.

6 Wu Jisheng, *Xindu jianwen lu* [What I Saw and Heard about the New Capital] (Shanghai: Guangming shuju, 1940), 14.

7 Li Zhiming, "Yige xingwu junren de huiyi: Li Zhiming xiansheng koushu lishi fangwen jilu" [Reminiscence of a common soldier: An oral history interview with Mr. Li Ziming], *Junshishi pinglun* 9 (June 2002): 106.

8 Hu Renyou, "Wo suo zhidao de suidao zhixi can'an" [What I know about the Tunnel Tragedy of 1941], *Lezhi wenshi ziliao xuanji* 8 (October 1985): 40.

9 Chen Jiying, "Chongqing da hongzha" [The great bombing of Chongqing], *Zhuanji wenxue* [Biographical Literature] 24, 4 (April 1974): 62; Li Tingying, "Kangzhan jishi" [A record

of the Anti-Japanese War], in *Jizhe bi xia de kangri zhanzheng* [The Anti-Japanese War in the Eyes of Journalists], ed. Song Shiqi and Yan Jingzhi (Beijing: Renmin chubanshe, 1995), 404.

10 *Guomin gongbao*, 30 August 1939.

11 Chongqing renmin fangkong bangongshi, ed., *Chongqing fangkong zhi* [A History of Air-Defence Works in Chongqing] (Chongqing: Xinan shifan daxue chubanshe, 1994), 219.

12 Ibid., 315.

13 Zhao Xiaoyi, "Fayang Chongqing jingsheng," *Zhongwai zazhi* 10, 6 (December 1971): 19.

14 "Shusan zazhui," *Shishi xinbao*, 13 May 1940.

15 Claire Lee Chennault, *Way of a Fighter* (New York: G.P. Putnam's Sons, 1949), 14.

16 Wang Zerui, "Kangzhan suoji" [Random notes on the Anti-Japanese War], *Jiangbeixian wenshi ziliao* 5 (1990): 14.

17 "Youguan shusan de liang ge wenti" [Two questions relating to evacuation], *Shishi xinbao*, 5 April 1941.

18 Liu Jihong, "Jiaoyu shengya mantan" [Random talks about my teaching career], *Dongfang zazhi* (after resumption of publication) 19, 5 (November 1985): 70.

19 Chen, "Chongqing da hongzha," 62.

20 "Chongqing fangkongdong guanlichu chengli jingguo ji jieshu banfa zhi jianyi, 27 August 1945" [Evolution of the Air-Raid Shelters Administration and Suggestions about its Closure, 27 August 1945], manuscript.

21 Fan Chaozhen, "Kangzhan qijian she zai Hualongqiao de Zhongguo Nongmin Yinghang zhongguanlichu" [The Central Administration of China Agricultural Bank located at Hualong Bridge during the Anti-Japanese War], in *Shapingba yi dangnian xuji* [A Sequel to Remembering the Old Days at Shapingba], ed. Chongqingshi Shapingba qu zhengxie wenshi weiyuanhui (Chongqing: Chongqingshi Shapingba qu zhengxie wenshi weiyuanhui, 1991), 359.

22 "Zhixi can'an de jiaoxun" [Lessons of one Tunnel Tragedy], *Xinshubao*, 11 June 1941.

23 Feng Siyi, "Chongqing yongyuan zai kuqi: Riben junji dahongzha qingli ji" [Chongqing weeps forever: An eyewitness account of Japan's great bombardment], typescript.

24 You Jianmin (interviewer) and Huang Mingming (recorder), "Zhang Wang Mingxin nüshi fangwen jilu" [An oral history interview with Mrs. Zhang Wang Mingxin], in Luo Jiurong, You Jianming, and Qu Haiyuan (interviewers) and Luo Jiurong et al. (recorders), *Fenghuo suiyue xia de Zhongguo funü fangwen jilu* [Oral History Interviews with Chinese Women Who Experienced the War Years] (Taipei: Institute of Modern History and Academia Sinica, 2004), 83.

25 Chen, "Chongqing da hongzha," 65.

26 *Zhongyang ribao*, 22 August 1941.

27 Qian, *Guo Gu hua piao po*, 218.

28 Maeda, *Chongqing da hongzha*, 250.

29 *Zhongyang ribao*, 26 May 1939.

30 "Shelun: duiyu jingjibu fangkongdong shijian guangan" [Editorial: Observations about the Ministry of the Economy Air-Raid Shelter Incident], *Shangwu ribao*, 4 August 1940.

31 Qin Chuange, "Yi Chongqing suidao da can'an" [Recollecting the Tunnel Tragedy of Chongqing], *Nanming wenshi ziliao xuanji* 4 (1986): 160.

32 He, *Aiguo yi shusheng*, 157.

33 Chongqing renmin fangkong bangongshi, ed., *Chongqing fangkong zhi*, 221.

34 Chongqing Municipal Archive, "Chongqing fangkongdong guanlichu gongzuo gaikuang (April 1942)" [General survey of the Chongqing Air-Raid Shelter Administration (April 1942)], *Dang' an yu shiliao yanjiu* 3 (1998): 9-10.

35 *Guomin gongbao,* 30 August 1939.
36 Chongqing Municipal Government, *Chongqing shizhengfu gongzuo baogao* [Work report of the Chongqing Municipal Government] (April, May, and June 1943) (Chongqing: Chongqing Municipal Government, 1943), 72.
37 Zhang Xiluo, "Yi Chongqing da hongzha" [Recollecting the great bombing of Chongqing], in *Zhonghua wenshi ziliao wenku,* ed. Quanguo zhengxie wenshi ziliao weiyuanhui (Beijing: Zhongguo wenshi chubanshe, 1996), vol. 5, 598.
38 Zhang Henshui, "Renjian canjing" [Human World Miseries], in *Zhang Henshui shuo Chongqing* [Chongqing as Told by Zhang Henshui], ed. Zeng Zhizhong and You Dexiu (Chengdu: Sichuan wenyi chubanshe, 2001), 157.
39 Cheng Yuchen, "Jiang Jieshi yu Chongqing de fangkongdong" [Jiang Jieshi and the air-raid shelters of Chongqing], *Dang'an yu shiliao yanjiu* 4 (1993): 92-94.
40 Yang Xiaoyan, "Duo Jingbao" [Evading air raids], in Luo, *Chongqing da hongzha jishi,* 426.
41 Tang Shourong, ed., *Kangzhan shiqi Chongqing de fangkong* [Air-Raid Defences in Chongqing during the Anti-Japanese War] (Chongqing: Chongqing chubanshe, 1995), 93.
42 Qin Chuange, "Yi Chongqing suidao da can'an," 160-61.
43 Zhao Xiaomei, "Kangzhan huiyi: Ji zhanshi etong bayou hui" [Recollecting the Anti-Japanese War: Notes on the Wartime Childcare Association], *Zhongwai zazhi* 138 (August 1978): 69.
44 Second Historical Archive of China, "Chongqing dashuidao can'an shiliao yi zu," *Minguo dang'an* 1 (1997): 27-28.
45 Gao Xunlun, "Chongqing suidao zhixi dacan'an zhenxiang" [The truth about the Tunnel Tragedy of Chongqing], *Lezhi wenshi ziliao xuanji* 8 (1985): 44.
46 Owen Lattimore, *China Memoirs: Chiang Kai-shek and the War against Japan* (Tokyo: University of Tokyo Press, 1990), 121.
47 "Zhixi an de jiaoxun" [Lessons of the Tunnel Tragedy of Chongqing], *Xin shubao,* 11 June 1941.
48 Ibid.
49 Zi Gang, "Chongqing de renli che" [Rickshaws of Chongqing], *Dagongbao,* 25 September 1939.
50 Tian Xun, "Hou fang zhandou de hanglie: Ji shourongsuo ji qi shenghuo" [Battle formation in the rear: Houses of refuge and the lives within], *Zhongyang ribao,* 2 September 1949.
51 Ye Gu, "Bingongting tingzhang Li Chenggan" [The Ordnance Department Head Li Chenggan], in *Peidu xingyun lu* [Recollections of Times and Tides at Chongqing], ed. Chongqing wenshi yanjiuguan (Shanghai: Shanghai shudian, 1994), 19.
52 "Changfang weifan fangkong faling buzhun gongren duobi kongxi" [The factory authorities forbid workers to evade air raids], *Xinhua ribao,* 3 June 1940.
53 Yi Fu, "Shancheng zase (Chongqing Tongxun)" [Mixed colours of a mountain city: Correspondences from Chongqing], *Jiefang* 129 (May 1941): 21.
54 "Kongxi xia de yingxiong" [Heroes under the air raids], *Dagongbao,* 13 June 1940.
55 Gao Xunlun, "Chongqing suidao zhixi dacan'an zhenxiang" [The truth about the Tunnel Tragedy of Chongqing], *Lezhi wenshi ziliao xuanji* 8 (1985): 42.
56 Wu, *Xindu jianwen lu,* 85.
57 Lao She, "Bafang fengyu" [In turbulent times], in *Lao She wenji* [Collected Works of Lao She] (Beijing: Renmin wenxue chubanshe, 1989), 298.
58 Su zhiliang et al., *Qu dahoufang* [Going to the Rear Area] (Shanghai: Renmin chubanshe, 2005), 392.

59 Tang Zong, *Tang Zong shiluo zai dalu de riji* [Tang Zong's Diary of Being Lost on the Mainland] (Taipei: Zhuanji wenxue chubanshe, 1998), 242.
60 Lin Rusi, *Zhanshi Chongqing Fengguang* [The Wartime Chongqing Scene] (Chongqing: Chongqing chubanshe, 1986), 90.
61 Zou Gaojing, "Kangzhan shiqi Chongqing fangkong hemu" [Inside stories about air-defence during the Anti-Japanese War], *Wenshi ziliao xuanji* 40 (1963): 231.
62 Qiu Shenjun and Ding Xuzeng, "Kangzhan shiqi Chongqing de dianxun fangkong gongzuo" [Air-defence work on the Chongqing radar system during the Anti-Japanese War], *Sichuan wenshi ziliao xuanji* 32 (1984): 96.
63 Wei Daming, "Zhenkong qingbaodui fangkong yu kongzhan zhi gongxian" [Contributions made by air intelligence to air defence and air battles], *Zhuanji wenxue* 39, 3 (September 1981): 112.
64 Feng Zikai, "Laozhe zige" [Songs sung by workers], in *Zhongguo kangri zhanzheng shiqi dahoufang wenxue shuxi* [Series on Literature in the Rear Areas during the Anti-Japanese War], ed. Qin Mu (Chongqing: Chongqing Chubanshe, 1989), series 5, vol. 2, 956.
65 Zhang Henshui, "Bashan yeyu" [Night rains at Baishan], in *Zhang Henshui shuo Chongqing* [Chongqing as Told by Zhang Henshui], ed. Zeng Zhizhong and You Dexiu (Chengdu: Sichuan wenyi chubanshe, 2001), 94.
66 "Wushiba nianqian Liangping canzao riji kuanghonglanzha" [Liangping was tragically bombarded by Japanese planes fifty-eight years ago], *Liangping zhi chuang,* 2008, http://www.tsy.8u8.com/lpxinwen4/010818.htm.
67 "Wo'men zai ge daozi" [We were reaping rice], *Dagongbao,* 19 August 1941.
68 Maeda, *Chongqing da hongzha,* 105.
69 Cheng, "Jiang Jieshi," 93.
70 *Dagongbao,* 29 July 1940.
71 Liu Wuji, "Fenghuo zhong jiangxue shuangchengji" [Recollections of my teaching experiences in Chongqing and Kunming during the war years], *Zhuanji wenxue* 32, 3 (March 1978): 57.
72 Han Suyin, *Birdless Summer* (New York: G.P. Putnam's Sons, 1968), 182.
73 Shi Xiuwen, "Fangkongdong zhong xiaohai tiku de wenti" [The problems of children weeping in the air-raid shelters], *Dagongbao,* 12 June 1941; Li Huafei, "Cong hongzha zhong chengzhang" [Growing up with the bombardments], in *Zhongguo kangri zhanzheng shiqi dahoufang wenxue shuxi* [Series on Literature in the Rear Areas during the Anti-Japanese War], ed. Qin Mu (Chongqing: Chongqing Chubanshe, 1989), series 5, vol. 2, 321.
74 Second Historical Archive of China, "Chongqing dasuidao dang'an shiliao yi zu" [A collection of archival source materials relating to tunnels in Chongqing], *Minguo Dang'an,* January 1997, 27.
75 Zhang Mingming, "Fuqing zai Chongqing de rizi" [The days when father stayed in Chongqing], in *Zhang Henshui shuo Chongqing* [Chongqing as Told by Zhang Henshui], ed. Zeng Zhizhong and You Dexiu (Chengdu: Sichuan wenyi chubanshe, 2001), 364.
76 Yan Chen, "Weida de cixin: Gei fangkongdong li de muqin men" [Great merciful hearts: For mothers of the air-raid shelters], in *Zhongguo duiri kangzhan shiqi dahoufang wenxue shuxi* [Collected Writings from the Rear Areas during the Time of China's Anti-Japanese War], ed. Zang Kejia (Chongqing: Chongqing chubanshe, 1989), series 6, vol. 1, 696-97.
77 Lin, *Zhanshi Chongqing fengguang,* 131-32.
78 Liang ma, "Ji'e xian shang de ertong" [Children on the line of starvation], *Xinshubao,* 26 September 1941.

4

Militarization and Jinmen (Quemoy) Society, 1949-92

Michael Szonyi

THE WORK OF DIANA LARY, along with many others, has shown us that war and its brutal consequences profoundly shaped Chinese society throughout the twentieth century. But even militarization short of open conflict can distort and scar society. In this chapter, drawn from my book *Cold War Island: Quemoy on the Front Line,* I explore militarization in one local Chinese setting, the small island of Jinmen (Quemoy) in the Taiwan Strait, in the decades after 1949.[1] Retained by the retreating forces of Chiang Kai-shek's Republic of China (ROC) army in the waning months of the Chinese Civil War, Jinmen became one of the most highly militarized local societies in the world. Local residents were conscripted into a universal militia and forced to provide logistical support for the troops of the garrison, whose numbers came to dwarf the civilian population. Largely spared the horrors of the great episodes of mass violence in twentieth-century China, Jinmen's experience of war since 1949 has been limited to two well-known episodes of geopolitical conflict, the Taiwan Strait Crises of 1954-55 and 1958, and the bizarre alternate-day shelling of the island by the People's Liberation Army (PLA) from 1958 to 1978. But local society has nonetheless been profoundly affected by militarization.

The chapter makes two arguments. First, I show that the complex trajectory of militarization on Jinmen cannot be understood by reference to military issues alone but must be located within the larger geopolitical context, the manifold ways Jinmen society was connected to national, regional, and international phenomena. Militarization of local society in Jinmen can thus serve as a case study for the interconnections between global geopolitics and everyday life. Second, I discuss some of the enduring legacies of militarization. Although the soldiers are largely gone from Jinmen today, the period of militarization continues to affect local society. I focus specifically on how remembrance of the militarized period functions in local politics today.

Because of its physical position on the frontline of the military and political standoff between the People's Republic of China (PRC) and the ROC, and its symbolic position as an image of Cold War tension, Jinmen has received much attention from scholars, who have written on the island's geopolitical role and on the significance of the various events in which it was involved. Jinmen figures with some prominence in the history of US foreign policy and of Sino-Soviet

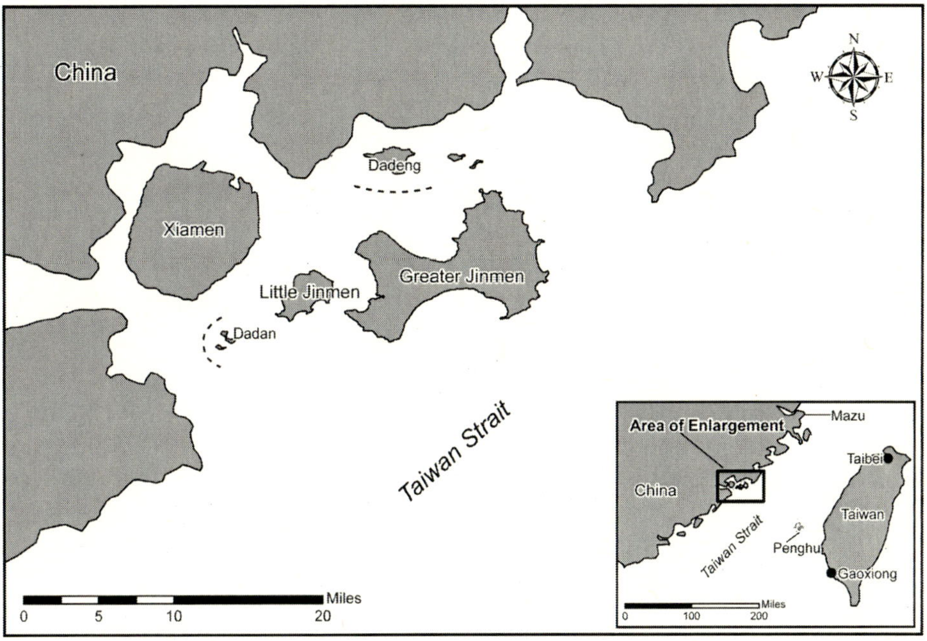

FIGURE 4.1 Jinmen and vicinity.

and Sino-American relations and in the theoretical literature on realism, deterrence, and brinkmanship.[2] This project considers Jinmen from a different perspective, one that has been almost entirely neglected in the English-language literature. It explores Jinmen as a human society, embedded in a larger world, and asks how the inhabitants of the island experienced these dramatic events.

The history of Jinmen must be traced by a dual chronology, in which one register records events, decisions, and campaigns launched in the centres of power and the other records corresponding experiences, struggles, frequent suffering, and less frequent triumphs in the island's villages. On Jinmen the upper register is not only at the national level but also at the global and geopolitical. It was not only decisions made in Taibei that shaped people's lives on Jinmen but also those made in Beijing, Washington, and Moscow. Two themes emerge from this chronology: militarization and geopoliticization.

By militarization, I do not mean the deliberate process by which states enhance their capacity to make or defend against war but rather "the step-by-step process by which something becomes controlled by, dependent on, or derives its value from the military as an institution or militaristic criteria." On this definition, as Cynthia Enloe argues, virtually anything can become militarized, even a can of soup.[3] On Jinmen militarization in this broader sense meant the mobilization of the populace to support the ROC military and the subordination of people's interests to military concerns. Among the things that became militarized on Jinmen were rats' tails, women's bodies, and cookie tins.

As with many other twentieth-century societies in China and elsewhere, militarization on Jinmen occurred under a condition of national emergency. Giorgio Agamben, who uses the term "state of exception" rather than "emergency," points out that such a condition is usually understood as a simple de facto response to crisis. But declaring a state of emergency is *always* a political decision. Agamben considers the state of exception to be a problem of legal philosophy and ethics. The state of exception is typically represented as a fact of law rather than as a question of law. But since it means not simply the suspension of laws but also the suspension of the legal order, the state of exception actually defines the limits of law.[4]

For much of the period covered by this chapter, the entire Republic of China was governed under a state of emergency, whose legal basis was martial law and the "Temporary Provisions Effective During the Period of Communist Rebellion." Jinmen's distinctive position, along with Mazu, the other main Taiwan Strait island group, meant that even martial law and the temporary provisions were considered inadequate to the situation. The distinctive systems created to administer Jinmen and the other offshore islands were thus a state of exception within a state of exception. Agamben's argument that the state of emergency or exception (I use these terms interchangeably) is not an objective condition but a problem to be explained can be very suggestive for the historian. Although the very terms "emergency" and "exception" suggest temporariness, the state of exception can also be seen as an increasingly important paradigm for political sovereignty in the twentieth century, not only in China but also around the world.

Militarization on Jinmen was inseparable from geopoliticization. By "geopoliticization," I mean not simply the military significance of the island to global geopolitics or how the island was directly affected by global issues and forces. Rather, I use geopoliticization to describe how regional and global tension affected different aspects of social relations and became an important frame through which the people of Jinmen understood their own experiences. The Cold War was at one level a struggle over mass utopias – that is, over competing ideological visions of how society should be organized.[5] But as Greg Grandin has written of the conflict in Latin America, "what gave that struggle its transcendental force was the politicization and internationalization of everyday life and familiar encounters."[6] For the people of Jinmen, the Cold War was seen at the time and is remembered today less as an ideological confrontation and more in terms of the minutiae of struggles of daily life: how they negotiated curfews, blackouts, and population-registration rules; how illiterate farmers learned new agricultural techniques to produce goods that could be sold to soldiers; and how families responded to the commodification of sexuality and danger of rape that seem universal wherever male soldiers gather. On Jinmen geopolitical conflict should also be seen in terms of the interaction between multiple power regimes operating in overlapping fields, from high-level diplomacy in Washington and Beijing to local village politics. Even before the heyday of contemporary globalization, local society on Jinmen was deeply embedded in the global. Another dimension of geopoliticization is the way Jinmen was used by various actors to communicate geopolitical messages – for example, to signal resolve, assert the superiority of one political system over another, or hint at dangers and threats.

A Chronology of Militarization on Jinmen

To oversimplify a complex chronology, the history of Jinmen since 1949 can be divided into five overlapping phases: (1) ad hoc militarization (1949-56), (2) formalization and institutionalization (1956-92), (3) development militarization (1960-68), (4) combat militarization (1968-80s), and (5) demilitarization and memory (1990s to present). In each phase, geopolitical developments inspired a set of responses from local authorities and the local populace, and the interaction of the larger developments, local policies, and individual behaviour profoundly shaped the experience of life on the island, often in unexpected ways.

Phase 1: Ad Hoc Militarization

Jinmen's geopolitical significance is a product of historical accident. In 1949, as the forces of the Republic of China retreated to Taiwan in the face of Communist victories and Mao Zedong's declaration of the founding of the PRC, ROC troops retained possession of Jinmen, Mazu (Matsu), and a number of offshore islands. The initial Communist efforts to take Jinmen were stymied by the Battle of Guningtou in October 1949. As the first major Kuomintang (KMT) victory in many months of the long Civil War, Guningtou soon became a symbol of the survival of the ROC on Taiwan. The island was invested with a large garrison to ensure that this valuable symbol was not lost. Within a few months, anticipating a Communist attack on Taiwan after the outbreak of the Korean War, President Harry S. Truman ordered the US Seventh Fleet to neutralize the Taiwan Strait, eliminating the possibility of further conflict over the island. The unfinished matters of the Chinese Civil War were thus internationalized.

In the months after Guningtou, the civilian government on Jinmen was dissolved, and political authority was vested in the commander of the Jinmen fangwei silingbu (Jinmen Defence Headquarters [JDHQ]). Civilians were pressed into labour after the battle in order to mop up the battlefield, bury the dead, and search for survivors and later to porter military and construction supplies as the army dug in against an anticipated second attack. From 1949 to 1956 civilian obligations were expanded. Adult men were organized into "duty teams" to provide logistical support for the large numbers of troops garrisoned on Jinmen both in peace and in war. Teenage boys and older men were organized into road-repair teams. Adult women were given training in nursing and emergency medicine. All of this was co-ordinated by the assignment of a low-ranking army officer to each village as political instructor, or commissar *(zhidaoyuan)*.

Phase 2: Formalization and Institutionalization

In 1953 a nominal civilian county government was restored, but it was entirely subordinate to the senior military commander. Three years later, a new administrative structure for Jinmen was introduced, in which authority over civilian affairs was given to a newly created, experimental Zhandi zhengwu (War Zone Administration [WZA]), led by the head of the Political Warfare Department of the JDHQ. The WZA's offices mirrored the civilian agencies of the county government, with a WZA cadre overseeing the work of every agency. There was thus an entire parallel structure to the civilian government made up of officers of the military headquarters, separate from but superior to the county administration.[7] As an official army history of the islands puts it, "The basic idea of the WZA ... is to implement a system that unites the military and political domains, to use the methods of scientific administration and political warfare to unify [civilian administration and] military power, and to organize and implement a total war encompassing the entire population in order to defeat the brutal government of the enemy on the Mainland."[8] The basic functions of the civilian government were subordinated to the fundamental task of supporting the military presence. "Developing an ideology of opposing Communism under the requirement that military [concerns] be foremost made it necessary to mobilize the entire populace in order both to develop the combat ability of all the people and to organize all political and economic efforts to carry out total war."[9] All of the functions of government under the WZA were aimed at the political conflict with the PRC.

The main factor behind this phase of institutionalization was Chiang Kai-shek's decision, in the face of US pressure, that for symbolic as well as practical reasons the offshore islands in the Taiwan Strait could not be relinquished to the PRC. Symbolically, they were a demonstration that the ROC still controlled at least some territory on (or at least close to) the Mainland. Practically, they would be crucial staging points in the anticipated counterattack on the Mainland. As it became apparent that ROC troops would be based on Jinmen for some time, planners developed more efficient ways to make use of the civilian population in order to ease some of the logistical burdens on the military. These efforts accelerated with the Taiwan Strait Crisis of 1954-55, initiated by heavy PLA shelling of the island. There is a general scholarly consensus (at least in Western-language and ROC scholarship) that Mao launched this bombardment in an attempt to deter the United States from signing a Mutual Defence Treaty with the ROC by sending the message that any nation that guaranteed aid if the ROC came under attack had to consider the possibility of war with the PRC.[10] This attempt failed, and the United States and the ROC signed the treaty in late 1954. One consequence of the negotiations around the treaty was a US commitment to come to the aid not just of Taiwan itself but also of other territories held by the ROC that were essential to the defence of Taiwan. This gave Chiang Kai-shek strong incentive to expand the garrison on Jinmen. By committing a significant proportion of his total forces to the island, such that its loss would mean such a weakening of his army that the survival of Taiwan would be at risk, Chiang was able to make Jinmen essential and therefore to secure US support for its defence. The garrison ultimately rose to a size of more than one hundred thousand, almost double the civilian population. The large military presence, and the likelihood that this presence would remain for the long term, convinced military planners that civilian government could not be allowed to interfere with military contingencies. Their response, the creation of the distinctive and elaborate bureaucracy of the WZA, illustrates a more general and unintended phenomenon of the state of exception: its tendency toward institutionalization and hence permanence.

The first big test of the WZA came in August 1958, with the second Taiwan Strait Crisis. On 23 August, PLA artillery launched a barrage of over thirty thousand shells onto Jinmen. For the next forty-four days, soldiers and civilians were forced into a life underground in shelters that had been built in every community after the 1954-55 crisis. By the time the PRC declared a temporary ceasefire, almost half a million shells had been fired, more than three thousand per square kilometre of territory. But even during the height of the bombing, the mobilized civilian militia was expected to provide vital logistical support to the military. In contrast to the scholarly consensus on 1954, a number of different explanations have been given for Mao's decision to bomb the islands in 1958. Perhaps it was a "strategic probe" of the US commitment to Taiwan, or a demonstration of Chinese independence from the Soviet Union, or a demonstration of Third World solidarity against US intervention in the Middle East.

Today, many scholars, notably Thomas Christensen, argue that the crisis should be understood in terms of the interplay of domestic and international factors. In 1958 Mao had launched an extraordinary social revolution, the Great Leap Forward, which imposed a huge physical and economic burden on the populace. To the challenge of generating support for this program, Christensen argues, Mao's solution was "manipulating conflict [and] militarizing society."[11] Mao launched the attack on Jinmen in part to heighten the sense of external threat and thereby arouse popular enthusiasm for his domestic agenda. Thus domestic mobilization issues within the PRC were at least in part behind the 1958 Taiwan Strait Crisis, and foreign policy adventurism was the tool Mao chose to achieve this goal.

In response to the 1958 shelling, civilian mobilization was also dramatically stepped up on Jinmen, with civilian labour enlisted to provide vital support to the military and, more generally, with the extension of military concerns and military goals into many new spheres of social life. Thus, when Mao exploited the threat from an external (although not foreign) enemy to mobilize the population in 1958, he unintentionally inspired a parallel response on the part of that enemy. The ROC state on Jinmen in turn shaped its policies in ways that emphasized the threat from the enemy on the Mainland. The result was heightened mobilization and militarization on Jinmen. PRC and ROC domestic politics moved virtually in lockstep, two gears linked by a third gear of Maoist foreign policy.

Over the next several years, the WZA formalized the previously ad hoc militarization of every aspect of life on the island – its economy, social life, and politics. In the years after Guningtou, the military had literally penetrated the household through the billetting of troops in every home (and this is to say nothing of the rape of civilian women). Now the troops were mostly withdrawn to purpose-built barracks, but in their place there developed an emergent biopolitics of militarization that regulated and monitored the civilian population, that classified civilians according to the role that they were assigned in supporting and assisting the military in war and in peace, and that enlisted them to regulate themselves in the service of the nation.

The years after 1958 saw further militarization of life on Jinmen. With the PRC decision to continue to bomb the island on alternate days, the rhythms of daily life were deeply shaped by military concerns. Domestic architecture was also affected. To ensure that Communist gunners could not use Jinmen houses to help sight targets, restrictions were imposed on the location and height of buildings. Every new house was required to have an air-raid shelter before it could be hooked up to power and running water systems when these were introduced to parts of the island in the 1960s.[12] The transfer of even more troops to Jinmen after 1958 oriented the economy even further toward the military, with supply of goods and services to the troops providing the basis of many household economies.

Phase 3: Development Militarization

In April 1960 Chiang Kai-shek called for Jinmen (and Mazu) to become "Model Counties [for the Implementation of] the Three Principles of the People." The Three Principles – nationalism, democracy, and people's livelihood – was the ideological formulation developed by Sun Yat-sen to which both the ROC and the PRC nominally pledged allegiance. By the 1960s it had become largely synonymous in the ROC with modernization. Because of Jinmen's strategic location, the danger of attack at any moment, and the need for ROC troops to prepare for a possible counterattack, the modernization of Jinmen was an especially challenging task. As Chiang elucidated later, "Jinmen is an island that is both on the farthest frontline of the war and also impoverished and underdeveloped." In a series of speeches in the early 1960s, Chiang laid out in great detail how he thought Jinmen's modernization should proceed.[13] In response, the WZA drew up a series of multiyear plans covering the development model up to 1987. The overall goal of these plans was to implement "modern political development in the war zone." In the first phase, the task was to "train the masses, improve their livelihood, and reduce the burden [they impose] on the military."[14]

This new focus on civilian construction after 1960 was not a reversal of the trend of militarization so much as a shift in its trajectory. The people of Jinmen certainly saw it as simply a new form of exaction. A former police officer recalls that after the policy was promulgated, "the local government concentrated all its effort into rural construction ... The work of the police officer was mainly stopping gambling, tearing down pigpens, tearing down homes [houses damaged in the previous conflicts were a major target for village reconstruction]. All of these meant being in opposition to the people. So I was happy to take a severance ... and went home to be a farmer."[15]

The call to construct Jinmen as a Model County based on the Three Principles, like the militarization of a few years earlier, was also a reaction to developments on the Mainland. By 1960 the failures of the Great Leap Forward on the Mainland were becoming evident. But whereas in the earlier phase changes on the Mainland resulted in Jinmen and Mainland society becoming more similar, in this case the ROC response was to attempt to distinguish Jinmen from the Mainland. Recognizing that the famine and economic crisis on the Mainland represented a propaganda opportunity, the ROC shifted the focus of policy on Jinmen to civilian social and economic development. As its official statement recognized, the development plan was really a form of "political warfare" whose aims were "to attack the enemy, to influence the world, and to fortify the spirit of the people ... Our free and democratic political construction will strike a deathblow to the bandit clique's People's Communes."[16]

The Model County campaign thus provides another example of how geopolitics could shape ordinary life. I argued above that Mao's motivations for launching the 1958 artillery war cannot be separated from the Great Leap Forward. The failure of this campaign was seen as a propaganda opportunity that generated a new focus on economic development on Jinmen: the Model County program. It was poverty on the island that made the new focus of the program necessary. When people today talk about the early 1950s, their recollections focus heavily on poverty and shortfalls. Villagers often begged for food from the soldiers. Students in primary school were fed with donations from US aid agencies. "There was cereal and powdered milk. The cereal was full of bugs; you boiled it up and then strained out the bugs that floated to the surface. The powdered milk had hardened into bricks. You had to bang it against the wall. We got steamed bread at school, but we'd hide it in our pockets to take home to our parents who had no food at all." The burlap sacks of relief food were recycled into clothing. "You'd have 'Gift of the United States people' written on your chest."[17] Jinmen could hardly be a poster-child for the superiority of the ROC under such conditions, and it therefore became necessary to construct the cross-strait propaganda policy in a way that dramatically improved living standards on the island.

For ROC propaganda to work effectively, it had to be transmitted to the Mainland. Although the Model County campaign sought to distinguish Jinmen from the Mainland, the methods by which propaganda was disseminated were actually very similar to those in use on the Mainland. In their comparative study of Cold War culture, Patrick Major and Rana Mitter call this phenomenon "mirror-imaging," noting that it was at some times deliberate and at others "unwitting and ironic."[18] The Model County campaign provides evidence of both. The two sides sought to isolate their own populations from the pernicious influence of the enemy while each simultaneously influencing the other side's population through propaganda. The result was that both sides used an identical range of propaganda techniques. Beginning in the early 1950s, radio stations and loudspeaker stations, reportedly with the largest loudspeakers in the world, were set up on Jinmen to broadcast day and night. Hundreds of thousands of helium balloons and sea-floats laden with propaganda materials were released from Jinmen. Besides propaganda materials, the floats contained food, clothing, cigarettes, soap, toys, watches, and radios, all items thought to be in short supply on the Mainland. Similar materials were enclosed in propaganda shells, hollow artillery shells that were designed to explode in mid-air, showering the materials onto the ground below.[19] But Jinmen was also on the receiving end of PRC propaganda by loudspeaker, artillery shell, balloon, and sea-float. Besides leaflets, in the early 1980s these items included videotapes, kites, balls, figurines, and seasonal fruits such as the famous Hami melons of western China.[20] Counterpropaganda measures were also identical. Residents of the Mainland opposite Jinmen have told me it was well known that these floats were booby-trapped and that the food inside them was poisoned.[21] Similarly, civilians on Jinmen were warned that the Mainland materials were poisoned. The danger of propaganda items was that they might "poison the thinking of soldiers and civilians and dull their anti-Communist and anti-Soviet commitment." There seemed no limits to the enemy's deviousness – in 1977 village officials were notified that four soldiers who had eaten from food tins that had come over with Mainland propaganda had lost their minds.[22]

Hygiene policies both before and during the Model County campaign offer another good example of the unwitting similarities across the Taiwan Strait. They also show the intertwining of military, geopolitical, and domestic political agendas, as well as how policies in support of these agendas could produce unintended effects. The danger of plague and other diseases on Jinmen was a serious military concern since outbreaks would weaken the fighting capacity of the garrison. In the first years of military administration, official discussion of plague conceived of it as a problem demanding technical solutions: inoculation, quarantine, and eradication of carriers. But over time, the issue came to be generally understood as a problem of civilian backwardness and poor hygiene.[23] Inculcating and enforcing new hygienic discipline was both a matter of military importance and part of a broader project of modernization, a project that it was possible to pursue using extraordinary measures because of Jinmen's distinctive geopolitical situation. By 1954 the need to eradicate rats to prevent plague had been converted into a problem of mass mobilization. Civilian households were required to meet a rat-killing quota that eventually was set at one rat per person per month. Compliance was ensured by requiring households to hand in the tails of the dead rats. In the second quarter of 1954, civilians turned in over twenty-four thousand tails.[24] Although the consequences of plague continued to be seen in military terms, the cause of transmission, the prevalence of rats, now came to be understood as a problem of the backwardness of the civilian populace. As an inspection team put it, "Jinmen's location is remote, and the people's minds are closed. They don't emphasize hygiene; one could say they don't even know what hygiene is. When there is sickness, they hire sorcerers and ask the gods to cure them. This illustrates their low level of knowledge."[25] Villagers could be punished with forced labour if they did not meet their quota. Residents of the smaller island Little Jinmen who were behind in their quota were required to produce a tail at the village office before they could obtain the necessary permit to take the ferry to Jinmen.[26] Residents were also mobilized for other hygiene-related campaigns, such as flea and sparrow eradication.

These campaigns against rats, sparrows, and other pests have an almost exact analogue in the campaigns that occurred on the Mainland in the same period. On both sides of the Taiwan Strait, antipest campaigns were tools intended to improve civilian hygiene. Campaign-style mobilization, including assignment of quotas and sanctions against any who failed to meet them, was also common to both regimes. There was one difference: whereas in the PRC these campaigns coincided with the fiercest repression of private business, on Jinmen the campaigns were perceived by some as a business opportunity. Soldiers were also given a quota of tails and were even more anxious than residents to fill it, for a shortfall meant they would be denied leave on Taiwan. The market for tails led some people to specialize in catching rats. Eventually, a kind of secondary market in rat tails emerged. Army cooks and procurement officers, shopping for vegetables for their canteen kitchens, would require civilian vendors to include a certain quantity of rat tails with their order; otherwise, they would threaten to switch to a different vendor. So vegetable sellers were also willing to pay a premium for rat tails.[27]

Other acts of everyday resistance were legion. A villager who was behind in his rat-tail quota could always borrow a tail from a neighbour. There were also more devious strategies. One villager remembers cutting up rat tails into shorter lengths and claiming that each clipping was the tail of a different rat. In 1982 an outraged hygiene officer reported that recently submitted rat tails were actually a kind of reed treated in lye. Residents recognized that so long as the duration of the campaign was uncertain, it was not in their interest to be too energetic in the capture of rats. In 1991 a dissident newspaper contained a deliberately humorous report that soldiers killed only male rats. If they caught a female rat, the best thing to do was to cut off its tail and release it, so that it could have more offspring, and ensure that the supply of rats did not run out. There were many live rats, the story concluded, running about with no tail.[28] The rat-tail campaign was but one of countless policies that inspired creative forms of resistance. Militia members slacked off from their duties, pilfered supplies, and grumbled. Fishermen scooped up propaganda floats at sea, made use of the household items inside, and used the buoyant containers themselves as floats for their nets. Such acts of everyday resistance in wartime are widespread, perhaps universal, and there is not much that is distinctive about them in the Cold War contexts, with two exceptions. First, the targets of this resistance undermine oversimplistic binaries between friend and enemy. Virtually all of the acts of resistance that villagers remember were targetted against the KMT, its cadres, and village officials, and occasionally the US Military Aid and Assistance Group on Jinmen, not the Communist enemy. Second, the politicization of everyday life heightened the risk of such acts since even the most trivial could be interpreted not just as resistance but also as treason, as a challenge to the regime.

Phase 4: Combat Militarization

In April 1968 Xiao Zhengzhi, head of the Political Warfare Department of the Jinmen Defence Headquarters, and therefore the secretary-general ex officio of the WZA Commission, began to lay plans for the wholesale reorganization of Jinmen society into combat villages *(zhandoucun)*. The basic principle of the program was, "Every person a combat fighter; every village a combat fort."[29] The militia, whose role was previously logistical, was now to be trained into a combat force:

> The militia's most important obligation is to defend the village. But it must also promote the virtues of guerrilla war ... Sentry duty need not be restricted to the sentry posts but extended to every militia member – the farmer working in the field, the woman washing clothes, and the children at their games should all be taught to do this.[30]

Xiao Zhengzhi had come to Jinmen from the ROC's Military Assistance and Advisory Group in South Vietnam.[31] While in Vietnam, he had apparently become interested in South Vietnamese anti-Communist programs, especially Ap Tan Sinh (New Life Hamlets), a rural pacification program that stressed funding of economic development and expanded farm credit.[32] In 1968 the ROC Ministry of Defence produced a long report on Ap Tan Sinh that suggested the program be adapted for use on Jinmen.[33] But this was just a cover story. The real influence on Xiao's thinking during his time in Vietnam was clearly the guerrilla activities of the National Liberation Front (NLF) (the Viet Cong).[34] The combat-village system sought to emulate the capacity of NLF supporters to guard their strength underground even when the US or Republic of Vietnam enemy entered the village. As a former deputy headman recalled, "the idea for combat villages came from Vietnam. But the two places are totally different. The topography and the geography are really different. The only thing that we could do was to dig tunnels. So he [Xiao] mobilized the village police to supervise the militia to dig lots of tunnels."[35] The combat-village system represents another sort of deliberate mirror-imaging. The inspiration for this system came not from the enemy across the strait but from another Cold War conflict entirely, the one in Vietnam. Here the similarities result from deliberate (yet concealed) borrowing from an enemy whose tactics had proved effective. Militarization could be as much about effective techniques of power as it was about ideologically inspired commitment.

In 1976 the system was expanded in a campaign to create "Underground Jinmen." Beginning with Qionglin, the first "Model Combat Village," a comprehensive tunnel network was to be dug beneath the villages. In combat, the entire militia could retreat to the tunnels, equipped with generators, stores of food, and ammunition, and harass the enemy through secret exits and firing holes.[36] This was the largest militia works to date on Jinmen. Over the next five years, it was duplicated in seventeen other combat villages.[37] During the same period from the late 1960s to the late 1970s, the army also engaged in underground construction on a massive scale, hewing two naval bases out of the coastal granite and expanding the underground army headquarters.

These developments of the 1970s and 1980s marked the apogee of Jinmen's militarization. Agamben argues that obfuscation is at the heart of the state of emergency: the state of emergency misrepresents itself as purely a matter of security when it is also a matter of politics.[38] His argument holds for the Jinmen case, as this high-point of militarization, in which every civilian became a potential combatant and every community a potential combat zone, was reached at a time when the actual military threat to Jinmen had receded considerably. Beijing was shifting to a more conciliatory approach to Taiwan even before Mao's death in 1976. The rise of Deng Xiaoping and the start of reform led to both a general withdrawal of the PRC state from society and a stronger commitment to a peaceful external environment. Both of these factors – a less militarized and mobilized society and a state that was generally interested in avoiding conflict – greatly diminished the likelihood of military action against Jinmen. Even as the combat-village system remade the topography of Jinmen, it became increasingly unlikely that the system would ever be put to the test. In January 1979, to mark the normalization of Sino-US relations and as a gesture of friendship to Taiwan, the PLA ceased its now decades-old alternate-day shelling of Jinmen.

If the military threat was so obviously diminishing, what explains the ongoing intensification of militarization on Jinmen? The answer is that this phase of militarization was driven not by military concerns but by political ones. These political concerns were both international and domestic. The ROC government hoped to use the combat-village system to exaggerate the threat posed by the PRC in order to garner international support. This meant representing the cross-strait conflict in terms of a stark bipolar Cold War world that in fact no longer existed. Although society on Taiwan had already liberalized considerably by the early 1970s, Jinmen could be built into a symbol that harkened back to that world and therefore inspired the unity of purpose of the earlier Cold War. Concrete evidence of this effort can be seen in the now abandoned cave complex known as Yingbin guan (Hall of Welcoming Guests), an underground bunker-cum-guesthouse for official delegations that was carved out of a mountainside in the late 1970s.[39]

This international propaganda strategy, however, proved completely ineffective. Taiwan's diplomatic and international standings continued their inexorable slide. The KMT regime also faced pressing challenges at home: demands for liberalization from a nascent middle class and a growing Taiwanese independence movement. In this context, the extraordinary levels of militarization on Jinmen in the 1970s also make sense as propaganda for internal consumption, intended to stress the persistent external military threat in order to justify continued authoritarianism and lack of political reform and, once that battle too had been lost, to justify the slow pace of the reform. Unlike in the previous phase of intense militarization, Jinmen now became even more militarized as Mainland society grew less so. But the key independent variable influencing the degree of militarization was no longer on the Mainland; now it was on Taiwan.

My basic argument here is that the trajectory of militarization must be explained largely in terms of political factors that operated at multiple scales of geopolitical magnitude and that shifted considerably over time. Thus, at each phase, global geopolitical and domestic factors intertwined to produce campaigns that were decreed at the national level, implemented by local officials and cadres, and responded to by Jinmen villagers. This combination often resulted in outcomes that were quite unexpected by policy makers. To give just one further example, in the period of the Model County, when Jinmen was intended to serve as a model of Chinese modernity for Taiwan, the Mainland, and the world, local officials sought to modernize marriage practices, eliminating such backward customs as child marriage and bride-price. In fact, these practices were themselves the products of earlier state decisions. The massive troop presence after 1949 had destabilized the gender ratio and hence the marriage market on Jinmen. Many village women married soldiers. In response, local families used personal connections to obtain brides for their sons by arranging marriages before their neighbours' daughters entered the marriage market. The result was that the age of marriage for girls fell dramatically. Bride-price, not traditionally associated with marriage on Jinmen, also rose dramatically to reflect the increased value of women on the market. Although local officials recognized in their hand-written reports that the problems of village marriage practices were due entirely to the presence of the troops, this insight was lost once the reports made it to higher-ups. At the county level, the problem was converted into one of peasant backwardness. Just as it had done with civilian hygiene, the modernizing state had again created the targets of its own interventions.

Phase 5: Demilitarization and Memory

The sudden announcement in November 1992, five years after the lifting of martial law on Taiwan, that martial law would also be ended on Jinmen initiated more than a decade of dramatic changes to the island. The War Zone Administration was dissolved and replaced by a county government with greatly enhanced powers. The militia was also dissolved. The garrison was reduced by 90 percent, from a height of over one hundred thousand to just over ten thousand.[40] The local economy, which had come to rely heavily on supplying goods and services to the soldiers, collapsed.[41] The ROC government legalized tourism on the island, partly to alleviate the situation. In 1995, to promote tourism and resolve the issue of dealing with land no longer needed by the military, about one-quarter of the total area of Jinmen was handed over to a newly created national park. Local residents also found their own ways of dealing with the economic shock. A flourishing smuggling trade began on the island's beaches. In a demonstration that larger geopolitical developments continued to have immediate impact on Jinmen society, in 2002, as cross-strait relations continued to deepen, the ROC government authorized direct transport links between Jinmen and Xiamen, known as Xiaosantong (The Three Small Links). The dense social and economic ties that had formerly linked Jinmen to the nearby Mainland but that had been cut off since 1949 began to revive. Local people reconnected with lost relatives. ROC soldiers who had settled on Jinmen went back to the Mainland to take young wives from the poor fishing villages of the coast. Wealthy Jinmen residents began to invest on the Mainland, and many people purchased property in Xiamen. A running joke on Jinmen today is that when older folk greet one another in the local dialect, they no longer ask "Have you eaten yet?" but "Have you been to Xiamen lately?"

As is common to many societies in the midst of rapid change, the past has become a topic of great interest on contemporary Jinmen. People on Jinmen, like people everywhere, use memory both to critique the past and to critique the present by affirming the past. In this part of the chapter, I discuss briefly some of the ways that the martial-law period is remembered on Jinmen today and the relevance of these memories for contemporary issues. I begin from the assumption that people's sense of the past is a reality that is as worthy of analysis as the past itself. The interesting question is not whether their sense is accurate but rather how it has taken form in people's minds and evolved over time and how it operates in contemporary life.

For the outside observer, it is hard not to see the people of Jinmen as pawns in the larger conflicts, "political capital," as one scholar has put it, used by regimes on both sides of the Taiwan Strait to test the United States's commitment.[42] This sense of victimization is shared by many people on Jinmen. "Whatever the soldiers wanted they took." "They stole all our crops in the field. It was as if we had worked for nothing." "At that time, [militia] service was obligatory. We didn't have any rights; we didn't get any benefits ... If you were told to work, you had to work; if you were told to do something, you just had to do it. You couldn't hesitate or you'd be punished under military justice."[43]

Besides this discourse of victimization, there is also a contradictory but co-existing mode of memory that might be called a discourse of agency. For virtually every historical moment where the people of Jinmen were put upon by forces beyond their control, there is a countermemory that puts them at the centre of events, their wits and determination undermining the schemes of the powerful and those who did not have their best interests at heart. Although this sort of countermemory is not unique, it is very highly developed on Jinmen. Here is how one former soldier from the Mainland, who settled on Jinmen and married a local widow, recalls the 1958 crisis:

> Mao Zedong said that if they could capture Jinmen, then it would be impossible to defend Taiwan ... On August 23 they started firing. Our side was ready, we loaded our shells, but we didn't fire. We waited for orders. Their guns were weak; the shells fell in the sea. We weren't afraid ... We drove away their planes. Their losses were much heavier than ours. They had many more casualties. We lost only one landing craft; they lost so many. After twenty days, they still hadn't won victory. So Mao Zedong was forced to leave office (*xiatai*). Liu Shaoqi took over from him. It was Liu who decided on the idea of shelling on alternate days ... We were really tired [from the fighting]. If you fought in a battle for two, three, or five hours, you'd be exhausted. You're an American – you'd have to go see a therapist. But we fought for twenty days. We were so tired. But we defeated them.[44]

Although it is not always ascribed to Liu Shaoqi, the idea that the alternate-day shelling was the PRC response to ROC victory in 1958 is common. "The Communists started to shell us every other day because they knew they couldn't defeat us."[45]

This sense of agency on the part of Jinmen people has its own history, tied to the deliberate decades-long construction of Jinmen by the ROC state as a crucial linchpin in world affairs. Today, having been told so often and for so long how important they were to the future of the ROC, of freedom, and of humanity, the people of Jinmen have accepted this vision of themselves. They remember how they made history. "In the past, we on Jinmen laboured so that Taiwan could democratize and indirectly contributed to economic development on Taiwan." "Without the Jinmen military miracle, there would have been no Taiwan economic miracle."[46]

Identifying when the vision of heroic agency took root in popular memory is difficult. It first enters the documentary record, in forms other than government propaganda, in the speeches and writings of political activists in the late martial-law period. A fully elaborated version appears in the manifesto of a 1993 demonstration of Jinmen natives living on Taiwan:

> Since the Battle of Guningtou and the August 23 [1958] artillery war up to the present day, the lives of many of our people have been sacrificed to the heartless artillery fire for the sake of the safety of the nation, and for the sake of protecting the stability and prosperity of Taiwan and Penghu ... [Referring to the inadequacy of local development plans] What about Jinmen? It is still a "battlefield." It is still the "frontline." It is still the same Jinmen, where the people are impoverished, where the damage has yet to be repaired ... What about Jinmen? What about the people of Jinmen, who have sacrificed themselves in countless numbers for the sake of the nation?[47]

Similar perspectives are today very widespread in the community. One former militia member, asked about his feelings toward the ROC government, answered, "I hate them. What makes me the most upset is that during the August 23 artillery war, the people gave so much for the government. The museum doesn't have any memorial to us; we haven't received any compensation. It's only because of our sacrifices that Taiwan exists today."[48]

During the martial-law period, the ROC state adopted a certain argument in order to justify its policies on Jinmen. Today, that same rhetoric is being appropriated by the people of Jinmen, who redeploy it for their own purposes. In this sense, the discourse of agency and the discourse of victimization converge in a common call for compensation. Either for their heroic contributions or for the suffering they have endured, the people of Jinmen deserve to be compensated. In 1992, a few days after the lifting of martial law, dissident Weng Mingzhi submitted a petition to the Jinmen county government demanding compensation for property seized or damaged, compensation for unpaid service and labour by the militia, and compensation for injuries suffered at the hands of both the Communists and the ROC government.[49] The rhetoric around compensation for militia service is remarkable for the way it exploits contradictions within official memory. Militia service was represented as the fundamental obligation of citizenship on Jinmen, just as military service was the fundamental obligation of adults males on Taiwan, yet only the latter received compensation. Jinmen's militia members therefore also deserve compensation, not only because of the principle of fairness but also because of the principles of economic liberalism, which are presumed (perhaps falsely) to be at the heart of Taiwanese political economy. Democratization *(minzhu hua)* and the recovery of local autonomy *(zizhi hua)* have come to be interpreted on Jinmen largely as a politics of redress. Popular memory plays a crucial role in this politics.

Many of the early claims for compensation were eventually settled in favour of the residents of Jinmen, although of course the amounts were never seen as adequate, and there has been much debate within Jinmen about the equity of distribution. But as an enduring political resource with which to make claims on the state, memories of past heroism and past suffering are proving less effective than Jinmen activists have hoped. Since the liberalization of ROC politics in the mid-1980s, some former dissidents have sought to articulate a distinctive Taiwanese identity as a rebuttal to the KMT and PRC claims that Taiwan is part of China. This vision of a distinctive Taiwanese identity, resting on Taiwan's distinctive history of migration, Japanese colonialism, and then rapid economic and social development since 1949, creates a challenge for the people of Jinmen, which shares little of this history with Taiwan. Recognizing that this situation would make it difficult for Jinmen ever to be incorporated into the polity of an independent Taiwan in the future, the chairman of the leading pro-independence party, the Democratic Progressive Party (DPP), once offered to renounce control over Jinmen, returning it to the Mainland, in exchange for a cross-strait settlement. This position proved hugely unpopular, and the DPP distanced itself from the proposal. But the very offer indicates the current double marginalization of Jinmen, internationally marginalized along with Taiwan and at the same time marginalized from Taiwan. As the people of Jinmen were adopting a rhetoric of the past in order to negotiate with the state that had created it, the state was simultaneously abandoning that rhetoric. Precisely as militarization became part of the public identity of Jinmen, it became increasingly irrelevant to Jinmen's most important political relations, namely with the ROC. Not surprisingly, this has given rise to a third type of collective memory on Jinmen, a discourse of nostalgia that harkens back to a martial-law period that is now seen as a time of stability and order in contrast to contemporary chaos and uncertainty.

Conclusion

The history of Jinmen's militarization, although often represented as a de facto response to military threat, was in fact shaped by a wide range of factors that did not always have much connection to military issues. It was at all times profoundly connected to larger geopolitical forces, including the dominant global system of the time, the Cold War. But the connections did not function in a consistent way. In the early phases, domestic policy considerations on the Mainland shaped foreign policy decisions, which in turn shaped militarization policies on Jinmen. In later phases, the key factors were global (the Sino-American relationship) and domestic (the internal politics of the ROC). Even though the overall trend was toward ever greater levels of militarization, the relationship between militarization and military threats was basically reversed over the course of the period. It was direct in the early phases and inverse in the later phases, as militarization became increasingly driven by political rather than military concerns. The changing geopolitical context generated changing policies that profoundly affected the everyday lives of Jinmen's residents, so to understand local society it is essential to consider the larger context, the subsequent policies, and the social consequences and responses they generated. The second part of the chapter suggests that among the lingering consequences of the symbolic construction of Jinmen as a crucial place in global geopolitics has been the incorporation of this image into local memory, where it co-exists with a contradictory image of Jinmen as victim. Whether they see themselves as heroic warriors or helpless victims, the people of Jinmen deploy their memories in contemporary political struggles. Reviewing this connection helps to explain some distinctive characteristics of contemporary politics. Greg Grandin has argued that one of the consequences of the Latin American Cold War was the elimination of social democracy from local expressions of democracy, leaving behind a washed-out version that focused exclusively on economic freedoms.[50] On Jinmen, Cold War militarization has had a similar impact, although on a more localized scale, resulting in a vision of democracy in which compensation and redress are paramount.

The extraordinary similarities between Jinmen and the Mainland, in terms of social experience and also the policies that shaped that experience, illustrate the phenomenon of mirror-imaging across the borders of Cold War–divided states. The similarities in policies across the two regimes on either side of the Taiwan Strait show that the two regimes were shaped by utopian visions that were both opposed and overlapping. James Scott has shown how in southeast Asia concerns from diametrically opposite points on the ideological compass could yield very similar outcomes.[51] Although he ascribes this to universal characteristics of modernizing states, the extraordinary similarities of the Chinese case probably also have something to do with path-dependency, the common trajectories created by the shared origins of the two regimes in the anti-imperialist modernizing movements of China in the early twentieth century.

The effects of militarization and geopoliticization on Jinmen might fruitfully be compared to their effects on other societies besides the Mainland. Many aspects of the Jinmen story resemble other highly militarized societies during the Cold War, such as Okinawa, or places to which great geopolitical symbolic importance have become attached, such as West Berlin. The propaganda value of Jinmen in the cross-strait relationship and the ROC-US relationship also reminds us that, like other Cold War islands and outposts, Jinmen's state of exception made it an exemplary site for the state to convey particular significations to its domestic populations as well as internationally. During the Cold War, Jinmen was at different times the "springboard for the attack to recover the Mainland from Communism," the "lighthouse of the forces of freedom," and the first domino, whose fall would signal the failure of those forces.[52] In this role, different Cold War outposts were in some sense interchangeable, which is why Jinmen was also the "Berlin of Asia" and the "Panmunjom of China." But attention to the social history of such places shows us that their residents in their daily lives made challenges to those significations that could be in their own way as important as the challenge posed by the enemy. A more general phenomenon was the instrumentalizing of many aspects of policy. In the Cold War context, many of what had previously been ends of modernization – economic development, infrastructure construction, even education – now became means in the pursuit of national security by ensuring military readiness, preventing enemy infiltration, encouraging domestic cohesion and international support, and demonstrating the superiority of one's own system over that of the enemy.

But although convinced of the value of comparisons across societies, I would not argue that Jinmen is representative of many other places in the world. Rather, I think Jinmen is best understood as an exemplar of broader phenomena that go beyond the limits of the cross-strait regimes or even the global Cold War. Despite claims to the contrary, militarization is never simply a response to military conditions but is always intertwined with other agendas and always produces a wide range of consequences, many of them unanticipated. Given the twentieth- and twenty-first-century history of militarization, perhaps there are useful comparisons to be made between Jinmen and the many other societies where the state of exception has given rise to novel forms of government, fully or partially extrajudicial, and where militarization and modernization have been intertwined, with profound consequences for people's lives and their memories.

Acknowledgment

I am very grateful for the help of many Jinmen people in allowing me to collect their oral history and providing me with many documents. I am also thankful for the great generosity of two fellow scholars of Jinmen, Jiang Bowei and Chi Chang-hui of the National Quemoy University. Research for this project was supported by the Social Sciences and Humanities Research Council of Canada.

Notes

1 Jinmen is the pinyin Romanization of the name of the island in modern standard Chinese; Quemoy is the common Romanization of the name of the island in local dialect; today the island is also known as Kinmen.

2 Key works in each field include Robert Accinelli, *Crisis and Commitment: United States Policy toward Taiwan, 1950-1955* (Chapel Hill, NC: University of North Carolina Press, 1996); Chen Jian, *Mao's China and the Cold War* (Chapel Hill, NC: University of North Carolina Press, 2001); and Gong Li, "Tension across the Taiwan Strait in the 1950s: Chinese Strategy and Tactics," in *Re-examining the Cold War: US-China Diplomacy, 1954-1973*, ed. Robert Ross and Jiang Changbin, 144-72 (Cambridge, MA: Harvard University Asia Center, 2001); Gordon Chang, *Friends and Enemies: The United States, China, and the Soviet Union, 1948-1972* (Stanford, CA: Stanford University Press, 1990); Zhai Qiang, *The Dragon, the Lion and the Eagle: Chinese/British/American Relations, 1949-1958* (Kent, OH: Kent State University Press, 1994); Thomas Christensen, *Useful Adversaries: Grand Strategy, Domestic Mobilization, and Sino-American Conflict, 1947-1958* (Princeton, NJ: Princeton University Press, 1996).

3 Cynthia Enloe, *Maneuvers: The International Politics of Militarizing Women's Lives* (Berkeley: University of California Press, 2000), 291.

4 Giorgio Agamben, *The State of Exception*, trans. Kevin Attell (Chicago: University of Chicago Press, 2005).

5 Susan Buck-Morss, *Dreamworld and Catastrophe: The Passing of Mass Utopia in East and West* (Cambridge, MA: MIT Press, 2000), 3.

6 Greg Grandin, *The Last Colonial Massacre: Latin America in the Cold War* (Chicago: University of Chicago Press, 2004), 17.

7 Wu Zongqi, "Jinmen diqu shiyan zhandi zhengwu ji qi zhidu zhuanxing zhi yanjiu" [Research on the experimental War Zone Administration on Jinmen and its institutional transformation] (PhD diss., Institute of Sun Yat-sen Studies, Wenhua daxue, 2004).

8 Guofang bu shizheng bianyi ju, ed., *Guojun waidao diqu jieyan yu zhandi zhengwu ji* [Martial Law and the War Zone Administration of the National Army on the Offshore Islands] (Taibei: Guofang bu shizheng bianyi ju, 1996) vol. 1, 188-89. All translations of quotations from non-English sources are mine.

9 Ibid., 192.

10 Accinelli, *Crisis and Commitment*.

11 Christensen, *Useful Adversaries*, 217; Chen, *Mao's China;* Xu Yan, *Jinmen zhi zhan, 1949-1959* [The battle for Jinmen, 1949-1959], reprinted in *Taihai dazhan*, vol. 1, *Zhonggong guandian* [The War in the Taiwan Strait, vol. 1, The CCP Perspective] (Taibei: Fengyun shidai, 1992).

12 If appropriate, houses were also required to be equipped with firing holes and other military facilities. See Lieyu xianggongsuo [Lieyu Township Office] Archives, Jinmen zhandi zhengwu weiyuan hui, *Zhandou cun zhandou shouce* [Combat Manual for Combat Villages] (1968), 3. It is an irony rarely lost on Jinmen people that although the propaganda sent from Jinmen to the Mainland trumpeted the sanctity of private property, their own rights in this regard were somewhat qualified.

13 Chiang Kai-shek, quoted in Guofang bu shizheng bianyi ju, ed., *Guojun waidao,* vol. 1, 191; *Jinmen xianzhi* [Jinmen County Gazetteer] (Jinmen: Jinmen xianzhengfu, 1992), vol. 1, 108.

14 Jiang Jieshi (Chiang Kai-shek), "Ruhe jianshe Jinmen wei sanmin zhuyi moufan xian" [How to build a Model County of the Three Principles of the People on Jinmen] (1963), in *Jinmen xianzhi,* vol. 1, 559-60.

15 Huang Pingsheng, interview, in *Jinmen jieyan shiqi de minfang zuxun yu dongyuan fangtan lu* [Record of Interviews on Militia Training and Mobilization on Jinmen under Martial Law] (hereafter *Jinmen jieyan fangtan lu*), ed. Dong Qunlian et al. (Taibei: Guoshiguan, 2003), vol. 1, 321-22. I have used pseudonyms for all interviews I conducted myself but not for interviews in published oral-history collections in which the informant's real name is given.

16 Jiang (Chiang), "Ruhe jianshe Jinmen," 559-60. There is no causal link with Jinmen, but within a few years the "bureaucratic restoration" in the PRC meant a demilitarization of the Mainland as well.

17 Chen Ganbu, interview by author, Shanwai, Jinmen, 20 June 2006.

18 Patrick Major and Rana Mitter, "East Is East and West Is West? Towards a Comparative Socio-Cultural History of the Cold War," *Cold War History* 4, 1 (2003): 1-22.

19 *Jinmen xianzhi,* vol. 3, 1258-59; propaganda materials displayed at the August 23rd Museum, Jinmen.

20 Lieyu xianggongsuo [Lieyu Township Office] Archives, Shanglin, "Jianjiao feiwei xuanchuan pin," [Inspection and collection of (Communist) bandit propaganda materials] c. 1984.

21 Wang Aimei, interview by author, Santa Rosa, California, 29 May 2005.

22 Lieyu xianggongsuo [Lieyu Township Office] Archives, Shangqi, "Jingwei zonghe," County government to Shangqi village office, 2 May 1977.

23 Guoshiguan [Academia Historica] Archives, files of the Nongweihui [Joint Committee on Rural Reconstruction], files 081-1083-9 and 081-1083-3, Taiwan Province Hygiene Office to Ministry of Internal Affairs, 18 April 1951.

24 Guoshiguan [Academia Historica] Archives, file 081-1083-14, "43 nian fangzhi shuyi" [Plague prevention in 1954], May 1955; Guofangbu and Jinmen xianzhengfu, eds., *Jinmen tongji nianbiao* [Jinmen Statistical Yearbook] (Jinmen, 1961-2006), vol. 32 (1985), provides annual tallies for rats' tails submitted. The highest number was 226,000, submitted in 1973.

25 Guoshiguan [Academia Historica] Archives, file 081-1083-9, "Fujian sheng jinmen xian fangzhi shuyi jihua shu" [Plague prevention plan for Jinmen county, Fujian province], April 1951. Common sense suggests a different explanation for the proliferation of rats. In 1949 the military presence on Jinmen meant that vast quantities of food had to be shipped regularly from Taiwan and stored on the island. Food reserves became an effectively inexhaustible food supply for rodents. The construction of large numbers of trenches, pillboxes, and underground bunkers created endless hiding places that poisoning campaigns were never able to penetrate thoroughly. Thus at least part of the reason why the military was troubled by rats on Jinmen was that its very presence made the island particularly hospitable to rats.

26 Li Zenghua, interview, in *Jinmen jieyan fangtan lu,* vol. 1, 524; Wu Mafu, interview, in *Jinmen jieyan fangtan lu,* vol. 1, 493-94.

27 Li Jinliang, interview by author, Lieyu, Jinmen, 2 August 2004. The secondary market is confirmed (although the article itself is intended to be humorous) in Wu Huasheng, "Jinmen de shan laoshu mei weiba" [The wild rats of Jinmen have no tail], *Jinmen baodao* [Jinmen Report], 6 November 1991, 14.

28 Wu, "Jinmen de shan laoshu mei weiba."

29 Yang Shiying, interview, in *Jinmen jieyan fangtan lu,* vol. 1, 229.
30 Qu Zhiping, interview, in *Jinmen jieyan fangtan lu,* vol. 1, 81. The combat village drew almost the entire population, including children, into military and paramilitary duties. From the mid-1950s to 1968, militia service was compulsory for teenage men and women aged 16 to 18, for males and unmarried women aged 18 to 45, and for males aged 45 to 55. In the new combat-village system, men between 16 and 35 were formed into a combat-ready "mobile team," older men and unmarried women into a "defensive team" to counter paratroop landings and to guard prisoners, married women into a "logistical team" to provide logistical support, do psychological warfare, and look after the wounded, and teens into the "youth team" to patrol the village. Even children under 11 and seniors over 56 in good health were trained as the "evacuation team" to assist in getting whoever was left into underground shelters.
31 On the ROC's Military Assistance and Advisory Group, see Stanley Larson and James Collins, *Allied Participation in Vietnam* (Washington, DC: Department of the Army, 1985).
32 On Ap Tan Sinh, see John Donnell, "Pacification Reassessed," *Asian Survey* 7, 8 (1967): 567-76.
33 Guojia anquan huiyi zhandi zhengwu weiyuan hui, *Yuenan Xinshengyi zhi yanjiu* [New Life Hamlets of Vietnam] (Taibei, 1968).
34 My interviews with men who served as officials in this period show that this is an open secret, but it is not clear whether it was also so at the time.
35 Zhang Qicai, interview, in *Jinmen jieyan fangtan lu,* vol. 1, 220.
36 Yang Shiying, interview, in *Jinmen jieyan fangtan lu,* vol. 1, 229.
37 Yang Xiaoxian, *Jinmen jindai shi yanjiu* [Modern History of Jinmen] (Jinmen: Jinmen xianzhengfu, 2005).
38 Agamben, *State of Exception,* 7.
39 *Jinmen xianzhi,* vol. 1, 276. In the same period, the JDHQ also built the world's first hospital carved entirely out of granite. The hospital, with over one thousand beds and nine thousand square metres of floor space, was reportedly able to withstand a direct atomic hit.
40 "Jinfangbu zuzhi xitong dishan duizhao biao" [Comparison chart of the transfer of units of the Jinmen Defence Headquarters], photocopy in author's collection.
41 One of the many interesting related developments was an abortive attempt to privatize military prostitution.
42 Chi Chang-hui, "The Politics of Deification and Nationalist Ideology: A Case Study of Quemoy" (PhD diss., Department of Anthropology, Boston University, 2000), 73.
43 Ou Ganmu, interview, in Xu Weimin et al., *Jinmen Daoshang Minfangdui shiji ji Guo-Gong zhanyi diaochao yanjiu* [Chronology of Militia on Jinmen and Investigation into the KMT-CCP conflict] (Jinmen: Guojia gongyuan, 2001), 162; Lin Weibing, interview by author, Bishan, Jinmen, 16 June 2006; Hong Futian, interview, in *Jinmen jieyan fangtan lu,* vol. 1, 384.
44 Zhang Caifang, interview by author, Zhushan, Jinmen, 15 June 2006.
45 Xu Shengyi, interview by author, Jincheng, Jinmen, 15 June 2006.
46 Ouyang Jinzhang, interview, in *Jinmen jieyan fangtan lu,* vol. 3, 204; Yang Shiying, interview, in *Jinmen jieyan fangtan lu,* vol. 1, 229.
47 Yang Shuqing, *Jinmen shehui diaocha* [Jinmen Social Investigation] (Taibei: Daotian, 1998), 99-100.
48 Weng Shuishe, interview, in Xu et al., *Jinmen Daoshang,* 148.
49 Weng Mingzhi, "San da yaoqiu, wu da xiwang" [Three demands, five wishes], in *Wuchao pengzhang* [Jinmen's Rising Tide], ed. Weng Mingzhi (Jincheng: Weng Mingzhi fuwu chu, 1994), 53.

50 Grandin, *Last Colonial Massacre.*

51 James Scott, *The Art of Not Being Governed* (New Haven, CT: Yale University Press, 2009).

52 Ming Qiushui, ed., *Jinmen (Jiang zongtong yu Jinmen)* [Jinmen (President Jiang and Jinmen)] (Jinmen: Jinmen zhandi weiyuanhui 1971), 5. The clearest early account of the domino theory as applied to Jinmen is "American Embassy Taipei Cable to Department of State," 19 September 1958, in US Department of State, *Foreign Relations of the United States (1958-1960),* vol. 19, *China* (Washington, DC: US Government Printing Office, 1996), 227.

Part 2: Institutional Engagement

5

The Blagoveshchensk Massacre of 1900: The Sino-Russian War and Global Imperialism

Victor Zatsepine

For most of the history following the Treaty of Nerchinsk in 1689, the Qing-Russian north-eastern frontier was peaceful and open for trade. By the 1850s, however, Russian elites had become interested in the Amur River as a convenient route linking Siberia with the Pacific Ocean. Backed by Tsar Alexander II (r. 1855-81), Count Nikolai Nikolaevich Muraviev, governor of East Siberia, expansionist, and ardent promoter of Siberian economic development, initiated the occupation of Qing territory north of the Amur River and east of the Ussuri River. The Aigun Treaty (1858) and Peking Treaty (1860) established the Amur River and its tributary the Ussuri as the new eastern border between the two empires. Russia annexed this territory claimed by the Qing without military confrontation, as Qing military fortifications in the region proved insufficient to offer any resistance.

Both the Qing and Russian Empires engaged in peaceful means to strengthen their new border. State-sponsored agricultural settlers from European Russia and northern China established new villages and towns along the Amur River. Russia sent numerous expeditions to the estuary of the Amur to study local conditions and encouraged the economic and administrative development of the newly occupied lands. In just two decades, Blagoveshchensk, Khabarovsk, and Vladivostok became vibrant centres of economic life of the Russian Far East, matching the cities in European Russia in terms of size and architecture. With the discovery of gold on both sides of the Amur River in the 1870s and the 1880s, cross-border trade flourished, increasing daily contacts between Qing and Russian traders, seasonal workers, and peasants. As peace prevailed, only a limited contingent of Cossack and Manchu frontier garrisons were stationed there.

Russian eastward expansion took a new turn during the reign of Tsar Nicholas II (r. 1894-1917) with the development of railways. Railway construction further facilitated Russia's economic expansion in Central Asia and beyond the Amur border. The Trans-Siberian Railway was constructed from 1891 to 1901 and linked Siberia with Vladivostok's ice-free port. The Chinese Eastern Railway (CER) became an extension of the Trans-Siberian Railway, running through Manchuria. Together with the South Manchurian Railway, the CER became a strategic shortcut to the Pacific.

Starting in 1895, the Russian government pursued a policy of economic expansion in Manchuria, hoping to turn it into an economic base for the development of the Russian Far East. Since the Amur frontier was sparsely populated and lacked strategic settlements, Russian expansion relied on Chinese labour and on the extraction of natural resources. The Chinese Eastern Railway Company (CERC) began to serve as a de facto institution of Russian economic colonization in Manchuria, pushing the frontier to that area. In 1898, based on unequal treaties and on assumed Imperial Russian supremacy, Russia negotiated a twenty-five-year lease of a part of the Liaodong Peninsula with the Qing Empire. Remarkably, no loss of human life or open clashes accompanied Russian colonial expansion beyond the Amur River.

But in 1900 the Russian army occupied Manchuria, adding a military aspect to Russia's railway expansionism. This led to a bloody conflict that surprised the Chinese and Russian communities living peacefully on the frontier. Mass killings of Qing subjects near the border town of Blagoveshchensk in July 1900 occurred when Russian Cossacks forced more than 3,000 Qing subjects living on the Russian side of the border to return to Qing territory. This tragic event was followed by the Russian military occupation of Manchuria in the summer and fall of 1900, as part of the invasion of China by other Western powers and Japan, under the pretext of suppressing the Boxer Rebellion (1900).[1] In Manchuria this action involved Russian, Qing, and Boxer troops scattered around several major CER settlements.

This chapter examines the events at Blagoveshchensk in July 1900, Russia's subsequent occupation of Manchuria, and how that history has been recorded. Although the Blagoveshchensk Massacre has been described in detail by Chinese and Russian historians,[2] the episode remains poorly understood. Was it cruelly planned, or was it simply a tragic accident caused by panic and fear? I argue that the Blagoveshchensk Massacre was not an accident but rather a calculated display of imperial power that Russian colonial authorities on the frontier allowed to happen. Russian military commanders, Cossacks, and commoners shared an attitude of cultural and racial superiority, of belonging to a league of European empires that was capable of educating "barbarians," by force if necessary. Along with other Western powers in China, Russia employed cruel methods against suspected Boxers and their supporters, a cruelty that has been minimized or erased by constructs of benevolent colonial rule in the heyday of global imperialism.

Russia's Road to War in Manchuria, 1900-1

Only limited contingents of the Russian military appeared in Manchuria in the 1890s. Russian finance minister Sergei Yul'evich Witte advocated a policy of "peaceful" economic colonization of Manchuria. In 1896 he and the Qing imperial commissioner Li Hongzhang signed an agreement to build the CER through Manchuria and to form an alliance between the two countries against a possible Japanese threat. However, this policy did not guarantee Russian colonizers peaceful relations with the local authorities and population. After 1898 the CER employed several thousand armed soldiers to protect the railway and its property.[3] In case of a military occupation of Manchuria, the future railway could serve as a major artery to relocate troops from European Russia.

In 1898 the Qing government leased part of the Liaodong Peninsula to Russia as a base for economic and military expansion in the region for a period of twenty-five years. Although an ice-free port in Dalny (present-day Dalian) was built to facilitate international trade, a new naval base in Port Arthur (present-day Lüshun) was opened to protect and advance Russian strategic interests in northern Manchuria and in Korea. In 1898 Port Arthur's military presence did not exceed 1,000 soldiers, and Dalny had even fewer.[4] But by the beginning of 1900, the number of Russian troops in and around these cities had grown to about 11,300.[5] They faced the immediate task of rebuilding Port Arthur's infrastructure, which had been destroyed during the Sino-Japanese War; roads, housing, sewage systems, and drinking water were lacking.

The Boxer Rebellion, which originated in Shandong and Zhili, spread into the three provinces of Manchuria. On 1 June 1900 the Boxers surrounded Beijing's foreign legation, but in Manchuria the situation remained calm until the end of June, when Boxers attacked the southern line and occupied Mukden. They burned the city, beheading local Christian converts. They captured a Russian stationmaster, then tortured and killed him.[6] The CER's armed defence proved insufficient and ineffective. Qing government troops and Chinese rebels occupied all the major settlements along the railway, blocking station guards in Harbin. For several months, construction of the railway was halted while the Boxers destroyed 970 out of 1,400 kilometres of railway, mostly in the western and southern branches; they also destroyed telegraph lines and burned all railway stations.[7] As a result, Chinese contract workers were forced to abandon the railway. In June 1900 Russia started to mobilize troops from the Amur and Maritime regions in order to address growing threats to its interests in Manchuria, such as the railway line, by supporting enterprises and new Russian settlements. Rumours of Boxer activities in Manchuria reached the Qing-Russian frontier settlements along the Amur River, and preparations were made for possible military action by provincial authorities on both sides of the border, thereby increasing already growing fears of an imminent war among the Chinese, Manchu, and Russian civilians.

The Blagoveshchensk Massacre (1900)

The first military clashes between Qing and Russian forces started at the Amur frontier. Indeed, the most violent events happened in the vicinity of the Russian town Blagoveshchensk and spread to Qing fortifications in Sakhalian and Aigun. Blagoveshchensk had been founded in 1856 as a Russian military settlement and since 1858 had served as an administrative centre of the newly founded Amur province. In the 1890s a gold rush in the upper Amur River transformed the town into a centre of Russian frontier trade with Manchuria.[8] Chinese traders, farmers, and contract workers supported the economy of Blagoveshchensk and surrounding areas. Dozens of Manchu villages on both sides of the Amur River had stable trade relations with the Russian settlements, even though Qing and Russian subjects did not assimilate culturally.

In early June 1900 Qing forces stopped and searched the Russian steamboat *Mikhail* twenty miles east of Blagoveshchesk. The steamboat carried arms and ammunition from Khabarovsk. When the Russian crew attempted to proceed, they were arrested. Qing soldiers occupied the right bank of the Amur, blocking river navigation for more than 100 miles between the Russian settlements of Ignatievskaya and Poyarkova.[9] According to a later Russian official account, the Qing army repeatedly fired at Russian military boats sailing along the Amur River between Blagoveshchensk and Aigun. A regiment of Amur Cossacks sailed from Blagoveshchensk and fired back at the Qing positions in Aigun. This led Qing forces to then fire directly at Blagoveshchensk across the river, causing panic in the city. The presence of more than 4,000 Chinese traders and labourers in Blagoveshchensk added to the panic among the Russian population. Fearing that the Chinese residents of the town might help the Qing forces to occupy the city, the military governor of the Amur region, K.N. Gribskii, ordered police to deport them to Qing territory by forcing them to cross the Amur River.[10] The border-crossing took place north of Blagoveshchensk.

On 17 July 1900 armed Russian Cossacks forced about 3,000 Qing subjects to be deported across the river, including women, children, and elderly adults.[11] Those who refused to cross were beaten or killed. According to a Russian witness, N.Z. Golubtsov, there was a shortage of boats, and most of the victims could not swim. Those who could swim started to cross the river but were met by Qing fire, probably by mistake. Only a few reached the other shore.[12] Russian Cossacks divided Chinese captives from around Blagoveshchensk into several groups and forced them to cross the river in at least four different shifts from 17 to 21 July. These deportations were accompanied by reckless killings of innocent people and by the destruction of their houses.[13] Meanwhile, Qing soldiers intensified sporadic armed attacks and gunfire from Aigun. On 21 July, Gribskii ordered Russian Cossacks to destroy all the enemy fortifications on the Chinese side of the Amur River.[14] Gribskii's orders could not be carried out immediately, as Blagoveshchensk did not have enough soldiers and arms to defend itself. In June a small contingent of Blagoveshchensk Cossacks was sent to Khabarovsk to join the expedition along the Songhua River to Harbin, which was besieged by the Boxers. For more than a month, Blagoveshchensk remained poorly defended. Only on 27 and 28 July did Russian troops from Siberia reach the city, turning it into a base for a full-scale attack on northern Manchuria.[15]

The accounts of this massacre remain controversial, as there have been no serious investigations conducted in Russia since 1900. From the very beginning, General Gribskii played a pivotal role in ordering the deportation of all of the Chinese residents and in allowing his subordinates to kill Qing subjects. The chairman of the Amur military government, Colonel V., whose full name was not disclosed, publicly told his staff that it would be no tragedy if all the Chinese were drowned and killed. He ordered the death of all of the Chinese appearing on the Russian side of the Amur River, without the need for further instruction.[16]

Arrangements for the river crossings suggest that the killings were carefully planned. The organizers chose a quiet place near Verhne-Blagoveshchensk, seven miles up the Amur River from Blagoveshchensk, in order to avoid accidental witnesses. Russian volunteers, and the Cossacks, armed with guns and axes, accompanied innocent Qing subjects, occasionally robbing and killing those who did not obey the orders. In Verhne-Blagoveshchensk no boats were waiting for the victims. Many Chinese were brutally killed before they were thrown into the water. Others either drowned or were shot while swimming. Table 5.1 gives details of the four documented "crossings":

TABLE 5.1

Details of the Blagoveshchensk Massacre, 17-21 July 1900

Crossing date	Qing subjects in each crossing	Russians in each convoy	Surviving Chinese
17 July	3,000-3,500	80-100	no more than 100
17 July	84	10	almost none
19 July	170	50	no more than 20
21 July	66	36	more than half

Source: V., "Blagoveshchenskaya 'Utopiya'" [The Blagoveshchensk "Utopia"], *Vestnik Evropy* [News of Europe] 10 (1910): 232-35.

As a result of the Blagoveshchensk Massacre, around 3,500 Chinese died; only around 160 managed to cross the river.

Similar methods were used against Qing subjects in other frontier settlements along the Amur River. Few living in Manchu villages near the Zeya River were able to escape the fate of the Chinese residents of Blagoveshchensk. After forcing all the Chinese residents out of Blagoveshchensk, Cossacks burned all the Manchu villages around the Zeya, killing several thousand Chinese, Manchu, and Daurs, without distinguishing between civilians and the military. One survivor of these killings later recalled that numerous corpses were thrown into the Amur River. Human blood covered the river's surface, contaminating the water.[17] Sporadic killings continued even after 20 July, when General Gribskii issued an order to stop killing innocent Qing subjects and to aim only at those armed Qing subjects attacking the Russians.

The evidence suggests that the regional military command organized the massacre as a tactic to scare the Qing troops across the border. The killings carried a message that anybody attempting to challenge Russian power on the Amur would suffer a similar fate. On the eve of the Russian occupation of Manchuria, General Gribskii announced that "the name of the Amur Cossack will thunder through all of Manchuria and strike terror among the Chinese population."[18]

Russian writer Alexander Vereshchagin, who visited Blagoveshchensk three weeks after the massacre, naively believed that the massacre was a tragic mistake resulting from fear and confusion over shootings from across the river. At the same time, he noted that local Russians were indifferent to the loss of life among the Qing subjects. He described the tragic scene he witnessed while travelling by steamer along the Amur River from Blagoveshchensk to Khabarovsk:

> "A Chinese!" – an old crew-member tells me in a low indifferent voice, as if talking about a snag ... His face covered with a thin brown beard, he shows a disparaging smile, as if asking me not to pay attention to such a trivial matter ...
>
> ... Our steamer passes a dead body. It is naked, of reddish and bronze colour, with hands hanging like whips, and widely open legs. It is floating, face down, as if thinking about something. The corpse is swollen, its legs and arms white as lime. Waves from the boat shake it, making it disappear in the water ... More bodies of the Chinese appear, and now they float along the width of the Amur as if haunting us. The passengers come out of their cabins to see such a rare scene. It will stay in my memory forever. These are, possibly, those unfortunate who drowned near Blagoveshchensk ...
>
> "Breakfast is served," announces a waiter ... The crowd goes inside. I do not feel like having breakfast. This horrible scene and poisoned air kill my appetite.

> I stay and continue to observe. The boat hits a corpse and the waves push it away. Its head is covered with a cloth. I think it must be a farmer. In Blagoveshchensk half of all farmers were Chinese.[19]

On reaching Khabarovsk, Vereshchagin met with the governor-general of the Priamur region, N.I. Grodekov, who boasted about Russian military successes in Manchuria but remained silent about civilian casualties. Later, the author travelled south along the Ussuri Railway, discovering that the news about the massacre was spreading slowly in the Russian Far East. At a dinner party thrown by the governor of the Maritime region in Nikolsk-Ussuriisk, attended by twenty Russian officers, he was "the first one to tell them about the Blagoveshchensk tragedy ... nearly one month after it happened."[20] The fact that his account of the massacre was published in 1903 in St. Petersburg was remarkable, as it exposed the ugly side of Russian expansionism to the Russian public in its then tightly censored imperial capital. Yet no further publications on this topic appeared, and no public discussion followed, as both could have undermined the news of the Russian army's success in Manchuria.

Russian Troops in Manchuria

In late July 1900, in response to Boxer disruptions, the Russian Cossack detachments crossed the Amur River and moved south toward major Manchu fortifications in Sakhalian and Aigun. On 2 August, with the help of artillery, the Russians took Sakhalian. On 5 August they occupied Aigun and burnt it to ashes. The remains of a 10,000-strong Qing army retreated south.[21] The Russian army continued its advance in Manchuria and occupied all major settlements along the old trade route between Aigun and Qiqihaer.

Another line of Russian attack followed the Songhua River. Alarmed by the news of a besieged Harbin, the Russians sent seventy-three boats from Khabarovsk to Harbin, burning Manchu settlements on their way. On 28 July they took over Sanxing and set it on fire. In August, Russian victory appeared imminent as the Russian horse cavalry, commanded by General Pavel Karlovich Rennenkampf, took Mergen and Qiqihaer. The troops of General Sakharov, commander of the Russian army in northern Manchuria, cleared up all armed resistance along the main line of the badly damaged CER, from Qiqihaer to Mudanjiang, and occupied Harbin.[22] Imperial Russia entered Manchuria from at least six different directions, coming from Manzhouli, Blagoveshchensk, Khabarovsk, and the Ussuri region.

Russian troops converged in Harbin to celebrate a fast victory. With the fall of Qiqihaer, the official residence of the Qing provincial government, the Qing army ended its organized resistance in north Manchuria on 28 August. It then

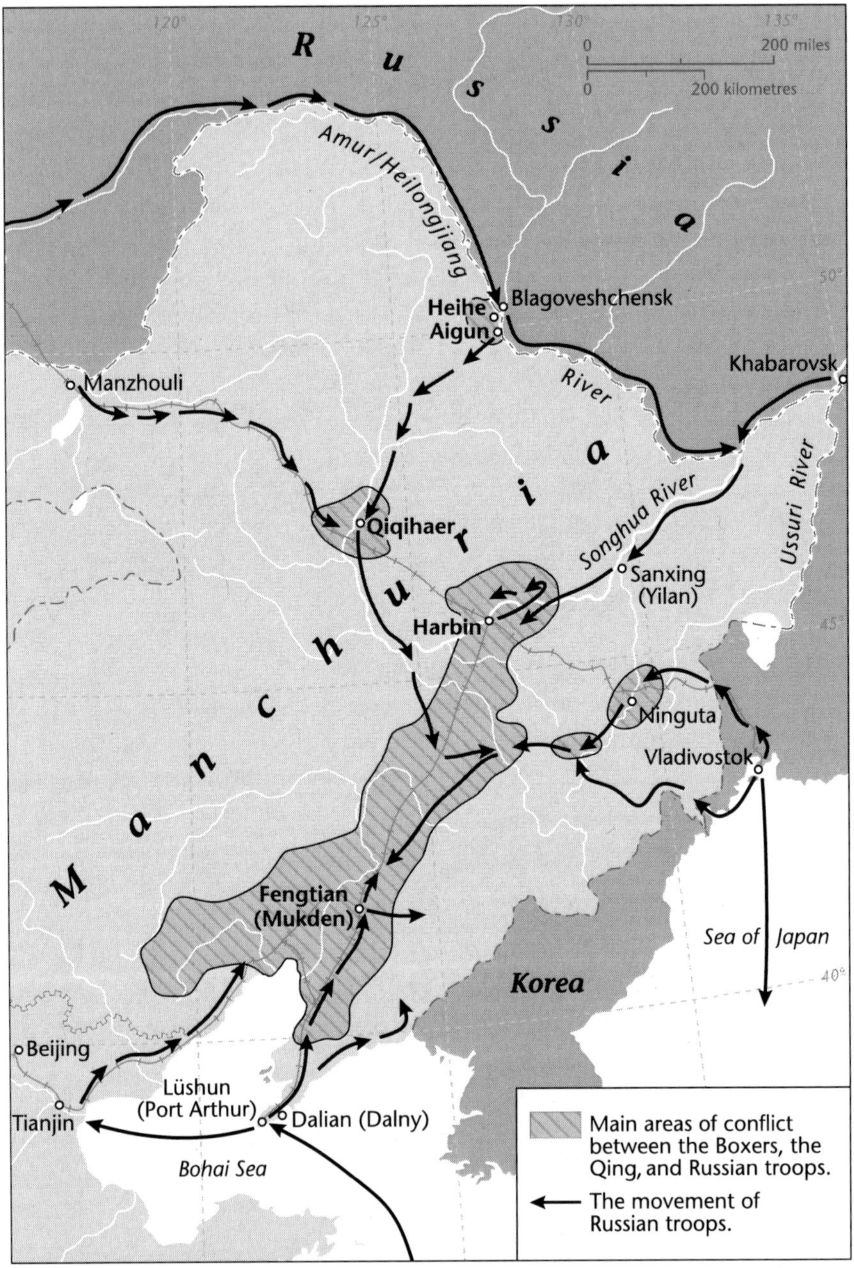

FIGURE 5.1 Boxer Rebellion in Manchuria and the Movement of Russian Troops, 1900. *Note:* The arrows show the direction of Russian troops. *Source: Zhongguo jindai shigao dituji (China's Modern Historical Map Collection)* (Beijing: Ditu chubanshe, 1984), 73.

took the Russian army two months to restore control over major settlements along the northern line of the CER. Imperial Russia started the war well prepared.

In northern Manchuria the Russians fought mostly with Qing troops, as Boxer influence did not spread to the north and west of Harbin. In southern Manchuria and along CER lines, Boxer influence was strong due to connections between the Boxers and migrants from Shandong, who worked as contract workers along the railway and travelled all over Manchuria in search of seasonal work. But although anti-Russian resistance was limited to the destruction of railways and of Russian property, the Boxer threat did provide the Russian army with freedom of movement and decision-making powers in occupied Manchuria. Sparse population and insufficient Qing defences facilitated the quick advance of the Russian troops and the conquest of major Manchurian settlements.

Domestic Tensions and Anti-Russian Sentiments

After the Manchu defeat in the north, the war in Manchuria was not over. Southern Manchuria, especially the area along the southern branch of CER lines, from Harbin to Dalny, was devastated and persistently raided by the Boxers. By the early autumn of 1900, the Russian government had sent an additional 100,000 troops to Manchuria by railway and by sea.[23] Most of them arrived from Siberia and from the Priamur and Ussuri regions, and a smaller number came from European Russia. This contingent of troops was not sufficient to cover the vast territory of Manchuria, but after occupying major settlements from Aigun to Qiqihaer, the Russian army concentrated its efforts on the south. For the purpose of conducting military operations, the Russian army divided Manchuria into northern and southern parts, conveniently divided by the main line of the CER.

Domestic tensions in Manchuria complicated Russian military strategy. First, there was no unified response to the presence of the Russian military, contrary to usual statements by later Chinese historians. The Chinese population of Manchuria was divided and in constant flux. Local bandits had ravaged the urban and rural areas of Manchuria before the Boxers had even arrived there. The lines between the regular Qing army, the bandits, and Boxers had been blurred, as armed men in Manchuria often switched their loyalty. These groups were far from being a unified force, wholeheartedly supported by the local population. Moving from Shandong and Zhili provinces north to Manchuria, the Boxers recruited young, single men from poor backgrounds with the promise of a better life or, more often, by force of death.[24] Neutral peasants, labourers, and merchants preferred to escape or to hide while disruptions caused by the

Boxers were resolved either by the provincial armies or by the Russian troops, who launched several campaigns through September and October of 1900.

The leaders of Manchuria were divided in their attitude toward the Boxers. Shou Shan, the military governor of Heilongjiang province, and Jin Chang, the *fu dutong* (lieutenant-general) of Shengjing (present-day Shenyang), sympathized with the Boxers' anti-Christian and antiforeign objectives. Zeng Qi, the military governor of Fengtian, on the contrary, advocated suppression of the Boxers.[25] The Russian military occupation of Manchuria inspired different responses from provincial governors. Shou Shan opposed Russians by fighting to the end. Surrounded by Russian troops in Qiqihaer, he chose to commit suicide to avoid being taken prisoner. After the fall of Qiqihaer, the Qing official Cheng Dequan, Shou Shan's aid, declined Russian offers to become the next military governor of Heilongjiang and jumped into a river. He was rescued and briefly imprisoned by the Russians.[26] On the other hand, Chang Shun, the military governor of Jilin province, chose to compromise with the Russians while secretly siding with the Boxers. This ambiguity in attitude toward the occupiers among the provincial leadership reflected the Qing court's lack of unified opinion about the Russian presence. Senior Qing official and seasoned diplomat Li Hongzhang, despite being unpopular with Empress Dowager Cixi, believed in the necessity of co-operating with Russia during the invasion of China by the Allied forces.

Facing military threats from a foreign power, Qing troops stationed in Fengtian and Jilin provinces were ordered to side with the Boxers in armed opposition to the Russian military presence. However, Russian Cossacks and artillery, in a series of battles during August and September 1900, defeated them and took over major cities along the southern branch of the CER. Russian troops moving from Harbin to the south occupied Kuanchengzi, Jilin, and Kaiyuan. Those moving from Dalny to the north took the towns of Anshan, Shahe, Haicheng, Liaoyang, and finally, on 2 October, Mukden. In most of the battles, Cossacks and Russian troops were outnumbered by the Qing armies.

How were Russian troops able to gain control of an area so densely populated by the Chinese and home to the two provincial Qing armies in a matter of several months? One reason was the gradual demoralization of Qing troops after humiliating defeats in northern Manchuria, which resulted in desertion. Another reason was the lack of popular support for Qing troops. The peasants found it difficult to distinguish between Boxer rebels, bandits, and fleeing solders. Devastated by marauders and intruders of all kinds, the local population hid food from their own troops. Russian generals then used tensions between the Qing military and civilians to their advantage. After their harsh treatment of

FIGURE 5.2 Russian Soldiers in Qiqihaer, Manchuria, 1900-1. *Source:* Photo album, "Manchuria, 1900." Provincial Library of the Khabarovsk Krai, Khabarovsk.

the Chinese civilian population on the Amur, Russian troops in southern Manchuria conducted themselves less cruelly once they took control of the areas within the Russian sphere of influence.

Finally, the changing policy in the Qing court from opposition to support and back to opposition toward the Boxers led to changing attitudes toward cooperation with Russians in administration of Manchuria. This may explain why in September 1900 a group of Cossacks headed by General Rennenkampf was able to take over Jilin, a fortified city of 120,000, without a battle. A day before the siege, the confused military governor of Jilin received an order from Beijing to suspend hostilities toward the Russian troops.[27] Occupying Russian forces did not meet unified opposition from local civilian-power groups either. For example, the administration, gentry, and merchants of Jilin were not interested in supporting armed opposition against the Russian presence, as a protracted war would have jeopardized mutually beneficial contracts in railway construction and commerce.[28] Russian economic success in Manchuria depended on co-operation between the local authorities, Chinese compradors, and small Chinese businesses, which in turn profited by providing labour, commercial services, and goods to the Russians.

Conquistadors' Glory Wrapped in Shame

After defeating the Boxers in August 1900 and declaring a victory over the weak Qing government, the Allied forces expected the contingent of Russian troops to leave China. In October 1900 General A.N. Kuropatkin decided that the Russian army was to stay on. This decision came at a time when the Russian army had already defeated the Qing troops and gained control of all of the major cities in Manchuria. Yet the war was not over. Russian military expeditions in Manchuria and in Zhili province continued for more than a year. They were directed at remaining Qing army units and bandits posing a threat to Russian positions in Manchuria.[29]

The provincial government in the Amur region and the Russian military command in Manchuria faced one crucial dilemma: how to justify the barbaric killings of Qing subjects. The Amur provincial government preferred to erase the massacre from public memory. Priamur governor-general N.I. Grodekov pretended to have limited knowledge about the killings and preferred not to talk about the massacre. No military tribunals were held. Local investigations of the massacre were carried out in secrecy. By whitewashing the killings, the Russian government distanced itself from the cruelties of other European nations in China, America, and Japan. Moreover, it covered up the widespread racial hostility among the Russian military toward Chinese and other Asian peoples. Hardened during the conquest of Central Asia, top Russian military commanders saw Chinese people as barbarians in need of civilizing. General Kuropatkin's ambivalent attitude toward China and Asian nations had deep roots in the Christian faith. He believed that "the twentieth century should bring a heavy struggle in Asia of Christian people against non-Christian. For the benefit of humankind, it is necessary for us to form a union with Christian England against the non-Christian tribes of Asia."[30]

As a result of an agreement between three Russian ministries (the Ministry of the Interior, the Foreign Ministry, and the Ministry of War), Gribskii and his subordinates were indicted. Yet Gribskii's record of achievement in the Russian army and his superb command of Russian forces in Manchuria saved him from jail. He was temporarily relieved of military duties but remained in the army on a colonel's pay. Other commanders were discharged and sentenced to several months in prison. The Cossacks and volunteers involved in the Blagoveshchensk Massacre were absolved of responsibility.[31]

Such a weak resolution suited both the administration of the Priamur Governor-Generalship and the tsarist government in St. Petersburg. They chose to celebrate the victory and to suppress the truth about the Blagoveshchensk Massacre. The "victory" was recorded as a symbol of Russian imperial glory. For this purpose, Nicholas II issued a medal "For the Military Campaign in China, 1900-1901." A silver medal was given to military staff participating in the battles. A bronze medal was awarded to those who stayed in the war zone. Governor-General N.I. Grodekov and Admiral E.I. Alekseev each received a diamond-encrusted golden saber. Numerous commemorative medals were given to the Cossacks and soldiers for occupying Chinese cities. Russian historian V.G. Datsyshen asserts that the large quantity of medals was disproportionate to the number and nature of military operations, especially considering the lack of organized resistance on the part of the Qing troops.[32] This special recognition with military honours reinforced the government's commitment to the use of force and terror in spreading Russian influence beyond its Far East borders.

Sentiments of expansionism were widespread among the military administration of the Priamur region. Grodekov was an open advocate of the colonization of Manchuria and of turning it into a vassal of Russia. He hoped that Russian troops, after occupying Manchuria, would stay on the right bank of the Amur forever. On 1 August 1900 he wrote to General Kuropatkin, the war minister from 1898 to 1904, that the Amur River, explored by Gennady Nevelskoi fifty years previously, should be an internal river belonging to Russia, not a border river. Russia's War Ministry shared his opinion. Yet the powerful Ministry of Finance, headed by Sergei Witte, advocated peaceful economic expansionism in China and was against a protracted military occupation of Manchuria. Pressured by the Allied powers, the tsar chose not to annex Manchuria and to restore friendly relations with the Qing government.[33]

The Russian government and media were silent about the atrocities of this war. One editorial in *Amurskii Krai (Amur Region)* on 27 July 1900 bravely raised the question of the moral cost of the Russian victory, criticizing the killings of innocent people on the Amur: "What shall we tell civilized people? ... We are mean and terrible people; we have killed those who hid in our place, who sought our protection."[34] For several weeks after the article was published, the Allied forces burned Chinese cities and villages and looted imperial palaces. The "civilized people" from Europe, the United States, and Japan organized punitive expeditions against suspected Boxers, in which many innocent people were killed. All of this escaped the attention of the Russian government and public. Russia, as a European monarchy, shared a prevailing imperialist attitude of cultural superiority over Chinese culture. "Christian civilization" was confronting the "barbarian culture" of the Qing state. James Hevia in his study of British imperialism in China has demonstrated Britain's reliance on war, violence, and terror in order to impose European law, culture, and religion on Qing territory. The purpose of this deliberate violence was to shake the political, economic, and cultural foundations of the Qing state.[35] Similarly, Russia used violence in order to punish, to teach, and to "civilize" the Qing government and its people.

The Russian public was more often exposed to publication of accounts of Russian suffering in the war. In October 1900 an account entitled "Poslednie Dni v Manchzhurii" ("Last Days in Manchuria") appeared in the monthly magazine *Russkoe Bogatsvo (Russian Wealth),* published in St. Petersburg. It was written by the wife of a senior engineer at the CER, with their names carefully omitted. It was an emotional story of the evacuation of 1,500 Russian civilians, mostly wives and children of the CER staff, from Manchuria to Khabarovsk along the Songhua River, the Amur River's main tributary, on the eve of Russian occupation of Manchuria. Yet the reader learned only about the attacks on Russian civilians and about the threat to Russian possessions in Manchuria. The author described a week-long journey (2-8 June) by steamboat from Harbin to Khabarovsk, escape from enemy fire, and the fear of being caught by Manchu soldiers. She highlighted the dangers of the journey, in which a passenger was killed and six people wounded by Qing gunfire, and portrayed Russians as the victims in a land of savages.[36] This one-sided account did not explain the reasons beyond Russia's military presence in Manchuria, nor did it reveal the cruelties that accompanied it.

The liberal press in St. Petersburg and Moscow did not mention the Blagoveshchensk Massacre for several years. Russia's defeat in the war with Japan five years later demonstrated the failure of Russian imperial expansion in Manchuria and the weakness of its military. Any negative publicity about the tsarist policies in Manchuria would have only added to the revolutionary fever spreading in Russia in 1905, further antagonizing the government and society. In 1910 an article in the St. Petersburg magazine *Vestnik Evropy (News of Europe)* finally exposed the ugly side of the Sino-Russian War and of the government's role in covering up the atrocity conducted by the Russians on the Amur River. The anonymous author of this article, entitled "Blagoveshchenskaya 'Utopiya'" ("The Blagoveshchensk 'Utopia'"), complained that in 1900 public opinion was kept in the dark, making it difficult to assess what ordinary people thought about the Blagoveshchensk tragedy at that time.[37] Former war minister Kuropatkin and his ministry may have been the target of criticism. The author's access to the official Russian legal archives suggests that opposition to the War Ministry, which whitewashed the massacre, was well alive among the Russian political elite a decade after 1900.

Consequences of the Sino-Russian War

The Russian military occupation of Manchuria had several long-term consequences for the development of the Amur frontier. The violent expulsion of Qing subjects from their legitimate settlements along the Amur River, and destruction of these settlements, became a painful reminder to the Chinese of the forced Aigun Treaty of 1858. Chinese traders, merchants, and seasonal labourers realized their vulnerable position on this frontier when no laws could guarantee their safety. The Russian looting and burning of sixty-four Manchu villages along the Zeya River, the tributary of the Amur River on the Russian side of the border, was a violation of earlier Qing-Russian treaties. According to the Aigun Treaty, all existing Manchu settlements on the Russian side of the Amur River were legitimate and subject to recognition and protection by Russian law.[38] Surviving Chinese victims and witnesses of forced repatriations from the Amur carried the news of slaughter, destruction, and looting to northern Manchuria, discouraging other peasants from going north of the river.

The Sino-Russian War in Manchuria increased anti-Russian sentiment among students and merchants in China's treaty ports, especially as a result of the slow withdrawal of Russian troops from Manchuria.[39] Admiral E.I. Alekseev, head of the Pacific Fleet and Russian army in the Liaodong Peninsula, stood for keeping the Russian troops in Manchuria. On 13 November 1900 an agreement signed by Admiral Alekseev and Fengtian's governor, Zeng Qi, established the position of a Russian military commissar to supervise military affairs in Fengtian province, undermining the power of the local military administration.[40] When the Allies withdrew from the capital, Beijing, in September 1901, a reduced contingent of Russian troops stayed in Manchuria. They were stationed along the main towns of the CER and continued to suppress separate attacks of Chinese bandits on the railway and on nearby settlements. Only after the Qing-Russian agreement of 26 March 1902 did Russia start a gradual withdrawal of its troops from Manchuria. At the end of September 1903, the last contingent of Russian troops left Heilongjiang province.[41]

This war interfered with daily life in Manchuria. Chinese and Manchu frontier settlements were destroyed. Killings, or fear of being killed, forced people to move. The lives of Chinese Christian converts were endangered. Peasants abandoned their fields, leaving summer harvest unattended. In November 1900 Dugald Christie, a medical missionary of the United Presbyterian Church of

Scotland, while travelling from Liaoyang to Mukden (present-day Shenyang) in southern Manchuria, observed: "The whole countryside was a scene of desolation: miles of millet-fields were uncut, trampled and spoilt; the villages were in ruins, the houses either burned or gutted and wrecked; few Chinamen and no women were to be seen."[42] Seasonal workers abandoned their jobs. In the cities, Russian forces occupied government buildings, seized official documents, and burned property. Qing administrative archives were partially removed from Qiqihaer and taken to the Institute of the Oriental Languages in Vladivostok.[43]

Once the Russian military occupation was over, life in the cities gradually returned to normal. Chinese workers were rehired to rebuild the damage done to the CER, and they continued to work for the Russians in different capacities after the railway was finished in 1903. Yet Russian destruction of the Chinese settlements along the Amur, occupation of the Manchu ancestral lands, and disruption of local governance went beyond Witte's policy of peaceful economic penetration of Manchuria. Military conflicts along the Amur frontier of 1900 marked the end of Russia's image as a peaceful ally of the Qing subjects who lived there.

Historical Memory of the Blagoveshchensk Massacre in China and in Russia

What happened near Blagoveshchensk was never repeated in the Manchurian interior. Public memory of the Qing-Russian conflict in Manchuria in 1900 was weakened by more bloody and brutal military conflicts in the region, such as Russia's war with Japan (1904-5), part of which was fought in Manchuria at the expense of the Qing state. Twentieth-century revolutions, civil conflict, and two world wars further overshadowed the memories of 1900, as millions died on both sides of the Sino-Russian border. As Blaine Chiasson demonstrates in this volume, the events of the Boxer Rebellion and the Russian occupation of Manchuria were used selectively for different political and ideological purposes in China and Russia. The Japanese occupation of Manchuria from 1931 to 1945 left harsher memories among the Chinese people than the earlier Russian presence.

Soviet and post-Soviet Russian historians and politicians consider the Blagoveshchensk Massacre an uncomfortable topic. At best, they avoid talking about it. They argue that Russia had never been in a state of formal war with China and that no war was declared during the Sino-Russian conflict of 1900. Friendly bilateral relations of the past two decades and worship of former imperial grandeur as a new ideology in post-Soviet Russia make it difficult for historians to objectively face the past. Recently, the Russian government commemorated the seizure of the Amur River in 1858 by issuing a 5,000-ruble note. Most work on the history of Sino-Russian relations mentions this war only briefly. In 1996 the Russian historian V.G. Datsyshen braved the topic and wrote a detailed history of the war. But the book received little publicity, as only 500 copies were published.[44]

In China the Sino-Russian War is officially seen from two perspectives: as aggressive tsarist policy in Manchuria and as part of European imperialist expansion in China. Chinese historical writings condemn Russian imperialism in Manchuria with strong nationalist language. Although the loss of human life was immense, the forced deportations of Qing subjects from the villages on the Amur River did leave some witnesses. In 1965 a group of Chinese scholars investigated the destruction of sixty-four Manchu villages, interviewing seventy-three elderly witnesses who had lived there or who had relatives who suffered from the atrocities committed by the Russian forces. The findings of this investigation were published only in 1979 after the Cultural Revolution. According to the study, the killings of the Chinese residents in and around Blagoveshchensk were planned by local Russian authorities, who even forbade Russian civilians to save the lives of innocent Qing subjects.[45] Paul Cohen points out that during the Cultural Revolution Chinese historians were forced to use the past to serve official anti-Soviet propaganda. They used the events of 1900 in Manchuria to accuse the Soviet Union of revisionism and hegemony. According to him, only in the early 1980s were they able to return to less ideological historical analysis of the Amur atrocities.[46] Yet, even today, different attitudes toward Russia's imperial past divide Chinese and Russian historians.

The best example of contrasting official interpretations of the Blagoveshchensk Massacre in Russia and China can be found today in the museums of local history in the border towns of Blagoveshchensk and Aigun, located only several kilometres from each other and separated by the Amur River. In the Russian museum, 1900 is mentioned only briefly, with no details of the massacre. The Chinese museum in Aigun has a separate section in which life-size dioramas display in graphic detail the brutal methods used by the Russian forces to kill innocent Qing subjects. This diorama is very similar to the panorama "Borodino" in Moscow, dedicated to a major battle of the Russo-French War of 1812, when Russian troops repelled Napoleon's army. Unlike the battle of Borodino, the Blagoveshchensk Massacre was a slaughter of helpless people who were not armed and who begged for their lives. The museum in Aigun, as well as the whole town, is closed to Russian visitors. Built for patriotic education at home, this museum demonstrates to the Chinese people the humiliation caused by

Imperial Russia. In 2007 the Institute of Chinese Modern History at the Chinese Academy of Social Sciences issued a new edition of *The History of Russian Aggression in China*.[47] Published in four volumes, this set serves as another critical reminder by Chinese historians of the destruction and suffering caused by Imperial Russian expansionism in China.

Russia's Manchurian Campaign and Global Imperialism

In 1900 the world's major empires were busy with different celebrations. The Christian civilizations of Europe and North America saw 1900 as the birth of a new Christian century. In Britain, Queen Victoria celebrated her eighty-first birthday. In Italy, Pope Leo XIII turned ninety. The European monarchy and the church remained powerful symbols of empires. European armies marched into non-European lands in the name of kings, queens, and God. The French marked the beginning of the twentieth century with the Paris Universal Exhibition despite water shortages in the capital.[48] In Russia the Trans-Siberian Railway made it possible to travel between Moscow and Irkutsk. Although the Boxer Rebellion and the Russian military campaign in Manchuria delayed the construction of the remaining section through Manchuria to Vladivostok for another three years, the Trans-Siberian became a celebration of Russian eastward expansion.

European empires celebrated their military victories abroad. The Qing-Russian military conflict in Manchuria never made it to the world news. European newspapers and news agencies, based in foreign concessions in Beijing, Tianjin, and Shanghai, reported the suppression of the Boxer Rebellion from the victor's point of view, with photographic images of looted imperial treasures and severed Boxer heads. Manchuria, where European influence was limited, received less attention. Apart from suppressing the Boxers in Beijing and Tianjin in 1900-1, the Western powers sent their armies to claim new territories and potential markets. German and Italian troops were in Africa. British troops were in north-western India, Sudan, and South Africa. After winning the Spanish-American War in 1898, US troops "defended" US imperial gains in Puerto Rico, the Philippines, and semicolonial Cuba. The cruelty of the Blagoveshchensk Massacre was not exceptional during this high tide of global imperialism. British troops committed serious atrocities against Boer farmers during the South African War (1899-1902), putting civilians, including women and children, in concentration camps. Manchuria may not have had much in common with the Transvaal, although both were rich in natural resources, particularly gold. Yet the two areas shared a similar history as objects of economic imperialism, with Russia and Britain both using military force against civilian populations. Military commanders E.I. Alekseev and H.H. Kitchener returned from their military campaigns not as war criminals but as heroes of their empires and remained so in official historical accounts of Imperial Russia and Britain a century later.

Wars and violence were seen as necessary to keep the empires strong. Whereas the Russian government and official press remained silent about St. Petersburg's "success" in Manchuria, the British military campaigns abroad were accompanied by lavish official propaganda. In South Africa, Rudyard Kipling boosted troop morale by contributing to the army newspaper the *Friend of the Free State*, and a promising war correspondent, Winston Rudolph Churchill, glorified the British Empire's course against the Boers in a series of dispatches published in 1900 as two books, *London to Ladysmith* and *Ian Hamilton's March*. In contrast, in 1902 the Russian writer Leo Tolstoy criticized, in an open letter, both the policies of Nicolas II in China and the government's abuse of the people. By not praising imperial victories, Tolstoy complicated his relationship with the Russian autocracy and with the Russian Orthodox Church.[49] However, for the majority of Russians living west of the Ural Mountains, China was too far away to cause concern.

In Qing China historical time was counted differently, and the talk of a new century occurred only in the treaty ports and major towns among Chinese reformers and intellectuals and among Western missionaries and their Chinese converts. In the countryside, where the majority of people lived, the months and days were counted according to the lunar calendar, and each year was named after a ruling emperor. Nineteen hundred was the Year of the Rat and the twenty-sixth year of the Guangxu reign, the latter part of which was plagued by natural disasters. It was an unhappy year for the Qing court, when the European powers forced the emperor and Dowager Empress Cixi to abandon the Forbidden City. The life of the government was disrupted by the Boxers and the foreigners. Allied troops looted the Imperial Palace, and a year later the Qing court was forced to sign the humiliating Boxer Protocol in order both to compensate for damage to foreign lives and property and to punish pro-Boxer officials. The foreigners were appeased and the empire was saved for another decade.

Conclusion

By 1900 the Qing state was too weak to protect its subjects in China proper, in Manchuria, or abroad. European Sinophobia was a common phenomenon where the Europeans came into contact with Chinese. Chinese workers and farmers encountered cruelty and racism in the Russian Far East as well as in North America, where they built railways and worked in goldmines and on farms, and this attitude was rife among the European communities in Harbin,

Qingdao, Shanghai, and Hong Kong, as well as Blagoveshchensk. More than 100 years later, the historical contribution of the Chinese workers to the development of the Russian Far East has not been acknowledged to the same degree as their contribution to the economic development of Canada. In Blagoveshchensk, Khabarovsk, Vladivostok, and other cities of the Russian Far East, Qing subjects were involved in urban construction and industrial development, in farming and fishing, in small trades, and in domestic services. The Russian Far East has always depended on Chinese labour and agricultural products from Manchuria. Russian colonial administrators and military commanders took their reliance on Chinese human and natural resources for granted. Tsar Nicholas II and his policy makers played with the idea of Russia's special relationship with the Qing government. Unlike England, Germany, and France, Russia did not rely on opium or aggressive missionary activities in advancing its interests in China. Yet, during the Boxer crisis, Russia contributed its military might to the Allied forces in a humiliating assault on Qing imperial institutions and symbols of power. Moreover, Russia used the crisis in the imperial capital to send a warning through Manchuria not to question its dominant position along the Amur River and to accept the legitimacy of its expansion in Manchuria.

Russian atrocities in Manchuria in 1900 can be compared to German colonial practices in Shandong. Russian tsar Nicholas II and German kaiser Wilhelm II, two royal cousins, were well informed about each other's policies in China. Both used similar imperialist practices, backed by religious institutions, of railroad expansion, European-style administration, land-lease, resettlement of local populations, architectural and racial segregation in the cities, and military force. Although the suppression of Qing subjects by Russian forces at Blagoveshchensk was brutal, no museum in Russia, Europe, or elsewhere tells the story of Russian misconduct in China in the name of European cultural and racial supremacy.

Notes

1 The Boxer Rebellion was an anti-Christian and anti-foreign movement. It originated in western Shandong and spread north through Zhili province. In the summer of 1900 Boxers briefly joined forces with official Qing militia in Shanxi, Inner Mongolia, and the north-eastern provinces of Manchuria. Apart from Russia and Japan, also involved in the fighting were Great Britain, Germany, France, the United States, Italy, and Austria. See Joseph Esherick, *The Origins of the Boxer Uprising* (Berkeley: University of California Press, 1987), 1, 317-21.

2 See Zhongguo shehui kexueyuan jindai shi yanjiusuo, ed., *Sha-E qin Hua shi* [The History of Imperial Russian Aggression in China] (Beijing: Renmin chubanshe, 1987), vol. 4, pt.

1, 237-54; and V.G. Datsyshen, *Russko-Kitaiskaya Voina: Manchzhuria, 1900* [Russo-Chinese War: Manchuria, 1900] (St. Petersburg: Tsytadel, 1996), 85-96.

3 Railway guards were a substitute for the regular army and were part of the Independent Corps of Frontier Guards under the Ministry of Finance. They performed the duties of railway police until November 1903, when a separate unit of the police force was established. See R.K.I. Quested, *"Matey" Imperialists: The Tsarist Russians in Manchuria, 1895-1917* (Hong Kong: Centre of Asian Studies, University of Hong Kong, 1982), 99-100.

4 P. Rossov, *Russkii Kitai: Ocherki zanyatiya Kvantuna i byta tuzemnogo naseleniya* [Russian China: Essays on the Occupation of Kwantung (literally "East of the Pass," part of Liaodong) and on the Daily Life of the Indigenous Population] (Port Arthur: Novyi Krai, 1901), 1-2. Dalny and Port Arthur were built as Russian towns on the foundation of the existing Chinese settlements of Dalianwan and Lüshunkou. Russian control of these towns, reflected in their new names, lasted for only eight years. After Russia's military defeat by Japan in 1905, Russia surrendered the South Manchurian Railway to Japan and lost all towns along it.

5 O.R. Airapetov, ed., *Russko-Yaponskaya Voina, 1904-1905* [Russo-Japanese War, 1904-1905] (Moscow: Tri Kvadrata, 2004), 368-75.

6 See Dugald Christie, *Thirty Years in Moukden, 1883-1913* (London: Constable, 1914), 130-39.

7 N.E. Ablova, "Rossiya i russkie v Manchzhurii v kontse XIX nachale XX vv" [Russia and the Russians in Manchuria from the late nineteenth to the early twentieth century], in *Russko-Yaponskaya Voina, 1904-1905,* ed. Airapetov, 188.

8 Alexander Kirillov, *Geografichecko-Statisticheskii slovar' Amurskoi I Primorskoi Oblastei* [Geographic-Statistical Dictionary of the Amur and Maritime Regions] (Blagoveshchensk: D.O. Mokin, 1894), 75-76.

9 *Voennyi Sbornik* [The Military Collection] 6 (1908): 206-7.

10 I.Ya. Korostovets, *Rossiya na Dal'nem Vostoke* [Russia in the Far East] (Peking: Tipografia Rossiiskoi Dukhovnoi Missii, 1922), 109.

11 The events of the Blagoveshchensk Massacre still remain obscure. According to the Julian calendar used in Russia at that time, the first massacre took place on 4 July 1900. In the twentieth century, the Julian calendar was thirteen days behind the Gregorian calendar used in Europe. This chapter uses the Gregorian calendar. The numbers of Chinese victims during the first "crossing" vary from 2,000 to 4,000, and the names of Russian officers in charge of persecution remain obscure. The details of the killings also vary. For a detailed account of the Blagoveshchensk Massacre in English, based on Russian published materials, see George Alexander Lensen, *The Russo-Chinese War* (Tallahassee, FL: Diplomatic Press, 1967).

12 V.N. Abelentsev, *Amurskoe Kazachestvo, XIX-XX vv* [Amur's Cossacks, Nineteenth and Twentieth Centuries] (Blagoveshchensk: Amur Region Museum of Local History, 2004), 41.

13 Zhang Zonghai, *Yuandong diqu shiji zhijiao de Zhong-E guanxi* [Sino-Russian Relations in the Far East at the Turn of the Century] (Haerbin: Heilongjiang renmin chubanshe, 2000), 132-35.

14 Ibid., 43.

15 Lensen, *Russo-Chinese War,* 111-13.

16 V., "Blagoveshchenskaya 'Utopiya'" [The Blagoveshchensk "Utopia"], *Vestnik Evropy* [News of Europe] 10 (1910): 236-37.

17 Zhongguo shehui kexueyuan jindai shi yanjiusuo, ed., *Sha-E qin Hua shi,* vol. 4, pt. 1, 252.

18 General K.N. Gribskii, quoted in Lensen, *Russo-Chinese War,* 108.

19 A. Vereshchagin, *Po Manchzhurii (1900-1901): Vostominaniya I rasskasy* [Across Manchuria (1900-1901): Memoirs and Short Stories] (St. Petersburg: Sklad v knizhnykh magazinakh V.A. Berezovskogo, 1903), 19-21. All translations of quotations from non-English sources are mine.

20 Ibid., 23-26.

21 Abelentsev, *Amurskoe Kazachestvo,* 44-46.

22 Ibid., 49-53.

23 Airapetov, ed., *Russko-Yaponskaya Voina,* 362.

24 On recruitment by bandits, see Shi Fang, ed., *Heilingjiang quyu shehuishi yanjiu, 1644-1911* [Study of the Social History of the Heilongjiang Region, 1644-1911] (Haerbin: Heilongjiang renmin chubanshe, 2002), 471-73.

25 Xue Xiantian, ed., *Zhongdong tielu hulujun yu dongbei bianjiang zhengju* [Chinese Eastern Railway Patrol Police and Political Situation of the North-Eastern Borderland] (Beijing: Shehui kexue wenxian chubanshe, 1993), 48.

26 Robert H.G. Lee, *The Manchurian Frontier in Ch'ing History,* Harvard East Asian Series No. 43 (Cambridge, MA: Harvard University Press, 1970), 140.

27 Lensen, *Russo-Chinese War,* 197.

28 E.Kh. Nilus, *Istoricheskii obzor Kitaiskoi vostochnoi zheleznoi dorogi, 1896-1923 gg* [Historical Overview of the Chinese Eastern Railway, 1896-1923] (Harbin: Tipografia Kitaiskoi Vostochnoi Zeleznoi Dorogi, 1923), vol. 1, 192. The different reactions of the authorities in Jilin and Mukden to the Russian military occupation are remarkable. Whereas the administration of Jilin nearly welcomed the Russian troops, the military governor of Mukden fled, together with local officials, fearing Russian retributions for their support of the Boxers. See Korostovets, *Rossiya na Dal'nem Vostoke,* 123-24.

29 S.A. Dobronravov, *Zametki Manchzhurskogo Strelka* [The Notes of a Manchurian Rifleman] (Harbin, Vladikavkaz: Tipografiia G.K. Turich s Mi, 1906), 62.

30 A.N. Kuropatkin, *Russko-Yaponskaya Voina, 1904-1905: Itogi voiny* [Russo-Japanese War, 1904-1905: Results of War] (1906; reprint, St. Petersburg: Poligon, 2002), 96-97.

31 V., "Blagoveshchenskaya 'Utopiya'" [The Blagoveshchensk "Utopia"], *Vestnik Evropy* [News of Europe] 10 (1910): 240.

32 Datsyshen, *Russko-Kitaiskaya Voina,* 129.

33 Ibid., 95-96.

34 Cited in Lensen, *Russo-Chinese War,* 103.

35 James L. Hevia, *English Lessons: The Pedagogy of Imperialism in Nineteenth-Century China* (Durham, NC: Duke University Press, 2003), 3, 4, 231.

36 A.I., "Poslednie Dni v Manchzhurii" [Last days in Manchuria], *Russkoe Bogatsvo* [Russian Wealth] 10 (1900): 163.

37 V., "Blagoveshchenskaya 'Utopiya'" [The Blagoveshchensk "Utopia"], *Vestnik Evropy* [News of Europe] 10 (1910): 241.

38 See V.S. Miasnikov, ed., *Russko-Kitaiskie dogovorno-pravovye akty (1689-1916)* [Sino-Russian Treaties and Legal Acts (1689-1916)] (Moscow: Pamyatniki Istoricheskoi Mysli, 2004), 62.

39 Between 1901 and 1905, Chinese patriotic societies, established in Shanghai and Tokyo, propagated anti-Russian and anti-imperialist sentiments. Despite the Qing court's official ban on anti-Russian activities, Chinese students in Japan and Chinese merchants were central in organizing patriotic societies in treaty ports. See Yang Tianshi, *Cong dizhi zou xiang gonghe* [From Monarchy to Republic] (Beijing: Shehui kexueyuan wenxian chubanshe, 2002), 87-101.

40 This agreement was negotiated between a Russian diplomat, I.Ya. Korostovets, and the military governor of Mukden, Zhou Mian. Both Zhou Mian and Zeng Qi were criticized by the Qing court for signing this agreement. See Korostovets, *Rossiya na Dal'nem Vostoke,* 130-35.

41 See Miasnikov, ed., *Russko-Kitaiskie dogovorno-pravovye akty,* 290-93.

42 See Christie, *Thirty Years in Moukden,* 154.

43 Vereshchagin, *Po Manchzhurii,* 87.

44 See note 2.

45 Heilongjiang jiang dong liu shi si tun wenti diaocha ju, "Sha-E bazhan jiangdong liushi si tun de qianqian houhou" [The whole story of seizure of the sixty-four villages by tsarist Russia], *Xuexi yu Shensuo* [Study and Investigation] 1 (1979): 71-72.

46 Paul A. Cohen, *History in Three Keys: The Boxers as Event, Experience, and Myth* (New York: Columbia University Press, 1997), 175, 285.

47 Zhongguo shehui kexueyuan jindai shi yanjiusuo, ed., *Sha-E qin Hua shi* [The History of Imperial Russian Aggression in China] (Beijing: Zhongguo shehui kexue chubanshe, 2007).

48 Rebecca West, *1900* (New York: Viking, 1982), 11-19.

49 See Tolstoy's letter to Nicholas II in S.P. Melgunov, ed., *Nicholas II: Materialy dlia kharakteristiki lichnosti I tsarstvovaniya* [Nicholas II: Materials for Characterizing the Person and His Reign] (Moscow: Izdanie Zhurnala "Golos Minuvshego," 1917), 117-23.

6

Victims and Victimizers: Warlord Soldiers and Mutinies in Republican China

Edward A. McCord

On a warm day in June 1921, a train bearing over 1,700 exuberant soldiers departed from Hubei's Hankou station. Most of these soldiers had served directly under the Hubei military governor, Wang Zhanyuan, some for as long as a decade. At midnight on 7 June, however, these soldiers had mutinied in Hubei's provincial capital, Wuchang, plundering its commercial and residential districts and leaving a trail of corpses and burned buildings. This mutiny was a serious blow to Wang's reputation for having kept Hubei at peace while other provinces were wracked by military conflicts. Nonetheless, Wang seemed willing to treat his errant troops magnanimously. Soldiers who agreed to disarm would be given their back pay and a special bonus and would be sent back to their north China homes with no charges against them. Since a large-scale disbandment of Wang's troops had already been announced before the mutiny, many soldiers decided to accept this offer. Carrying the loot taken from the city, and in many cases accompanied by wives and children, they crowded onto the train specially prepared for their journey. When the train reached the Xiaogan station a short distance from Hankou, the troops were invited to disembark for a meal supposedly arranged for them by the governor. Instead, the soldiers found themselves facing a bank of machineguns. After a tense confrontation between the soldiers and the commander in charge, the guns opened fire. When the guns stopped, most of the mutineers were dead. Wang Zhanyuan had taken his revenge.[1]

Atrocities perpetrated on civilians by warlord armies were a common occurrence of the early Republican period. Diana Lary has shown, however, that common soldiers in this era were, in an interconnected way, often both the perpetrators and the victims of violence. Warlord soldiers learned their "brutal ways" in a military society where their own officers brutalized them.[2] The Xiaogan Massacre illustrates the dual role of warlord soldiers as victims and victimizers in even more complicated ways. By studying the chain of events that led to this massacre, this chapter reveals the special function that mutinies, real or threatened, played in the complicated intramilitary and military-civil politics of warlord China. Certainly, there were real grievances behind the Wuchang mutiny, which led the mutineers to release their anger on the city's innocent people. At the same time, the mutiny was also the result of a broader contest among Wang

Zhanyuan, his officers, and the Hubei people for military, political, and financial power. Thus, despite appearing as the primary agents in mutinies, soldiers were frequently also pawns in struggles over which they had little control.[3]

Military Financing and Troop Mutinies

The underlying context for the Wuchang mutiny was the strain placed on Hubei's financial resources by a steady growth of military forces. Although a three-way struggle ensued between individual commanders, Wang Zhanyuan, and the central government over the provisioning of these troops, common soldiers were the ones who actually suffered from this fiscal crisis. Frustrated and angry troops finally took matters in their own hands in a series of mutinies that would serve as a prelude to the final outrage at Wuchang.

Wang Zhanyuan had overseen a steady increase in military forces following his arrival in Hubei in 1913 with his northern 2nd Division. The original two divisions and a brigade of provincial forces in Hubei would eventually be dispersed following a failed 1917 revolt. But Wang more than made up for this decrease by spinning off new units from his 2nd Division and recruiting additional troops to create a new 18th Division, two infantry brigades, and five mixed brigades under his control. The ebb and flow of successive military struggles deposited additional troops on Hubei soil. These included a Henan mixed brigade given refuge in Hubei after the 1916 Anti-Monarchical War, the northern 8th and 20th Divisions that retreated to Hubei after a failed invasion of Hunan in 1917, and several brigades under Wu Guangxin (brother-in-law of the Beiyang Anhui faction leader Duan Qirui) that settled in west Hubei after a failed invasion of Sichuan. In 1920 a successful southern attack against northern forces that had occupied Hunan in 1918 also forced the retreat of the northern military governor, Zhang Jingyao, into Hubei with his 7th Division and other affiliated units. By late 1920, then, Hubei was host to at least five divisions and nearly a dozen brigades, totalling over 100,000 soldiers.[4]

From the beginning, Wang pursued a number of methods to make sure these expanding forces were paid. For example, he pushed add-on taxes through a complacent Provincial Assembly to cover the costs of new "provincial" forces.[5] Over time, provincial funds originally set aside for other purposes were increasingly shifted to military uses.[6] With control over the Hubei Mint, Wang could also simply print more currency. For example, in 1916 new currency was issued under the guise of redeeming old notes, but 1 million yuan in notes was issued beyond the value of notes actually redeemed.[7] Finally, using Hubei government property or revenues as collateral, Wang was able to negotiate large loans from foreign banks.[8]

By the summer of 1919, however, meeting the payrolls for all the troops in Hubei had become increasingly difficult. One cause of this crisis was the declining financial circumstances of the central government. Armies with "national" designations stationed in Hubei (including Wang's 2nd Division) were in theory supposed to be paid directly by the central government. The Beijing warlord government's continued efforts to regain control of southern provinces, however, had depleted its Treasury. By August 1919 troop pay for many national units in Hubei was three to four months in arrears. By October, 8th Division soldiers in west Hubei were owed seven months' pay. As central payments became unreliable, Wang Zhanyuan began "advancing" one-third to one-half of the troop pay for some national forces from provincial sources. To ensure the stability of his own 2nd Division, he also advanced its entire pay from Hubei funds.[9] To meet these demands, Wang continued to raise funds from a variety of sources. First, he continued to reallocate other provincial and local funds to meet military needs.[10] He borrowed 1 million yuan from an American bank.[11] And he continued to print money. Notes valued at 8 million yuan were issued in 1919, supposedly replacing old notes, although only 2 to 3 million yuan in old notes were reportedly collected.[12]

By the fall of 1919 the sources Wang had relied on to meet payroll shortfalls were drying up. Given the growing amount of unbacked paper notes, printing more money became increasingly untenable. When the central government pressed Wang to seek another foreign loan, he also found no bank willing to extend additional credit.[13] In November, over Wang's opposition, the central government issued Treasury bonds worth 200,000 yuan to help pay troops in west Hubei. After negotiations with Wu Guangxin, the Yichang Chamber of Commerce agreed to issue "script" that could be used as currency by troops with these bonds as backing, even though the value of these bonds was uncertain.[14] Such stopgap measures, however, failed to resolve the problem of accumulating payroll deficits.

Troop dissatisfaction over pay problems in late 1919 resulted in a number of disturbances. In Yichang and Badong unpaid soldiers simply seized goods they wanted from local merchants.[15] In Shashi merchants considered calling a market strike to protest similar robberies; meanwhile, soldiers attacked a shop whose owner dared to call them "bandit troops."[16] Eventually these merchants, with much difficulty, advanced 300,000 yuan for troop pay, but military-civil relations continued to deteriorate. The last straw occurred when the merchants, forced to accept the valueless military script issued to troops in west Hubei, declared a market strike. In response, on 2 December the 8th Division troops at Shashi mutinied.[17] Sporadic troop disturbances would continue, mainly over pay issues, through 1920, with mutinies in Yichang, Tianmen, Xinyang, Shayang, and Puzhi.[18] In Shayang conflict also arose over merchant reluctance to accept military script. Ultimately, troops attacked the local Chamber of Commerce, beat chamber members, and held the chamber head for ransom.[19]

A new factor in troop instability arose as a result of the outbreak of the Anhui-Zhili War in July 1920. Initially, Wang had avoided identifying himself too closely with either side in the emerging Anhui-Zhili factional dispute. The outbreak of the war, however, gave Wang an opportunity to deal with Wu Guangxin, whom he considered an unwelcome interloper. On 16 July Wang had Wu arrested as he passed through Wuhan (ironically on a mission to seek financial aid from Wang) and charged him with a plot to seize Hubei for the Anhui cause.[20] While Wu's fate hung in the balance, Wu's troops were concerned – rightly as it turned out–about their own future. By eliminating such "guest" armies, Wang could better guarantee payrolls for his own forces. Seeing the writing on the wall, the troops that had accompanied Wu to Wuhan mutinied, hoping for at least some gain through plunder. Wang's troops moved quickly, however, to disarm them and expel them from the province.[21] Wang then prepared to disband other parts of Wu's forces. But the two to three months' pay Wang offered as a disbandment "bonus" was far short of the back pay the soldiers were owed. In several locations Wu's troops mutinied on receiving their disbandment orders and had to be forcibly suppressed.[22]

Wang's treatment of Wu's forces served as a warning to the troops under Zhang Jingyao, who had just fled into Hubei from Hunan. Zhang's troops were notoriously ill-disciplined, and Wang's hospitality could not be counted on for long.[23] On 5 August a group of Zhang's troops rose up to plunder Xinshui city. Wang quickly arrested and executed Zhang's younger brother, Zhang Jingtang, whom he charged with having fomented this looting in order to acquire resources to support the move of his forces to a new base farther down the Yangzi River. The trouble with Zhang Jingyao's troops did not end here. On 10 September 500 soldiers mutinied in Luotian, broke open the prison, and plundered stores and the local yamen. Disturbances with other 7th Division remnants continued into the following year.[24] Attempts to disband these remnants, meanwhile, often provoked more mutinies. Thus a detachment of Zhang's former troops patrolling outside Guangji city refused to return on hearing that their comrades inside the city had been disarmed and disbanded. Taking their guns, they fled east, pillaging, killing, and raping as they went.[25]

Although troop disbandment was one solution to the problem of growing military costs, it obviously also had its own problems. Besides direct resistance by soldiers seeking to preserve their livelihood, disbanded troops with no other options often turned to banditry.[26] Meanwhile, for most commanders, troop expansion, not reduction, was the path to increased power. Thus few people believed Wang when he pledged in 1919 to reduce his own forces by 20 percent. Indeed, even as Wang made this pledge, he was recruiting 3,000 additional troops for a new "provincial defense regiment."[27] Although Wang could fulfil his pledge in part by disbanding Wu Guangxin's and Zhang Jingyao's armies instead of his own, he also made plans to expand his own power by incorporating their best soldiers into his own forces.[28]

What disbandment took place in Hubei, then, did little to dent the enormous cost of paying all the troops garrisoned there. Meanwhile, Beijing's difficulty in paying for "national" units had gone from a temporary problem to a permanent condition. By late summer of 1920, Hubei province was simply expected to take responsibility for all the troops stationed within its borders.[29] One account set the military payroll for "provincial forces" in Hubei at over 640,000 yuan per month.[30] Using a conservative estimate of 100,000 yuan as the normal payroll for a division based on this accounting, over 300,000 yuan per month would have been needed for remaining "national" units in the province. Thus nearly 1 million yuan was needed per month to cover troop payrolls. Meanwhile, on average, only 425,000 to 475,000 yuan per month was "officially" allocated for troop expenses in Hubei's budget, the total of which did not exceed 900,000 yuan.[31] Wang therefore continued to pursue extraordinary measures to meet these costs. On the one hand, he used the Hubei Mint as collateral to borrow another 1 million yuan from an American bank.[32] On the other hand, he withheld central tax and fee revenues to exert pressure on Beijing to increase its contribution.[33] Even these efforts did little to redress back-pay issues in many units, particularly the less favoured forces outside Wang's core army. The end result was a series of new troop disturbances and mutinies driven by pay issues in late 1920 in Tianmen, Dazhi, Chongxiang, Yichang, and Shashi.[34]

The mutiny at Yichang on 29 November 1920 was the most devastating to date. Yichang, a major commercial centre on the Yangzi in west Hubei, was garrisoned by the 13th Mixed Brigade (a Wu Guangxin unit that Wang Zhanyuan hoped to incorporate into a new division) and by some portions of the 18th Division. The main mutineers were from the 13th Mixed Brigade, although some 18th Division soldiers were rumoured to have joined in. Troop-pay issues were again behind this mutiny; in November 1920, 13th Mixed Brigade soldiers had not been paid for nine months.[35] Immediately before the incident, 18th Division officers received messages warning of an impending rising by soldiers driven by "necessity" and asking them not to interfere.[36] As they rose, the mutineers took out their frustration on Yichang's citizens. Most shops in the city were looted, nearly one hundred buildings destroyed by fire, and several dozen people injured. Even Yichang's foreign residents were not spared. Nearly fifty foreigners were robbed, and several foreign businesses were burned. Total losses were estimated at 5 million yuan.[37]

Deteriorating Military-Civil Relations

As one mutiny followed another, a growing tension emerged in Hubei's military-civil relations. Wang Zhanyuan had always taken pride in his ability to maintain order and to keep Hubei free of the warfare that had washed over other provinces in the early Republic.[38] These mutinies now began to taint his reputation. Additional tension arose when, faced with the inadequacy of official funds, Wang increasingly began to seek "advances" from the Hubei public, mainly from chambers of commerce, to meet military payrolls. As mutinies continued despite these efforts, the "threat" presented by these incidents seemed to shift in meaning. Rather than seeking funds to prevent the threat of mutinies, Wang increasingly seemed to be using mutinies as a threat to extract funds to feed an insatiable military regime.

It was not unusual for Republican-era military commanders to seek "emergency" loans or advances for military expenses from private sources in the communities they controlled, whether local banks, rich individuals, chambers of commerce, or other public organizations. Likewise, issuing bonds or military script was another means to force an "advance" of funds from local communities in order to meet troop payrolls. Given persistent military finance problems, however, there was usually little expectation that these advances or loans would be repaid or that the bonds would be redeemed. As Wang Zhanyuan stretched his normal sources of revenue to the limit, he also sought more direct funding from Wuhan's financial and commercial communities.

Amid the military tensions surrounding the outbreak of the Anhui-Zhili War in the summer of 1920, Wang approached the Hankou and Wuchang Chambers of Commerce for a 600,000-yuan loan to be used to "calm" the military, and each chamber pledged 300,000 yuan toward this goal.[39] In the immediate wake of the Yichang mutiny, Wuhan, which had so far largely escaped trouble from disgruntled troops, was suddenly awash in rumours that Wang's troops around Wuchang were on the verge of rioting over pay arrears. In the face of this *naoxiang* (clamour over troop pay), Wang again approached the chambers of commerce for assistance. Warning of a "great upheaval" if this pay problem was not resolved, he now reported a need for 2 million yuan. The two chambers were hard pressed to raise such an amount so soon after their previous 600,000-yuan contribution. Alarmed by the threat, however, the two chambers eventually agreed to try to raise a 1-million-yuan "loan" by the end of December while Wang sought more funding from the central government. But they would do so only if Wang could, in return, guarantee troop stability.[40] When Wang took this proposal back to his military commanders, they argued that if the chambers could raise 1 million yuan, they could raise more. Thus they demanded that means be found to pay off all owed pay – 7 million yuan. Wang then returned to the chambers with additional proposals, including a 2-million-yuan bond issue, a 2-million-yuan loan, and a new issue of 10 million yuan in banknotes to be backed by a 20 percent increase in a range of taxes.[41]

At the time, many in Hubei were suspicious of the origins of this naoxiang. Wang's Wuchang troops were generally better and more regularly paid than were any of the other troops in Hubei. Their pay was, in fact, only two months in arrears, whereas troops garrisoned in west Hubei were owed seven to nine months' pay. Contemporary press accounts suggested that the real origins of the "clamour" lay in a broader political conflict that had soured military-civil relations in the province, namely a power struggle between Wang and a centrally appointed civil governor backed by provincial interests.[42]

Even as Wang had consolidated his control over Hubei, considerable submerged resentment remained against his "occupation." A desire for greater Hubei "self-government" was in part a reaction against Wang's reliance on non-Hubei natives to fill military and civil-government positions, which deprived Hubei natives of these opportunities. Broader concerns were also raised about the damage done to Hubei's society and economy by Wang's fiscal policies, including tax increases and currency manipulation, which were of course largely driven by his relentless military expansion. The success of other "self-government" movements in 1920, including Zhang Jingyao's ouster from Hunan, gave new hope to Hubei self-government advocates. This submerged anti-Wang sentiment soon focused on taking control of Hubei's civil governorship as a first step toward undermining Wang's power.

Wang originally gained control of Hubei's civil administration in 1916 by convincing the central government, which needed his support following the Anti-Monarchical War, to appoint him concurrently as Hubei's military and civil governor. In 1919, in a nod toward the principle of the separation of military and civil powers, Wang gave up the civil position, but he maintained control by ensuring that the governorship went to his own chief of staff, He Peirong (who by coincidence was a Hubei native).[43] He Peirong, however, also had very close ties to the Anhui faction, which became a liability for Wang at the conclusion of the Anhui-Zhili War. So in August 1920 Wang recommended He's replacement by a relative from Shandong with minimal administrative experience.[44] This recommendation was greeted by widespread outrage. Leading Hubei figures in Beijing, with the support of former president Li Yuanhong (a Hubei native), organized a campaign to force the Beijing government to reject Wang's recommendation. After an intense struggle, in mid-September the central government gave in to this popular opposition and appointed Xia Shoukang, a Hubei native who had served as Hubei's civil governor in the early Republic, as He's replacement.[45]

Wang was angered by this opposition and by the threat to his control of Hubei's civil administration. He therefore turned the growing military instability in Hubei into a tool to oppose Xia's appointment. Wang announced that Xia's arrival in Hubei would be certain to cause "disorder" *(luan)*.[46] He then went on sick leave and repeatedly proffered his resignation. This was appropriately recognized as a form of passive resistance designed to force central authorities to acknowledge that Wang was still needed in Hubei to maintain order.[47] Making this point more explicitly, Wang announced that he could not guarantee order if Xia took up his position. This threat was accompanied by a renewed demand for central funds for troop pay in Hubei, in effect shifting the blame for any possible disturbance over lapsed pay to Beijing.[48]

After long negotiations, Wang was, at least on the surface, convinced to make peace with Xia and welcome him to take up office, which he finally did on 22 November. The day after his arrival, however, Xia's office was suddenly surrounded by troops. The officer in charge presented Xia with a letter from his superior explaining that the troops were there for his protection since local soldiers might blame Xia, as the new civil governor, for continued pay shortages. Rather than welcoming this "protection," Xia saw an implied threat aimed at forcing him to yield his post. The next day, Xia moved his office to the security of the foreign concessions across the Yangzi in Hankou.[49] He then wired Beijing, charging the commander of these troops, Sun Chuanfang, with using a show of force to prevent him from taking office. Xia's supporters then organized a Punish the Ringleader Movement against Sun, accusing him of interfering in civil government and violating central orders.[50]

This then was the political atmosphere in which the Wuchang naoxiang of early December had occurred. As the civil-governor controversy fed anti-Wang feelings among the Hubei people, many concluded that recurring troop mutinies and the "clamour" over troop pay were all simply tactics used by Wang to defend his political power. Thus the Punish the Ringleader Movement charged that Sun Chuanfang had incited the November Yichang mutiny as a way for Wang to put more pressure on Xia.[51] At the same time, safely outside of Wang's territory, Hubei residents in Beijing led an outcry against Wang's financial demands on the Wuhan chambers of commerce. After meeting with representatives of these chambers in an emergency meeting, they denounced Wang's use of the "preservation of local order" as a threat to demand funds from the chambers. They noted that it was his duty to guarantee the maintenance of order, not something he could use as a political bargaining chip. They also expressed their opposition to proposed new taxes or banknote issues to cover troop pay. Instead they argued that military costs could be reduced by cutting the Hubei army's size and by removing guest armies from the province. Finally, they asked for a government inquiry into Wang's own troop pay accounts.[52] This last point reflected growing resentment over the apparent personal wealth Wang had acquired as military governor, which many suspected was the result of the embezzlement of public funds.[53]

Wang's demands for new taxes and for a new banknote issue quickly emerged as other major points of controversy. Wang again used the possibility of disorder as the ultimate threat, announcing that if his plans were not accepted, he would simply leave the province and not take further responsibility for local order. Not surprisingly, Xia Shoukang declared his opposition to these financial measures from his office-in-exile in Hankou. The normally compliant Provincial Assembly also held a secret meeting where a majority voiced their opposition to Wang's proposals, noting that the Hubei people were not responsible for the arrears in the payroll of national forces. While decrying the increased burden on the people from a 20 percent tax increase, they also warned that another increase in banknotes threatened a dangerous drop in the value of Hubei's currency. Finally, Wang's opponents in the Assembly noted that, even if Wang did not care about his own reputation, he could not simply shirk his duty to uphold order. Meanwhile, there were reports that various public organizations in Hankou, which had often feuded with the Hankou Chamber of Commerce, were now totally united with the chamber in opposing Wang's proposals. If Wang could not maintain order, they proposed that the city organize a merchant militia for its own defence.[54] Finally, the Hubei Natives Association in Beijing also continued its own campaign of opposition to any new exactions on the Hubei people.[55]

Military-pay issues continued to play a role in a broader struggle between Wang Zhanyuan and Xia Shoukang that dominated Hubei politics in late 1920 and early 1921. This conflict would finally end with Xia' resignation in early February 1921 and his replacement with a compromise candidate, Liu Cheng'en, who, although a Hubei native, as a Beiyang Military Academy graduate, also had good relations with Wang and other northern generals.[56] Meanwhile, there would be no real solution to the military-pay problem. Rather, a hodge-podge of measures was introduced, and fought over, to meet payroll deadlines, including the reallocation of provincial funds, the "borrowing" of national tax and fee revenues, and a package of loans, tax increases, and bond and banknote issues.[57]

The politicization of the military-pay issue probably increased rather than decreased the danger of troop mutinies. Wang's attempt to shift responsibility for meeting military payrolls onto Hubei public organizations, such as the chambers of commerce, fostered military grievances against Hubei people. Opposition to Wang and his proposals by chambers of commerce, local organizations, the Provincial Assembly, and Hubei residents in other provinces certainly may have suggested to soldiers a lack of sympathy for their financial distress. This weakened soldiers' inhibitions against seeking their own "solution" to the pay problem.[58] At the same time, Wang's frequent protests that he would or could not accept responsibility for troop disturbances if his financial demands were not met appeared to condone troop action in the face of continued pay deficits. These conditions fed continuing troop disturbances around the province and ultimately contributed to a second major mutiny in Yichang by Wang's own troops, followed by another in the Hubei capital itself, which wreaked enormous devastation on both cities.

Wang's Disbandment Scheme and the Yichang and Wuchang Mutinies

Meeting troop pay was not just a problem in Hubei but also a crisis of national proportions. In early 1921 Wang reiterated his willingness to meet central disbandment goals by reducing troops in Hubei by 20 to 25 percent.[59] At a subsequent military conference called by the premier at Tianjin, and attended by other leading northern military figures, Wang renewed this pledge.[60] Wang had, of course, already carried out a number of disbandments, but none involved his own core troops. Early reports suggested that "guest" troops were still his main disbandment targets.[61] After returning from the Tianjin conference on 1 June, however, Wang initiated a plan to cull older soldiers within his own units, mainly by disbanding all soldiers over forty.[62] This was the immediate spark for mutinies by Wang's troops at Yichang on 4 June and at Wuchang on 8 June.

Behind the scenes, Wang's disbandment proposal was actually a scheme to increase, not decrease, his overall troop strength. This scheme originated in a conference of Wang's military officers and advisers where he outlined a basic problem. On the one hand, he actually wanted to increase his troops to enhance his military power. On the other hand, this increase would be impossible if funds were insufficient to support existing troop numbers. One commander, Liu Zuolong, offered a solution to this dilemma. He proposed disbanding more expensive older troops to free up funds to recruit a larger number of less expensive, new troops.[63] The original troops who had followed Wang to Hubei were indeed more highly paid due to a number of significant raises given over the years. They had also received a bonus for their role in the 1913 campaign against the bandit White Wolf, which was subsequently incorporated into their regular pay.[64] Thus the elimination of one older soldier could free up funds for at least two new recruits.[65]

Most of Wang's advisers and officers were opposed to this proposal. First, they noted that older troops had more value because of their experience, which new recruits would need considerable training to match. Many were also concerned about handling an expected negative reaction from the troops to be disbanded. They likewise argued that the cavalier treatment of soldiers with a long record of loyal service could undermine the morale of soldiers who remained, as well as new recruits, who would see a similar fate facing them in the future. Finally, one adviser argued that Wang's own moral reputation, and thus popular support, might suffer from this obvious disregard for basic principles of loyalty.[66]

Behind these rational arguments, there was also a power struggle among Wang's officers. Liu Zuolong's unit was mainly made up of new recruits who would be largely unaffected by this proposal. Commanders with large numbers of older troops, such as Sun Chuanfang, saw Liu's proposal as a scheme to undermine their positions. Sun became so angered that he pulled a gun on Liu and had to be restrained. Liu meanwhile protested that he was only thinking of the greater good and giving Wang a solution to the problem he had presented.[67] Despite the overwhelming opposition of most of his officers, Wang was enamoured of Liu's plan and was determined to implement it.[68] This decision set off a chain of events that would lead to the Yichang and Wuchang mutinies. (As an appropriate end to Liu's role as the advocate of this policy, Wang later assigned him to carry out the massacre of mutineers at Xiaogan.)

According to one of Wang's top advisers, the conflict between Liu and Sun had an even more direct role in inciting these mutinies, as Sun, angry over the disbandment decision, leaked the information to the affected troops.[69] Nonetheless, once the proposal was announced, the soldiers hardly needed anyone to provoke them into action.[70] Men who had served under Wang for many years were dismayed that they could be so casually dismissed. They were angered even more by the disbandment terms. First, pleading financial difficulty, Wang had already announced the elimination of the bonus they had collected since 1913.[71] Now they learned that Wang also intended to send them off with less than the full back pay and three months' severance pay official disbandment regulations required. Since most of these troops were still owed at least two months' pay, they should have received a total payment of five months' pay. But Wang was willing to offer only a reduced amount (accounts vary between one and three months' pay), despite special pleas for full payment from officer and troop delegations.[72] Finally, Wang's troops were particularly outraged over his niggardly treatment of men who had helped him to gain both high office and enormous wealth. Indeed, the contrast between Wang's wealth and the miserable future they expected after forced retirement was an important catalyst for the mutiny.[73]

There was little doubt about the wealth Wang had accumulated in his term as Hubei military governor. Memoirs written by one of Wang's financial managers reveal a stunning picture of the wide array of properties, investments, and bank accounts that made Wang one of the wealthiest men of his era.[74] Although an exact reckoning of this wealth is unknowable, Wang himself once commented that his net worth was "only" 40 million yuan – implying his dissatisfaction with this figure.[75] Wang acquired this wealth by taking every advantage of his position to skim off official revenues and to manipulate currency and official loans for his own profit. Wang's personal enrichment also had a direct effect on his soldiers. Any official funds he pocketed obviously meant less left to cover official expenses, including troop pay. An important source of Wang's wealth was, in fact, the direct embezzlement of troop pay.[76] He did this in several ways. First, foreshadowing his disbandment scheme, unit payrolls were kept constant even as older troops retired and were replaced with new recruits at lower starting salaries, allowing Wang to pocket the difference.[77] Second, he regularly maintained unit strength below the reported standard and then had the pay of "ghost" soldiers sent to the governor's yamen, where they were supposedly "assigned."[78] It is hardly surprising, then, that Wang also sought to squeeze extra funds out of his troops in his proposed disbandment scheme. According to a bureaucrat in the Provincial Treasury, there were more than enough funds in provincial accounts to provide the troops with the full back pay and severance pay they were owed. Wang, however, arbitrarily set a lower payout to generate increased financial savings.[79] Wang's greed thus had a direct connection to the mutinies that were to follow.

Although Wang's disbandment plans may have been the immediate catalyst for the mutiny by his troops, the form taken by the mutiny, namely the plunder of Yichang and Wuchang, actually made the Hubei people bear the brunt of troop dissatisfaction. As noted above, this action was no doubt influenced by the building tension in military-civil relations that had arisen over the civil-governorship issue and Wang's attempt to press the local community to cover military deficits. The portrayal of the Hubei people as unsympathetic to the military's financial needs predisposed Wang's soldiers to see them as deserving targets.[80] And this perception may have had some foundation. The Hubei people may indeed have had little sympathy for the suffering of individual soldiers in what they may have seen as an unnecessarily bloated army of outsiders imposed on them by Wang's occupation.

The decision to plunder was surely also encouraged by the relatively light consequences suffered by previous mutineers. In earlier mutinies, other military units were usually sent to suppress mutineers who refused to return to order of their own accord. Many escaped any retribution, however, by simply deserting and returning to civilian life (or to banditry). At the same time, punishments were few for troops who returned to their camps of their own accord. The general lack of consequences for mutinying soldiers was obvious in the 1920 Yichang case. Most of the troops involved simply returned to their encampments after a night of plunder. Only a small number of soldiers, thirty to forty, were arrested for their actions that night.[81] Subsequent reports reveal that most of the remaining mutineers remained free and kept possession of the goods they had plundered. Thus in the aftermath of the incident idle soldiers were frequently seen gambling with the loot they had acquired, while powerless local police looked on. Yichang's silk shops were actually able to reopen after soldiers, finding no use for the silk they had stolen, sold it back to the very shops they had taken it from. Moreover, while ignoring loot retained by the mutineers, troops supposedly sent to restore order prolonged the city's plunder by searching residences and confiscating "suspicious" goods they claimed were looted by common people during the disturbance.[82] The organized way that the soldiers had looted the city, and the little punishment they suffered for it, led many citizens to believe that Wang had actually condoned the mutiny as a way for local soldiers to solve their own pay problems.[83]

The result of a rehabilitation conference held after the 1920 Yichang mutiny also revealed another way that soldiers may have seen it as a "success." To prevent further disturbances, the conference decided to raise 1.5 million yuan from the Hubei government and the local Chamber of Commerce to meet military pay deficits.[84] The only real downside for some soldiers was Wang's decision to disband the 13th Mixed Brigade, which had been the main force in the mutiny, rather than to incorporate it into a new division as originally planned.[85] Nonetheless, for the troops involved, the combination of loot and the postmutiny contributions to their back pay may have seemed better than continuing military service with little expectation of regular pay.

To the extent that the advantages of a mutiny seemed to outweigh its disadvantages, press reports at the time noted the potential danger of "contagion" of the idea of mutiny from one unit to another.[86] This might have been particularly true for troops garrisoned at Yichang in the summer of 1921 as they learned of Wang's disbandment plans. With the example of the 13th Mixed Brigade before them, a mutiny might have seemed a good opportunity to gain at least some additional benefits before being severed from military service.

The 1921 Yichang mutiny, which broke out on 4 June, involved most of Sun Chuanfang's 21st Mixed Brigade and portions of the 18th Division, both core Wang forces.[87] Large portions of the city were burned by rampaging troops, including 60 percent of the stores and two-thirds of the homes. As before, foreign property in the port was not spared. More shockingly, the military governor's office reported that nearly one thousand people died at the hands of rioting troops. Total damages, including the losses from the first mutiny six months earlier, were estimated at 12 million yuan.[88] Although the damages in Yichang were great, they were in the end overshadowed by those of the mutiny that occurred in the provincial capital.

There is evidence again of "contagion," as the Yichang mutiny provided a model for soldiers in Wuchang. When some Yichang mutineers were escorted under guard to Wuchang, 2nd Division troops, many of whom were also slated for disbandment, could not help but note the loot they carried. Thus they saw firsthand the advantages of following the Yichang example.[89]

The Wuchang mutiny started soon after midnight on 8 June 1921 and involved large parts of Wang's 2nd Division. It was widely noted that the soldiers left their camps and headed into the city in an orderly fashion. They then attacked the Provincial Assembly building, the governor's yamen, the Provincial Treasury, and the Wuchang Mint. The shops and homes of common people were then systematically robbed, and large sections of the city, particularly its commercial districts, were set afire.[90] Philanthropic organizations later estimated total property losses at between 30 and 40 million yuan.[91] Rampaging soldiers also committed numerous rapes, and many accounts later appeared of women who were killed or who committed suicide while resisting rape, including a provincial assemblyman's daughter.[92] Although there was no complete list of casualties, several hundred people were estimated to have been seriously injured or killed.[93]

Because the Wuchang mutineers entered the city in organized groups that seemed to have specific objectives, and because they met with so little opposition, many suspected that Wang ordered the mutiny to serve his own purposes. One theory was that Wang used the mutiny to revenge himself on the Hubei people for their political opposition. Another theory was that Wang, as a basis for reneging on his disbandment commitment, ordered the mutiny to show the central government the difficulty of disbandment. Since one target of the mutineers was the Provincial Treasury, another theory was that Wang used the mutiny to destroy evidence of currency manipulation, which had been a source of ongoing political controversy.[94] But if Wang had planned the mutiny, he certainly would have safeguarded the approximately 1 million yuan actually stolen from the Treasury and the Mint.[95] In the end, Wang's angry response to the mutiny, reflected in his eventual harsh treatment of the mutineers, suggested that the mutiny had caught him by surprise.

Even if not directed by Wang, the mutiny seemed well organized by the mutineers themselves. Various accounts suggested that soldiers in camps outside the city were in communication with each other prior to the event and had pre-arranged the time to rise, entry routes into the city, and specific targets to be attacked. Many officers were apparently aware of these preparations yet did nothing to stop them.[96] Some lower officers even led their troops into the city to join the mutiny.[97] Many of these officers had opposed the proposed disbandment and were reportedly dejected by their failure to block it.[98] This mutiny, then, was perhaps as much a demonstration of the loss of confidence in Wang by his officers as it was a protest by his soldiers.

As dawn arrived on the morning of 8 June, some of the mutineers deserted but most returned to their camps with their loot.[99] It was fairly obvious that they expected to suffer few consequences for their actions. They would learn differently only when they disembarked from the train that took them to their deaths at Xiaogan. The extent to which many of Wang's troops simply could not believe that he would punish them for their destruction of the Hubei capital can be seen by angry letters sent after the massacre to the chambers of commerce by troops who had remained behind in Wuhan. Believing that the city's merchants had forced Wang's hand in this action, they warned that if forced to rise again, due to continued pay problems, no one in the city would be spared.[100] These letters clearly showed the extent to which military relations with the people of Hubei had deteriorated. But they also show how Wang's use of the threat of mutinies, and his attempt to shift responsibility for them onto others, had encouraged his troops not only to think that the indifference of the Hubei people was at least partially responsible for their suffering but also to assume that Wang would turn a blind eye if they sought to remedy their situation through plunder and pillage.

The Fall of Wang Zhanyuan

Although many cities across China in the early Republic suffered the effects of civil war and military atrocities, Wuchang had up to this point survived relatively unscathed.[101] Even the Wuchang uprising initiating the 1911 Revolution had resulted in little physical destruction to the city. (Revolutionary battles were fought mainly across the Yangzi in Hanyang and Hankou.) Indeed, to find the level of devastation suffered by Wuchang in 1921, one would have to go back to the mid-nineteenth-century Taiping Rebellion. The enormous public outcry in the aftermath of the incident was therefore hardly surprising. It was also a serious blow to Wang Zhanyuan's carefully cultivated image as the person who had kept the Hubei capital free of disorder while the rest of China descended into civil war, an achievement that led many Hubei natives to accept both his occupation of their province and his corruption.[102] The weakness of Wang's control over his own troops revealed by the Yichang and Wuchang mutinies encouraged both Wang's political enemies to redouble their attacks and his erstwhile military allies to look with avarice at his base. In just two months after the mutinies, Wang would be forced from his position.

In the immediate aftermath of the Wuchang mutiny, Wang initially tried to downplay the incident and to obscure his own troops' role in it. Thus in various announcements he blamed the disturbance on a small number of soldiers (either unspecified or identified as being from "guest" armies) who had been incited by "bandits" or other outside agitators.[103] But the scope of the disaster was too great, and there were too many witnesses, for this cover story to work.[104] In response to the fast-emerging outcry, Wang went through the ritual of offering his resignation, with the usual expectation that it would be rejected.[105] In an attempt to restore discipline and hold someone accountable for the mutiny, Wang immediately executed nine soldiers who had been caught the night of the mutiny by government-office guards. Angry citizens gathered around the corpses to stab them with knives and pelt them with vegetables.[106] Shortly after, Wang also cashiered several regiment commanders and executed several lower officers for failing to control their troops during the mutiny.[107] And, of course, the massacre of mutineers at Xiaogan was meant to be the ultimate bone thrown to outraged public opinion.[108] This gesture's effect was somewhat blunted, however, by Wang's fear that the truth of this event might provoke troops remaining in Wuhan to further violence. Thus a story was put out that local troops at Xiaogan had been forced to open fire when soldiers on the train became disruptive and discipline could not be restored.[109] Put on their guard, however, other mutiny participants who were still to be disbanded insisted that they be allowed to retain their weapons, for their own self-defence, until they reached their homes.[110] Meanwhile, the scam of Wang's entire disbandment program was uncovered, to even more outcry, when he unveiled a proposal to recruit new troops to fill the holes that disbandment had created in the ranks of his forces.[111]

Even as Wang attempted to manage the crisis, the Wuchang mutiny became the catalyst for a reinvigorated anti-Wang campaign.[112] Responding to this, Wang tightened his political controls in Wuhan to prevent open protests.[113] As in the past, Hubei residents in Beijing then took the lead in organizing the anti-Wang opposition. A meeting called immediately after the news of the mutiny reached the capital resulted in an unprecedented gathering of over one thousand Hubei residents. In this and subsequent meetings, motions were passed denouncing

Wang's crimes and demanding his removal.[114] After one meeting, the entire gathering marched through Beijing's streets to demonstrate outside the president's office for Wang's removal. They also met with representatives from the president's and premier's offices, who expressed sympathy but could not promise any action.[115] They even appealed to the foreign diplomatic corps, hoping that international pressure could be brought to bear on the government for Wang's removal.[116] Meanwhile, Hubei residents' associations in Tianjin, Shanghai, Hunan, Guangdong, and even Singapore also joined in these demands.[117] Despite Wang's political controls, organizations in Hubei also found ways to show their support. For example, the Hankou Chamber of Commerce provided secret funding for an anti-Wang paper published in Beijing.[118]

The anti-Wang activists were under no illusion that the pressure of public opinion alone could force Wang from power. Therefore, they also sought military assistance. Rising public opinion against Wang might, it was hoped, provide cover for a military challenge to his position. In the North, anti-Wang delegates called on the emerging leader of the Zhili faction, Wu Peifu, but did not find him receptive. In the South, they approached the new "self-government" regime in Hunan led by Zhao Hengdi, and Zhao expressed sympathy for the Hubei cause. With his approval, Hubei activists met in Changsha on 22 July 1921 to organize an alternate Hubei government. Zhao meanwhile also sought an alliance with Sichuan commanders, who had just ousted Yunnan militarists from their province. In late July, Hunan and Sichuan forces advanced on Hubei in what became known as the Aid-Hubei War.[119]

With northern control over Hubei threatened, Zhili faction leaders Cao Kun and Wu Peifu decided to seize Wang's territory for themselves. In an effort to placate Hubei provincialist sentiment, a native Hubei commander under Wu Peifu's command, Xiao Yaonan, was sent to "aid" Wang. After reaching Wuhan, however, Xiao refused to advance his troops and assist Wang's beleaguered forces at the front. Seeing the writing on the wall, Wang resigned his position and left the province. Xiao then mobilized his forces to block the further advance of Hunan and Sichuan troops and replaced Wang as military governor.[120]

Conclusion

Mutinies in warlord China were rarely limited to a refusal to obey orders or a rejection of military authority. Rather, they were usually acted out with attacks on government offices and assaults against the homes, shops, and persons of the general population. Thus, for the people of China, mutinies were one of the many tribulations they had to endure in an era of military ascendancy. Under these circumstances, the relationship of warlord soldiers to the Chinese people was that of victimizer to victim. Nonetheless, the soldiers who participated in these mutinies were themselves often reacting against conditions in which they themselves were victims. As seen in this chapter, the most consistent reason for mutinies was the hardship endured by soldiers when their pay, quite small to begin with, was withheld, delayed, or even embezzled by their commanders or higher political authorities. A second major reason was the threat to soldiers' livelihoods represented by often-arbitrary disbandment. In all these situations, soldiers were pawns in broader conflicts that included wars over territory among warlord factions, struggles over resources between warlord commanders and the societies they dominated, and internal disputes within individual warlord commands. Sometimes, then, mutinies enabled soldiers to become active players in these conflicts in pursuit of their own interests – for example, by forcing authorities to deal with their pay issues. As political tools, mutinies could also be a two-edged sword. Wang Zhanyuan used the threat of mutinies to strengthen his political position and to increase his control of provincial resources. However, in expressing their anger over their disbandment, Wang's soldiers also used the Yichang and Wuchang mutinies to undermine Wang's reputation as a military commander, to bring down on him the full power of outraged public opinion, and finally to make him the target of rival commanders who coveted his territory. Thus, although Wang wreaked his vengeance on these mutineers in the Xiaogan Massacre, the mutineers had their own revenge, as the controversy arising from their mutiny ultimately drove Wang from power.

Notes

1 Liu Cuochen, *Ezhou canji* [Hubei's Tragic Record] (n.p., 1922), 84-85; Ni Zhongwen, ed., *Beiyang junfa tongzhi Hubei shi* [History of Beiyang Warlord Rule of Hubei] (Wuhan: Hubei renmin chubanshe, 1989), 147; United States Department of State, "Decimal File, 1910-1929: Internal Affairs of China" (hereafter USDS), 893.00/3848 (Huston, 10 June 1921) and 893.00/3950 (Huston, 15 June 1921); *Hankou zhongxibao* [Hankou Chinese-Western News], 12 June 1921. These accounts differ as to whether the train left Hankou the morning or evening of 8 June or on the following day. They also cite a variety of sources placing the number of mutineers killed at between 300 and 2,000. There seems to be some basis, however, for accepting Liu Cuochen's precise figure of 1,784 dead. A contemporary military report cited by Ni Zhongwen stated that 1,700 troops had left on the train to Xiaogan (followed by another train with an additional 150). A wire from Wang Zhanyuan to Hubei residents in Beijing, reprinted in *Hankou xinwenbao* [Hankou News], 21 June 1921, also noted that over 1,700 troops had been enticed onto the train and that only a few had escaped. Finally, an account of a report by Wang to Wuhan's merchants on the massacre in *Hankou zhongxibao,* 12 June 1921, says over 1,700 were killed.

2 Diana Lary, *Warlord Soldier: Chinese Common Soldiers, 1911-1937* (Cambridge, UK: Cambridge University Press, 1985), 87-90.

3 Even a representative for Wuchang refugees at a postmutiny rehabilitation conference warned against simply blaming the troops for "troop mutinies" *(bingbian).* He charged that the real blame lay with those (namely Wang and his officers) who "condoned troops in their harm of the people" *(zongbing yangmin).* See Liu, *Ezhou canji,* 128.

4 Edward A. McCord, *The Power of the Gun: The Emergence of Modern Chinese Warlordism* (Berkeley: University of California Press, 1993), 278-82; *Shibao* [Eastern Times], 19 September 1920 and 10 October 1920; USDS, 893.00/3742 (Huston, 16 December 1920).
5 *Shibao,* 28 September 1917.
6 *Shibao,* 4 May 1919.
7 *Shibao,* 4 and 7 October 1916. By 1919 it was estimated that notes equal in value to 90 million *chuan* (cash strings) had been printed. See *Shibao,* 19 April and 20 November 1919.
8 In 1918 Wang borrowed 1 million yuan from a Japanese bank. See *Shibao,* 4 May and 18 August 1919.
9 *Shibao,* 11 November 1919.
10 *Shibao,* 24 July 1919.
11 *Shibao,* 18 and 28 August 1919.
12 *Shibao,* 29 September and 3 October 1919.
13 *Shibao,* 18 October 1919.
14 *Shibao,* 6 October and 2 November 1919.
15 *Shibao,* 29 August 1919.
16 *Shibao,* 23 October 1919. All translations of quotations from non-English sources are mine.
17 *Shibao,* 6 and 12 December 1919; USDS, 893.000/3331 ("Hubei 1919 Annual Report").
18 *Shibao,* 10 and 12 December 1919; *Shibao,* 18 April, 3 May, and 19 and 25 June 1920.
19 *Shibao,* 3 May 1920.
20 *Shibao,* 21 July 1920; Fei Zepu, "Wu Guangxin zai changjiang shangyou de xingbai" [The rise and fall of Wu Guangxin on the upper Yangzi], *Wenshi ziliao xuanji* [Selected Historical Materials] 41 (1963): 75-76.
21 *Shibao,* 23 July 1920.
22 *Shibao,* 29 and 31 July 1920; Fei, "Wu Guangxin," 76-77.
23 On the ill-discipline of Zhang's troops, see Edward A. McCord, "Burn, Kill, Rape and Rob: Military Atrocities, Warlordism, and Anti-Warlordism in Republican China," in Diana Lary and Stephen MacKinnon, eds., *Scars of War: The Impact of Warfare on Modern China* (Vancouver: UBC Press, 2001).
24 *Shibao,* 2 and 6 October, 26 November, and 8 December 1920.
25 *Shuntian ribao* [Shuntian Times], 15 May 1921.
26 The connection between troop disbandment and banditry was commonly noted. See, for example, *Shibao,* 29 August 1919.
27 *Shibao,* 10 November 1919.
28 In late 1920 Wang proposed the formation of a new division by combining one of his core units, the 21st Mixed Brigade under Sun Chuanfang, with the 13th Mixed Brigade, a former Wu Guangxin unit, and one of Zhang Jingyao's remnant units. The Beijing government refused to sanction this new unit, and both the 13th Mixed Brigade and the Zhang unit rose in mutinies before the year was out. See *Shibao,* 10 October and 8 December 1920.
29 *Shibao,* 2 August 1920.
30 *Shibao,* 12 August 1920. By this time, Zhang Jingyao's original "national" 7th Division is listed as a Hubei provincial unit.
31 *Shibao,* 9 January and 4 October 1920.
32 *Shibao,* 6 November 1920.
33 *Shibao,* 4 and 27 July and 8 August 1920.
34 *Shibao,* 7 December 1920.
35 *Shibao,* 3, 5, 7, 8, and 10 December 1920; USDS, 893.00/3709 (Huston, 9 December 1920).
36 *Shibao,* 8 December 1920.
37 Ni, ed., *Beiyang junfa tongzhi Hubei shi,* 145; *Guomin xinbao* [Citizen's News], 5 January 1921; *Shibao,* 7 December 1920.

38 Wang was known to boast, "Who but I has the ability to maintain local order in Hubei?" See Liu, *Ezhou canji*, 2.
39 *Shibao*, 13 December 1920.
40 *Shibao*, 11, 12, 13, and 18 December 1920.
41 *Shibao*, 21 and 24 December 1920.
42 *Shibao*, 11, 13, 17, and 18 December 1920.
43 McCord, *Power of the Gun*, 242-43, 272-73.
44 USDS, 893.00/3675 (Huston, 18 November 1920); *Shibao*, 2 and 9 August and 1 and 13 September 1920.
45 *Shibao*, 19 and 22 September 1920.
46 *Shibao*, 25 September 1920.
47 *Shibao*, 2, 7, 12, and 13 October and 26 November 1920.
48 *Shibao*, 16 and 17 November 1920.
49 Liu, *Ezhou canji*, 11-12; *Shibao*, 30 November 1920; Lu Fu, "Wang Zhanyuan, Xiao Yaonan bachixiade Hubei zhengju" [Hubei's political situation under the control of Wang Zhanyuan and Xiao Yaonan], *Wuhan wenshi ziliao* [Wuhan Historical Materials] 12 (1983): 3 (Lu Fu was an anti-Wang activist who served as a secretary to Xia Shoukang in 1921).
50 *Shibao*, 28 November 1920.
51 *Shibao*, 12 December 1920. The 13th Mixed Brigade, which had been involved in the Yichang mutiny, came under Sun's control as part of Wang's scheme to create a new division. The Beijing government, however, refused to approve this new unit and Sun's promotion as division commander. There was suspicion, then, that Sun's role in the Yichang mutiny and the threats against Xia also reflected his own personal antagonism toward the central government. See *Shibao*, 29 December 1920.
52 *Shibao*, 29 December 1920.
53 For example, a pamphlet appeared on Wuhan's streets charging Wang with pocketing 7 million yuan he had received from the central government, which had been intended for troop pay. See *Shibao*, 13 and 17 December 1920.
54 *Shibao*, 24 December 1920.
55 *Shibao*, 28 and 29 December 1920.
56 USDS, 893.00/3840 (Huston, 9 March 1921); *Shuntian ribao*, 3 March 1921; Liu, *Ezhou canji*, 45-47.
57 *Shuntian ribao*, 1 January, 1 February, 3 and 6 March, 11 and 24 April, and 5 and 13 May 1921.
58 Liu, *Ezhou canji*, 14.
59 *Shuntian ribao*, 29 March and 7 April 1921.
60 USDS, 893.00/3917 (Huston, 20 May 1921); Jiang Yannan, "Huo-E baniande Beiyang junfa Wang Zhanyuan" [The Beiyang warlord who devastated Hubei for eight years, Wang Zhanyuan], in *Wuhan wenshi ziliao* [Wuhan Historical Materials] 12 (1983): 25 (Jiang was an adviser in Wang Zhanyuan's military governor's office); *Shuntian ribao*, 24 April and 4 June 1921.
61 *Shuntian ribao*, 27 April 1921.
62 Xu Yisu, "Hubei bingbian zhi yinguo" [The cause of the Hubei mutiny], *Hubei wenshi ziliao* [Hubei Historical Materials] 27 (1989): 84; USDS, 893.00/3949 (Huston, 11 June 1921).
63 He Yanwen, "Wang Zhanyuan zhi-E de Wuchang bingbian neimu" [Inside story of the Wuchang mutiny during Wang Zhanyuan's rule of Hubei], *Hubei wenshi ziliao* [Hubei Historical Materials] 5 (1982): 101-2; Wang Guowei, "Wang Zhanyuan lanjie bianbing lieche muji ji" [An eyewitness record of Wang Zhanyuan's interception of the train of mutinous troops], *Wuhan wenshi ziliao* [Wuhan Historical Materials] 12 (1983): 35.
64 Liu, *Ezhou canji*, 83.

65 Wang, "Wang Zhanyuan," 35. Other estimates of the number of new recruits that could be supported from the pay of one older soldier range from two and a half to four. He, "Wang Zhanyuan zhi-E," 102-3; Wang Yaqiao, "Cong pashang dujun zuo dao zidong cizhi de Wang Zhanyuan" [Wang Zhanyuan from his climb to the military governor's seat to his resignation], *Hubei wenshi ziliao* [Hubei Historical Materials] 27 (1989): 53.

66 Jiang, "Huo-E baniande Beiyang junfa," 25; Yan Jingzong, "Wo ren Wang Zhanyuan baodui yingzhang shi jingli de bingbian qingkuang" [The mutiny situation I experienced while serving as Wang Zhanyuan's artillery corps battalion commander], *Hubei wenshi ziliao* [Hubei Historical Materials] 27 (1989): 88-89; He, "Wang Zhanyuan zhi-E," 103.

67 He, "Wang Zhanyuan zhi-E," 102-3.

68 Jiang, "Huo-E baniande Beiyang junfa," 25; He, "Wang Zhanyuan zhi-E," 103-4; Yan, "Wo ren Wang Zhanyuan baodui yingzhang," 89.

69 He, "Wang Zhanyuan zhi-E," 104 (which mistakenly sets the mutiny in 1919). This account was related to He Yanwen by his father, He Peirong, who was Wang's chief of staff.

70 Yan, "Wo ren Wang Zhanyuan baodui yingzhang," 89.

71 Liu, *Ezhou canji*, 83, 94; USDS, 893.0/3950 (Huston, 15 June 1921).

72 Du Ruicheng, "Wuchang 'wu-er' bingbian zhi suojian" [What I saw of the Wuchang "5-2" mutiny], *Wuhan wenshi ziliao* [Wuhan Historical Materials] 12 (1983): 28. Du, who worked in the Hubei Treasury and was present at the Treasury the night of the mutiny, recorded that Wang offered the troops three months' pay. The memoir of a platoon commander from the 2nd Division states the troops received only one month's severance pay; see Chen Runqing, "Wuchang bingbian qinliji" [A personal account of the Wuchang mutiny], *Wuhan wenshi ziliao* [Wuhan Historical Materials] 12 (1983): 32. Another source also asserts that only one month's pay was given; see Xu, "Hubei bingbian," 85.

73 *Shuntian ribao*, 11 and 15 June 1921; Liu, *Ezhou canji*, 84, 104-5; Wang, "Wang Zhanyuan," 35.

74 Zhao Shixian, "Wang Zhanyuan de jiazu he caichan" [Wang Zhanyuan's family and property], *Wuhan wenshi ziliao* [Wuhan Historical Materials] 12 (1983): 40-49; Zhao Shixian, "Wo suo jingbande Wang Zhanyuan caichan ji jiufen" [My management of Wang Zhanyuan's properties and disputes], *Hubei wenshi ziliao* [Hubei Historical Materials] 27 (1989), 102-17.

75 Jiang, "Huo-E baniande Beiyang junfa," 27.

76 Liu, *Ezhou canji*, 118.

77 Jiang, "Huo-E baniande Beiyang junfa," 24-25; Yan, "Wo ren Wang Zhanyuan baodui yingzhang," 88.

78 Wang, "Cong pashang dujun," 52.

79 Du, "Wuchang 'wu-er' bingbian," 28.

80 *Shuntian ribao*, 15 June 1921.

81 *Shibao*, 8 December 1920.

82 *Shibao*, 26 December 1920.

83 *Central China Post*, 10 December 1920, enclosed in USDS, 893.00/3704.

84 *Shibao*, 25 December 1920.

85 *Shibao*, 17, 23, and 25 December 1920.

86 *Shibao*, 2 October 1920.

87 *Shuntian ribao*, 7 and 8 June 1920.

88 Liu, *Ezhou canji*, 93, 116; *Guomin xinbao*, 19 October 1921.

89 Wang, "Cong pashang dujun," 54.

90 Liu, *Ezhou canji*, 74-81, 92-93; USDS, 893.00/3947 (Huston, 9 June 1921).

91 *Hankou xinwenbao*, 21 June 1921; *Hankou zhengyibao* [Hankou Justice News], 17 June 1921; Liu, *Ezhou canji*, 80.

92 *Hankou xinwenbao,* 21 June 1921; Liu, *Ezhou canji,* Appendix, 4, 7, 12.

93 Liu, *Ezhou canji,* 93. Liu provides detailed accounts of specific atrocities in an appendix of over fifty pages.

94 *Shuntian ribao,* 15 June 1921; Liu, *Ezhou canji,* 105; USDA, 893.00/3947 (Huston, 9 June 1921). Soldiers did plunder old bills gathered in the Treasury that were to be redeemed by a new banknote issue, preventing an exact accounting of these bills. The soldiers discarded these bills when they discovered they had been marked as invalid. See Du, "Wuchang 'wu-er' bingbian," 29.

95 Currency losses from the Treasury totalled 700,000 yuan, whereas the Mint lost 300,000 yuan; see Du, "Wuchang 'wu-er' bingbian," 31. Another source, *Hankou zhengyibao,* 17 June 1921, reported that the Mint also lost over 400,000 yuan of its silver holdings and over 200,000 strings of copper cash.

96 One platoon commander reported to his brigade commander that some of his soldiers and squad commanders had met to plan their role in the mutiny. He claimed that his own attempt to stop the participation of his troops was unsuccessful. See Chen, "Wuchang bingbian," 32-33.

97 Wang, "Cong pashang dujun," 54.

98 Xu, "Hubei bingbian," 85.

99 Chen, "Wuchang bingbian," 33; Yan, "Wo ren Wang Zhanyuan baodui yingzhang," 89. One estimate was that among the 7,000 troops in the 2nd Division at the time of the mutiny, 2,000 "disappeared" at some point, thus escaping the massacre at Xiaogan. See *Central China Post,* 13 June 1921, enclosed in USDS, 893.00/3950 (Huston, 15 June 1921).

100 Liu, *Ezhou canji,* 95-96; *Hankou xinwenbao,* 22 June 1921.

101 Liu, *Ezhou canji,* 75-76.

102 Even leaders of anti-Wang movements acknowledged that the Hubei people had been willing to overlook Wang's corruption in exchange for peace. See Liu, *Ezhou canji,* 152.

103 *Shuntian ribao,* 22 and 25 June 1921; *Hankou zhongxibao,* 12 June 1921; *Hankou xinwenbao,* 21 June 1921; Liu, *Ezhou canji,* 82-83.

104 Liu, *Ezhou canji,* 107.

105 Ibid., 90, 94-95, 101; *Hankou xinwenbao,* 21 June 1921. As expected, the president rejected Wang's resignation. See USDS, 893.00/3951 (Huston, 16 June 1921).

106 Liu, *Ezhou canji,* 87, 92.

107 *Shuntian ribao,* 25 and 30 June and 2 July 1921; Liu, *Ezhou canji,* 98-100.

108 Wang took credit for the ambush of the mutineers in statements to Hubei organizations; see *Hankou zhongxibao,* 12 June 1921; and *Hankou xinwenbao,* 21 June 1921. Wang was reportedly pleased with the massacre and saw it as his apology to the Hubei people; see Du, "Wuchang 'wu-er' bingbian," 30-31.

109 *Shuntian ribao,* 5 July 1921. Some members of Wang's staff also took this line in their memoirs, perhaps wanting to downplay the severity of the massacre. See Yang Wenkai, "Wo zai Wang Zhanyuan muxia de huodong pianduan" [A fragmentary account of my activities on Wang Zhanyuan's staff], *Wenshi ziliao xuanji* [Selected Historical Materials] 41 (1962); Wang, "Wang Zhanyuan," 36.

110 *Central China Post,* 13 June 1921, enclosed in USDS, 893.00/3950 (Huston, 15 June 1921).

111 *Shuntian ribao,* 5 and 6 July 1921; Liu, *Ezhou canji,* 97-98, 108-9.

112 Lu, "Wang Zhanyuan," 9.

113 Liu, *Ezhou canji,* 109-13.

114 Ibid., 116-29; Rao Xiaowen, "Lu Jing Hubei tongxiang de dao-Wang yundong" [The Hubei Beijing residents' oust-Wang movement], *Hubei wenshi ziliao* [Hubei Historical Materials] 27 (1989): 94.

115 Liu, *Ezhou canji,* 129-31, 140-43; Rao, "Lu Jing Hubei tongxiang," 95.
116 Liu, *Ezhou canji,* 133-34.
117 Ibid., 101-3.
118 Rao, "Lu Jing Hubei tongxiang," 95.
119 *Hankou xinwenbao,* 21 and 22 June 1921; Zhang Fangyan, "1921 nian Zhi jun yuan-E de jingguo" [The experience of the Zhili armies' aid to Hubei in 1921], *Wenshi ziliao xuanji* [Selected Historical Materials] 41 (1962): 105-6; Liu, *Ezhou canji,* 147-52.
120 Zhang, "1921 nian Zhi jun yuan-E de jingguo," 107; Liu, *Ezhou canji,* 173-74.

7

Turning Bad Iron into Polished Steel: Whampoa and the Rehabilitation of the Chinese Soldier

Colin Green

For the Chinese, the warlord era of the early 1920s was a terrible period characterized by the breakdown of social, economic, and political order, and the destruction brought about by endemic warfare threatened to overwhelm even the remarkable recuperative powers of the long-suffering peasants. Much has been written about the hardships experienced by civilians during this turbulent era, and rightly so, for they were usually the innocent victims of the events that swirled around them, but the damage inflicted by the warlords extended to institutions as well as individuals. Odd as it might seem, the Chinese military was itself a victim of warlordism, suffering from a precipitous decline in its prestige as armies degenerated into congeries of armed gangs, and officers forsook loyalty to any cause other than their own self-interest. This decline in status was especially noticeable because the military had enjoyed an unusually high degree of popularity in the years leading up to the 1911 Revolution.

In the final decade of the Qing Dynasty, intellectuals flirted with militarism as a solution to China's weakness, and the military came to be seen as a vanguard institution in the nation's struggle to modernize.[1] As in Wilhelmine Germany and Meiji Japan, the soldier was held up as a model for all citizens, and as the military profession gained respectability patriotic young Chinese men flocked to the colours in droves. For example, Li Zonghuang (1888-1978) was typical of the generation that came of age in the last years of the Qing, when China was reeling under intensifying imperialist pressure. Like many of his peers, he felt compelled to take action, and he found inspiration in Yue Fei's biography. The story of the Song Dynasty general's heroic efforts against foreign invaders and his concurrent battle with a capitulationist court seemed all too familiar to Li, and like his hero he eventually opted to pursue a military rather than a civil career in order to demonstrate his "absolute loyalty to the nation."[2]

The military's newfound prestige did not go unnoticed, and even foreigners felt moved to comment on the noticeably improved status enjoyed by soldiers.[3] But this did not last, for the endemic violence of the warlord era quickly eroded whatever respect the Chinese had recently developed for their soldiers. Public disenchantment was reflected in the renewed popularity of old anti-military sayings such as "good iron is not used to make nails, and good men do not become soldiers."[4] Less than a decade after the 1911 Revolution, an English officer on his way home from a posting in Japan expressed shock over the low status of the military in China:

> This is simply one amongst many striking differences between Japan and her large, though feeble, neighbour, China. In the former country, the profession of arms is regarded as one of great honour, whilst in China, on the other hand, the soldier is regarded as a necessary evil, and, far from being looked up to, is considered a thief and a murderer – a reputation not infrequently well merited.[5]

The deterioration of the military was something China could ill-afford at that particular time. Although the forces of imperialism were in abeyance in the early 1920s, China was far from safe, and the need for a strong, modern military was just as pressing as it had been at the turn of the century. The warlords only made the situation worse, for although they commanded some of the largest armies in Chinese history, their political squabbling weakened the nation and actually increased the likelihood of foreign intervention. For many Chinese this was an immensely frustrating situation, and the warlords were roundly condemned for their self-serving politics and the mindless brutality of their troops. Yet despite the bad press received by soldiers in general, there were still those who continued to place their faith in the potential of the military as a force for modernization and nation building. Not surprisingly, the most ardent advocates of this view were themselves military officers, and by the early 1920s many of these disaffected men had made their way south to join Sun Yat-sen at his revolutionary base in Guangzhou, where, as historian Michael Gibson notes, they remained determined to pursue "the earlier goal of a modern, professional army that was dedicated to the nation and its defense against the foreigners."[6]

As Sun's military adviser and commandant of the Guomindang's newly established Whampoa Military Academy, Chiang Kai-shek would emerge as the leader of this group. Like many of his peers, Chiang had been deeply influenced by the popular flirtation with militarism in the last years of the Qing Dynasty, and his experience in Japan as a military cadet had served only to reinforce his conviction that soldiers ought to take the lead in the struggle to build a modern nation. The problem he faced in the early 1920s was that his fervent militarism was out of step with the public mood. The warlord era had effectively shattered the Chinese people's faith in the military as a positive institution, and soldiers were regarded as little better than bandits. Chiang was well aware that he would have to restore the tarnished image of the soldier before the military could act as the vanguard in a national revival, and he intended to have the Whampoa cadets play the leading role in this process.

In this chapter, I first examine the origins of Chiang Kai-shek's militarism and situate his views within the context of the early twentieth century. Next, I show how the proponents of militarism suffered a serious setback when the internecine warfare of the warlord era eroded popular faith in the military. Finally, I examine how Chiang sought to undo this damage by using the Whampoa cadets to restore the reputation of the military. Far from training the cadets to be nothing more than obedient servants of the Guomindang, Chiang was from the beginning intent on preparing them to assume what he believed to be the soldier's proper role in a modern society – that of champion and moral exemplar for all citizens in the struggle to build a rich and powerful nation. To achieve this goal, Chiang set out to rehabilitate the military profession by means of a spiritual training program that emphasized a strict code of ethics. Chiang believed that the emphasis on ethics would serve to distinguish the revolutionary soldiers from the warlord rabble in the eyes of a skeptical public and restore popular trust in the military.

The Origins of Militarism in China

If one looks at militarism not through the prism of the twentieth century's two great wars but rather from the standpoint of the late nineteenth century, it appears in a more positive light. To the Germans and the Japanese, militarism was a key component in the emergence of their nations as great powers. Widespread emulation of military values and universal conscription turned peasants and burghers into patriotic citizens, and the military as an institution was seen as a leading force in the quest for modernization and national power. Even Max Weber saw the military as a model for the bureaucratic rationality he so admired.[7] The world wars may have tainted militarism in Western eyes, but this cannot change the fact that as a developmental strategy it contributed in many ways to the creation of strong nations. For those untouched by the horrors of Europe's wars, especially the First World War, this was the lesson that stuck.

During the last years of the Qing Dynasty, when the threat of partition at the hands of the great powers seemed very real, the military took on new importance in China. Driven by fear that China was on the verge of becoming a "lost country" *(wangguo)*, many politically engaged Chinese intellectuals took up the cause of militarism, arguing that to survive in a hostile world the Chinese people would have to overcome their spiritual malaise and lack of martial vigour.[8] Intellectuals traced the origins of this malady back to the periods of Mongol and Manchu rule, when nervous alien dynasties tried to declaw their Chinese subjects by forbidding martial pursuits. For example, Gu Hongming (1847-1928), a conservative Confucian scholar, noted that whereas the Japanese had been able to preserve the Tang Dynasty's elegant culture and views on loyalty and courage, the Chinese themselves had succumbed to the corrupting influences of the Mongols and Manchus.[9] Even today, some Chinese scholars cite two centuries of Manchu rule as a major reason for the deterioration of the Chinese martial spirit.[10]

Liang Qichao is representative of the patriotic intellectuals who took up the cause of militarism, and his writings incorporate many of the themes found in the works of other Chinese intellectuals who struggled to come to terms with the Darwinian world around them – fear of racial/cultural degeneration or even extinction, as well as fear of China succumbing to imperialism and becoming a "lost country."[11] In his 1902 essay "On the Appreciation of Martial Values," Liang advocated what Stanislav Andreski calls "militolatry," or civic militarism, as a solution to China's chronic weakness.[12] Liang ridiculed the idea that only barbarians should esteem strength, noting that Rome's advanced civilization had not saved it from the Goths. He praised the civic militarism of the ancient Spartans and equated it with the German "iron and blood" policy promoted by Otto von Bismarck.[13] Nor did Liang think that this "martial spirit" *(shang wu jingshen)* was somehow limited to the West, for he pointedly reminded his readers that even China's tiny neighbour Japan had successfully instilled such a spirit in her people.[14] Unfortunately, the Chinese people displayed no such spirit; on the contrary, whereas the Europeans and Japanese emphasized sports and other physical activities to ensure that their children developed into healthy citizen-soldiers, the Chinese had become a weak and enfeebled race, addicted to opium and soft living. How could such a people ever stand up to the fierce martial races?[15]

Liang admitted, "The strong do not become powerful overnight, nor do the weak become feeble in a day."[16] He believed that for much of their history, China's people had enjoyed unity, peace, and stability, which led to the supremacy of *wen* (the civil) over *wu* (the martial). According to Liang, these periods of prolonged peace, far from being a blessing, actually turned the Chinese people into a race of weaklings and left China at the mercy of its more warlike neighbours. Liang also blamed China's weakness on the distortion of Confucianism. He linked the West's martial spirit with Christianity's faith in an afterlife, and argued that even Japanese Buddhism taught its followers to treat death lightly. The Chinese, on the other hand, had been taught to be submissive and yielding, with the predictable result that they were timid and fearful in times of war. This was not Confucius's fault, for he had emphasized courage in the cause of righteousness. The problem was that in the centuries after Confucius's death, his teachings were distorted through a one-sided emphasis on yielding and compassion as opposed to courage and resoluteness. As Liang noted, "They did not copy his firmness, but rather his softness. They did not copy his yang, but rather his yin."[17] Their submissiveness had caused the Chinese people to endure "shame and humiliation that even slaves would not have tolerated, and to endure hardships that even oxen and horses would not have endured. Not once had they fought back with bared arms and fire in their eyes."[18]

Liang feared that in his own time the degeneration of the Chinese people had reached the point where not even the sages of old could transform these "soft, spineless, spiritless people into an indomitable race."[19] Although Liang recognized that soft living had led to the physical degeneration of the Chinese people, he saw China's weakness as primarily psychological in nature and believed a spiritual renaissance based on civic militarism was required to remedy the debilitating effects of the preceding 2,000 years. Liang was all for training troops and building arsenals, but unless these reforms were accompanied by the development of a national martial spirit, it would be akin to covering a sheep with a tiger's skin.[20] If the Chinese people could develop a true military spirit, Liang hoped that his compatriots would be able to "raise their heroic spirits and muster their courage, and stop destroying their self-confidence through overcaution and self-doubt."[21]

Historian Edmund Fung argues that these attacks on the Chinese tradition were overstated for rhetorical purposes:

> The modern scholars of the early twentieth century who urged rapid development of Chinese military power tended to ignore, deliberately perhaps, the military aspects of Chinese history and culture. Rather, they emphasised, even exaggerated, its pacifist features to show how they had prevented China from becoming a strong nation. They found it necessary not only to update the defence system but also to reorientate the psychology of the Chinese people towards military values.[22]

Given his exceptional knowledge of Chinese history, it seems obvious that Liang knowingly distorted the historical record in order to make his point, but he did so in order to goad his countrymen into embracing martial values like courage, self-sacrifice, patriotism, and duty.[23] Not surprisingly, the military was seen as the most effective institution for instilling this martial ethos in the larger society, and reformers echoed their German and Japanese counterparts in arguing that as a "repository of moral resource" for the nation, the military had a responsibility to train both good soldiers *and* good citizens.[24] This enthusiasm for militarism would have a significant impact on many young Chinese, including future military leaders like Cai E and Chiang Kai-shek.

Like many of his generation, Cai E (Cai Songpo, 1882-1916) had started studying for the imperial examinations at an early age, but he abandoned his traditional studies after being caught up in the currents of reform that were sweeping through China in the aftermath of the 1894-95 Sino-Japanese War.[25] In the fall of 1900 Cai enrolled in a military preparatory school in Japan, and in 1902 he was accepted by the prestigious Rikugun Shikan Gakkō officer's academy, where he and classmates Jiang Baili and Zhang Lizhun were collectively known as the "Three Chinese Heroes."[26] When he first arrived in Japan in 1899, Cai could not help but notice the difference in status between soldiers in Japan and China. At the time of his enrolment in the military academy, he wrote an article for Liang Qichao's *New Citizen* journal titled "On Civic Militarism." In the article he vented his anger over the fact that in China his fellow countrymen looked down on those who, like him, had dedicated their lives to protecting the nation:

> There is a saying that good men do not become soldiers, just as good iron is not used for nails. Although these are the words of foolish bumpkins, one hears them everywhere, and elders still recite them as a warning to the younger generation. Alas! Soldiers are the shield and wall of the nation, a sacrifice for the people, and objects of respect, honor, and veneration – there is nothing quite like a soldier! They offer their lives and their deaths; they forsake advantage and desire; they exchange all those things that bring joy to life for bitterness and hardship; and they set aside their individual interests for the benefit of the public good – is there any greater benevolence than this? This despising of such great men – is it not strange?[27]

Cai was clearly disgusted with the anti-military attitudes of his fellow Chinese, although his own decision to pursue a military career was proof that these attitudes were changing. Like Liang, Cai ridiculed his fellow Chinese not only for their lack of martial enthusiasm but also for their feebleness, noting that their poor physiques and bad habits left the nation vulnerable to foreign aggression. Although this passage stops well short of any eugenics-based or Social Darwinist–inspired call for the purging of weak elements in Chinese society, Cai clearly sees China as handicapped by its large population of drug addicts, bookworms, and other undesirables:

> We have 400 million people, but of these, 50 percent are women who are not suited for soldiering. Ten to 20 percent of the people are addicted to opium, and another 10 percent have immersed themselves in studying to the extent that they resemble senile old men. The handicapped, deaf, blind, mute, chronically sick,

> young, and old together constitute another 10 to 20 percent. All told, the so-called fit population amounts to only 10 percent. Of this 10 percent, it is hard to guarantee that they will all be suitable for military service. When looked at this way, even if the great powers abandoned fighting with bullets in favour of boxing, we would still all be killed on the spot![28]

In sharp contrast to his disdain for his fellow Chinese, Cai was clearly impressed with the martial spirit of the Japanese people, and he especially admired how conscription had turned the army into the school of the nation, teaching not only martial virtues but patriotism and citizenship as well. Just before his early death in 1916, Cai published his most important original contribution to Chinese military thought, "A Plan for Military Affairs," which reflected his experience in Japan. The architects of the Meiji Restoration had viewed conscription as an excellent tool for developing a sense of civic duty in the people, and in "A Plan for Military Affairs" Cai saw this strategy as equally applicable to China:

> If one is clear about the principles of conscription, then one knows that in peacetime the army serves as the military school of the nation. Soldiers are the pick of the nation, so their education can influence local customs and affect the spirit of the people. The martial disposition formed during military training is sufficient to improve social mores and behaviour. Indeed, if the citizens are strong and robust, the nation will flourish. Therefore, those who are responsible for educating the troops need to know that making a good soldier is the way to make a good person; the education of soldiers is the way by which citizens are moulded.[29]

The Chinese students who had trained at Japanese military schools had seen firsthand what an efficient conscription system could do, not only for a nation's military power but also for its national spirit. This message was certainly not lost on the young Chiang Kai-shek when he underwent military training in Japan on the eve of the 1911 Revolution.

Following his direct admission into the accelerated program at the Baoding Military Academy in China, Chiang was selected to attend a preparatory school of the Japanese military. He started his three-year course in 1908 at a time when Japanese military education was undergoing an important change. In December of that year, the Japanese army issued a new manual of interior administration that reflected what it perceived to be the lessons of the Russo-Japanese War. Historian Leonard Humphreys notes that as far as the Japanese were concerned, "the overriding lesson of the war appeared to be the decisive role of morale or spirit in combat. Japan's centuries-old samurai tradition had strongly emphasized the importance of the intangible qualities of the human spirit in warfare, and this war served to reestablish their primacy."[30] As part of this new emphasis on the cultivation of spirit, the Japanese army introduced *seishin kyōiku* (spiritual education) as a component of regular training. The object of this training was to teach the conscripts to live according to *bushidō* (the way of the warrior), the idealized normative code of the former Tokugawa samurai class. As one contemporary observer noted:

> As the whole object of *seishin kyōiku* is to train the soldier to regard these standards of living as the ideal for which he must strive, it comes about that the army becomes a form of propaganda centre for such ideas, and that the more men it can train the greater becomes the proportion of the population imbued with these ideas, for, after all, every man who enters the army returns to civil life after the completion of his colour service, and the lessons learned during the period of his military training are bound to affect his whole outlook on life.[31]

The Japanese military used lectures, special ceremonies, and trips to historic sites to teach recruits the "seven duties of a soldier" – loyalty, valour, patriotism, obedience, humility, morality, and honour – with the expectation that soldiers would continue to embrace these virtues on their return to civilian life and help to disseminate them among the civilian population.[32] Chiang Kai-shek was intrigued by the fact that Chinese students were not allowed to attend the lectures on spiritual training given to their Japanese classmates, so he started to look into bushidō on his own. Chiang was of course familiar with the standard Confucian works from his youth, but he first realized the connection between Confucianism and military values while in Japan, and like Liang Qichao and Cai E, he came to realize that bushidō was actually the Chinese *wushidao* and very much a product of China's own traditions.[33] This realization had to be of some comfort to those young Chinese who, like Cai and Chiang, were forced to swallow their national pride in order to learn from the very people who had humiliated China in 1894-95.

Like Cai E before him, Chiang Kai-shek did not let national chauvinism blind him to Japan's example, and by 1911 he was part of the growing chorus of support for what Edmund Fung calls "positive, national militarism," where "the dominant desire was to strengthen the national polity through a military and psychological reorientation of the entire population as well as through an updating of the defence system. To be militaristic was to be modern."[34] For many Chinese, Japan's rapid emergence as a great power provided both the incentive and the model for China's own modernization, and civic militarism was seen as a major part of that model. At the very least, a modern military could protect China from predatory powers, but the advocates of militarism hoped that it would do much more. As a "repository of moral resource," the military would take the lead in transforming Chinese society from a collection of enervated individuals into a nation of heroic citizens. However, much to the frustration of those who shared these views, domestic events in the aftermath of the 1911 Revolution rapidly put an end to popular faith in the soldier as the role model for the citizen.

Grey Rats and Grey Wolves – the Warlord Era

The Qing New Armies had been a breeding ground for both revolution and warlordism, with the one eventually creating the opportunity for the other. The decisive role played by military force in the 1911 Revolution had the unintended but predictable effect of pushing soldiers to the forefront of national politics. Once in control, soldiers such as Yuan Shikai proved unwilling to surrender the powers handed them by chance or seized through their own machinations, and within a few years the new Republic of China was torn apart by rival military cliques. The recently revived prestige of the military now took a distinct turn for the worse. Whereas in the period immediately preceding the Revolution a broad cross-section of Chinese society had been actively advocating militarism as the solution to China's weakness, the self-serving manoeuvres of Yuan and his successors eventually convinced many that far from being a cure for China's ills, the soldiers were themselves the source of most, if not all, of the current troubles.

The warlord era represented a nadir in Chinese civil-military relations. The biggest threat to the Chinese people in the decade between 1916 and 1926 came not from the forces of imperialism but from their own soldiers. In her book *Warlord Soldiers,* Diana Lary paints a grim picture of the terrible toll exacted by warlordism:

> The violence was pervasive. On the battlefields, soldiers fought each other constantly. Leaving aside the innumerable small-scale clashes in which soldiers were involved, there was an average of eight full-scale wars per annum between 1912 and 1930. Only two years, 1914 and 1915, were free of conflict. In the worst single year, 1928, there were sixteen separate wars. Each year an average of seven provinces was hit by war. These wars caused major turbulence and disruption on their own, but the violence did not end there. Men with guns were just as likely to use them against civilians as they were against other soldiers. Chinese civilians were subjected to a capricious, arbitrary, chronic terrorism, at the hands of the "defenders of the nation."[35]

When contemplating the sorry state of the Qing military in the 1850s, Zeng Guofan had once been moved to lament that "if Yue Fei came back to life, he could probably train these soldiers to fight in half a year, but Confucius himself would need more than three years to change their evil habits."[36] Many Chinese would have agreed with Zeng when it came to the soldiers who victimized them during the warlord era.

Arthur Waldron has shown that the general repugnance generated by warlord depredations eroded public support for militarism.[37] Politics may have been militarized in the sense that armed strength became the determining factor in political struggles, but the earlier enthusiasm for the martial spirit disappeared as soldiering increasingly became associated with warlord-army excesses. In his study of warlord atrocities, Edward McCord quotes a 1919 account from Hunan that succinctly sums up popular disgust with soldiers during the warlord era:

> Since the beginning of the war in Hunan, the Hunan people have suffered from the violence of soldiers. How can one bear to speak of this? ... A nation establishes an army to protect its people. Today, because of the army, the people have no way to protect themselves. Therefore the original purpose in establishing an army has indeed been completely lost.[38]

Warlord behaviour effectively put an end to what Hans van de Ven calls a "naive faith in the military as a positive institution."[39] Moreover, he notes that the damage was irreversible: "One of the lasting consequences of warlord warfare was that the innocent militarism of the reformers and revolutionaries of the late Qing and early Republic was rejected. Militarist values remained important, but a purely militarist solution to China's problems became impossible."[40] Chiang Kai-shek, however, refused to concede that the military must give up its leading role in China's struggle to modernize. For Chiang, the problem was not the military per se but the warlords' appropriation of public military power for personal profit. They privatized what should have been a national resource and in the process replaced the individual soldier's ethic of service with the mercenary's ethic of self-service. It was therefore essential to defeat the warlords, for once they were out of the way and the soldiers returned to their proper role as protectors of the nation, Chiang was confident popular faith in the military would be restored. Thus for Chiang, the pressing issue was how to eliminate the men who were ruining the reputation of the military and destroying the nation they had sworn to serve. He shared this goal with the man who would eventually pluck him from obscurity and set him on the road to power, Sun Yat-sen.

Sun Yat-sen had experienced his own problems with the warlords, having been betrayed repeatedly by his military allies as he struggled to put the Revolution back on track in the decade after 1911. Sun recognized early on that a man armed only with principles would not last long in Republican politics, but circumstances never presented him with the time, secure base, or financial resources necessary to create an army of his own.[41] Instead, Sun was forced to wander China as a sort of political Blanche DuBois, dependent on the kindness of strangers for his military needs. With no other viable options, he sought to "borrow [friendly] warlords to control [hostile] warlords" *(jie junfa zhi junfa),* but this was a policy fraught with risk.[42] The inconstancy of his military backers, who were allies of convenience rather than ideological brethren, frequently played havoc with Sun's plans, forcing him to flee for his life on more than one occasion. Despite these frequent betrayals, Sun persisted in his attempts to win over warlords and their troops through appeals to what can only be described as their better nature. As part of these efforts, he made a series of speeches in 1921 and 1922 to the nominally revolutionary armies from Yunnan, Guangxi, and Guangdong aimed at fostering a deeper commitment to his revolution on the basis of principle rather than profit.[43] These speeches are interesting not only for what they tell us about Sun's political beliefs but also for what they reveal about the role and characteristics of the revolutionary soldier as envisioned by Sun. In particular, the speech titled "The Spiritual Education of Soldiers," delivered in Guilin in early 1922, clearly demonstrates that Sun saw the revolutionary soldier as a modern-day version of the Confucian "superior man," or *junzi.* Just as the Confucian superior man differed from the "petty man" *(xiao ren)* in adhering to a higher standard of conduct, Sun's revolutionary soldier would be distinguished from ordinary soldiers and citizens by his commitment to a code of ethics that placed nation before self.[44]

Sun's moral exhortations fell on deaf ears at the time. Only a few months after the Guilin speech, Chen Jiongming's revolt would highlight the dangers of relying on warlord allies, and Sun was finally forced to acknowledge that he would have to build his own revolutionary army from scratch. Yet the message of his speech was not lost on everyone. The image of the revolutionary soldier-as-junzi described by Sun in "The Spiritual Education of Soldiers" corresponded well with the self-image of military figures like Chiang Kai-shek, men who saw themselves as part of a vanguard spearheading the Chinese struggle to create a modern nation. Clearly, Sun hoped his revolutionary soldiers would set an ethical standard for all Chinese to emulate, and in at least this respect his views corresponded with Chiang's own belief that the soldier ought to be the embodiment of the nation's martial ethos and civic spirit. It was this shared vision that led Sun to appoint Chiang as commandant of the new Guomindang military academy to be opened at Whampoa in 1924.

Whampoa and the Missionaries of Militarism

With the founding of the Whampoa Military Academy in the spring of 1924, Chiang Kai-shek finally had the opportunity to put into practice some of the ideas he had been exposed to in Japan. However, the decline in the quality of the military that resulted from China's descent into warlordism meant that before the public would accept the soldier as moral exemplar for the citizen, something would have to be done about the sorry state of the military itself. For Chiang and the other officers who gathered at Whampoa, the first step was obvious: they had to restore traditional military values within the ranks of the revolutionary forces gathered at Guangzhou. Richard Gabriel, although writing about a different army in a different time, sums up this task well. In response to the crisis of confidence that plagued the United States Army in the post-Vietnam period, Gabriel called for a renewed emphasis on traditional military ethics:

> If we are to stop the erosion of our ideals and rebuild the profession, if we are to steel the psyche of the soldier against the horrors of battle, if we are to give meaning to the sacrifice of those who have gone before, and if we are to expect those now in service to follow their example even unto death, we must reconstitute the brotherhood of arms along lines of ethics. Without a code of ethics, the task of the soldier degenerates into senseless violence.[45]

That last line essentially echoes the conclusions drawn by Sun and Chiang with respect to the sorry state of China's military forces in the early 1920s.

From day one, it was intended that the handful of graduates from Whampoa would be distributed throughout the Guomindang's allied armies in order to raise professional standards and spread the message of militant nationalism. In his speeches to the cadets at Whampoa, Chiang Kai-shek frequently reminded them of their intended role as models for both the army and the nation:

> After each of you has been posted to a unit for your practicum, we want you to guide and instruct everyone. At all times and in every action, you must act as a model for others. When you were students, your superiors instructed you, but now it will soon be time for you to instruct others. If one is capable of presenting others with a good model, they will be transformed for the better.[46]

The expectation that a few hundred military-college graduates could play a missionary role within the larger army was not unique to China. Few armies draw their officers exclusively from military academies, but as military historian Louis Sorley notes, there is a very real expectation that those who do graduate from institutions like West Point and the Royal Military College will go on to "set standards for the entire officer corps in terms of dedication and ethical standards."[47] Modern armies have long recognized what Gabriel calls the "missionary approach":

> The missionary approach assumes that somehow academy graduates will be instructed in codes of honor and ethics that are different from and far above those found in the profession at large. These academy graduates will then go forth and act as missionaries; by their own examples and honor, they will engender within the profession a sense of ethical behavior that will lift the rest of the profession to these high standards.[48]

Gabriel's words accurately describe Chiang's plans for the Whampoa cadets: technical proficiency would not be overlooked, but the missionary role had to be emphasized if the handful of cadets was to have any impact on the conduct of both the larger army assembled at Guangzhou and the people of China as a whole.

This belief in the power of "good men" to transform others has a long history in China. Confucian superior men, or junzi, were in fact expected to act like a sort of moral vanguard dedicated to instructing those who had yet to find the Way (or Tao).[49] Nor was it solely a matter of lecturing those who were less enlightened on the error of their ways – the personal conduct of the superior man itself constituted a form of propaganda by deed that could inspire others to reform. It was therefore assumed that just as heaven had used Confucius as a bell to arouse the masses, the Whampoa graduates would use the power of positive example to transform the ragtag armies of the Revolution into an unstoppable force. There is no reason to believe that military men like Chiang Kai-shek saw anything odd or old-fashioned about the idea of a small vanguard leading and transforming others by the power of example. Indeed, many of those who had attended Japanese military schools in the late Qing and early Republic had done so in the belief that on their return to China they would perform precisely that role.

In 1951, while reminiscing about the founding of the academy, Chiang commented on his early ambition to train such a crack force:

> Prior to the founding of Whampoa, I had one desire – I hoped that at some point in my life I would be able to open a military school and train dedicated youths according to my own ideals in order to complete the task of building the army

> and the nation. Moreover, at the time, I believed that if I could realize my desire, China's military education would definitely be successful and that *the officers produced by this education system would not only be able to complete the Northern Expedition and unite China but would also establish a modern army and a modern nation.*[50] (Emphasis added)

From the above quotation it is clear that Chiang believed the military could act as a vanguard institution in the struggle to establish a modern nation and that the officers he trained could play the role of missionaries of militant nationalism not only within the military but in society as well. Of course, to be effective in their missionary role, the cadets would have to develop both a strong martial ethos and esprit de corps. If they did not develop esprit de corps and the sense of common purpose that goes with it, they would in all likelihood be corrupted and assimilated by the very people they hoped to reform.[51] Indeed, Sun's former military adviser Zhu Zhixin (1885-1920) had already warned the Guomindang leader about the corrupting influence of life in a warlord army:

> Before researching the psychology of soldiers, we must first acknowledge that this psychology is probably entirely a product of the soldiers' lifestyle. Nowadays, those who serve as soldiers come from all walks of life: students, businessmen, workers, farmers, robbers, swindlers, smugglers – they are all gathered together in the army. Before joining up, their ideals and habits vary widely, but once in the barracks, they gradually and unconsciously develop the same psychology. After serving for a few years and obtaining the status of "old soldiers," they all appear to have been printed from the same press, and one cannot find two who are not alike in temperament. Unless we admit that their psychology has been shaped by their lifestyle, there is no way to explain this.[52]

Chiang emphasized spiritual training at Whampoa precisely in order to provide the cadets with the moral armour they needed to withstand the temptations of such a corrupting environment.

The first class of cadets reported to Whampoa in early May 1924 to undergo basic military training prior to commencing their formal program in June. The arriving cadets were left in no doubt as to the high ethical standards expected of them as revolutionary soldiers. As they disembarked on the island, they were confronted by exhortatory scrolls bearing the following grim messages: "The blood of the martyrs, the flowers of our ideology" and "Loyal unto death."[53] The front gate of the school itself was emblazoned with the warning: "Those looking to become officials and get rich please go elsewhere. Those who only care about life and fear death cannot enter this gate."[54] The school buildings were covered with similar messages: "Carry on the past and open a way for the future," "Sacrifice and struggle," "Do what is right," "Prepare for a fight to the death," "Die for a just cause," "Await the dawn with weapon in hand," "Steel yourself for the struggle to come," "Greatness comes from strength of character," and "Start training at the cock's crow."[55]

The main lecture hall and the commandant's office were also festooned with banners containing messages personally selected by Sun and Chiang, including the following: "Nourish the all-encompassing air of righteousness and model yourselves after the great men of the past and present," "Be at ease on the battlefield and abide in benevolence and righteousness," "In safety and in peril we will depend on each other, together we will taste bitterness and sweetness," and "When the Great Way prevails, all under heaven belongs to the people."[56] Even the mess hall was not exempt, and while the cadets ate their meals they were reminded of who provided their food and why: "[This food is the] flesh and blood of the people," so "love the nation and the people."[57] Veterans of that first class recalled how these banners conjured up images of determination and heroic sacrifice, which is of course precisely what they were intended to do.[58] What is striking is that so few of these banners referred to revolution or politics; instead, most appealed to the Chinese heroic tradition with its emphasis on courage and resolve in the face of hardship and defeat. Confronted with these slogans, the cadets would have seen themselves as the inheritors of that heroic tradition, and although the words may have presaged the hard work and sacrifice that lay ahead, they also struck a chord with the cadets' own pre-existing ideas about war and heroism.

Chiang Kai-shek had his first opportunity to speak to the corps of cadets shortly after their arrival at Whampoa. His speech did not pull any punches – in his first sentence, he proudly proclaimed that from this day forward the cadets and their instructors would live and die together.[59] He went on to warn them that their task was a difficult one, for China was torn by internecine fighting, the people were dispirited, and the Guomindang was depending on the Whampoa cadets to rescue the nation:

> You see how difficult and monumental our task is. We therefore have no choice but to struggle with all of our might ... In future, we must view the cultivation of our spirit and the improvement of our knowledge like the refining of iron and steel – they must be refined in order to make you unstoppable heroes of steel. If a man wants to accomplish great deeds, he can succeed only by passing through many hardships.[60]

Chiang assumed that all students embraced the ethic of self-interest, or the pursuit of personal gain as the highest good. Such an ethic clearly clashed with the selfless service required of the soldier. As General John Hackett once observed, the military profession is unique in obliging its members to operate under a "clause of unlimited liability."[61] In his pioneering work on military ethics, Gabriel argues that it is this unlimited obligation that separates the soldier from the civilian:

> Given the life and health risks that soldiers are likely to face, the requirement that one may be obliged to observe obligations even unto death truly constitutes a special and unique sense of ethics, obligation, and responsibility ... What makes the military sense of ethics different from the ethics of the society at large is precisely this requirement of service instead of self-interest.[62]

The first step in developing this ethic of service was to redefine what sociologist Sidney Axinn calls the "moral object," or the person/object/idea external to the actor for which he or she is willing to sacrifice.[63] In other words, what exactly were the cadets expected to die for? To answer this question, Chiang Kai-shek had the cadets study Sun's "The Spiritual Education of Soldiers."

In that speech, Sun Yat-sen had set out to define the proper moral object for the revolutionary soldier. For both Sun and Chiang, the Confucian concept of *ren* (benevolence, humaneness, altruism, selflessness) was the key to understanding what was expected of the revolutionary soldier. Sun equated the Confucian concept of ren with his own concept of universal love, or fraternity *(bo ai),* but the good of humanity as a moral object was simply too abstract to provide a realistic motive for individual sacrifice, at least for those untouched by religious zeal.[64] Sun therefore set the nation up as the moral object for the revolutionary soldier: "The purpose of a soldier's benevolence is to rescue the nation. Therefore, ever since there have been soldiers, there has never been one who did not give his all for the nation."[65] But in reiterating the old adage *dulce et decorum est pro patria mori* (how sweet and fitting it is to die for one's country), Sun made it quite clear that in his republic the true locus of military loyalty had to be the people/nation rather than the ruler:

> But there is a difference between the soldiers of an autocratic state and those of a republic. In an autocracy, the state is the personal possession of the monarch, and the ruler is in fact synonymous with the state. Therefore, soldiers in an autocratic state can be said to be loyal to one person or one ruling family, and they will give their all for the ruler rather than sacrifice for the people. In a republic,

> the state is subordinate to the people as a group, so those who sacrifice for the people will at the same time sacrifice for the state.[66]

Sun was well aware of the dangers inherent in setting up an individual as the locus of a soldier's loyalty. After all, the warlord forces that plagued China were classic examples of personal armies, in which soldiers were loyal to whoever paid them. For Sun, the difference between the revolutionary soldier and the warlord soldier was as clear as night and day, with the former being a selfless servant of the nation, whereas the latter was little better than a bandit. Sun went on to note that the problem with China was that at the present time state power had been seized by warlords who knew nothing about republicanism or enriching the nation, and their unwillingness to take responsibility for defending the nation opened the door to foreign interference. If the benevolence of a soldier was equated with patriotism, then love of nation and the people ought to compel the true soldier to rescue them from their present plight by joining the revolutionary struggle against the warlords.

Chiang's own speeches at Whampoa focused on the same themes. He started by pointing out that there was more to life than the pursuit of personal comfort and that those who were preoccupied with such things were little better than beasts. If the students and staff at Whampoa were interested only in fine food and warm clothes, they were definitely in the wrong place. Like Sun, Chiang argued that the true meaning of life was to be found in sacrifice for the greater good:

> You have to understand that looking out for ourselves is not the only purpose of our lives. Our goal in life is to improve the lives of all men ... And what is the meaning of life? Before I explain this to you, there is one important point I must make: As soldiers, we know only the word "death," and the goal of our lives as soldiers is also "death." Aside from death, there is only cowardice. If one fears death and prefers to live in disgrace, then not only can one not be a soldier but one cannot even be considered a man. The ancients said, "If to live I must turn my back on righteousness, then I prefer death to living." These words were spoken with the common people in mind, and if they are expected to live up to this standard, what about us? ... If our deaths are as substantial as Mount Tai, then we will have died a proper death. If we die for our principles, or in rescuing the nation or the party, how can we begrudge our deaths?[67]

Like Sun Yat-sen before him, Chiang sought to shift the moral object away from the individual by positing the greater good as the only object worthy of sacrifice.

In "The Spiritual Education of Soldiers" Sun even went so far as to argue that those who "died a proper death" *(si de qi suo)* by sacrificing themselves for the greater good would achieve a sort of immortality. Perhaps carried away by his own enthusiasm, Sun attempted to convince his audience that the task at hand was so exceptional that those who were unable to participate would regret it for the rest of their days, whereas the names of those who died would live forever:

> We live in today's new world, a revolutionary world, so one could say that this is the perfect time to carry out great deeds and establish our names. Confucius extolled the revolutionary changes wrought by Tang and Wu, but these were only the revolutions of kings and heroes. However, our revolution is a people's revolution, a revolution for the ordinary people, and thus a unique and unprecedented sacred undertaking! Those who came before us were too early, whereas those who come after us will regret that they arrived too late, and they will envy us. Therefore, we who live at this moment – we were born for the revolution, and we should die for the revolution. There is no time like the present to die a noble death![68]

We must not assume that the cadets regarded such admonitions with skepticism, for Chinese history is full of military heroes who achieved a form of immortality in song and story. Two such heroes – Guan Yu and Yue Fei – were actually enthroned as gods in the pantheon of Chinese deities, despite having fought and died for lost causes. Nor were modern examples lacking: Sun and Chiang both made frequent references to the martyrs who had fallen before, during, and after the 1911 Revolution, and the Whampoa slogan "blood of the martyrs, flowers of our ideology" was a constant reminder of those who had made the ultimate sacrifice.

Chiang argued that for soldiers, sacrifice on behalf of the nation was not only the right ethical choice but also a sacred duty. Chiang emphasized that although the people were oppressed by the warlords and the imperialists, and were struggling to stay alive themselves, they gave what they could to support their champions, so the cadets had a moral duty to repay this trust, with their lives if necessary. On the occasion of their first pay parade, Chiang reminded the cadets where their food and equipment came from and why:

> Whether we are in the army or at school, we consume and have no way of producing. Soldiers are people who partake of the social wealth without contributing anything, and thus one might say they are the most unreasonable creatures in the world. But if you look at our present national situation, if it were not for us, the nation would be helpless. Why? Look at the warlords, who talk only of power and

> ignore the public good while exploiting the people, who have robbed the people of their rights and plunged them into peril and poverty – if the Revolutionary Party had not stepped forward in the name of justice and resisted these warlords, would these traitors not have committed still more evil? Therefore, we revolutionary soldiers must bear the great responsibility for reforming society, protecting the rights of the people, liberating them, and supporting their livelihood. This way, most people will be willing to use the money they earn with their own sweat and blood to support the Revolutionary Army.[69]

The cadets' question-and-answer drill served to reinforce these ideas on a daily basis:

Q: *Do we see the suffering of the people?*
A: *We see it.*
Q: *Where do our food, clothing, and shelter come from?*
A: *The people.*
Q: *Why do we want a revolution?*
A: *To rescue the nation and the people.*

Q: *How can we implement the Three Principles of the People?*
A: *We must do away with the oppressors and, by sacrificing ourselves, restore equality and prosperity to all of the people.*
Q: *Are we willing to shoulder the responsibility for this great task?*
A: *We will do our best to shoulder it.*

Q: *What is our duty in rescuing and protecting the people?*
A: *We must serve them loyally as best we can until death.*

Q: *How do we know when we have fulfilled our duty?*
A: *Unless we are dead, our duty is never fulfilled.*[70]

Like Sun, Chiang deliberately used epic language in describing the revolutionary task in order to link it with the great undertakings of other periods in Chinese history. In speech after speech, Chiang emphasized how special the cadets were:

> What makes humans different from oxen and horses is our nature and our sense of righteousness, and what makes us revolutionaries different from ordinary people is our ability and our will to embrace our principles and brave hardship and insults in order to expel the violent and bring peace to the good, to restrain the strong and assist the weak, to do what others cannot do, to endure what others cannot endure, to sacrifice our individual prosperity and happiness in order to

> bring prosperity and happiness to others, and to sacrifice our individual freedom in order to seek freedom for all – this is what is noble in humanity, and this is what makes us more noble than other men.[71]

Although it is not evident in the English translation, many of the phrases in the original Chinese text are popularly associated with heroic tasks and the "knight-errant" *(youxia)* spirit. Having entered Whampoa with certain preconceived ideas about the nature of heroism and courage, the cadets would have been receptive to such language. Aside from the continued popularity of older traditional novels like *All Men Are Brothers, The Romance of the Three Kingdoms, Three Heroes and Five Gallants, Seven Swordsmen and Thirteen Gallants,* and the knights-errant chapters in the *Historical Records,* the last decades of the Qing and the first years of the Republic witnessed the rapid growth of newspapers and magazines, many of which carried serialized tales about knights-errant. These stories, old and new alike, exerted a powerful influence on their youthful readership, moulding their conceptions of heroism and prompting them to emulate the ideals and actions of their heroes.[72] The cadets would not have missed the meaning behind Chiang's language and would have seen themselves as following in the footsteps of real and fictional Chinese heroes.

Chiang also promoted the singing of certain songs that were rich with heroic imagery designed to arouse the cadets' patriotism and their sense of duty. Without doubt, the songs with the most symbolic value were the two commonly attributed to the great Song Dynasty patriots Yue Fei and Wen Tianxiang. First classman Deng Wenyi recalled how important these two figures were as symbols for the students: "To provide the Whampoa students with concrete examples in order to teach them how to nourish their sense of righteousness and model themselves after the great men of the past, Commandant Chiang specially selected the two great martyrs Yue Fei and Wen Tianxiang as models of patriotic sacrifice."[73]

Yue Fei was an obvious choice as an example for the cadets. Not only was he a famous martial hero, but he was also a patriotic symbol of China's struggle against foreign invaders. His life story was known to every child, especially the part where his mother sought to give him a permanent reminder of his duty by tattooing his back with the stirring phrase "To serve the nation with absolute loyalty." He was also reputed to have made another famous comment that seemed especially appropriate to warlord China. Asked when the empire would again enjoy peace, Yue Fei allegedly replied, "When the civil officials do not love money and when the military officials are not afraid to die, then all under heaven will be at peace."[74] *Bu pa si* (do not fear death) became the motto of the revolutionary forces, and judging from the cadets' performance on the battlefield, they must have taken Yue Fei's exhortation to heart.

In addition to Yue Fei's *Man Jiang Hong (The River Runs Red),* a song replete with bloody images and revanchist passion, Chiang also promoted the use of Wen Tianxiang's *Zheng Qi Ge (Song of Righteousness).* Wen Tianxiang was the epitome of the soldier-scholar, having been both a high official and a battlefield commander. Captured by the Mongols, he refused to work for his captors, preferring death to a life of shame. When he was finally executed for his stubborn refusal to collaborate, a paper was allegedly found in his pocket containing the following famous lines: "Confucius spoke of dying for a righteous cause; Mencius spoke of doing what was right. Only by persevering in what is right can benevolence be attained. Study the works of the sages and worthies to learn how to conduct yourself, and in future you will probably have a clear conscience."[75] Wen Tianxiang's *Zheng Qi Ge* is an ode to the righteous spirit of China's ancient heroes. The song proclaims that the spirits of past heroes provide a reserve of righteous energy that men of exemplary moral integrity can tap into during times of crisis. These heroes are immortalized in the historical records, and the song lists the deeds of famous figures like Zhang Liang and Zhuge Liang. The lyrics state that through their selfless service and loyalty, these heroes actually became part of the all-pervading spirit of righteousness after death and that their virtue continued to shine "as bright as the sun and the moon." The song is a moving testament to China's heroes and the nobility of sacrifice, and like Yue Fei's *Man Jiang Hong,* Wen Tianxiang's *Zheng Qi Ge* served to remind the cadets that they were the trustees of a long tradition. The illustrious heroes of the past were held up as examples to be emulated, and given the praise heaped on these past champions, how could the cadets doubt that they in turn would be similarly honoured if only they could rise to the challenge of their own time?

Having defined the revolutionary soldier's moral object and explained why it was worthy of individual sacrifice, Chiang now turned his attention to character building. He knew that in order to abandon the civilian ethic of self-interest in favour of a martial ethic based on sacrifice and duty, the cadets would have to search out and discard all of the bad habits and corrupt values they had brought with them from their outside life. Chiang saw contemporary Chinese society as corrupt and decadent, and although the cadets were presumably well motivated, he believed that they carried with them the taint of the outside world. All of the norms and values associated with that world would have to be abandoned as the first step in creating the model soldier. Chiang demanded role-stripping, or since it was supposed to be voluntary, role-surrender – the replacement of the cadets' original value systems with a new one tailor-made for their role as revolutionary soldiers and moral exemplars:

> Therefore, I hope that after entering the academy today each one of you will sweep away all of the old habits, old thinking, and old behaviour and start anew to create a proper person, a person who can shoulder the responsibility for our great enterprise. If a person truly understands what it means to be a person and the purpose of one's life, then afterward, even if one is caught in the midst of a furious battle, one will feel no fear. No matter whether the obstacles are as vast as the Pacific Ocean or as high as the Himalayas, one will be able to surmount them without the slightest misgiving. Even in a time of great tumult, we will forge ahead with our righteous task and deliver the people from their calamity. If our will is truly firm, our task can be accomplished and our ideals realized.[76]

To assist the cadets in this process of self-cultivation, Chiang made use of traditional Chinese philosophy. In October 1924 he issued his own annotated version of Cai E's *Record of Zeng Guofan's and Hu Linyi's Writings on Military Leadership* for the cadets to study. Chiang had been struck by the similarities between his own problems and those faced by the famous nineteenth-century scholar-soldiers Zeng Guofan and Hu Linyi, and he realized just how applicable their experience was to his situation.[77] Tactics and strategy were of course subject to changes in technology, but Chiang believed the techniques for leadership and personal cultivation promoted by Zeng and by Hu were timeless. In particular, their emphasis on the need for leaders to manifest exemplary character struck a chord with Chiang's own thoughts.

Like Hu and Zeng, Chiang emphasized personal cultivation and self-discipline. In his first address he warned the students that as cadets at a military school run by the Guomindang, they would be required to strictly observe not only the party rules but the school rules as well. The combination of party and military rules meant that the cadets would be subjected to stricter discipline than the ordinary civilian party members. In comments that echoed the ancient Chinese strategists' approach to rules and punishment, Chiang noted that strictness was essential to military life.[78] However, discipline had to be internalized to be effective, so the cadets were called on to monitor themselves at all times. As Chiang repeatedly stressed, the way that the cadets conducted themselves as they carried out even the most insignificant and routine of their duties was a reflection of the degree to which they had embraced self-discipline. The cadets were to be "quiet, solemn, neat and tidy" and to maintain a soldierly bearing – "head up, shoulders back, be quick and agile." Chiang also noted that it was the soldier's lot in life to endure "pain, cold, heat, and hunger" and that they must be "diligent, hardworking, and live frugally and simply."[79] Clearly, Chiang believed that soldiers must demonstrate their dedication to a higher purpose and their willingness to die by living a life devoid of all but the most basic necessities. Just as the superior man served as an exemplar for the common man, the austere morality of the revolutionary soldier was expected to set the standard for all citizens. In his classic work on the role of the military in developing nations, Morris Janowitz observes that such puritanism is not unusual in soldiers:

> A second and widespread element [in the military mindset] is a strong puritanical outlook and an emphasis on anti-corruption and anti-decadence. This again seems to be a rather universal characteristic of the military profession and reflects, to some degree, the underlying motives of those who select this career. The desire to be strong and unyielding is reinforced by the rigour and routines of daily existence. But the military demands these qualities not only for itself but for society as a whole, and it sets itself up as a standard-bearer of hard work and unflinching dedication.[80]

Chiang likely developed his faith in the character-building benefits of hardship while undergoing military training in Japan. The Imperial Japanese army was famous for both its discipline and its frugality in pay, rations, and quarters, so it is possible that Chiang came to associate these with the development of soldierly qualities. However, it is interesting to note that this emphasis on a Spartan existence echoed Zeng Guofan's own belief in frugality and simplicity as essential elements of the self-control so esteemed in Confucian circles. Zeng firmly believed that an ordered exterior was a reflection of a disciplined mind, and Chiang frequently made the same point in his speeches.

Although Chiang did not outline a comprehensive set of military ethics for the cadets when the academy was founded, in the course of his forty-nine speeches during the first year, he gradually put together the core elements of what would become a code. By the time of the Second Eastern Expedition against Chen Jiongming in late 1925, the code had taken written form as a set of admonitions for the revolutionary soldiers.[81] The very first section put the soldiers on notice that service to the revolution/nation might very well require them to sacrifice their lives: "The soldier's ultimate goal is death. This is what the ancients meant when they said, 'The hero *[hao han]* dies on the battlefield,' and this is what Confucius meant when he said, 'Sacrifice oneself for a just cause *[sha shen cheng ren]*.'"[82]

The norms and values outlined in this code are drawn from the Chinese tradition as embodied in the works of the Qing commanders Zeng Guofan and

Hu Linyi and of the Ming Dynasty general Qi Jiguang. This code of ethics also stressed that under no circumstances could the soldiers harm the people: "Protect the people (do not conscript labour, do not steal their goods, do not extort supplies, do not occupy their homes) – this is how we put our Three Principles into practice. If we harm the people, then we are an army of bandits that betrays our principles and opposes the revolution."[83]

Chiang himself repeatedly reminded his cadets that ultimately they had to rely on their ethical conduct to persuade the people that they were different from the bandits and warlord troops who preyed on them. This exhortation echoed Zeng Guofan's own admonitions to his anti-Taiping forces in his training song *Ai Min Ge (Cherish the People).* As Chiang once noted, "the main points of *Ai Min Ge* are these six: 'bandits harm the people, and only we can save them'; 'an army that loves the people will be welcomed everywhere, but an army that disturbs the people will be hated everywhere'; and 'soldiers and the people are members of the same family, so never take advantage of them.'"[84]

In sum, the code of ethics prepared for the Eastern Expedition explicitly laid out what was required of the soldiers, such as fearlessness in the face of death, incorruptibility, obedience, discipline, dedication to protecting the weak, honour, duty, tenacity, and esprit de corps. Chiang believed that if cadets could adhere to this code, they would be able to shoulder the responsibility for rescuing the nation and the people. The school anthem used during this period reiterated Chiang's message that the cadets were a select band held together by a shared higher calling and code of ethics and that the very future of China depended on their efforts:

> All we many students, united in our efforts.
> The Three Principles of the People are our model.
> Revolutionary heroes are the people's vanguard.
> We must strive to continue the martyrs' success.
> Schoolmates and comrades in arms, students and teachers,
> From beginning to end, through life and death,
> None will forget today's school.
> Discipline is sacred and more precious than our lives.
> Obedience and compliance are inherent qualities of the revolutionary soldier.
> Making blossoms of our blood, the school has become our home.
> Enduring countless hardships, we strive to build China.[85]

Given the sacrifices made by the cadets and the honours they won on the Eastern Expedition, it would appear that Chiang's faith in the power of spiritual training was not misplaced.

Conclusion

As Chiang Kai-shek noted, the Whampoa cadets were relatively well educated and could easily have found good civilian jobs, and he repeatedly warned them that if they were motivated by nothing more than concern for their own material well-being, they were free to go elsewhere. He could not have been any blunter about what lay ahead for those who stayed when he stated that "the goal of a soldier is to die!" The tribulations of school life and campaigning quickly weeded out those who were not willing to accept the demands of the ethic of service; for those who survived, however, shared hardships promoted the development of a strong collective identity based on the core values of sacrifice, duty, and unity. If one were to look back on Whampoa not through the lens of the Nationalists' ultimate defeat in 1949 but from the perspective of 1928, it would be difficult not to credit Chiang and the Whampoa staff with achieving something of a miracle, albeit a limited one. From a revolutionary base that barely extended beyond the city limits of Guangzhou in 1924, the Revolutionary Army had by 1928 brought much of China under Guomindang control, and the Whampoa cadets played a prominent role in this campaign. It has long been accepted wisdom that the Revolutionary Army's victories were facilitated by the advance work done among the peasants and workers by political organizers associated with the Left Guomindang and the Communist Party, but Donald Jordan makes a strong case for giving the Whampoa cadets much of the credit. It was their exemplary conduct that distinguished the Revolutionary Army from its warlord enemies, thereby earning the support of the people and effectively rehabilitating the military in the eyes of a skeptical public.[86]

Despite his success in defeating the northern warlords, serious barriers remained in the way of Chiang's plan to rebuild China on the basis of a strong and modern military. His faith in "positive, national militarism" as the solution to China's ills remained unshaken, but circumstances still prevented him from realizing his vision. The restored prestige of the military as a result of the Northern Expedition confirmed the effectiveness of his emphasis on spiritual training, but the campaign itself seriously depleted the number of Whampoa graduates while simultaneously swelling the ranks of the Revolutionary Army with unrepentant warlord soldiers. In a very real sense, the Revolutionary Army fell victim to its own success, as the surviving Whampoa graduates found themselves badly outnumbered by soldiers who did not subscribe to their martial ethos or the ethic of service. Thus, having finally restored a semblance of unity to China, Chiang immediately found himself confronted with the need to reunify his army. In 1934 Whampoa alumnus Liu Yongyao recalled that the immediate aftermath of the Northern Expedition was a dangerous period for the revolutionary forces:

> In the midst of all the rapid developments, the revolution unexpectedly encountered great danger. We had destroyed our visible enemies, but many more invisible ones appeared within the revolutionary camp itself. We overthrew the old warlords but produced untold numbers of new ones in their place. We also overthrew the old bureaucrats but produced untold numbers of new, even more low-grade, and greedy ones in the process. The emergence of these new warlords and new bureaucrats wrecked our revolutionary enterprise, corrupted our revolutionary spirit, and pushed the Chinese people off the path to a new life and back onto the road to destruction.[87]

The split with the Communists in 1927 also dealt a serious blow to Chiang's plans for the Whampoa cadets. Chiang had tried very hard to suppress the growing political factionalism within the academy as early as 1926 when he ordered an end to unofficial student groups, but this was at best a stopgap measure.[88] When he turned on the Communists in early 1927, many of the graduates serving in the Revolutionary Army sided with his enemies, leaving Whampoa alumni on both sides of the ideological divide. It seems that neither Sun nor Chiang anticipated that Sun's Three Principles of the People would have to compete with another ideology for the loyalty of the cadets and that they therefore overlooked the possibility that Communist soldiers could make competing and perhaps equally valid claims to be "serving the people and the nation." Although it is difficult to assess the influence of Whampoa alumni within the Communist military, it is clear that both the Nationalist and Communist militaries bear the imprint of their common origin as consciously constructed alternatives to the corrupt and predatory warlord forces. In the end, it would be the Chinese people themselves who would decide which army best served the people, but in the twenty-year struggle leading up to 1949, both sides hurled accusations of warlord-like behaviour at the other while simultaneously claiming the ethical high-ground for themselves. Even today, it is no coincidence that the militaries on both sides of the Taiwan Strait continue to promote strict ethical codes in a manner that seems overstated, even exaggerated, by the standards of Western armies.

Chiang also did not make things easier for himself by insisting on the unquestioning loyalty of the army as its supreme leader. Notwithstanding his frequent speeches on the subject of the soldier's loyalty to the state, Chiang did not hesitate to exploit his position as commandant of the Whampoa and Nanjing Military Academies in order to create a personal following among the cadets, and he used the Whampoa Clique to control the army. Chiang clearly understood the meaning of Mao Zedong's famous dictum about political power growing out of the barrel of a gun, and throughout the Nanjing Decade (1927-37) he refused to relinquish control of the military. Benjamin Schwartz once noted that the generalissimo's place atop both the civil and military hierarchies was a constant reminder of "the melancholy fact that the subordination of military to civil power had not yet taken place."[89] Chiang's position as head of both the government and the military encouraged him to conflate his interests with those of the nation, and his frequent *l'état c'est moi* moments made it increasingly difficult for both partisan and nonpartisan observers to determine exactly how his army differed from the personal armies of the warlords. Political rivals like Li Zongren and Feng Yuxiang certainly were not fooled, and they regarded the so-called "National" army as Chiang's personal power base. This perception made it difficult to see China's new soldiers as anything other than pawns in a partisan political struggle.

Yet despite the numerous obstacles that remained following completion of the Northern Expedition, Chiang persevered in his efforts to turn the military into a vanguard institution in China's struggle to modernize. We can see his faith in militarism reflected in many government policies during the early years of the Nanjing government. The following resolution on conscription, passed by the National Assembly in 1929, echoed Japanese policy and might well have been penned by Cai E himself:

> All military training and education will be conducted in accordance with the national defence plan to indoctrinate troops in the Three Principles. The way to do this is according to the principle of unifying military and political education. The first step in implementing this principle is to enable soldiers on active duty to return to society as law-abiding and productive citizens. The second step is to enable law-abiding and productive citizens to become the nation's active-duty soldiers. This will establish a politicized military education system using good citizens as the basis for good soldiers and *good soldiers as models for good citizens.* (Emphasis added)[90]

Chiang retained his faith in the benefits of militarism for China's modernization, along with his firm conviction that the soldier ought to serve as the model for the citizen. Knowing this, many of his policies during the Nanjing Decade become more comprehensible. For example, historians have long viewed the New Life Movement's obsession with hygiene and orderly appearance as a wholly inadequate, even farcical, response to China's serious problems, and it is tempting to see the movement as little more than a pathetic attempt at mass mobilization based on outdated Confucian values. However, if the movement is viewed as an attempt to promote the militarization of Chinese society through the regimentation of social life, it takes on new significance. As the 1929 resolution on conscription makes clear, Chiang originally hoped that compulsory military service would serve to disseminate martial virtues throughout society, but by the early 1930s it was apparent that China's tremendous size and huge population made the creation of a viable conscription system almost impossible. Faced with his government's inability to reshape civilian attitudes through conscription, Chiang initiated the New Life Movement with the intent of turning the entire country into one gigantic boot camp through the promotion of martial values and the imposition of military norms of behaviour on the civilian population.[91] The Confucian flavour of the movement can be explained away by the fact that Chiang, like Zeng Guofan before him, saw Confucian and military virtues as virtually identical.

Throughout the Nanjing Decade, Chiang struggled to militarize Chinese society not only in order to break it to the bit of Nationalist rule but also because he genuinely believed that the creation of a disciplined citizenry was critical to China's nation-building efforts. Chiang Kai-shek was first and foremost a soldier, so it was natural for him to look to the military to set the example for society at large, and he liked to point out that "good people are the basis for good soldiers, but good soldiers are the model for good people."[92] Chiang saw himself as a soldier, he viewed things from the standpoint of a soldier, and like many soldiers in other times and places, he was convinced that society could learn a few things from the men in uniform – but only if they were his soldiers. Chiang might have been in the minority when it came to his stubborn advocacy of militarism as an ideology of national development, but he was never alone in his beliefs, even after warlordism soured most Chinese on the idea. As Hans van de Ven reminds us, "in the late Qing and again after the rise of the Nationalists and Communists, dominant perceptions of how to construct a state or conduct revolution did view the military as the midwife of a modern and cohesive China."[93]

Notes

1 Stanislav Andreski's definition of "militarism" remains the most comprehensive: "Sociological analysis would be facilitated by defining militarism as the compound of militancy, militarization, militocracy and what might be called militolatry, that is to say adulation of military virtues. Where all four components are present to a high degree, we have a clear case of militarism." Stanislav Andreski, *Military Organization and Society* (London: Routledge and Kegan Paul, 1968), 186.

2 Li Zonghuang, *Li Zonghuang Huiyi Lu* [The Memoirs of Li Zonghuang], 4 vols. (Taibei: Zhongguo Difang Zizhi Xuehui, 1972), vol. 1, 70. All translations of quotations from non-English sources are mine. The phrase used by Li comes from the legend of Yue Fei, who allegedly had been tattooed with the characters "jin zhong bao guo" (repay the nation with absolute loyalty). Li would go on to graduate with the first class at the new Baoding Military Academy.

3 For example, see the comments of George Morrison in the *Times,* 8 March 1910, 5, as quoted in Edmund Fung, *The Military Dimension of the Chinese Revolution* (Vancouver: UBC Press, 1980), 87. In Chapter 4 of this work, Fung provides a detailed analysis of changing social attitudes toward the reformed military in the years before the 1911 Revolution.

4 "Hao tie bu da ding, hao ren bu dang bing."

5 Malcolm Kennedy, *The Military Side of Japanese Life* (London: Constable, 1924; reprint, Westport, CT: Greenwood Press, 1973), 218.

6 Michael Gibson, "Chiang Kai-shek's Central Army, 1924-1938" (PhD diss., Department of History, University of Washington, 1985), 8.

7 For a discussion of Weber's views on military organization, see Robert D. Miewald, "Weberian Bureaucracy and the Military Model," Public Administration Review 30, 2 (March-April 1970): 129-33.

8 For a detailed discussion on the origins of militarism in the late Qing and early Republic, see Fang Guoan, "Qingmo Minchu Zhongguo Junguomin Jiaoyu zhi Yanjiu" [Research on education for civic militarism in the late Qing and early Republic] (MA thesis, Department of History, Chinese Culture University, Taibei, 1976).

9 Quoted in Anatol M. Kotenev, *Zhongguo Junren Hun* [The Soul of the Chinese Soldier] (Shanghai: Commercial Press, 1937), 36. It is interesting to note that this is precisely the argument put forward by the Japanese scholars who tried to naturalize Confucianism. Although it was impossible for them to deny the Chinese origins of Confucianism (or bushidō for that matter), they argued that it had been corrupted in China after the fall of the Tang Dynasty, whereas its original meaning had been preserved in Japan.

10 Wei Rulin, *Zhongguo Junshi Sixiang Shi* [A History of Chinese Military Thought] (Taibei: HuaGang Chubanshe, 1979), 238.

11 For an insightful discussion of these themes in late-Qing and early Republican writing, see Rebecca Karl, *Staging the World: Chinese Nationalism at the Turn of the Twentieth Century* (Durham, NC: Duke University Press, 2002). As Karl demonstrates, at the beginning of the twentieth century many Chinese intellectuals came to see the Chinese as having more in common with other colonized and vanquished peoples than with the Japanese. After all, the Japanese had succeeded where the Chinese had failed, so it was only logical for China to find common cause with the other "lost countries."

12 Liang Qichao, "Lun Shang Wu" [On the appreciation of martial values], in *Yin Bing Shi Congzhu: Xin Min Shuo,* 183-200 (Shanghai: n.p., 1917); Andreski, *Military Organization,* 186. The Chinese equivalent of "militolatry" – the embracing of martial values by civilians – is *shang wu jingshen.*

13 Liang, "Lun Shang Wu," 183-84.

14 Ibid., 185.

15 Ibid., 198-99.

16 Ibid., 188.

17 Ibid., 191.

18 Ibid.

19 Ibid.

20 Ibid., 195.

21 Ibid., 198.

22 Fung, *Military Dimension,* 91.

23 Liang demonstrated his excellent knowledge of Chinese military history in several of his essays, including "China's Way of the Warrior," a fascinating piece in which he argued that Japanese bushidō was actually a naturalized version of China's own way of the warrior. See Liang Qichao, *Zhongguo zhi Wushidao* [China's Way of the Warrior] (Shanghai: Zhonghua Shuju, 1936).

24 The concept of the military as a "repository of moral resource" for the state comes from General Sir John Hackett, "The Military in the Service of the State," in *War, Morality, and the Military Profession,* ed. Malham Wakin (Boulder, CO: Westview Press, 1986), 119.

25 Xie Benshu, *Cai E Zhuan* [The Biography of Cai E] (Tianjin: Tianjin Renmin Chubanshe, 1983), 2-3; Guojia Chubanshe Bianshen Bu, *Hu Guo Mingjiang Cai Songpo* [The Famous General and Protector of the Nation Cai Songpo] (Tainan: Guojia Chubanshe, 1982), 4-6.

26 Ibid., 14, 24.

27 Cai Songpo, "Jun Guo Min pian" [On civic militarism], in *Cai Songpo Ji* [The Collected Works of Cai Songpo], ed. Zeng Yeying (Shanghai: Shanghai Renmin Chubanshe, 1984), 20-21.

28 Ibid., 22.

29 Cai Songpo, "Junshi Jihua" [A plan for miltary affairs], in *Cai Songpo Ji* [The Collected Works of Cai Songpo], ed. Zeng Yeying (Shanghai: Shanghai Renmin Chubanshe, 1984), 1309.

30 Leonard Humphreys, *The Way of the Heavenly Sword* (Stanford, CA: Stanford University Press, 1995), 12-13.

31 Kennedy, *Military Side of Japanese Life,* 311.

32 Ibid., 54-55.

33 Guofangbu Zong Zhengzhi Zuozhan, *Lingxiu Xingyi* [Our Leader's Deeds] (Taibei: Guofang Bu, 1966), 14-17. For the Chinese origins of bushidō, see Liang, *Zhongguo zhi Wushidao.*

34 Fung, *Military Dimension,* 99.

35 Diana Lary, *Warlord Soldiers* (London: Cambridge University Press, 1985), 5.

36 Cai Songpo, *Zeng Hu Zhi Bing Yu Lu* [A Record of Zeng Guofan's and Hu Linyi's Writings on Military Leadership] (Taibei: Liming Wenhua Shiye Gongsi, 1999), 97.

37 Arthur Waldron has described in detail how disgust with the militarization of politics was reflected in the pejorative use of the term "warlord" *(junfa)* to describe the leaders of military factions. Arthur Waldron, "The Warlord: Twentieth-Century Chinese Understandings of Violence, Militarism, and Imperialism," *American Historical Review* 96, 4 (1991): 1073-100.

38 Quoted in Edward McCord, "Burn, Kill, Rape, and Rob: Military Atrocities, Warlordism, and Anti-warlordism in Republican China," in *Scars of War: The Impact of Warfare on Modern China,* ed. Diana Lary and Stephen MacKinnon (Vancouver: UBC Press, 2001), 42.

39 Hans van de Ven, "The Military in the Republic," in *Reappraising Republican China,* ed. Frederic Wakeman and Richard Edmonds (London: Oxford University Press, 2000), 103.

40 Ibid., 107.

41 Huang Zhenliang, *Huangpu Junxiao zhi Chengli ji qi Chuqi Fazhan* [The Founding of the Whampoa Military Academy and its Early Development] (Taibei: Zhengzhong Books, 1993), 12-13.

42 Ibid., 18.

43 Lü Fangshang, *Xian Zongtong Jiang Gong yu Huangpu Junxiao de Chuangjian* [Former president Chiang and the founding of the Whampoa Military Academy], in *Huangpu Junxiao Liushi Zhounian Lunwen Ji* [Collected Essays on the Sixtieth Anniversary of the Founding of the Whampoa Military Academy], ed. Guofangbu Shi Zheng Bianyi Ju (Taibei: Guofangbu Shi Zheng Bianyi Ju, 1984), vol. 1, 27.

44 See Sun Yat-sen, "Junren Jingshen Jiaoyu" [The spiritual education of soldiers] (1922), in *Zongli Yizhu* [The Premier's Commemorative Book], 1-54 (Taibei: Yangmingshan Zhuangyin, 1950).

45 Richard Gabriel, *To Serve with Honor: A Treatise on Military Ethics and the Way of the Soldier* (Westport, CT: Greenwood Press, 1982), 229. This work is an example of the post-

Vietnam soul-searching that took place in the United States Army. The author, a serving officer, identifies careerism – what Sun and Chiang called the "shang guan fa cai" attitude – and a widespread ethical malaise as contributing factors in the American failure in Vietnam.

46 Chiang Kai-shek, "Geming Jun Teshu de Jingshen he Zhanshu" [The special spirit and tactics of the Revolutionary Army], in *Huangpu Zhongyao Wenxian* [Important Materials on Whampoa], ed. Lujun Junguan Xuexiao (Fengshan: Huangpu Chubanshe, 1984), 118.

47 Louis Sorley, "Duty, Honor, Country: Practice and Precept," *American Behavioral Scientist* 19, 5 (May-June 1976): 638.

48 Gabriel, *To Serve with Honor*, 134.

49 The idea of a vanguard was best expressed by Mencius when he noted, "Shi xian zhi jue hou zhi, shi xian jue jue hou jue ye" (Heaven intended those who understood first to teach those who had yet to understand). Mencius, *Mengzi: Wan Zhang*, pt. 1, ch. 7, sec. 5.

50 Chiang Kai-shek, "Guoqu Junshi Jiaoyu zhi Jiantao yu Gaojiban Chengli zhi Mudi" [A critique of military education in the past and the objectives for the founding of the advanced class], in *Zongtong Jiang Gong Sixiang Yanlun Zongji: Di ershisi juan* [The Thought of President Chiang Kai-shek: Collected Speeches] (Taibei: Zhongguo Guomindang Zhongyang Weiyuanhui, 1984), vol. 24, 85.

51 Chiang Kai-shek, "Xiaozhang di Ershisi Xunci" [The commandant's twenty-fourth address], in *Huangpu Congshu* [Whampoa Collection], ed. Zhongyang Lujun Junguan Xuexiao Zhengzhi Bu (Nanjing: Zhongyang Lujun Junguan Xuexiao Zhengzhi Bu, 1928), 141.

52 Zhu Zhixin, "Bing de Gaizao yu qi xinli" [Psychological implications of military reform], in *Zhu Zhixin Ji* [The Collected Works of Zhu Zhixin], ed. Jianshe She (Shanghai: Minzhi Shuju, 1925), 370-71.

53 Huang Zhenwu, "Huangpu Yiwang" [Recollections of Whampoa], pt. 1, *Yiwen Zhi* [Journal of Art and Literature] 4 (January 1966): 8.

54 Huang Renyu, *Cong Da Lishi de Jiaodu Du Jiang Jieshi Riji* [Chiang Kai-shek's Diary from a Historical Perspective] (Taibei: Shibao Wenhua, 1994), 33.

55 Leng Xin, "Huangpu Shenghuo Zhuiyi" [Recollections of life at Whampoa], *Ziyou Tan* [Liberty] 15, 3 (March 1964): 9.

56 Wang Zibu, *Wang Zibu Xiansheng Bashiwu Huiyi Lu* [The Memoirs of Mr. Wang Zibu at Eighty-Five] (Taibei: privately published, 1986), 90.

57 Huang, "Huangpu Yiwang," pt. 1, 8.

58 Wang, *Wang Zibu Xiansheng Bashiwu Huiyi Lu*, 90; Huang, "Huangpu Yiwang," pt. 1, 8.

59 Chiang Kai-shek, "Junxiao de Shiming yu Geming de Rensheng" [The mission of this military academy and the revolutionary life], in *Huangpu Zhongyao Wenxian* [Important Materials on Whampoa], ed. Lujun Junguan Xuexiao (Fengshan: Huangpu Chubanshe, 1984), 39.

60 Ibid.

61 General John Hackett, "The Military in the Service of the State," in *War, Morality, and the Military Profession*, ed. Malham Wakin (Boulder, CO: Westview Press, 1986), 119.

62 Gabriel, *To Serve with Honor*, 57.

63 Sidney Axinn, *A Moral Military* (Philadelphia: Temple University Press, 1989), 11.

64 Sun Yat-sen, "Junren Jingshen Jiaoyu" [The spiritual education of soldiers], in *Zongli Yizhu* [Sun Yat-sen's Writings] (Taibei: Yangmingshan Zhuang, 1950), 23. The equation of ren with bo ai was originally made by Han Yu; see Zhang Dingyu, *Zhongguo Daode Sixiang Jingyi* [The Essentials of Chinese Ethics] (Taibei: Zheng Zhong Shuju, 1983), 100.

65 Sun, "Junren Jingshen Jiaoyu," 26.

66 Ibid.

67 Chiang Kai-shek, "Xiaozhang di yi ci Xunci" [The commandant's first address], in *Huangpu Congshu: Jingshen Jiaoyu* [Whampoa Collection: Spiritual Education], ed. Zhongyang Lujun Junguan Xuexiao Zhengzhi Bu (Nanjing: Zhongyang Lujun Junguan Xuexiao Zhengzhi Bu, 1928), 15-16.
68 Sun, "Junren Jingshen Jiaoyu," 43-44.
69 Chiang Kai-shek, "Xiaozhang di jiu ci Xunci" [The commandant's ninth speech], in *Huangpu Congshu: Jingshen Jiaoyu* [Whampoa Collection: Spiritual Education], ed. Zhongyang Lujun Junguan Xuexiao Zhengzhi Bu (Nanjing: Zhongyang Lujun Junguan Xuexiao Zhengzhi Bu, 1928), 48.
70 Chiang Kai-shek, "Jun Guan Xuexiao Ri Ke Wenda" [Officer school daily recitation], in *Huangpu Congshu: Di San Ji Fulu* [Whampoa Collection: Part 3 Annex], ed. Zhongyang Lujun Junguan Xuexiao Zhengzhi Bu (Nanjing: Zhongyang Lujun Junguan Xuexiao Zhengzhi Bu, 1928), 35-41.
71 Ibid., 53.
72 For a discussion of late-Qing and Republican knight-errant literature, see Cao Zhengwen, *Xia Ke Xing* [The Way of the Knight-Errant] (Taibei: Yunlong Chubanshe, 1998); Robert Ruhlmann, "Traditional Heroes in Chinese Popular Fiction," in *Confucianism and Chinese Civilization,* ed. Arthur F. Wright, 122-57 (Stanford, CA: Stanford University Press, 1964); and James Liu, *The Chinese Knight-Errant* (Chicago: University of Chicago Press, 1967).
73 Deng Wenyi, *Huangpu Jingshen* [The Whampoa Spirit] (Taibei: Liming Wenhua Shiye, 1976), 361.
74 Zhou Yanmou, ed., *Jing Zhong Yue Fei* [The Loyal Yue Fei] (Taibei: Jingyi Shuju, 1976), 38.
75 Guofang Bu Shi Zheng Bianyi Ju, ed., *Zhongguo Zhanshi Da Cidian: Renwu zhi Bu* [A Biographical Dictionary of Chinese Military History] (Taibei: Guofang Bu Shi Zheng Bianyi Ju, 1992), 308.
76 Chiang, "Junxiao de Shiming yu Geming de Rensheng," 40.
77 See Chiang's introductory comments to "Zengbu Zeng Hu Zhi Bing Lu" [Annotated record of Zeng Guofan's and Hu Linyi's writings on military leadership], in *Huangpu Congshu: Di San Ji Fulu* [Whampoa Collection: Part 3 Annex], ed. Zhongyang Lujun Junguan Xuexiao Zhengzhi Bu (Nanjing: Zhongyang Lujun Junguan Xuexiao Zhengzhi Bu, 1928), 1-2.
78 Chiang Kai-shek, "Xiaozhang di yi ci Xunci" [The commandant's first speech], in *Huangpu Congshu: Jingshen Jiaoyu* [Whampoa Collection: Spiritual Education], ed. Zhongyang Lujun Junguan Xuexiao Zhengzhi Bu (Nanjing: Zhongyang Lujun Junguan Xuexiao Zhengzhi Bu, 1928), 19.
79 Chiang Kai-shek, "Xiaozhang di er ci Xunci" [The commandant's second speech], in *Huangpu Congshu: Jingshen Jiaoyu* [Whampoa Collection: Spiritual Education], ed. Zhongyang Lujun Junguan Xuexiao Zhengzhi Bu (Nanjing: Zhongyang Lujun Junguan Xuexiao Zhengzhi Bu, 1928), 23; Chiang, "Xiaozhang di jiu ci Xunci," 51.
80 Morris Janowitz, *Military Institutions and Coercion in the Developing Nations* (Chicago: University of Chicago Press, 1977), 140.
81 Chiang Kai-shek, "Chongzheng Dong Jiang Xunjie" [Admonitions for the Second Eastern Expedition], in *Huangpu Congshu: Di San Ji Fulu* [Whampoa Collection: Part 3 Annex], ed. Zhongyang Lujun Junguan Xuexiao Zhengzhi Bu (Nanjing: Zhongyang Lujun Junguan Xuexiao Zhengzhi Bu, 1928), 1-3.
82 Ibid., 1. Chiang rarely used the term *hao han,* and his use of it in this passage indicates that he may have been paraphrasing Qi Jiguang, who had once urged his troops to "zuo yige hao han si!" (Die a hero's death!). See Qi Jiguang, "Lian Bing Shiji: Lian Dan Qi," in *Qi Jiguang Bingfa* [The Military Methods of Qi Jiguang], ed. Pu Yinghua (Taibei: Zhaowen She, 1997), 103.

83 Ibid., 1.
84 Chiang Kai-shek, "Shi De Sheng Ge" [Explaining the meaning of the "Victory Is Ours" song], in *Zongtong Jiang Gong Sixiang Yanlun Zongji: Di shiyi juan* [The Thought of President Chiang Kai-shek: Collected Speeches] (Taibei: Zhongguo Guomindang Zhongyang Weiyuanhui, 1984), vol. 11, 80.
85 Lujun Junguan Xuexiao, ed., *Huangpu Jian Xiao Liushi Zhounian Jian Shi* [An Outline History of the Whampoa Military Academy on the Sixtieth Anniversary of its Founding] (Fengshan: Lujun Junguan Xuexiao, 1984), 12.
86 Donald Jordan, *The Northern Expedition* (Honolulu: University of Hawai'i Press, 1976), 291.
87 Liu Yongyao, "Huangpu Xuesheng yu Zhongguo Geming" [Whampoa students and the Chinese Revolution], in *Zhongyang Lujun Junguan Xuexiao Chengli Shi Zhounian Jinian Ce* [A Commemorative Book Marking the Tenth Anniversary of the Central Military Academy], ed. Zhongyang Lujun Junguan Xuexiao Chengli Shi Zhounian Jinian Dianli Choubei Weiyuanhui (Nanjing: Zhongyang Lujun Junguan Xuexiao, 1934), 31.
88 For an inside look at the political struggle waged at Whampoa, see the memoir written by first classman Deng Wenyi, *Huangpu Jingshen* [The Whampoa Spirit] (Taibei: Liangming Wenhua Shiye Gongsi, 1976).
89 Benjamin Schwartz, "Themes in Intellectual History: May Fourth and After," in *The Cambridge History of China*, vol. 12, *Republican China, 1912-1949*, ed. John Fairbank (Taipei: Caves Books, 1989), pt. 1, 447.
90 "Di San Ci Quan Guo Daibiao Da Hui Dui Junshi Baogao zhi Jueyi An" [The Third National Assembly's resolution with regard to the report on military affairs] (March 1929), in *Cai Bing Jian Guo zhi Yiyi* [The Meaning of Demobilization and National Construction], ed. Junshi Weiyuanhui (Nanjing: Junshi Weiyuanhui, 1930), 18.
91 For a discussion of the link between Chiang's militarism and the goals of the New Life Movement, see James E. Sheridan, *China in Disintegration* (New York: Free Press, 1975), 218-19; and Hans van de Ven, *War and Nationalism in China, 1925-1945* (New York: Routledge Curzon, 2003), 163-68.
92 Chiang Kai-shek, "Jiao Fei Chengbai yu Guojia Cunwang (1933)" [Bandit extermination and the fate of the nation (1933)], in *Jiang Zongtong Ji* [The Collected Works of Chiang Kai-shek] (Taibei: Guofang Yanjiuyuan, 1960), 216.
93 Van de Ven, "Military in the Republic," 99.

8

Orphans in the Family: Family Reform and Children's Citizenship during the Anti-Japanese War, 1937-45

M. Colette Plum

Orphans as Idealized Citizens

In 1940 the staff of Jiangxi Diyi Baoyuyuan (Jiangxi Number One Wartime Children's Home) hoped to establish plots of vegetable gardens but had insufficient land. The administrators did not abandon the project. Rather, they presented the problem to the child residents and asked them to propose solutions. The children purportedly met and discussed the problem and collectively made a decision: they would move a large mound of earth from the east side of the school and use it to fill a wide ditch at the west side of the school.[1]

The next afternoon, the work began. The older children dug up the soil and carried it in baskets slung on each shoulder. The smaller children worked in pairs to lift and balance their loads between them. The very youngest of the children carried fistfuls of soil. The children levelled the earth, measured the area, and mapped, plotted, and divided the sections, and the planting began. When the bright green of newly sprouted rapeseed spread across the field, the children reportedly came to see it, shouting, "Look! This is our field! This is our vegetable garden!" They were delighted with the fruits of their labour. The social worker who reported this story ends her narrative celebrating the implications of this endeavour for the child participants: "Once these vegetables are grown and harvested, how delicious they will taste to the children who planted and grew them with their own toil and sweat!"[2]

The narrator, Zhao Shihui, spent nearly two weeks at the children's home, observing and evaluating the lives of institutionalized war orphans. Her observations were published in the periodical *Jiangxi Funü (Jiangxi Women)*. Her accounting of facts and figures is peppered with colourful anecdotes like the one above, all seemingly aimed at convincing the reader of a great discovery: children have tremendous value, which has hitherto gone unrecognized.

Zhao attributes the emergence of the valuable, enterprising child to the founding of wartime children's homes, which presumably enabled children to realize their fullest potential:

> The great strength of children, the astonishing talents of children: these never emerged until the creation of wartime children's homes ... All 500 of these children ... are leaders. They take turns chairing the morning, evening, and weekly

> assemblies ... (they) line up in a public square, and their management and directions do not feel chaotic. They have organizational talent, leadership strength, courteous manners, and discipline. They have every decent moral virtue accorded to humanity. If anyone in this world is worthy of praise, we must first extol children.[3]

During the war, the pedagogical method of encouraging children in self-sufficiency and leadership was not unique to the Jiangxi Number One Wartime Children's Home, nor was enthusiasm about children's abilities unique to the above narrator. Wartime writings by educators, child-welfare officials, journalists, government bureaucrats, and party propagandists lauded the special strengths and resourcefulness of children.[4]

The school that the narrator describes has familiar, progressive, and modern characteristics. But this story is peopled with characters and themes strikingly *un*familiar when compared with China's prewar orphanages: a woman social worker, dispatched to carry out an inspection; a body of student governance, entrusted with decision making and leadership; a women's magazine whose editors believe that the content of this article is of interest; a public into which students are sent forth to civilize and to bring order; and a readership whom the author feels compelled to persuade of the value and worth of these orphans. But perhaps most important, the language that Zhao selects to narrate her story heralds the "talent," "strength," "manners," and "discipline" of a set of children who have been through the most horrific and harrowing of human experiences – the loss of family and community to the traumas of war – before arriving at this new home. We are not asked to avert our eyes from these orphaned children, most of whom were recently lice-ridden, filthy, tattered, and sickly. Instead, we are invited to see them as the embodiment of all things good about children, orphaned or not.

Why is it that, in the midst of a war, childhood was being celebrated and children held up as ideal leaders? How is it that the residents of this children's home – who were for the most part war orphans – were taken to represent idealized versions of the best traits of children in general and even of humanity as a whole? How do we read this discourse? Whose interests, dreams, or fears might it represent? This chapter examines these questions in order to understand better the puzzling celebration of the Chinese orphan in the midst of the flames of the Anti-Japanese War.

Orphan Relief during the Anti-Japanese War

The violence and dislocation brought about by the Anti-Japanese War resulted in at least two million Chinese war orphans. With funding from the Nationalist government and private donors, newly formed child-relief organizations under the direct control of China's National Relief Commission built and subsidized wartime children's homes throughout China from October 1938 until December 1944, mostly in the interior but also in occupied China and in Communist-base areas. These children's homes housed approximately 220,000 war orphans during the war, and the National Relief Commission appropriated US$334 million for the education of wartime refugee children – which amounted to over one-third of the total relief funds appropriated by the commission.[5]

One of the most basic human instincts may be to protect the young. But war orphans will not survive without a concerted and organized effort to care for them. Written accounts by relief workers and oral histories of survivors from this period speak of parents and relatives abandoning children on roadsides or throwing children overboard from boats as families escaped with throngs of other refugees.[6] Many children were separated from their families during air raids or ground-troop invasions and were never reunited with them. Others recount that they wandered about in populated areas for days, starving, before they were given care by formally established relief units.[7] Despite these risks, many Chinese war orphans not only survived but were also raised in wartime children's homes and grew to adulthood with a strong sense of national belonging and with images of themselves as contributing members of what was described to them during their childhoods as a "future China" *(jianglai de Zhongguo)* of which they were expected to be a part.

Something unique in Chinese history occurred in the treatment of orphans during the Anti-Japanese War. Orphanages and foundling homes existed in other periods of Chinese history, funded and operated by philanthropists, foreign missionaries, and local or provincial authorities. But the wartime children's homes were the first created as part of a large-scale project at the initiative and with the involvement of the state itself, with the purpose not simply of caring for children in need but also of providing them with a particular set of skills and indoctrinating them with a set of ideologies deemed necessary to shape them into modern citizens.[8] Elsewhere in this volume, Norman Smith describes how opium addicts became an increasing concern of both the Japanese occupation's regime and Chinese reformers. The Manchukuo state built opium-rehabilitation centres aimed at shaping more productive and compliant subjects. This chapter describes a similar process in the shaping of future citizens within "Free China" – a process engendered by the conditions of war.

Ideas of "the child," and of "the orphan" in particular, were also imbued with a representational value unique to this period. War orphans became an important rallying point for both the Nationalists and the Communists during the Anti-Japanese War. Rather than be drowned out in the din and rubble of wartime violence, the "war orphan" was refined and shaped into a potent cultural symbol infused with nationalist ideology. Changed concepts about the value and roles of war orphans as citizens were instantiated in practices in wartime children's homes.

One way of understanding this unique value placed on orphans during the Anti-Japanese War is to examine the wartime conception of children as the recipients (and future transmitters) of culture and values: orphans as "children of the ancestral homeland" *(zuguo de haizimen),* as "children of the *minzu*" *(minzu de ertong),*[9] and as "the nation's children" *(guojia de ertong).* During the war, Nationalist propagandists, concerned with creating a "New China," were still dealing with a puzzle that had preoccupied the nation in the two decades preceding the war with Japan: how to create a New China when those transmitting culture to children had not yet themselves been modernized. Traditionally, parents were a child's primary teachers, but the Guomindang saw parents as unreliable transmitters of a modern culture supportive of a modern nation. The Guomindang had confused and contradictory ideas about families in its ideology, and this translated into tensions in the valuing and treatment of orphans, who were a subset of children needing to be modernized and made into citizens and who were presumably independent of family influences. The Nationalist treatment of orphans, who were without parents, highlights the conflicted role of the family in wartime Guomindang ideology.

"War Orphans" and "Refugee Children"

Before proceeding, it is vital to define some terms. The Chinese perception of the children being rescued and housed within children's homes during the war is best discerned by looking at the discursive space in which these children are discussed rather than simply translating, in isolation, the terms used to refer to these children. Chinese-language, wartime newspapers and journals rarely used the word "orphan" *(gu'er)* but rather the words "refugee child" *(nantong)* and "child" *(ertong),* almost always in conjunction with the other appellations discussed in this chapter ("children of the nation," "children of the ancestral homeland," and "the nation's children"). However, these wartime writings rarely discussed all refugee children in general or all Chinese children in general. Rather, the essays advocating that children be rescued, and describing the plight of child war victims, referred to children who were without parents. The reality was that most child refugees did not know whether or not they had surviving parents. As a result, they were treated as orphans – alone in the world, without the care or influence of their parents or families, in need of replacement caregivers, and perhaps most important, available for appropriation by others.

The status of "orphanhood" – both historically and in present-day applications – has more to do with a child's relationship with his or her family of origin, the state's assumption of responsibility for certain categories of children, and the broader political landscape in which state policy is initiated than it has to do with any verifiable conditions of one or both parents being deceased. Although Chinese texts during this period rarely used the word *gu'er* (orphan) to refer to children in wartime children's homes, the discourse surrounding these children assumed that they were parentless. In fact, "orphan" and the 1930s neologism "warphan" were the preferred English terms used in wartime China to cover this broad class of children.

Prewar Chinese Views of the Orphan

In traditional Chinese models of rulership, the family was perceived as the basic unit of society, and proper filial relationships within the family were the root of good governance. It was through the family system that a person learned to behave properly within hierarchical relationships; these habits of relating were then expected to be extended to other relationships lying outside of the family circle. The proper functioning of the family was thus considered an essential ingredient in maintaining social and political stability and served as the fundamental social, economic, religious, and legal unit throughout Imperial Chinese history.

It is no exaggeration to say that in such a system, the individual was not truly a person unless he or she was a person within a family. In most societies, cultures, and times, orphanhood, like widowhood, has been considered an unfortunate state. When parents or family elders are a child's main caregivers and advocates, the loss of such nurturance, guidance, and protection is indeed a great loss.

In her study of children and childhood in late Imperial China, Ping-Chen Hsiung found that the loss of one or more parental figures was commonplace in the lives of early-modern children. The loss of a mother to a nursing infant often meant death, and the loss of a father to a child of any age meant nearly certain economic hardship. Children who lost both parents were often sent to live with uncles or grandparents (either paternal or maternal) but could expect mistreatment from rival family factions or the loss of protection once a grandparent died. Orphaned children often needed to hire themselves out for such jobs as tending animals or collecting firewood in exchange for food and shelter, or they were "adopted" out as servants of other families or as future daughters-in-law or sons-in-law. Some sought emotional and physical shelter in Buddhist monasteries.[10]

Despite the disadvantaged position of the orphan in Chinese society, historical studies of philanthropy and social welfare have shown that throughout Imperial China the state rarely provided for orphan care in any systematic or far-reaching way. Orphans have existed throughout Chinese history, but something happened during the war years that elevated war orphans to a national priority and created the symbol of the war orphan as a national treasure, worthy of state protection and its own concomitant discourse.

Two factors helped to change the value, and hence the place, of the orphan in wartime China. The first was prewar cultural and intellectual antecedents concerning the relationship between the family and the nation. Twentieth-century critiques of the traditional Chinese family improved the orphan's image, for orphans were presumably free of influences that might instill objectionable habits and dispositions thought by reformists to be nurtured within traditional families and perceived as obstacles to the development of a modern state. Norman Smith's chapter in this volume argues that resistance writers in Manchukuo blamed a perceived degeneration of the Chinese family on the Japanese occupiers and their support of the opium industry. Family reformers in Free China still held up traditional Chinese culture as the primary obstacle to the creation of healthy and productive citizens.

The second factor altering the value of orphans was the war itself and how it was used by the Nationalists to promote a vision of the nation under state control. The valuing of orphans during the war years cannot be divorced from the Nationalist propaganda disseminated to garner support for the War of Resistance, which charged that the Japanese were set on exterminating the Chinese *minzu* by killing off Chinese children. These charges, widely circulated in Chinese newspapers, altered the value of one particular class of children by deeming them especially valuable to purported Japanese genocidal schemes: the war orphan, without the family as protectorate, was considered especially vulnerable either to extermination by the Japanese or to manipulation for occupation and collaborationist projects. The dislocation and disruption of families in the chaos and violence of the wartime context provided an opening through which the nation could emerge as "parent" to the *minzu*. Within Nationalist discourse, the war orphan embodied all the state wished to communicate about the perceived threat the Japanese posed to the *minzu*: the pitiable state of orphanhood might fall to anyone who did not contribute to the Nationalist nation. Those who went it alone, who failed to add their strength to the collective, who collaborated with the enemy, or who gave their allegiance to the presumably untrustworthy Communists (painted by the Nationalists as antifamily) should fear the loss of the family of the nation. War orphans were thus embraced in

Nationalist discourse as the state positioned itself as the protector of orphans, and hence as the protector of the *minzu*. Though bereaved and alone, war orphans were also protected because they could be readily appropriated as symbols.

War Orphans as "Children of the *Minzu*"

Stephen MacKinnon's work on 1938 Wuhan has shown how women leaders and journalists joined with high-ranking members of both the Nationalist and Communist Parties to make the rescue and care of war orphans a national priority and disseminated stories about the flight of refugees in Wuhan's numerous newspapers and periodicals.[11] But the writings of wartime child-relief advocates indicate that, although the United Front government's propagandists extolled war orphans as national heroes, relief advocates could expect very little enthusiasm for their efforts from the population at large. Much of the early wartime writings in newspapers and journals regarding war orphans was aimed at convincing readers that orphans were not what the reader assumed. Child-relief advocates and educators took on the task of convincing the public, and their very own childcare personnel, that orphans should be saved because orphans had a new value, suggesting that in the past their value had been overlooked. They also attempted to cut against a perceived fear that orphans came from backgrounds that would make them less teachable and hence less valuable to the nation. The discourse created around war orphans attempted to make the reader sympathetic to their plight by eliciting feelings of nurturance and care.

In her address to childcare workers in 1937, the writer and child-relief advocate Jun Hui (1904-81) utilized the term "the nation's children" *(guojia de ertong)* to evoke a sense of responsibility on the part of childcare workers toward the orphans in their care:

> You should have an attitude of selflessness toward childcare. We are participating in childcare work and nurturing children for the country's *minzu*. This is not some kind of fleeting interest, nor is it passive relief work. Therefore, regardless of the kind of child, all children must be given the opportunity to receive a rich education. They are all the nation's children, and all have a right to care. Even if there are differences among children ... childcare workers should not be partial.[12]

In this passage, Jun was writing against an attitude of indifference on the part of the Chinese toward children who were not their own. Although child-welfare reformers began their writings by advocating protection of children against the Japanese, most of their rhetoric was aimed at convincing the Chinese reader to respond appropriately to the plight of children, suggesting the Chinese had not been responding as they should. Her writing also valorized motherhood and encouraged women to make gendered contributions to the nation by impartially nurturing the nation's children.[13]

Children's relief advocates occasionally made their case for child rescue and relief by specifying that child relief in the wartime context was not simply benevolent or humanitarian work. Thus in the above quotation, Jun insisted that orphan care was part of broader-reaching nation-building projects. Likewise, the women's journal editor Shen Zijiu (1898-1989) argued that the rescue of children from war zones was not the same as the "pure-hearted" work of other benevolent organizations of the past.[14] According to Shen, a child surviving Japanese slaughter was valuable as a "seedling of the *minzu*" and, as such, when taken in by others, should be seen as a "priceless orphan guest" *(guojia guke).*[15]

The positioning of these "seedlings of the *minzu*" within the family of the nation meant that the special position wartime children occupied as "children of the *minzu*" was one loaded with expectation and responsibility, not one of simple privilege and protection. In his "Report on the Work of Developing Middle-School Wartime Travelling Painting Exhibitions," the educator Tang Yingwei began with a stern call to arms for students: "In our sacred fight for the *minzu,* every child of the Chinese *minzu* has the great mission of bearing the responsibility of saving the nation from extinction ... no one can evade this responsibility and [should] devote all of his or her strength completely to the nation."[16] In using the term "child of the *minzu*" to characterize the relationship between the child and the nation, propagandists and educators were utilizing powerful cultural models about the place of the child in the system of the traditional Chinese family. Confucian models of the parent-child relationship emphasized filiality and devotion extending from the child to the parent, which reciprocated the benevolent care of the child by the parent. The term "child of the *minzu*" substitutes the *minzu* for the parent.

Family-based concepts of the appropriate relationship of citizens to the state were very much a part of Guomindang visions of authority. This family-based conceptualization of children could do a great deal more discursive ideological work than the terms *ertong* (child), *nantong* (refugee child), or *gu'er* (orphan) could do on their own. The phrase "child of the *minzu*" could be inserted into a text and conjure up a more complex set of meanings about the relationship between children and the nation. The term was used throughout the war to refer to the place of the Chinese child, and the war orphan in particular, within the nation-state.

The Place of the Family in Prewar Guomindang Nationalism

Critiques of the traditional Chinese family entered the discursive landscape of the nation with the social and political disruptions accompanying the fall of the Qing Dynasty. Reform-minded intellectuals and students posed their most formidable challenge to prevailing hierarchies during the New Culture and May 4th Movements, when the family and clan foundations of Confucian society were attacked as the primary obstacles to a modern, democratic society.

The slogan "Save the Children," so ubiquitous in the wartime child-relief movement, made its debut at the end of Lu Xun's 1918 short story "Kuangren Riji" ("Diary of a Madman"). Lu and other New Culture Movement writers were deeply concerned with the perceived need to create a radical break from traditional Chinese culture. "Save the Children" was taken by New Culture Movement writers and later literary critics as a call to save Chinese children not from the Japanese but from their Chinese forbears, who were transmitting to children the crippling and stupefying effects of the culture of the traditional Chinese family.[17]

Critiques of the family continued into the Nanjing Decade (1927-37). One of the main Guomindang priorities was to create public order under the hierarchy of the state by reconfiguring conventional family allegiances. This priority was codified with the 1931 Civil Code of the Republic of China. The code, formulated by urban elites, had very little social impact on rural households, but it was an indicator of mistrust on the part of the Nationalists for the hold that the patrilineal system had on citizens.

Although the Nationalist legal code sought to deliver a blow to corporate kinship structures and the particular interests of lineages, Nationalist ideology was not exactly antifamily, and some intellectuals made a concerted effort to reconceptualize the family in ways that would lend support to the authority of the state.[18] Robert Culp has shown that two competing visions of a modern society were articulated during this period, conveyed to students in Guomindang civics textbooks, and that the family held a different place in each of these visions. The first vision conceived of society as a cohesive, social whole under the leadership of the party-state. The second was a vision of society rooted in the family that sought to revive the Confucian hierarchies and social patterns of Imperial China.[19]

The primary vision taught to students was the supremacy of the state over the system of the traditional family. But some textbooks presented the affective ties formed in the family as the basis of patriotism and encouraged students to extend these feelings toward the family of the nation. [20] Such textbook authors saw the emotional connections that were deemed to normally develop within families as the fundamentals necessary to developing national consciousness and patriotism. If orphans were missing these building blocks of filiality and emotional connections, how could they then be bound to the family of the nation? Did this mean they could not develop national consciousness?

In the project of creating loyal subjects of the state, the family could be either ally or impediment. Any party concerned with the consolidation of state power or with cultural reform could not ignore the importance of the family in traditional Chinese culture and its role in shaping the values and practices of citizens. In the shared project of turning orphans into assets of the state and symbols of nationalism, orphanhood was met with ambivalence. On the one hand, orphans, being *family-less,* were lacking something of vital importance: without affective ties and filial relations, orphans might not be loyal or disciplined. On the other hand, orphans, being *family-free,* were manipulable: without the influences of and loyalties to the family, orphans could be utilized for national purposes.

In sum, there were different strains of ideologies concerning the family before the war. Although the Guomindang codified prohibitions against certain patrilineal practices, its leaders also aimed to reform family culture in those ways deemed useful for consolidating state power and cultivating a disciplined citizenry. Yet despite the promotion of Confucian values that reinstated hierarchies of authority, the Guomindang remained highly skeptical of most Chinese families and thus instituted campaigns such as "family-education" programs that brought the reach of the state into families and homes.[21]

Wartime China operated from a different geographical, institutional, and ideological vantage point than that of the Nanjing Decade. The Second United Front between the Nationalists and the Communists ushered in a host of progressive intellectual writers who lent their voices to the prevailing critiques of the family. If families were not always an asset to the development of national consciousness, war orphans presented an opportunity for state builders to shape the future "masters of the nation" – the "children of the *minzu*" – without interference from family loyalties. Free from their families of origin, orphans were rescued by the "family of the nation."

The Role of Parents in New China

The needs of war orphans and refugee children were immediate and urgent, but the ideologies behind child-rescue efforts were – like all ideologies – abstract. Child relief was fuelled by a future-oriented vision in which the place of parents was at best murky. In his essay "The Meaning of the Rescue and Care of Refugee Children," originally published in the journal *Guohun (National Spirit),* the Guomindang's chief propagandist, Chen Lifu, made the case that the rescue and care of refugee children should be a priority over the rescue of parents. Chen proposed that relief efforts focus on children who were "the second generation of citizens" and "the next generation of masters of the nation." Revitalizing the *minzu* was conceived of as a long-term project, and the present generation had not yet been revitalized.[22] Parents, lacking the qualities essential for the modern citizen, were thought to pose a hindrance to revitalization projects and, as a result, to be a potential danger to the nation's progeny.

In addressing educated women in *Funü Shenghuo (Women's Life)* about how to propagandize among women about the rescue and care of refugee children, Shen Zijiu suggested not only that children needed to be rescued from the Japanese but also that they needed to be rescued, in part, from wartime families: "Most ordinary families in China do not know scientific methods for raising children, and therefore, although they give birth to many, half of them die ... large numbers of our children are being swallowed up by enemy bombs and huge numbers are dying ... We must ... go to every family to advise, inspect, and guide them."[23] Another child-welfare reformer challenged the innateness of parenting skills, claiming that most parents go blindly into parenting without having the qualifications necessary to educate and raise their children properly.[24] A 1937 article on children's citizenship training cites families as the primary obstacle to making modern citizens out of children.[25] Without state intervention, parents were deemed to be untrustworthy protectors of the *minzu*'s children.

The Nationalists proposed a solution to mitigate the problem of poor family influences by attempting to reform families. In 1939 Chen Lifu (who was then the director of the Ministry of Education) proposed a curriculum of *jiating jiaoyu* (family education) to be instituted in girls' schools in order to prepare the nation's future mothers to properly raise children and run orderly households.[26] The Ministry of Education also began to work with women's colleges to develop programs to dispatch women college students to Sichuan and Gansu provinces to bring modern knowledge and technologies into homes in order to improve the welfare of children.[27]

By 1940 education journals were publishing articles that explained the importance of the Ministry of Education's order to carry out family education and that told primary-school teachers about the importance of going to the homes of students to eradicate "irrational" childcare practices and to promote modern practices. But the goals of family education extended beyond mere training in childcare practices. One 1940 article listed stimulating "consciousness of the *minzu*" *(minzu yishi)* as one of the main objectives of family education, saying that caregivers needed to become more patriotic in order to instill patriotism in their children.[28]

Critiques of the family were also depicted in wartime cartoons aimed at garnering support for nationalist reform policies. A cartoon in the journal *Zhanshi Houfang (Wartime Homefront)* bears the caption "Family Education."

FIGURE 8.1 Family Education. *Source: Zhanshi Houfang (Wartime Rearguard),* 21 March 1941, 4.

In the middle of the frame sits a large mahjong table, and the four players are enthusiastically engaged in their game: one kneels forward on his chair, intently focused on the tiles lined up neatly in front of him; another sits with arms folded, waiting patiently for her opponent to make a move; the third stands on her chair and leans forward over the table, sneaking a peek at her opponent's tiles; and the fourth player scrambles to the floor to collect a tile he has dropped. All of the players are small children and winsome at that, their shoes large on their feet, legs dangling from their chairs. They appear to be model modern students, the girls with bobbed hair and the boys with knee-length shorts. A woman seated to the side, watching with what appears to be amusement, smoking an opium pipe, supervises the game.[29] Clearly, the education these children are receiving within the family falls far short of what reformers envisioned for the modern child.

Two pages later in the same edition of *Zhanshi Houfang* another cartoon bears the caption "This generation compared to our next generation."

A mother dressed in a traditional Chinese slit-skirt gown and high heels appears to have been stopped by her small son as they are walking down the street together. She is in a hurry to move him along, her large hand resting firmly on his head in an attempt to steer him along their course. The son is looking at a sign, which reads, "War bonds sold here." The boy says, "Mama, that man says

FIGURE 8.2 "This generation compared to our next generation." *Source: Source: Zhanshi Houfang (Wartime Rearguard)*, 21 March 1941, 4.

those are war bonds to save the nation. Let's buy one!" The mother replies, "Great. Wait while I go win at cards first, and then we'll buy two." Although the mother's intentions appear to be in line with nationalistic priorities, her practices are a concern, and the cartoon suggests that her gambling will harm the war effort, not save the nation. The cartoon is optimistic about the next generation of citizens: the boy hears the call for help and is eager to answer it, and he appears sincere in his efforts to meet the wartime needs.

In the wartime context, parents were not necessarily an asset to the nation but could be a liability, especially if they had habits and ways of thinking that ran counter to those viewed as essential to a modern and strong nation. As a result, parents were not necessarily a part of New China, but their children were, and wartime propaganda embraced these children, making them the *minzu*'s very own. Hope was wagered on the next generation, but in order to nurture these children, they would need to be cultivated not within their family of origin but within a new kind of family: the family of the nation.

Creators of wartime children's homes set out to build alternative families within state institutions and strove to modernize and make more scientific the combined tasks of educating and rearing children. These aims were discussed in institutional surveys and were reflected in the names given these institutions during the war, *baoyuyuan* (welfare-education-institution) and *jiaoyangyuan* (teach-nurture-institution), which were chosen by reformers to convey the dual function of wartime children's homes to educate and nurture.[30] In October 1938 the Executive Yuan ordered all city governments from every province to consolidate their existing orphanages[31] *(gu'er yuan)* into one institution and call it a jiaoyangyuan.[32] Parents might not be qualified to care for children, so the logic went, but with training, modernized childcare workers were qualified.

It is significant that in strategizing ways of confronting the crisis of refugee children and war orphans, relief advocates did not propose foster-care or adoption programs where children would be placed with new families, nor were resources poured into reuniting children with their families. And no attempts seem to have been made to keep orphaned siblings together. One oral-history participant, a child refugee from Anhui province, reported that he and his elder sister were placed in separate children's homes from the time they entered the child-welfare system until three years after he had arrived in Sichuan province. By apparent chance, they both tested into the same middle school in Chengdu but were not notified of each other's presence there. One day, he encountered his sister on the playground, and in recounting this event, he said, "By then so much time had passed that we were no longer like brother and sister. We were embarrassed in each other's presence because we didn't know one another any longer."[33] The preservation of the family was not seen as a solution to the problem of refugee children and war orphans. In fact, the dissolution of families by circumstances of the war was taken as an opportunity to cultivate young citizens free of family systems.[34]

The lack of attention given to preserving families is noteworthy given a historical precedent for child-welfare policies to privilege the preservation of families over the creation of institutions. The Song Dynasty state (960-1279) used allowances from granaries and exemptions from public-labour duties to encourage impoverished families to care for their small children when they might otherwise abandon them and encouraged the adoption of the children of poor families by wealthier families.[35] The post-Taiping Qing gave impoverished families allowances to encourage them not to abandon their small children.[36] Yet something very different occurred with the devastation of the Anti-Japanese War. Dislocated families, replaced by institutions, were being emptied out, not reconstructed. This is a radical alteration of the traditional relationship between the family and the nation.

The Orphan as Both Opportunity and Danger

If there is one thing that was sought by twentieth-century radical social reformers, such as the May 4th intellectuals, it was a definitive rupture from the past that would allow the nation to start anew on a path toward modernization. The wartime period was treated as a historical break – a chance to extract children from the historical trajectory by taking advantage of the ruptures of war: the loss of their homes, their families, their places of origin.

The view of the orphan as the ideal raw material out of which to create modern and loyal national subjects was not one that relief workers and Nationalist ideologues could assume was popularly held. War orphans were not necessarily from family and economic backgrounds that were likely to propel them into positions as future national leaders. Of the 431 children residing in the Shijie Hongshizihui Beiquan Ciyouyuan (International Red Cross Beiquan Loving Children's Home) in Sichuan in 1942, only 68 came from families whose occupations might traditionally predispose them toward government service: education, military, government, law, and medicine. The remaining 363 children were from family backgrounds such as labour, small business, agriculture, and unemployment.[37] A similar demographic in family backgrounds appeared in the composition of children residing at the Number One Temporary Children's Home in Wuhan in 1938. Of the 550 residents, only 75 came from occupations such as education, military, national salvation, government, and medicine. The remaining children were from backgrounds such as merchants, farmers, and labourers, and 167 were from the ranks of the unemployed.[38] If these children were to be transformed into modern citizens, with values embodied by the urban elite, they would need training, and their caregivers and teachers would need to be convinced that the training was worth their efforts.

Relief advocates and educators were aware that they conceived of the Chinese child differently from those who held traditional perspectives on the position of the child in the Chinese family. For example, in her 1938 letter to childcare workers in wartime children's homes, published in the popular journal *Funü Shenghuo (Women's Life)*, the child-relief advocate Jun Hui (cited earlier) argued that the war had changed children, particularly orphans. According to Jun, in the past children had been regarded as "accessories of their parents," "playthings," "family slaves," or "bright pearls clutched in the hands of parents." Because of their wartime experience, Jun argued, war orphans, which she referred to as "children of the *minzu*," were less selfish and more loyal than adults, making them a great asset to the nation:

> The artillery fire of the war has taken [today's children of the *minzu*] from schools, from street corners, and from their mothers' arms and gathered them in one

> place. Transient lives and the enemy's brutality have given them a profound understanding of the meaning of the war; they have more hatred for the enemy in their little pure souls than adults do. They are more passionate about pursuing truth than adults and have fewer individualistic worries.[39]

From Jun's perspective, all that was necessary was to give them training that would strengthen their resolve: "With proper training, they will display a strength as great as anyone's strength."[40]

In a survey of the Beiquan Loving Children's Home in Sichuan, the author – a Grade 5 teacher at the home – suggested that the patriotism of children and a child's own national consciousness were enough to counter any corruption a child may have received from his or her family of origin. The director of the home told the following story of a playground brawl between two students, which reads as a parable of the redemptive power – both for the children and for the nation – of viewing institutionalized children separately from their family histories:

> The patriotism of children is very strong. If you ask them what they will do when they grow up, they will definitely answer that they will fight the Japanese. Once a child called another child a "traitor" while they were fighting. The child started crying, and a teacher ran over and asked one child why he and the other children had called this child a "traitor," saying, "How can you tell?" The child answered, "He said his older brother is a soldier and went to fight the Japanese. But he never went ... he sold the gun for 20 yuan and he never went to fight the Japanese. Instead, he sold the nation's gun. Isn't that a traitor? So we beat him up." The teacher asked, "Is this true?" The child who was being attacked said, "Yes, it's true, my brother's a traitor. He is bad, and so I'm being beaten." The teacher said, "What you children did was wrong. Everyone must take responsibility for his own actions. Even if his brother is a traitor, this child can still be a patriot. If you say that he can only be a traitor because his brother is a traitor, aren't you then teaching him to be a traitor, and so you yourself are creating traitors?" When the children heard this, they let the child go.[41]

The optimism and idealism of Republican reformers about the true nature and potential of children, coupled with a faith in scientific methods for child-rearing and Western theories of child development, were finally given an arena where theory could meet practice, seemingly untainted by the influences of the past. Orphans were deemed by child-relief leaders to be the ideal raw material for the shaping of national citizens.

Not only were orphans appealing to reformers because they were without the bad influences presumed to come from families, but most were also without the influence of prior education. Of the 550 orphans of the Wuhan Number One Temporary Children's Home in 1938, only 164 had previously been students. Most of the others had been working as labourers or apprentices, scavengers, beggars, firewood collectors, and porters. Twelve were classified as former soldiers.[42] Their new institutional "parents" would also be their first teachers, which presented a tremendous opportunity for those who wished to fashion them into a new kind of citizen. Many wartime child-relief workers were educated and progressive refugees from occupied areas, transplanted to the interior and in need of meaningful work. They found this work and actively participated in nation building by creating wartime child-welfare institutions, and they had the perfect subjects for their new calling. War orphans presented an opportunity for education reformers to demonstrate the importance of education in Nationalist plans to revolutionize the nation.

But despite the opportunities that war orphans presented to reformers, these children were not without risks. Some child-welfare workers were concerned that orphans were more dangerous to the nation than were children with families. In an essay published in a 1938 collection on how to care for refugee children, one of Republican China's foremost child-development experts, Chen Heqin (1892-1982), posited that parents were a child's first teachers of patriotism and nationalism: "Parents should train children to have loving feelings toward others. People will be able to love society and the nation only if they developed loving feelings toward others when they were children."[43] Deprived of love from family, orphans might be stunted in their ability to develop a love for the "family" of the nation. The directors of wartime children's homes and the teachers employed there were acutely aware that one of their most important tasks was to instill war orphans with an experience of nationalism that would translate into work for the nation.

Conclusion

Ideas of the place of the family in rearing children were packaged by prewar agendas. Prewar intellectual, political, and cultural antecedents challenged the naturalness of the Chinese family and identified the family as a societal unit that could be created, reformed, or revolutionized. Although the discourse of family reform had been present during much of the early twentieth century, the wartime period marked, from the reformer's perspective, a kind of rupture with history. The special circumstances of the war allowed the unique role of the orphan to emerge. Orphans could now be valued, utilized, and even exploited.

There is a relative lack of scholarship on the family and general social history for this period, but the history of the family did not come to a standstill during the war years. The war created a moment that brought orphans into political and national discourse, and those seeking family reform had a new opportunity to enact theories that had been floated over the past decades. The war orphan came to be seen both as an opportunity to usher in a new kind of citizenry and as a risk to nation-building projects, and it is the tension between these two perspectives that animated much of the wartime discussion of orphans and the practices that spun from these discourses.

Historically, orphans had receded from the public view and had had no valuable identity within society or the state. Nationalist propaganda repositioned orphans as members of the greater national family, citizens who transcended blood ties and provided hope for the future. A distinctive political identity developed for orphans during the war as a result of this repositioning, and new orphan institutions were created during the war. This new identity and these institutions did not simply offer charity and protection to orphans but also extended new expectations and responsibilities to orphans that carried currency in postwar political eras. Former Chinese Communist Party (CCP) leader Jiang Zemin was publicly recognized as an orphan and used his status to spearhead a national campaign in the early 1990s to improve orphanages through increased donations and medical volunteers. The famous Communist martyr Lei Feng is also frequently depicted as an orphan who gave his life in service of the nation. The orphan, if properly shaped by the *minzu* and state as parent, was assumed to be unabashedly loyal to the nation.

The various ideologies concerning the family helped to shape the rhetoric and treatment of orphans. Critics of the traditional family saw the orphan as opportunity (family-*free*). Supporters of the family saw the orphan as risk (family-*less*). Practices in orphan homes reflected both of these concerns, but neither concern won out: family was still an important unit, and precautions were still taken to ensure that orphans would develop a sense of family. It was precisely the societal and cultural value placed on families that led to the orphan becoming a potent symbol for national propaganda.

Notes

1 Zhao Shihui, "Jiangxi Di Yi Baoyuyuan Shicha Guilai" [An inspector returns to the Jiangxi Number One Children's Home], *Baoyusheng Tongxun* [Newsletter for Children's Home Alumni] 1, 8 (1997): 7-10; originally published in *Jiangxi Funü* [Jiangxi Women] 5, 2 (1940).

2 Ibid., 8. All translations of quotations from non-English sources are mine.

3 Ibid., 8.

4 The most influential Chinese experts on child psychology and early childhood education during the Republican period were Chen Heqin (1892-1982) and Tao Xingzhi (1891-1976). Both received graduate degrees from Columbia University's Teachers College under the mentorship of John Dewey and were highly influenced by Dewey's model of progressive

education. Dewey travelled throughout China from 1919 to 1921 under the invitation of Tao Xingzhi and Hu Shi, visiting twelve provinces and lecturing – usually to packed halls – on his theories of education and democracy, school and society. I have written more extensively on John Dewey's influence on Republican-era educators and child psychologists in M. Colette Plum, "Unlikely Heirs: War Orphans during the Second Sino-Japanese War, 1937-45," ch. 5, "Lost Childhoods: The Political Construction of Child-Citizen-Workers," 210-52 (PhD diss., Department of History, Stanford University, 2006).

5 Hollington K. Tong, ed., *The China Handbook, 1937-1945: A Comprehensive Survey of Major Developments in China in Eight Years of War* (New York: MacMillan, 1947), 527-28. This chapter is not a comprehensive study of wartime relief work per se but a study of the meaning of children and war orphans to state-building projects and how this meaning was articulated in wartime practices by Nationalist-supervised institutions. Figures of numbers of orphans rescued by missionaries are not the focus because they are not part of the "puzzle" of the new place of orphans in the national body.

6 See Wu Yanyin, "Shishi jiuji ji jiaoyang nantong de yuanze yu yaodian" [Principles and essentials in the rescue and care of refugee children], in *Nanmin Ertong de Jiuji yu Jiaoyang* [The Rescue and Care of Refugee Children], ed. Duli Chubanshe [Indendent Publishing House] (Chongqing: Zhengzhong shuju zong zazhi tuiguangsuo [Central Publishing House Magazine Popularization Division], 1938), 26.

7 Wu Dehui (pseudonym), interview by author, Chongqing, 4 October 2002.

8 On the novelty of widespread public and political interest in child welfare during the war years, see Chen Zhenzhen, "Kangzhan qijian de nantong jiaoyu (1937-45)" [Child refugee education during the War of Resistance (1937-45)], paper presented at the Fourth Symposium of Seminars on Educational Philosophy and History, National Taiwan Normal University, 10 December 2004, 2; available at National Taiwan Normal University webpage, *Seminars on Educational Philosophy and History,* http://www.ed.ntnu.edu.tw/~seph/paper.htm.

9 One possible translation for *minzu* is "national race." I transliterate rather than translate this term because the content of *minzu* is importantly different from the nearest English equivalents, "race" and "nationality." *Minzu* has a racial component but also includes cultural and national – in the sense of nation-state – connotations. From a strictly semantic perspective, the nearest English term is "ethnicity," but translating *minzu* in this way is cumbersome and inaesthetic, and it misses the nation-state aspect of the meaning.

10 Hsiung Ping-Chen, *A Tender Voyage: Children and Childhood in Late Imperial China* (Stanford, CA: Stanford University Press, 2005), 165-69.

11 Stephen MacKinnon, "Refugee Flight at the Outset of the Anti-Japanese War," in *Scars of War: The Impact of Warfare on Modern China,* ed. Diana Lary and Stephen MacKinnon, 126-33 (Vancouver: UBC Press, 2001).

12 Jun Hui, "Xiegei Nantong Baoyu Gongzuozhe" [Letter to childcare workers working with refugee children], *Funü Shenghuo* [Women's Life] 6, 9 (1938); reprinted in *Kangri Fenghuo Zhong de Yaolan* [Cradle during the Flames of the War of Resistance], ed. Jin Futang, 90-95 (Beijing: Zhongguo Funü Chubanshe [China Women's Press], 1991).

13 The care and education of orphans in wartime children's homes was also gendered. Orphans in wartime children's homes were divided into family groups and called their primary teachers by the Chinese term for "mom" *(mama)* regardless of whether or not the teachers were male or female. Girls and boys studied many of the same academic subjects but were given gendered work training that encouraged them to make gendered contributions to the nation as child-citizens. For more on the training and education of orphans in wartime children's homes, see Plum, "Unlikely Heirs," ch. 6, "Child Citizens at Work in Wartime Children's Homes," 253-96.

14 Shen Zijiu, "Jiuji Ji Jiaoyang Nanmin Ertong De Xuanchuan" [Propaganda about refugee children rescue and care], in *Nanmin Ertong de Jiuji yu Jiaoyang* [The Rescue and Care of Refugee Children], ed. Duli Chubanshe [Indendent Publishing House] (Chongqing: Zhengzhong shuju zong zazhi tuiguangsuo [Central Publishing House Magazine Popularization Division], 1938), 22.

15 Ibid., 24.

16 Tang Yingwei, "Peiyang Zhongxue Kangzhan Huihua Liudong Zhanlanhui Gongzuo Jingguo Baogao" [Report on the work of developing middle-school wartime travelling painting exhibitions], *Zhanshi Yishu* [Wartime Art] 2, 2 (1938): 3.

17 Andrew F. Jones, "The Child as History in Republican China: A Discourse on Development," *Positions: East Asia Culture Critique* 10, 3 (2002): 708. Lu Xun's story inspired other critiques of the family system in May 4th literature. See, for example, Wu Yü, "Chiren yu lijiao" [Cannibalism and ethics], *New Youth* 6 (November 1919): 578-80.

18 Chiang Kai-shek's New Life Movement was a state-building effort that utilized Confucian family concepts such as loyalty and filiality in an attempt to produce a disciplined citizenry that was respectful of hierarchy and thus obedient to the state.

19 Robert Culp, "Setting the Sheet of Loose Sand: Conceptions of Society and Citizenship in Nanjing Decade Party Doctrine and Civics Textbooks," in *Defining Modernity: Guomindang Rhetorics of a New China, 1920-1970*, ed. Terry Bodenhorn (Ann Arbor: University of Michigan Center for Chinese Studies, 2002), 69.

20 Ibid., 72-73. You Hui wrote that "modern citizens should love the nation as they love the family"; see You Hui, "Guonan Zhong De Xiaoxue Jiaoyu Ying Ruhe Shishi" [How to implement primary education during national crisis], *Sichuan Jiaoyu* [Sichuan Education] 1 (1937): 71.

21 On women's involvement in wartime family reform, see Helen Schneider, *Keeping the Nation's House: Domestic Management and the Making of Modern China* (Vancouver: UBC Press, 2011).

22 Chen Lifu, "Jiuji Ji Jiaoyang Nantong De Yiyi" [The meaning of the rescue and care of refugee children], in *Nanmin Ertong de Jiuji yu Jiaoyang* [The Rescue and Care of Refugee Children], ed. Duli Chubanshe [Indendent Publishing House] (Chongqing: Zhengzhong shuju zong zazhi tuiguangsuo [Central Publishing House Magazine Popularization Division], 1938), 17; originally published in *Guohun* [National Spirit], n.d., 6.

23 Shen, "Jiuji Ji Jiaoyang," 24.

24 Chen Peilan, "You Zhanqu Nantong De Jiaoyang Tandao Ertong Baoyu De Shiji" [A discussion of the care of child war refugees and the realities of childcare], *Jiaoyu Zazhi* [Education Magazine] 30, 1 (1940): 21.

25 Chen Ying, "Ertong Gongmin Xunlian Wenti" [Problems with children's citizenship training], *Ertong Jiaoyu* [Children's Education] 7, 9 (1937): 84-89.

26 Helen Schneider, "On the Homefront: Women's Work Corps and Social Welfare in the Sino-Japanese War," paper presented at the Annual Meeting of the Southeast Chapter of the Association for Asian Studies, Lexington, Kentucky, 16 January 2005, 12. Schneider cites Chen Lifu, *Zhanshi jiaoyu fangzhen* [The Direction of Wartime Education] (1939; reprint, Zhonghua Minguo shiliao congbian series, Taibei: Dangshi weiyuan hui [Contemporary Committee], 1985), 179, 205, 206, 275.

27 Schneider, *Keeping the Nation's House*.

28 Wu Ding, "Xiaoxue Ruhe Tuixing Jiating Jiaoyu" [How primary schools should carry out family education], *Jiaoyu Zazhi* [Education Magazine] 30, 4 (1940): 38. See also Mai Canshi, "Dao Xuesheng De Jiating Qu!" [Go to students' homes!], *Jiaoyu Zazhi* [Education Magazine] 30, 4 (1940): 33-35.

29 *Zhanshi Houfang* [Wartime Rearguard], 21 March 1941, 4.

30 "Jiuji Nantong: Ge Shengshi Gukuyuan Jiang Kuoda Zuzhi, Guangshi Shourongsuo Jiaoyang" [Refugee children's relief: Every province's city orphanages shall be expanded and enlarged to include shelters for the care and education of children], *Zhongyang Ribao* [Executive Yuan Daily], 3 October 1938, 1. See also a fundraising pamphlet created by one of the wartime relief associations, Zhongguo Zhanshi Ertong Jiuji Xiehui [China Wartime Child Relief Association], *Zhongguo Zhangshi Ertong Jiuji Xiehui Yuanqi* [Origins of the China Wartime Child Relief Association] (Hankou: Zhongguo Zhanshi Ertong Jiuji Xiehui, 1938), 1; and Xingzhengyuan [Nationalist Executive Yuan], *Ertong Baoyu* [Child welfare] (Nanjing: Xingzhengyuan Xinwenju [Nationalist Executive Yuan's News Bureau], 1947), 1.

31 The intentional renaming of these institutions is significant. The change of the name from "orphanage" to a name emphasizing teaching and care of children communicated that these were a new kind of institution with new priorities for children, different from traditional philanthropic organizations.

32 "Jiuji Nantong."

33 Wei Yongli (pseudonym), interview by author, Chengdu, 26 April 2002.

34 In contrast, Soviet Russia created foster families and adoption programs to care for war orphans during the same period. See Nathan Berman, "The Place of the Child in Present-Day Russia," *Social Forces* 21, 4 (May 1943): 446-56; Margaret K. Stolee, "Homeless Children in the U.S.S.R., 1917-57," *Soviet Studies* 40, 1 (January 1988): 64-83.

35 Raymond David Lum, "Philanthropy and Public Welfare in Late Imperial China" (PhD diss., Department of History, Harvard University, 1985).

36 See Angela Ki Che Leung, "Relief Institutions for Children in Nineteenth-Century China," in *Chinese Views of Childhood*, ed. Anne Behnke Kinney (Honolulu: University of Hawai'i Press, 1995), 259, 265.

37 Jiang Kaixin, *Shijie Hongshizihui Beiquan Ciyouyuan Gaikuang* [A survey of the International Red Cross Beiquan Loving Children's Home] (Beiquan: Shijie Hongshizihui [International Red Cross], 1942), 29b. This book can be found in Chongqingshi dang'an guan [Chongqing Municipal Archives], "Beiyuan Folder," catalogue 1, vol. 1.

38 Jing, "Wuhan Di Yi Linshi Baoyuyuan Kaimu Yi Pie" [An overview of the opening of Wuhan's Number One Temporary Children's Home], *Funü Wenhua Zhanshi Tekan* [Women's Culture: Special Wartime Edition] 11 (1938): 15.

39 Jun, "Xiegei Nantong Baoyu Gongzuozhe," 90-91.

40 Ibid., 91.

41 Jiang, *Shijie Hongshizihui Beiquan Ciyouyuan Gaikuang*, 39b.

42 Jing, "Wuhan Di Yi Linshi Baoyuyuan Kaimu Yi Pie," 15.

43 Chen Heqin, "Zenyang Jiao Xiaohaizi" [How to teach children], in *Nanmin Ertong de Jiuji yu Jiaoyang* [The Rescue and Care of Refugee Children], ed. Duli Chubanshe [Independent Publishing House], 46-51 (Chongqing: Zhengzhong shuju zong zazhi tuiguangsuo [Central Publishing House Magazine Popularization Division], 1938), 50-51.

Part 3: Memory and Representation

9

Controlling Soldiers: The Memory Scars of Late Imperial China

Alexander Woodside

WHAT HAVE BEEN THE consequences of militarism and war for Chinese politics, culture, and society? Such consequences may be assessed in magisterial overviews of the Chinese republic's history between 1912 and 1949, as Diana Lary has done in her many books;[1] in contrast, they may also be examined (as Michael Szonyi does elsewhere in this volume) in small local settings like the islands in the Taiwan Strait during the post-1949 Cold War. The results of militarism, and efforts to contain them, may be studied in connection with the project of a military leader like Chiang Kai-shek to train a vanguard officer corps imbued with neotraditional moral and political values, undertaken at the Whampoa Military Academy in the 1920s, as Colin Green demonstrates in this book; failures to contain them may be explored by looking at the "pay problems" of warlord armies and, as Edward McCord's chapter shows, at the soldiers' mutinies that resulted when pay problems could not be resolved.

But all these analyses fit inside an even bigger and much older story. Anxiety about war – the ways it could distort politics, bankrupt the government, and ruin society, especially if military controls broke down – has a long history in Chinese political thought before 1911. Confucian scholar-officials were the leaders in keeping the anxiety alive. Contradicting their not wholly deserved reputation for pacificism, they were often involved in China's actual wars themselves. Wang Chang (1725-1806), a celebrated teacher and academy head who had also been an adviser and commander in an ill-starred Qing Dynasty invasion of Burma, was a good example. In a suggestive and much anthologized essay, Wang wrote that of all the tasks of political governance, the number-one problem was the problem of controlling or "governing soldiers" *(zhi bing)*. The moral spirit that would inhibit armies from threatening political stability could be instilled only in good generals and select troops.[2] But how could these be found or created?

Of course, the difficulty of controlling the military establishments that governments themselves build up, so as to prevent soldiers from turning either to political subversion or to informal savageries outside the plans of strategists remote from the battlefields, was a concern Chinese thinkers shared with European and Ottoman Empire leaders and, more recently, with Japanese and American ones. But the great size of the Chinese Empire after 1368, and the scale of its armies, made the concern especially problematic for Chinese thinkers like Wang Chang. At the beginning of the 1500s, for example, Ming Dynasty China (1368-1644) had a hereditary-"guards" *(weisuo)* army with 2.7 million soldiers recorded in its registers.[3] How could they be managed?

The Control of Soldiers: A Chinese and Universal Management Risk

All political systems need to generate codes of accountability for themselves that lie outside the more formal means of ensuring such accountability, such as written law codes or constitutions. Cautionary memories, or storytelling practices about past military experiences that turned out badly, could be incorporated into such codes, strengthening their reflexes of risk management. In China the development of such reflexes was part of a great debate about the proper degree of the centralization of power. For rulers of China after the eighth century, some of the most powerful cautionary tales about past wars were probably the ones that concerned An Lushan, the Tang Dynasty's Turkic-frontier general. His rebellion against the Tang central government supposedly showed the dangers of a weak political centre, especially one that decentralized military power too much, as the Tang court seemingly had before the rebellion's outbreak in 755.

But for many Chinese scholar-officials, there were even more potent cautionary tales that warned against too much centralized power. This theme is probably less well known. For such scholar-officials, the bloody meltdown of the eleventh-century Song Dynasty's capital-city army, which had a paper strength of 800,000 men but could not successfully defend its court against frontier pressures or save about half of its soldiers from eventually drifting into banditry, also survived as a memory in subsequent centuries. This memory influenced the Chinese thinkers who wished to reshape the structure or military arrangements of the empire. So did yet another memory, that of the decline of the Ming Dynasty's military establishment in the 1500s and 1600s, before, during, and after what Huang Zongxi (1610-95), one of China's most famous political theorists, called Dong shi (the Eastern Incident). The Eastern Incident was a brutal war between China and Japan over Korea. This war began in 1592 with a Japanese invasion of Korea aimed at China. It ended only when the Japanese military expansionist who had begun it, Toyotomi Hideyoshi, died in 1598.

Beyond politics lay philosophy. Debates about how to control soldiers raised even broader issues than the political one of how much power should be concentrated at the centre or devolved on more local authorities. Such debates also became a specialized variant of mainstream Chinese discussions about the formation and preservation of human moral character itself. The specific concept of "military virtue" *(wu de)* appeared very early in Chinese thought. The term even became the name of a Han Dynasty court dance in which dancers clutching shields and axes acted out military scenes in order to exorcise the spirit of rebellion. One recent history of the development of a Chinese culture of military virtue begins in the Zhou Dynasty and divides the evolution of its subject, from then to modern times, into five periods. The book suggests that military virtue – the "value concepts" of armies and of the soldiers in them – amounts to a special form of moral self-control that cannot be compared to other types.[4]

But in Chinese history the question of military morality's relationship to more general morality was a grey area whose tensions and conflicts had to be endlessly negotiated. The fragility of the connections between Confucian humanism and the management of military power was an important worry in Chinese politics long before the twentieth-century warlords and the emergence of modern leaders such as Chiang Kai-shek. Ming and Qing Dynasty literati wrote eloquently about the need to integrate thinking about military issues more closely with general political and ethical theory. They warned that soldiering was undervalued and that it was dangerous to allow so great a separation to exist between civil learning and military life. Such a separation encouraged the norms of civil learning to become less real and the practices of military life to become less principled.

Are there, then, such things as perennial political problems? Some critics of this assumption might say no, on the grounds that, over the centuries, there have been too many changes in human thought in terms of both epistemologies and uses of language. These changes supposedly make it impossible for us fully to recapture the concerns of past ages. This argument, however, could be said to be self-refuting: the critics explain what they regard as the alienness to us of the concerns of former centuries in our own contemporary language, thus acknowledging backhandedly that this language can be used to access that past after all. And if ever there were an instance of "all history being contemporary history," we can find it in what Wang Chang, in the 1700s, called the primary political problem of governing soldiers.

European kingdoms, before the rise of professional armies, had to divide their political systems' legal uses of violence between monarchs and their nobilities; the nobilities' very "honour" lay (according to Montesquieu) in going to war.[5] The problem of controlling armies was conceived more bureaucratically in China. As a transcontinental empire, its defence often seemed to require troop-mobilization levels so high, by pre-industrial standards, that scholar-officials despaired of finding any known theoretical recipe for successfully managing them, either inside or outside classical thought.

But beyond differences in scale, we may see the universality of this problem. The British (and, by extension, Canadians, Australians, and New Zealanders) might not have a monarchy now if Oliver Cromwell's successors, in the English republic he created, had not lost control of Cromwell's increasingly undisciplined army between 1658 and 1660, prompting people of property to restore the monarchy and give its crown to Charles II and, in the long run, to Elizabeth II. Edward Gibbon's history of the decline and fall of the Roman Empire is generally supposed to be about the triumph of "barbarism" and religion; but it could equally be said to be a chronicle of the dangerous illicit power of armies in politics, especially that of the brutal praetorian guards who so casually enthroned and then murdered Roman emperors. In the 1700s, the century in which Gibbon actually lived, the vulnerability of the Ottoman sultans in Istanbul to their own armed janissaries offered Gibbon a contemporary confirmation of the importance of this theme. Japanese civilian politicians' losing struggle to restrain the Japanese army and navy in the 1930s moves this perennial problem much closer to us, as well as to the painful subject matter – in the history of the Chinese republic – that Diana Lary has explored so well. President Dwight D. Eisenhower's famous 1961 warning about the unwarranted and potentially misplaced power of the American military-industrial complex merely adds the necessary industrial and capitalist flavouring to what is a very old anxiety.

The problem of controlling soldiers was (and is) related to the question of how to produce and maintain trust in human societies. Were trustworthy armies best created by their soldiers' childhood socialization and by their moral or ideological training as they matured? Or were such armies best created by excellent administrative and legal arrangements? To put the matter even more simply: should a political system give greater weight to the creation of people who were loyal or to the creation of institutions and laws that would make people loyal?

In Classical China this was the debate over "government by virtue" versus "government by laws." In the somewhat pompous language of contemporary American political science, it is the "culturalist" approach versus the "institutionalist" approach to explaining political trust and loyalty formation. "Culturalists" think that models of moral and social behaviour govern us, whereas "institutionalists" maintain that the goals we choose to pursue are shaped by the institutional arrangements through which we operate.[6] In China a catastrophe like the collapse of the Ming military system in the 1500s and 1600s can be explained in "institutionalist" terms as having been caused by too high and too costly a level of military mobilization at the centre and by failed arrangements for reconciling military people directed by the centre with the needs of local communities and their claims. But it can also be explained in "culturalist" terms as amounting to a failure to use the central moral traditions of the civilization, supposedly best upheld by scholar-officials, to inspire and subdue potentially disobedient soldiers. One great seventeenth-century thinker, Huang Zongxi, chose the latter approach, in what remains a cogent but somewhat subjective analysis of one dynasty's loss of control of its soldiers and of its military downfall.[7]

The Politics of Interpreting Ming Military Decline

The Ming military defeat in the 1600s, when the dynasty foundered, has generated an enormous amount of commentary, from the end of the Ming era itself to the present. The full range of this commentary can hardly begin to be surveyed adequately here. Huang Zongxi addressed the subject in the early 1660s, shortly after the Manchus' Qing Dynasty had replaced the Ming. Huang's "culturalist" explanation of the Ming Dynasty's loss of control of its military establishment is an important example of the genre. Huang's father was a well-known figure in the Donglin Academy, a stronghold of critical dissent in the late Ming; his father was also a victim of the eunuch "police-state" terror that helped to destroy the dynasty. (By one calculation, the late Ming court had some 100,000 eunuch officials, as contrasted with about 20,000 or so regular civil bureaucrats.)[8] Huang himself defended the Ming to the bitter end, even serving in the war ministry of one of the last Ming princes. Then he turned to writing.

One hundred or more of Huang's works have survived to the present, including landmark histories of the learning of Ming Dynasty and Song-Yuan Dynasty literati. His chief Western interpreter and translator, William Theodore deBary, has called Huang an outstanding figure in the history of Chinese thought.[9] He was all of that; but he was also the member of a social class (scholar-officials) that was determined, in such a time of troubles, to recover its political position by projecting its values as the values and interests of humanity itself. For Huang, restoring the position of the scholar-official was associated with the extreme view that the monarchy itself was hopelessly degraded. (This has subsequently earned Huang the not wholly deserved reputation, three centuries after he lived, of having been a precocious "liberal.") Human history had gone through three stages: a bad period without monarchy; a good era of monarchy in which personal self-abnegation and hard work were so intrinsic to monarchs that nobody wanted to be one; and a bad period with a monarchy in which monarchs manufactured the false belief that their private interests were really public ones. Huang inherited the neo-Confucian predisposition of earlier centuries to think that principle and desire were polar opposites that could be separated from each other, as could righteous behaviour from profit seeking; scholar-officials supposedly embodied desire-proof principle. Unfortunately for Huang, the growing commercialization of Chinese society – the Ming China of the Huizhou,

Suzhou, and Shanxi merchant networks – weakened the practical plausibility of such claims, either for scholar-officials or for the soldiers they hoped to influence.[10]

Ming political and military institutions between the late 1300s and the 1600s had been remarkably complex. Kenneth Lieberthal and Michel Oksenberg, two American political scientists, have pointed to the "fragmentation of authority" as being a key feature of the politics of the present-day People's Republic of China.[11] But the principle of fragmented authority is far older in China than is Communist rule there. It goes back many centuries, it may have acquired its most extreme forms in the Ming Dynasty's empire, and it is at least arguable that the critical question of how to "govern soldiers" was at the root of its persistence.

In his writings about Ming military decline, Huang Zongxi called the Ming Dynasty's fragmented authoritarianism by a more poetic name: it was the "dog's teeth" *(quan ya)* pattern of administration. By this, Huang meant a system of checks and balances, especially in the governance of military affairs, that resembled the interlocked, jig-sawed appearance of dogs' teeth. Power fragmentation of this calculated dog's teeth type had been thought to be a barrier against the early rise of disloyal regional army commanders such as the infamous An Lushan. In effect, the calculated fragmentation substituted for the more intense hierarchical loyalties of a feudal culture that had eroded too much over the centuries as a result of the influence of examinations-based bureaucratic rule.

In practice, the dog's teeth formula meant that Ming China had both a central war ministry, which controlled troop movements and military strategy, and five central "chief military commissions," which controlled the military registers and the training of the empire's hereditary-guards soldiers. (China's contemporary Communist leaders, on the other hand, make do with just one central military commission.) In the provinces, the Ming court deployed three different types of military authority figures. These were the civil grand co-ordinators, who controlled military planning and military supplies; the military regional commanders, who led the troops; and the "inner-court ministers" (i.e., court eunuchs), who were intended to be a counterweight to the first two in the proper checks-and-balances, dog's teeth manner.

The purpose of the dog's teeth state, and its deliberate fragmentation of control, was to create a rebellion-proof political community. But as Huang Zongxi scoffed, this was more or less trying to build a rebellion-proof community on the basis of pure proceduralism. There had never been, and never could be, "laws" that foreclosed all possibility of military rebellion.

As Huang saw it, Ming military power had evolved through three stages, in all of which the result had been failure. The first stage had featured the hereditary-guards soldiers. These soldiers were supposed to remain relatively isolated from nonmilitary Chinese village society and to obey generals they did not know. The generals themselves were sent out from the capital city to command them only for specified military operations. But the empire's perceived defence needs were so grandiose that they were thought to require hereditary-guards armies of up to three million men; Huang believed that the tax revenues of a "single empire" could not afford to pay for such armies. The second flaw in the hereditary-guards experiment, Huang thought, was its weak and artificial military-obedience system, which detached soldiers from rural society and their natal communities. The human longing for home (literally the soldiers' "thoughts of their village well") could not be repressed in these soldiers.

When the hereditary-guards system declined, its registers containing the names of soldiers who had long since died or deserted, two other types of army replaced it, embodying the second and third stages of the Ming military tragedy. First came an army of mercenaries. Financially, these mercenaries crippled the Ming government during the 1592-98 Sino-Japanese War. They also caused havoc in society and, as fighters, were not worth one-third of their number of old regular soldiers in their heyday. Lastly, the Ming turned to a reliance on the personal armies of local commanders in the early 1600s. But many of the local commanders used their personal armies to kill and loot, disobeying the crumbling political centre. Military men of this category who did create loyal model armies, like Qi Jiguang (1528-88), were the exception, even if they were also inspirations later to Zeng Guofan in the 1800s and no doubt to Chiang Kai-shek after 1911.

Representations of past military crises, needless to say, have ideological implications. This is as true of the first Sino-Japanese War in the sixteenth century as it is of the second one in the 1930s and 1940s. For Huang Zongxi, the Chinese Empire was a giant moral problem. How were codes of accountability for soldiers to be created that would stretch beyond "thoughts of the village well"? Huang's solution, in an era before mass nationalism, was pure Confucian elitism. He had argued that no mere military institutions could ever be designed that were disorder-proof or rebellion-proof. Only people could be created who would not rebel. Such people, he maintained, could be found only among the ranks of high Confucian scholars, who had been wrongly excluded from Ming military commands. The Chinese bureaucratic culture that divided civil and military officialdoms was a mistake. Reconciling the two worlds was crucial. It would allow Confucian scholars both to understand military strategy better and to teach less educated military men that "love of the people" was the real basis of military conduct. But who might the prototype be of the broadly learned scholar whose moral integrity was so strong that he could command big armies without their ever rebelling? Huang chose Du Mu (803-52), the Tang Dynasty poet who had also been a military expert. But Du Mu belonged to a Chinese society of eight centuries earlier.

Much of Huang Zongxi's thought may be seen to serve as a kind of preview of later Chinese concerns – about the politics of military establishments – in the nineteenth and twentieth centuries. Yet it was also an obvious effort to universalize the aims and values of the upper strata of the Confucian-scholar class, to which Huang belonged. Even in the 1500s and 1600s, it was hardly the only analysis of Ming military troubles.

As a contrast, consider the views of Zhang Juzheng (1525-82), the strong-willed Ming grand secretary of the 1560s, about a century before Huang Zongxi. Zhang had tried to plan a Ming military revival from inside the system, at a time when such a thing still seemed possible. According to Zhang, China in the 1500s lacked the willpower to defend its frontiers. The Ming bureaucracy was increasingly unable to adapt to its environment, disguising its weaknesses by too much discussion and by proposing the existence of illusory material scarcities, of soldiers, provisions, and commanders, as a means of concealing its declining effectiveness. The remedy was a return to emperors who were sufficiently martial to review their own soldiers on horseback and a restriction of policy discussions inside the government in order to make administration more "solid." Unlike Huang, Zhang did not see scholar-officials as omnicompetent worthies or as moral leaders. Indeed, Zhang wanted to intensify surveillance of scholar-officials, whose weaknesses worried him, and to convert academies, their strongholds outside the government, into office buildings.[12]

In this light, Huang's "culturalist" approach to the question of how to control soldiers may be seen as an extraordinarily sophisticated restatement of the timeless romance of the idealized Chinese mandarin, using a military crisis as support for it. This romance was especially strong in an empire whose real-life civil officials were so vulnerable. But its notion of a military regeneration based on the medieval Confucian separation of "principle" from "desire," as incarnated by virtuous scholar-officials, needed some imaginative policing to keep its anachronisms from colliding with Chinese social realities after the 1400s.

The growing commercialization of Chinese society seems in retrospect to have doomed the old Ming hereditary-guards army at least as much as the decline was caused by its soldiers' frustrations at being uprooted from their own communities and their accompanying "thoughts of their village well." One Ming observer had pointed out, as early as the mid-1400s, that soldiers were deserting their guards units in order to augment their incomes as merchants or artisans. As he put it, Ming soldiers' energy was being converted into "gold and silver," with a mercantile craftiness displacing their original honest natures. Asking such soldiers to resist a military enemy in a crisis would be like asking "sheep" to resist "wolves."[13] Economic prosperity and its accompanying growth of non-military employment opportunities, especially as these were not shared by China's less prosperous, more "wolfish" neighbours, were in effect psychologically demilitarizing the Ming Dynasty's empire. But growing imbalances between a dynamic civilian economy and a military establishment whose standard of living is in relative decline are a threat to war-making power in other polities besides early-modern China.

The Problem of Military Control after the Ming

If the growth of commerce was one threat to China's older military-control theories, especially the "culturalist" ones, the sheer scale of the empire was another.

One famous Chinese academician, Yao Nai (1732-1815), who had served in the Beijing Ministry of War, thought the problem was almost hopeless. Yao made the usual contrast between ancient China's small city-states and the giant, seemingly dehumanized empire in which he lived. The city-states' armies, Yao alleged, had been so small that their soldiers could be successfully conditioned by ritual to behave politely in people's houses, controlling their aggressiveness and reserving it only for battlefields. But the infinitely extendable empire required armies with millions of soldiers that had to be deployed in remote regions. Such large masses of military men could not be reached by moral conditioning or indoctrination. Their soldiers had lost their basic human empathy with other people. They were "abandoned in conduct" and could not be absorbed into normal village life.[14]

Yao Nai was a contemporary of Wang Chang, whose claims about the supremacy of the political problem of governing soldiers initiated this discussion. Both were scholar-officials of the multi-ethnic Qing Dynasty (1644-1911), which had destroyed the Ming. And for a time, the Manchu warrior people who created this dynasty appeared to have succeeded where previous Chinese dynasties, especially the Ming, had failed. The Qing ruled China, and much of Central Asia, with a smaller, better-financed military establishment than that of the Ming. The Qing court was helped in this in part by the extrabudgetary contributions to its war machine of eighteenth-century China's wealthy merchant houses, especially salt merchants. But it was helped even more by a strong, non-Chinese, feudal, warrior ethic, supplied by the loyal Mongols as well as by the Manchus themselves. This universal empire constituted itself through "multiple hierarchies of lordship based on differing types of authority," in Mark Elliott's words; Xinjiang alone, after it was conquered and added to China in 1759, had three different civil and military administrations, deriving from

Chinese, Mongolian, and Turkic traditions, in Peter Perdue's summary.[15] This could be regarded as a sort of multicultural feudal revival, interacting with Chinese traditions of merit-based bureaucracy.

Morever, the dominant Qing emperor of the 1700s, Qianlong, on the throne from the 1730s to the 1790s, was the ruler whom both Yao Nai and Wang Chang served; and he was a military expansionist. Qianlong was perfectly capable of personally reviewing his troops, as Zhang Juzheng had wanted the less effective Ming emperors to do. What Qianlong called his "Ten Great Campaigns" included the conquest of Xinjiang (1755-59), plus several wars in Burma, a failed invasion of Vietnam (1788-89), and costly wars in west Sichuan in the 1740s and the 1770s to suppress a Tibetan hill people then known as the Jinchuan (Golden Stream) community. Wang Chang himself had served in one of the Burma wars and had written an invaluable account of this Burma campaign. He had also participated in the bloody struggle to suppress west Sichuan's Tibetans and was a chief compiler of the official court history of the west Sichuan war. The famous boast of Wang Chang's English contemporary Edward Gibbon – that being a captain of the Hampshire Grenadiers had helped him to write his history of the decline of Rome – suggested a military experience that was quite trivial by the standards of Wang Chang and of at least a few other Chinese scholar-officials in the 1700s.

Under these circumstances, it might seem surprising that Wang Chang, addressing his own stated problem of how to govern soldiers, should have resurrected the old "institutionalist" approach of controlling them by procedural arrangements more than by Confucian moral education. Even more surprising, Wang Chang revived a seemingly anachronistic formula from the Tang Dynasty of 1,000 years earlier as a remedy for the problem. There was something of a parallel here with Huang Zongxi's retrieval in the 1600s of the example of the Tang scholar-official Du Mu.

The formula that Wang revived was the Tang Dynasty's "garrison-militia" *(fubing)* system. It had featured men who were lifelong soldiers but who were stationed in community-like farming garrisons throughout the empire. The number of tours of actual frontier warfare duty to which such soldiers might be rotated was carefully prescribed and limited, rather like the duties of American National Guard soldiers before George W. Bush's war in Iraq. Such soldiers were also allowed to retire from soldiering at sixty years of age. Only when the garrison-militia system was abandoned, Wang Chang wrote, did Tang Dynasty China founder in the military disorder epitomized by the warlord rebel An Lushan.[16]

Yet the Ming hereditary-guards system itself had been inspired, in part, by the Tang garrison-militia system. And it had collapsed when commercial expansion, and the greater economic opportunities the expansion generated, had made the lives of hereditary soldiers less attractive and mass desertion from the guards for other economic pastimes a way out. Why then should Wang Chang have been so nostalgic for this medieval model of military control? He must have known that it would be difficult to reproduce in eighteenth-century China. The explanation probably lies in his argument that the excellence of the Tang farmer-militia system resided in its principle of recurrently taking a "rest from toil" *(xiu xi)*. In the debate about how to govern soldiers, this principle assumed that military "rest" periods had to be cycled and recycled because no dynasty could ever end the horrors of war on its frontiers and then disarm itself. There would always be frontier wars.

An approach that favoured decentralized military colonies and farmer-soldiers remained popular, despite its anachronism, because it could be used to control not merely soldiers but also war-loving rulers. Such rulers had been in short supply in the Ming Dynasty but not in the 1700s. As Wang Chang well knew, it was unlikely that an emperor like Qianlong, who used his soldiers to fight enemies as distant from Beijing as the Gurkhas of Nepal, could have sent a national militia of farmer-soldiers on his invasions of Burma, Vietnam, or Tibet. The debate about how to control soldiers was also, therefore, in the end, a specialized variant of the debate about the very nature of the imperial state in China.

The Qianlong emperor's Ten Great Campaigns presupposed an expansionist view of that state. Governments of China in the twentieth century, having inherited the "China" (including Xinjiang) that Qianlong bequeathed them, have on the whole been eager retrospectively to legitimize it. Wang Chang's celebration of the medieval garrison-militia system, on the other hand, implied a different view of the imperial state. In his perspective, the empire became a sort of homeostatically self-renewing polity, devoted to the need for "rest from toil." This meant energy-saving modes of attempted equilibrium, designed for a state that might manage endless frontier instabilities without allowing itself to be exhausted by them. The disagreements might even be called a battle about crypto-federalism in purely military-administrative terms. In the same way, the disagreements inside the more "culturalist" approaches to the control of soldiers could also be called a struggle over just how far literacy, and virtue-encouraging moral indoctrination, could be spread among the people. Here, there were both optimists and pessimists.

In the world of Wang Chang, local community ties, and the soldiers' loyalty to such ties as garrison-militia men, were used as supplements for moral education, not to mention for the more hierarchical feudal loyalties that were no longer strong enough to control armies in China in the 1700s. But unlike the assumptions we find among scholars who suppose that China was an innately cellular society, rich in psychologies of "personal connections" *(guanxi)*, "rest from toil" military thought took for granted a society in which soldiers were not only excluded from the more ambitious forms of Confucian conditioning but also had to have the proper community ties endlessly created and recreated for them.

After 1840

We must not underestimate the variety of pre-Republican China's attempted solutions to its military-control problems. We must also take note of pre-Republican China's failure to find long-term solutions that could either cure the corrosive effect that economic growth had on the attractiveness of soldiering careers or produce a state structure that would permanently checkmate the dangers of local warlordism. But such problems exist outside China too. China's subjection to Western and Japanese colonialism between 1840 and 1945 meant a rare period in Chinese history when the loss of control or accountability in other people's armies probably concerned the Chinese people even more than the potential "wildness" of their own soldiers. But as other chapters in this volume show, with the coming of the Chinese republic the problem of the governance of military establishments reasserted itself. Diana Lary's painstaking scholarship addresses aspects of the problem in the twentieth century, when at least two new means of trying to govern armies came into play. The first was the encouragement of mass patriotism, with its national flags and anthems, its conscript armies, and its techniques of indoctrination. Loyalty to the nation-state might finally move soldiers' minds beyond what Huang Zongxi called "thoughts of the village well" in the 1600s. The second was specialized military laws, beginning with China's first modern military criminal code, promulgated by the Beiyang government in 1915. This new legal approach reflected the growing "internationalization" of the Chinese state, now a republic, and its search for military management remedies in the practices of other states rather than in those of previous dynasties. But in military terms, this "internationalization" did not end struggles over the form of the state; it merely complicated such struggles.

Older approaches to the problem persisted, however, albeit in new guises. European, and then Japanese, military advisers dominated military education in China in the late 1800s. They did so even to the point where Chinese army officers' commands became phonetic equivalents of English-language terms (like *fawei maqi*, for "forward march").[17] But when the great reformer Zhang Zhidong, under such influences, declared that China must use Western-style military academies to train military officers and that such officer candidates must be drawn exclusively from the children of bureaucrat-gentry families that had been important for generations, he was fusing imported European and Japanese aristocratic prejudices about whom the new officer academies should recruit with the old Huang Zongxi instinct that only the scholar-official elite, with its supposed moral magnetism, was capable of providing officers who could command rebellion-proof armies.

Far more recently, the People's Republic of China (PRC) has also had to confront the old Chinese fear that an army whose leaders were too dangerously detached from the accountability codes of the "best and the brightest" among the more general elite might be a resentful long-term threat, too conscious of its growing relative deprivation in professional terms. As just one example, therefore, in 2007 the PRC Central Military Commission approved regulations by which the Chinese armed forces could attract and retain "socially high-quality people of talent" *(shehui youzhi rencai)*. This was to be done by recruiting "postdoctoral researchers" and "decision-making consultants" from the science academies, who would be given privileged salaries and lives, as well as by introducing an "academic study-leave system."[18]

The claim that military virtue is a special form of moral self-control can never be left entirely to philosophers to debate. The potentially uncontrollable beast that lurks at the heart of even the most seemingly restrained war-making machinery is too formidable not to be a general statecraft issue, as was seen by Wang Chang and other Chinese academicians with direct experience of war.

Notes

1 See in particular Diana Lary, *Warlord Soldier: Chinese Common Soldiers, 1911-1937*. Cambridge, UK: Cambridge University Press, 1985.

2 Wang Chang, "Tang-Song bingzhi deshi lun" [On the achievements and failures of the Tang and Song military systems], in *Huangchao jingshi wenbian* [Statecraft Essays of the Imperial Court], comp. He Changling (1826; reprint, Taibei: Wenhai chubanshe, 1972), no. 70, 3b-4. All translations of quotations from non-English sources are mine.

3 Wu Han, *Dushi zaji* [Notes on a Reading of History] (Beijing: Sanlian shudian chubanshe, 1957), 92-141.

4 Wang Lianbin, *Zhonghua wude tongshi* [A Comprehensive History of Chinese Military Virtue] (Beijing: Jiefangjun chubanshe, 1999).

5 Henry Kamen, *Early Modern European Society* (London and New York: Routledge, 2000), 70-77.

6 Brian J. Glenn, "The Two Schools of American Political Development," *Political Studies Review* 2 (April 2004): 153-65.

7 The following discussion draws from *Huang Zongxi quanji* [Complete Works of Huang Zongxi] (Hangzhou: Zhejiang guji chubanshe, 1985), vol. 1, 29-35; and Huang Zongxi, *Waiting for the Dawn: A Plan for the Prince*, trans. William T. deBary (New York: Columbia University Press, 1993), 139-49.

8 Yu Huaqing, *Zhongguo huanguan zhidu shi* [A History of the Chinese Eunuch-Officials System] (Shanghai: Renmin chubanshe, 1993), 11.

9 Huang, *Waiting for the Dawn,* 4.

10 Liu Zehua, comp., *Zhongguo zhengzhi sixiang shi: Sui-Qing juan* [A History of Chinese Political Thought: Sui to Qing volume] (Hangzhou: Zhejiang renmin chubanshe, 1996), 600-18, esp. 601-2.

11 Kenneth Lieberthal and Michel Oksenberg, *Policy Making in China* (Princeton, NJ: Princeton University Press, 1988), 137.

12 Ding Shouhe, comp., *Zhongguo lidai zhiguo ce xuancui* [Selected Highlights of Chinese State Administration Policies through the Centuries] (Beijing: Gaodeng jiaoyu chubanshe, 1994), 636-42.

13 Quoted in Wu, *Dushi zaji,* 114.

14 Yao Nai, "Yi bing" [Proposals about soldiers], in *Huangchao jingshi wenbian* [Statecraft Essays of the Imperial Court], comp. He Changling (1826; reprint, Taibei, Wenhai chubanshe, 1972), no. 70, 7b-8.

15 Mark C. Elliott, *The Manchu Way: The Eight Banners and Ethnic Identity in Late Imperial China* (Stanford, CA: Stanford University Press, 2001), 4; Peter C. Perdue, *China Marches West: The Qing Conquest of Central Eurasia* (Cambridge, MA: Harvard University Press, 2005), 340.

16 Wang, "Tang-Song bingzhi deshi lun."

17 Wang Jianhua, "Lun lieqiang dui wan Qing junshi jiaoyu jindaihua de yingxiang" [On the influences of the great powers on late-Qing military-education modernization], *Shehui kexue* [Social Sciences] 10 (2004): 101-8.

18 *Xinhua yuebao: Jilu* [New China Monthly Report: Chronicles] 9 (2007): 59.

10

Chinese Savages and Chinese Saints: Russians and Chinese Remember and Forget the Boxer Uprising in 1920s China

Blaine Chiasson

JUST AS NO TWO persons will remember an event in the same manner, neither will persons on opposite sides of a national conflict remember and memorialize that conflict the same way. What one remembers and celebrates, or chooses not to remember and celebrate, is also affected by the political, economic, or social conditions within which one's reflections take place. China's Boxer Uprising of 1900 is one such contested event. As Paul Cohen has demonstrated in *History in Three Keys,* both the "meaning" of the Boxers and how the Boxers are remembered have changed for each generation of Chinese, and each generation's understanding of the uprising has been transformed according to different political and social contexts that affect remembrance.[1] Thus one generation's superstitious peasants are the next generation's proto-Marxist nationalists. Cohen demonstrates that in the traditional heartland provinces of China, the Boxer Uprising has since remained an event to which succeeding cohorts of Chinese intellectuals and political activists could attach their own changed understandings.

Not so in the Chinese Northeast, a region of confused national, political, and ethnic identities. In 1900 the Chinese Northeast was a frontier region of recent settlement by Chinese, Russians, and Japanese. Politically, the region belonged to China, but both the Russian and Japanese governments regarded the region as within their spheres of influence and thus as a possible colony. In his chapter in this volume, Victor Zatsepine demonstrates that the uprising was crucial to the extension of Russian military and colonial power in Manchuria. Rarely acknowledged is the fact that the uprising was equally important because it forced the Qing Dynasty to transform the region from a Manchu ethnic homeland, distinct from China proper, into three Chinese provinces that would be integrated politically and ethnically with the Chinese heartland. Therefore, the 1900 Boxer Uprising created the conditions for competing Chinese and Russian administrative and colonial projects in Manchuria, a competition that China would win following the Russian Revolution of 1917.

In the 1920s, just twenty years after the event, and despite the importance of the Boxer Uprising in determining Manchuria's ultimate political identity as Chinese, the uprising drew few comments from either Chinese or Russian refugees and settlers. On the one hand, this may not seem surprising given that following 1900 both peoples had experienced political and social revolutions that had completely altered their lives. In the case of Russians resident in China, these changes had resulted in exile, statelessness, and a new dependence on the benevolence of the Chinese government and people, whom the Russians had once treated with imperial disdain. China, in contrast, used the reversal of colonial roles in the Northeast to firmly establish the region's political and administrative identity as Chinese. On the other hand, the Boxer Uprising is crucial to understanding how Imperial Russia reinvigorated a colonial project in the Chinese Northeast and how the Chinese state met this response with its own project of administrative reform. Sources, both Chinese and Russian, should point to the Boxer Uprising as the single most important event that pushed both empires to solidify their "claim" to the Chinese Northeast. Yet for the most part, the event is ignored; at best, it appears as a footnote in the competing histories of Russian and Chinese frontier colonialism.

This chapter's subject is the political and social uses of selected memories, by the Russians and the Chinese, of the Boxer Uprising. These memories, it is argued here, were formed and selected in the postcolonial context of the Chinese Northeast during the 1920s. It is this postcolonial context of declining Russian and rising Chinese influence in the 1920s that rendered it impossible for Manchuria's two founding communities to have the same memory of the event. Indeed, Russian memories of the uprising would experience a dramatic shift, one that paralleled the shift in Russian colonial power in the Northeast. Although the two communities could not share the same memories, and indeed each side chose to suppress the memory of the most traumatic event, the choice of what to remember or forget is indicative of how each community's political and social position was reversed in the 1920s. These uncommon memories also demonstrate the limits of any attempt to find a common memory (and by extension a common history, even a common military history) for a multi-ethnic, multicultural, and multipolitical region. Nevertheless, the few references to the Boxers that did surface in the Northeast's history during the 1920s are indicative of how changed circumstances for both Chinese and Russians reflected what each community believed important in the context of declining Russian and rising Chinese regional colonialism. The task of thinking about how the Russians and Chinese remember the Boxer Uprising is, of course, complicated by the multiple players and ideologies that have swept the region. Interpretations differ not only between Chinese and Russians but also between Russian socialists and anti-socialists, between Russian settlers of recent arrival and those with longstanding residence, between Qing Chinese and Republicans, and between pre- and post-1949 Chinese understandings of events.

This chapter examines the absence of a shared memory of the uprising through three sources: a Russian religious icon, a Chinese administrative biography, and a peculiar absence of memory of the uprising's most violent border incident, the Blagoveshchensk Massacre. The icon of the 220 Holy Chinese Martyrs of the Boxer Rebellion is a visual representation of 220 Chinese Russian Orthodox victims, murdered in Beijing in 1900. Prior to 1917, the icon was used by the Russian Orthodox Church to illustrate and memorialize a narrative of heroic Orthodox (i.e., "civilized") Christians who fell victim to "savage" Chinese. It was a narrative that reflected Russian power and self-confidence vis-à-vis the Chinese prior to the reversal of Russian fortune in 1917. After 1917 the narrative around the icon changed to one that emphasized Chinese, not Russian, victims and Russian Orthodoxy's long history in China, in essence "sinifying" Russian Orthodoxy in China. The Chinese "icon" of the 1900 uprising is the biography of Harbin mayor Ma Zhongjun, a 1920s publication that celebrates Ma's administrative rise in the context of new Qing, and Chinese Republican, administrative bodies put in place after 1900 to hold and turn back Russian imperial pretensions in the Northeast.[2] This narrative only peripherally refers to the Boxers and their uprising; instead, it places Ma in the heroic position of deflecting Russian imperialism and extending Chinese sovereignty in the Northeast. As a patriotic icon, Ma represented a particular 1920s "North-eastern" Chinese nationalism, one that celebrated both Russian and Chinese contributions to the region and that differed considerably from the later forms of Chinese nationalism that erased non-Chinese influences in the region. Finally, the absence in the 1920s of any reflection from either side on the Blagoveshchensk Massacre, the forced deaths of perhaps 4,000 Chinese and Manchus resident on the Russian side of the border at the time of the Boxer Uprising, is examined in the context of a event that revealed the racism and racist, paranoid undercurrent of Russian imperialism in the region. The massacre, as memory in the 1920s, would have disrupted the fragile ethnic compromise that allowed the Chinese Northeast to prosper.

Both Russian and Chinese selective memories of the Boxer Uprising were determined by the political and colonial context in which the "remembering" of the uprising took place. For the Manchurian Chinese elite, the most important fact was not the uprising itself but that the Russian government used the uprising as an excuse to further the Russian colonial project in the Chinese Northeast. In the 1920s, when the principal Chinese sources cited in this chapter were published, the Northeast was still a site of geopolitical struggle between China, Japan, and the Soviet Union. Therefore, it is not surprising that North-eastern Chinese sources choose to remember the event differently than did their compatriots in China proper. The Boxer Uprising originated as a spiritually inspired peasant movement that was set off by the repercussions of an economic depression in the Grand Canal region due to new patterns of foreign trade, by the effect of missionary activity on local society, and by drought and the resulting poor harvests in Shandong province. Therefore, in the opinion of the men and women who would be known by the foreign-applied label of "Boxers" (in reference to the qigong exercises that were part of their rituals or to the mistranslation of their early name of "Righteous Fists"), foreign incursion and economic dislocation were connected. After forging an alliance with the Qing court in the summer of 1900, the Boxers spread across north China, attacking foreigners and the Chinese associated with them. As a result, the impact of the Boxer Uprising was most significant in the region of north China that surrounded the capital city of Beijing. In the Chinese Northeast, also known as Manchuria, the Boxer Uprising did produce isolated attacks on the Russian-owned railways, a "siege" of the Russian railway's hub city of Harbin, and a general feeling of panic among the Russian settlers in Manchuria.[3] As Victor Zatsepine's chapter makes clear, the uprising's principal effect on the Russians in Manchuria was damage to the Chinese Eastern Railway (CER), the symbol of Russia's economic invasion. The main incident of Chinese violence against Russians was the bombardment originating in the Chinese settlement of Aigun aimed at the Russian side of the river, the event that provoked the Blagoveshchensk Massacre. Despite these events, in Chinese sources published in Manchuria, the Boxer Uprising was regarded primarily as an event localized in the region surrounding Beijing. In these 1920s Chinese sources, surveyed for this chapter, little attention was paid to the presence of Boxers and their activities in Manchuria, other than acknowledging that the Boxer Uprising occurred. Instead, the focus was on the increased penetration of Russian state power in the region following the uprising, demonstrating that Manchurian Chinese elites saw the event, some nineteen years later, as a means to a Russian imperial conquest of the region. In contrast, Russian sources emphasized the threat posed by the Boxers themselves rather than post-Boxer Russian efforts to detach the region from Chinese control.[4]

The Boxer Uprising took place in Shandong province and the Beijing region, an area unquestionably identified as Chinese. Despite this, for the Russians and the Chinese living in Manchuria, the uprising's meaning was also caught up with the identity of the Chinese Northeast, a political and ethnic identity that had until 1900 had been in flux. The region had been something of a buffer zone between the Russian and Chinese Empires throughout most of the nineteenth century. Although the border was delineated in 1664, 1858, and again in 1860 – the final two treaties removing vast tracts of territory from Qing rule – by 1900 the region's "true" identity was still yet to be determined. As the homeland of the ruling Manchu Dynasty and technically closed to Chinese settlement, it was conceptually and politically impossible to equate the Chinese Northeast with the heartland of Chinese culture. Even today, some Chinese view the Northeast as not quite Chinese. It is possible to argue that only after the sinification of the region since 1949 and the accompanying obliteration of Manchuria's other histories and identities has it been possible to claim that the Northeast is truly and unequivocally Chinese. Before the Boxer Uprising, both the Russian and Japanese Empires eyed the region with interest, although it was only Russia, prior to 1905, that was able to carve out its own sphere of interest in Manchuria, or the Chinese Northeast, in the form of the CER concession.

The building of the CER concession and the Russian settlements that followed its track constituted a virtual Russian colony in the Chinese Northeast and an attempt to economically detach the region from China. Zatsepine's chapter illustrates how the CER concession was used by Imperial Russia to "extend the frontier" of the Russian Empire deep into Chinese territory. Rhetorically, Russian sources before 1917 celebrated the CER as an example of Russian economic prowess versus Chinese economic ineptitude and disorganization. For this reason, the post-1917 Russian understanding of the icon of the 220 Holy Martyrs of the Boxer Rebellion represented a significant departure from traditional Russian understandings of the Boxer Uprising and the overall Russian project in Manchuria. Rather than the pre-1917 interpretation of the Boxers as bloodthirsty rebels, the icon introduced a new post-1917 Russian discourse of the Boxers as victims of Western imperialism and the Chinese martyrs as representatives of Russian Orthodoxy's deep roots in, and connection to, China. To clarify this point, it is necessary to examine Russia's conflicted relationship with China and with the Chinese Northeast.

Although the Russian Empire had a longer diplomatic relationship with the Qing than did any other European power, Russian penetration of the Chinese Northeast was recent, dating from the empire's defeat in the Crimean War. Following this setback, Russia's imperial ambitions were projected eastward, capitalizing on the declining Qing. The Russian government was somewhat schizophrenic in its approach to the Qing. On the one hand, Russia aggressively took, by treaty, millions of kilometres of Qing territory, proclaiming itself destined to rule in the East because of its superior civilization. On the other hand, the Russian government, claiming to be an "Asiatic" power bringing peace and order to the region, proclaimed that it had a special relationship with China and that it would protect China from the rapacious greed of the imperial powers, among which Imperial Russia did not count itself. In reality, this special relationship took the form of the Russian government using its influence to squeeze more territory from the Qing, as it had done following the Sino-Japanese

War (1894-95) when Russia blocked Japan's attempt to create a Manchurian concession. Instead, the Russian government obtained that concession for itself and proceeded to create a transportation and military network centred on the Chinese Eastern Railway and the cities of Harbin, Dalian (in Russian, "Dalny"), and Port Arthur.

Zatsepine argues that the Blagoveshchensk Massacre was a deliberate attempt on the part of local Russian authorities to cleanse the Russian side of the border of its Chinese and Manchu inhabitants. This chapter argues that, in addition, the ferocity of the Russian reaction to the Qing bombardment was an indication of the anxiety felt by most Russians concerning the tenuous position of the recent Russian settlement in the Far East. Despite the apparent strength of the Russian presence in the region before the 1917 Revolution, the regional economy was completely artificial, based on military and civil subsidies from the empire's centre. Russian settlers did not flourish in the Far East, and many returned to European Russia. The groups that did prosper in the Russian Far East were the resident Chinese, Manchu, and Korean populations; some members of these groups were permitted to remain by the treaties that established national borders, and others had immigrated to the region for its economic opportunities. Able to exploit appropriate regional agricultural practices and established trading connections, these groups prospered in the Russian Far East but were perceived by the Russian government as a potential threat to Russian control.[5] The region's Asian populations were valued for their economic acumen but were also considered a demographic threat to the goal of making the Far East Russian. Well before 1900, Russian intellectuals and politicians agonized over what was to be done with the region's Asian population: absorption or exile? The very presence of a large, long-settled Chinese and Manchu population was a physical and demographic repudiation of Russia's recent claim to the Far East. Hence the Blagoveshchensk pogrom against the city's Asian residents during the Boxer Uprising was indicative of Russian fears of these residents' economic and demographic power to return the region to an "Asiatic" status.

Although Russia's legal economic and political influence in Manchuria was limited to the CER concession, its ambitions extended far beyond the concession's borders. Imperial Russia had long advocated, at the highest levels of government, the eventual annexation of the Northeast to the Russian Empire. Although Sergei Witte, architect of the policy of railway imperialism that moved Russian power to the Pacific Coast, publicly advocated for peaceful economic penetration, he privately considered the region a future Russian colony.[6] Others in the Imperial Russian Ministries of War and Finance openly advocated the detachment of Manchuria, or Manzhou, as they called the region to indicate what they saw as the area's weak political affiliation with China and its inclusion in the Russian Far East.[7]

Despite some expressions of sympathy for the Boxers from St. Petersburg, those Russians who witnessed Boxer activity characterized them in an almost completely negative fashion. Although there was some acknowledgment of how foreign, especially Catholic missionary, activity had contributed to the uprising, Russian eyewitnesses described the Boxers as wild, uncontrollable, and savage.[8] In the end, however, the true extent of Russians' anxiety and profoundly negative feelings for their Chinese neighbours was proven by the actions of Russian populations and officials living on the Russian side of the border who actively persecuted and murdered thousands of Chinese.[9]

In the uprising's aftermath, Russian forces quickly assumed the duties of local administration, usurping Chinese administrative privilege and political sovereignty.[10] Before the Boxer Uprising, the Russians were politically restricted by the Chinese Eastern Railway's concession boundaries. In November 1900, following the uprising's suppression, Russia pressured Qing representatives into signing an agreement that allowed Russia to assume all military and administrative power in Manchuria. The final provision determined that Russian supervision would end only when Russia determined that order had been restored, rendering the possibility of Russian withdrawal unlikely.[11] Russian troops patrolled the Northeast until they were forced, due to pressure from Japan, England, and France, to withdraw in 1902. Nonetheless, many Russian troops remained, exchanging the uniforms of the Russian army for those of the CER guards.

In 1903 Nicholas II created the imperial lieutenancy of the Far East, a position that included authority over all administrative matters within the CER-concession zone, an area outside of Russia's national boundaries, a clear signal that Russia considered the administration of this Chinese territory to be within the sphere of national Russian interests.

The imperial lieutenant of the Far East is invested with supreme power in respect of civil administration over Pri-Amur province on the Russian side and Kuantung province on the Chinese side, and the position is independent of different ministries. He is also given supreme authority regarding the maintenance of order and security in the localities appropriated for the benefit of the Chinese Eastern Railway. Due care and protection in regard to the interests and wants of Russian subjects in the neighbouring territories outside of the border of the imperial lieutenant's jurisdiction are also confided to him.[12]

Admiral Evgenii Alekseev's appointment to the position indicated the Imperial Russian government's position on the Chinese Northeast. Alekseev was a committed Slavic nationalist, convinced of Russia's special presence in Asia and that the goal of Russian domination of the region should be pursued by military and economic means. He was a devoted advocate of the eventual annexation of the Chinese Northeast by Russia. His bellicose attitude undermined Witte's policy of peaceful economic domination and eventually provoked the Russo-Japanese War.

Further proof of Imperial Russia's intention to annex the Chinese Northeast can be found in comparing Russia's colonial tactics in Manchuria to its tactics in formerly independent regions incorporated into the Russian Empire. Russia's expansion of its administrative power through military occupation and the creation of imperial lieutenancies, along with economic and cultural penetration of formerly non-Russian peripheries, had been standard Russian colonial practice. The former borderlands of Russia – the Khanates of Khiva, Bukhara, Kazakhstan, and Turkistan – were absorbed into the empire as Russian provinces. The process of colonization and annexation in all these areas was the same and identical to that carried out in Manchuria. In these regions, first a Russian economic presence, often centred on a railway and the creation of Russian settler communities, was established. Russians justified their presence with an argument based on Russian superiority, namely that Russia brought a higher level of economic, cultural, and administrative development to the area. Once Russian settlement was established, it was necessary to protect the Russian population from hostile native groups, which resisted Russian colonization and its resulting economic dislocation. Full incorporation of the region into the Russian Empire followed the military and administrative intervention that resulted from these uprisings. The same pattern – protection of Manchuria's Russian population and Russia's investment from Boxer savagery – was therefore employed to expand Russian conquest of the Chinese Northeast.

In sum, the Boxer Uprising and the resulting Russian expansion into the Chinese Northeast took place in the ideological and political context of an attempt to create a Russian "fact" in the Northeast, in the presence of the very real fact of the region's native Chinese population. The resulting project of colonial propaganda, which portrayed the Chinese as unfit to rule, can be seen in Russian publications before and following the Boxer Uprising. The Chinese were depicted as completely hopeless and incompetent at best and as criminally negligent at worst.[13] Imperial Russia, armed with the tools of modernity, would develop the region to its full potential, a discourse of modernity through colonial administration also seen in Japanese texts that sought to both lessen China's claim to the region and discredit China's political and administrative efforts. In the competing Chinese discourse after 1900, Chinese officials, such as Ma Zhongjun, responded to this charge of administrative incompetence with an administrative reorganization of the Northeast. Within this context of colonial anxiety, the Blagoveshchensk Massacre of 1900 took place as the culmination of Russian fears as to the demographic, economic, and cultural future of the region – an event covered in more detail by Victor Zatsepine.

Thus, beginning with the uprising itself, there is little commonly agreed-on meaning between the two peoples. What was for the Russians a deeply antimodern, antiforeign movement that justified a complete occupation of Manchuria by the Russian state was remembered by the Chinese as an opportunity for the Russian state to expand beyond its Chinese Eastern Railway concession in an attempt to seize the entire region. What can be interpreted from what both Russians and Chinese remember, and forget, of the uprising's impact on the Chinese Northeast? The three "documents" brought to this exercise – the Russian Orthodox icon of the 220 Holy Chinese Martyrs of the Boxer Rebellion; the biography of Harbin mayor Ma Zhongjun, whose career began with his act of heroism during the Boxer Uprising; and finally, the notable absence of material on, and memory of, the Blagoveshchensk Massacre – demonstrate that each document was a means to remember or forget the Boxer Uprising, but these memories are specific and do not intersect; the icon is important to Russians, Mayor Ma has significance for the Chinese, and the massacre was too controversial in the 1920s for either community to touch.

These three examples demonstrate how both sides used the memories and memorialization of the uprising to renegotiate a changed political and colonial situation in the 1920s Chinese Northeast. The geographical, colonial, and cultural context of this renegotiation was conditioned by the respective claims on the "empty" space of the Chinese Northeast and by the accompanying anxiety that both Imperial and Soviet Russia and Imperial and Republican China experienced over who would ultimately control the region. Although both sides had very different interpretations of the Boxer Uprising, their response to the event – to the political vacuum that opened in the Chinese Northeast – was remarkably similar. The political and administrative result of the Boxer Uprising would be an increased effort on the part of both Chinese and Russians to colonize the Northeast in order to draw firm ethnic, political, and cultural lines on the map, a colonization that also demanded a reconfiguration of the region's identity as either Russian or Chinese.

The icon of the 220 Holy Chinese Martyrs of the Boxer Rebellion was originally painted in the 1920s for the Spiritual Mission of the Russian Orthodox Church in Beijing.[14] Founded to care for the spiritual needs of Russian Christians captured by the Qing in the seventeenth century who settled in Beijing, the mission became an important listening post for the Russian Empire and instrumental for Russian tribute and trade missions to Beijing. As Russian imperial power expanded in the nineteenth century, the mission's importance and size also expanded. By the 1920s, however, the mission had been cut off from its parent organization, now under Bolshevik control, and was searching for a new spiritual and economic role to justify its existence. The memory of the 220 martyrs was part of the project undertaken by the Russian Orthodox Church in China to remake itself in order to move the church away from its associations with discredited Russian imperialism and to make the institution relevant, not only to its stateless and increasing indigent Russian parishioners but also to its protectors within the Chinese government.

The icon is painted in traditional Russian style and portrays a number of the 220 Chinese members of the Russian Orthodox Church's mission who were massacred in 1900 for their Christian faith and their foreign connections.[15] It is a striking work of art that depicts a group of Chinese men, women, and children in Chinese dress, although the women have their heads covered in the Russian Orthodox fashion. There is an Orthodox church depicted in the icon's left-hand corner and a Chinese building – perhaps to emphasize the group's Chinese connection – on the right. Some of the martyrs have their Russian names written over their heads, which are also surrounded by golden halos indicating their sainthood. Although the icon's context is unmistakably Russian Orthodox, it is also unmistakably Chinese, a remarkable deviation for the Russian Orthodox Church in China. Despite the church's 400-year history in China and a small but significant number of Chinese believers, the church had up to this point (with few exceptions hereafter) depicted itself in liturgy, iconography, architecture, and nationality as a Russian institution.

What of the 220 Chinese martyrs of Beijing? How did the creation of Chinese martyrs serve the Russification project in the Far East? Although the martyrs were elevated to sainthood just after their deaths in 1900, they were elevated as Russian Orthodox Christians of Russian ancestry. What Russians emphasized about the martyrs before 1917 was their Russian characteristics, their names, their religion, their Russian-style dress – in fact, what the Russians perceived as their cultural distance from the Boxers who murdered them. After the Russian Revolution of 1917, it was the martyrs' "Chineseness" that was emphasized.[16] It is worth noting that there was never one single project of Russian domination in the Russian Far East and the Chinese Northeast. It is more appropriate to conceive of intersecting projects of legitimacy and justification. The Russian Orthodox Church was an important component of Russian state, national, and cultural identity. The church had been subsumed within the Russian state since the reign of Peter the Great, and as a branch of the Russian government, the church followed the Russian government into the newly colonized areas of the Russian Empire. In a multilingual, multicultural, and multi-ethnic empire, the Russian Orthodox Church provided the useful binding agent for the components of a fragile Russian identity, both in Qing Manchuria and in non-Russian regions of the formal Russian Empire, such as the Muslim territories of the southern Russian Empire that constituted the empire's most recent conquests. To be truly Russian, despite one's ethnic origins, was to be Orthodox, although prejudice against non-Russian converts never completely disappeared. That Russian identity was tied to Russian state identity was seen in the late-imperial slogan "Pravoslaviye, Samoderzhaviye, i Narodnost" (Autocracy, Orthodoxy, and Nationalism). The Russian Orthodox Church also benefited from its status as the official religion of the empire through its government subsidies, subsidies that were administered through the Chinese Eastern Railway.

Although extending Orthodoxy was perceived as extending Russianness, Orthodoxy was not a religious tradition that emphasized missionary work. Despite the presence of the church in China since the 1600s, there was a relatively limited conversion rate among Chinese. Many who converted did so because they either married Russian spouses or wished to become accepted as citizens in the Russian Far East. The biographies of the 220 holy Chinese martyrs are few and short. We do know many were descended from the Albazinians, Russians seized from the settlement of Albazin by Qing forces in the first boundary disputes and brought to Beijing, where in the spirit of accommodating foreign communities, they were permitted an Orthodox priest and church. Gradually, they intermarried with Chinese but kept their identity as Orthodox Albazinians, although in appearance and culture (other than religion) they were northern Chinese. The Orthodox mission to Beijing was established to tend to their religious needs. Before 1920 it was the martyrs' Albazinian identity, a pseudo-Russian identity, rather than their Chinese cultural identity that was stressed.

The Orthodox Church, like its Russian imperial sponsor, was in the process of creating a Russian "fact" in the form of a parish system in the Chinese Northeast. As the Russian population in China expanded, so did the church, and establishing the church was seen as part of the establishment of Russian identity in that "empty" land – witness the financial support that the Chinese Eastern Railway extended to the church until the mid-1920s. The Boxer Uprising was remembered by the Russian Orthodox Church before 1917 as an uprising of the "heathen Chinese" against the "good Christian Russian/Albazanian people," who had always "wished the Chinese well." In this way the memory of the Boxer Uprising differed little from narratives of the event held by other Christian faiths in China. The martyrs' identity was emphasized as being rooted in an Albazinian/Russian community of long standing, whose members had been massacred by the "savage" *(dikii)* Chinese.[17]

Following the Russian Revolution and Civil War, Russian Orthodoxy in China found itself in a precarious financial and legal situation. With this changed context came a different remembrance of the 220 martyrs. The newly established Soviet state disavowed the former imperial regime's colonial possessions. Added to the sudden orphaning of the Orthodox Church in China was the Soviet critique of Imperial Russian culture and the religion that accompanied it. After 1917, China's Russians were truly on their own. The large Russian population in China, swollen with tens of thousands of refugees, found itself in the unique position of a colony not only abandoned by the mother country but also denounced as the representative of a feudal, antisocialist, and archaic political, cultural, and religious tradition. China's Russians turned inward, protecting their economic and cultural institutions in China as the best expression of pre-revolutionary cultural brilliance. In terms of religion, the Orthodox was cut off from the mother church in Petersburg and Moscow. The Soviet Union quickly re-established the Moscow Patriarchy, technically separating church and state. In reality, the church in the Soviet Union would be even more a tool of the new regime, alternately persecuted and used to disguise the anti-religious policies of the Bolsheviks.

The Orthodox Church in China declared itself free of the new, "heretical" Bolshevik-controlled Orthodox Church. Buttressed by thousands of faithful, and having a large establishment in China, the church proclaimed itself the true representative of Russian Orthodoxy.[18] Nevertheless, the church had to make a new accommodation to the changing political circumstances, and new allies were needed. Chinese governments, both national and provincial, were re-establishing sovereignty over former Russian concessions and also claiming to govern and protect stateless Russians. Russian extraterritoriality was abolished, and various levels of the Chinese state moved to take over Russian institutions, staff them with new Chinese directors, teach Russians the Chinese language and China's customs, and in general, demonstrate to the Russian population that a new regime was in control. Although the Chinese solutions were largely bilingual and bicultural, the Chinese effectively reversed the previous colonial balance of power by asserting the equality of their language and staff.

In this changed political context, the Orthodox Church used the memory of the 220 martyrs as a means to negotiate a new identity in China – one that emphasized less their Russianness and more their Orthodox and Chinese identities. Rather than stressing the Russianness of the Russian Orthodox Church, the memories of the 220 martyrs enabled the church to stress the long history of Russian Orthodoxy in China. Rather than the glory of Russian power in China through the church, as had previously been asserted, the glory of Orthodoxy in

China and its long connections with the Chinese people assumed priority.[19] Chinese names suddenly appear in the list of patrons of the church in China.[20] This was undoubtedly aided by the re-immigration of the Chinese Orthodox population from a hostile Bolshevik Russian Far East. Once in the Chinese Northeast, these individuals employed their linguistic and cultural skills and status in both communities, moving quickly to take advantage of a changed political context that demanded bilingual staff and merchants.[21]

What also disappeared from the Orthodox memory of the 220 martyrs was the emphasis on the "savage, barbarian" nature of the Chinese Boxers. Boxers continued to be remembered as persecutors of all Christian communities, a view incidentally that focused on the equality of the Russian Orthodox Church as one denomination among other Christians in China, something the church had not emphasized before 1917. By the 1920s it was the church's opinion that the Boxer Uprising had been caused by the arrogant rapacity of the colonial powers themselves. The colonial powers, Imperial Russia included, had contributed, by their arrogance, greed, and racism, to the xenophobic response that was the Boxer Uprising.[22] By emphasizing the Orthodox Church's Chinese connection through the medium of the 220 martyrs, as well as distancing itself from the imperial project of building Russian power in China, the Orthodox Church was using history, memory, and the martyrs to insert itself into a Chinese, in contrast to an exclusively Russian, narrative.

From the Chinese perspective, one of the longest accounts of the Boxer Uprising, dating originally from a 1920s gazetteer and later reproduced in a 1980s journal, was an administrative biography that concentrated on the uprising's effect on the career of a former Harbin mayor.[23] This biography of Mayor Ma Zhongjun, like the icon of the 220 Holy Martyrs of the Boxer Rebellion, was an attempt to pay homage to persons and events and, again like the Russian icon, is a textual window into a changed social and political context emerging from the Boxer Uprising. The biography traces Ma's administrative career, beginning with his successful negotiation with a Russian general of the withdrawal of Russian troops from the Chinese-controlled territory near Dalian under Ma's jurisdiction. The biography then follows Ma from one administrative success to another within the increasingly sophisticated administrative complex created after the uprising to solidify Chinese control of Manchuria. In fact, the Ma biography is a celebration of Ma's, and by extension Chinese, heroism in the face of Russian imperialism and a celebration of the administrative capacity of the Chinese to lay claim to Manchuria after the Boxer Uprising. The Ma biography therefore is a textual manifestation of an increasing Chinese confidence, growing out of successful measures to reassert Chinese sovereignty in the former Russian-controlled areas of Manchuria.

What of the Chinese and their memories? There are many accounts post-1949 that praise the Boxers as representatives of Chinese nationalism and even proto-socialism.[24] This sentiment is not present in Harbin's Chinese-language city gazetteer published in 1922 by a proud, in some cases bilingual, modernizing Chinese elite, who referred to the Boxers as uneducated bandits.[25] The Boxers did not fit into the developing identity of the North-eastern Chinese elite who praised Imperial Russia's attempts at regional development and who made it their goal not only to match Russian achievements but to surpass them. For Harbin's elite, the Boxer Uprising was remembered not so much for the uprising itself but more for the region's previously politically ambiguous status and thus as the object of Russian colonial ambitions. In the Ma biography the uprising is remembered as a moment when Imperial Russia illegally overextended its political and commercial rights in the Northeast and attempted to colonize the entire region. The Russians, however, were checked by the Chinese administrative response, which created Chinese institutions and affirmed the area's Chinese identity, a project that was personified in the figure of Ma and his success within this newly created Chinese provincial administration.

Following the Boxer Uprising, the region was transformed from the homeland of the Manchu Dynasty into the three Chinese provinces of Jilin, Heilongjiang, and Liaoning, which accepted and encouraged Chinese immigration. Before 1900 the region, as the homeland of the Qing Dynasty, had been officially closed to Chinese colonization, although illegal Chinese migration was tolerated. Manchuria had been administered separately as a part of the Qing imperial household. Chinese settlement had first been banned and then restricted to southern Manchuria. Specific Chinese administrative reforms began in 1907 with the division of the region into the three distinct provinces. The military governorship of the region was abolished, signalling that the area was to be administered by a civil, not a military, administration. Instead, a regional governor-general was appointed along with a governor for each new province. No longer would the area have a distinct and separate administrative identity. A system of provincial governments was introduced on a trial basis.[26] The entire region was opened to Chinese settlement, which the Qing government actively encouraged.[27]

The Qing created and staffed magisterial offices and negotiation bureaus across the Northeast. Branch offices of the negotiation bureaus were also built at every station on the Chinese Eastern Railway.[28] These magisterial offices and especially the negotiating bureaus filled the function of keeping the Russians within the physical and legal boundaries of the concession agreements.[29] Each new province also had a bureau of foreign affairs, specializing in the Russian agreements. Between 1904 and 1907, while Russia prepared to create and impose

Russian municipal governments on and in the CER concession, the governor of Heilongjiang province submitted proposals to Beijing to extend Chinese jurisdiction in that province.[30] These included appointing a Chinese official to the Harbin mixed court, establishing Chinese imperial customs in Harbin and other concession communities, posting Chinese troops to Harbin, and requiring that Russians carry passports when travelling outside the concession zone.[31] All of these measures were a means to assert Chinese sovereign rights in a context of creeping Russian colonialism resulting from the Russian invasion following the Boxer Uprising. Therefore, in the years after 1900 the Chinese, through their deft interpretation of the original agreements, managed to check Russian territorial and colonial ambitions in the region. Although the pressure to pull troops out of the region came primarily from the great powers, this largely unstudied impetus from the Chinese state itself helped to block Russian territorial and administrative ambitions.

The Boxer Uprising in the Northeast, beyond the initial accounts of Russian perfidy and illegal acts, ended in a Chinese success story. Just as the Russians used the opportunity to remake the Russian Orthodox Church's identity in China, the Chinese used the opportunity to establish a Chinese administrative context within a region where administrative identity was ambiguously Chinese at best. This success story was best symbolized by the biography of Mayor Ma Zhongjun of Harbin. Published in the city guidebook and later reproduced in a gazetteer from the 1980s, Ma's biography represented the Chinese making the best of the Boxer Uprising while at the same time asserting Chinese control over the region. Like many Chinese immigrants to the Northeast, Ma was a native of Shandong and came to the Northeast in 1897 as an appointee to the Chinese-Russian negotiation bureau, where he began his studies in Russian. The uprising itself received only a peripheral comment, being described as "breaking like a wave across the Northeast," and the emphasis was placed on the Russian army, which "invaded, occupied, and murdered with impunity." Ma was sent to Lüshun (Port Arthur) to negotiate with Admiral Alikesiyefu, probably Alekseev, who taunted Ma by stating Ma was too junior to negotiate. Ma's response summarized the North-eastern Chinese position on the Boxer Uprising, namely that the Russians were usurping Chinese sovereignty and administrative privilege. "The Russian army could occupy Chinese soil, but they did not have the force to rob China of her sovereignty. They could defeat the Chinese army, but they could not defeat the Chinese in their hearts, and they did not have the power to appoint Chinese officials." Surrounded by Russians, Ma stood his ground, negotiated a ceasefire, and thereby earned the praise of his Russian captors, who called him "General Ma," whereas his Chinese staff called him "Brave Ma," a title that, according to the text, was used until his death.[32] Ma used his superior negotiating skills to obtain a Russian withdrawal and the establishment of a bureau for further negotiations with the Russians, a bureau that successfully blocked further Russian administrative incursion while at the same time creating a viable Chinese state presence in the former Manchu homeland. From 1900 onward, Ma's rise mirrored the creation of the new provincial and regional administration that passed from the Qing to the Republican government and that established China's claim to the region. He moved from the new negotiation bureaus, where his Russian-language skills ensured his advancement within the local administration, eventually attracting the attention of Zhang Zuolin's government. This resulted in his appointment to Harbin's new municipal bureau and his rise to the mayoralty of Harbin.

Interestingly, although he was acknowledged as a great Chinese patriot and a proud son of the Northeast, his bilingual and bicultural skills were also celebrated. Indeed, his Russian-language skills, European lifestyle, and ease with both dominant cultures of the region were part of his patriotic persona, not deviations from a model of "pure" Chinese patriotism. After he moved to Harbin, Ma married and bought a home in the most prestigious neighbourhood, an area once restricted to Harbin's Russian bourgeoisie. He created for himself an equally bourgeois lifestyle, patronizing Chinese and Russian cultural events, sending his daughters to prestigious Russian schools, and celebrating their skill as pianists in the Russian musical tradition.[33]

Ma's narrative of administrative success, which began with the Boxer Uprising, was one celebrated by the region's Chinese elite during the 1920s. Nevertheless, Ma's patriotism does not fit contemporary Chinese history of the Northeast, a history that erases the contributions and presence of the region's non-Chinese populations. Rather than privileging a Chinese identity confined to the traditional markers of "Chineseness," Ma's biography emphasizes a hybrid identity that within the context of Chinese control of the former Russian concession was free to celebrate the region's multiple identities and possibilities of being Chinese. After the 1949 Revolution, the forced exile of the region's Russian populations, the moratorium on any discussion of the region's alternative Russian, Japanese, Korean, and Manchu identity(ies) and history(ies), and the sinification of this formerly multi-ethnic territory, it is no surprise that his biography could not be republished in Chinese until the 1980s. Only after Mao's death and the decentralization of power to the provinces were regional identities, priorities, and histories reasserted.

The final event, notable for its absence in the collective memory of both Chinese and Russians, is the massacre of up to 4,000 Chinese and Manchus by Russian civilians and officials in the Russian border town of Blagoveshchensk.

This was a long-established Chinese-Manchu population whose residence predated the Russian conquest of the former Qing territory. These communities' right of abode was protected by Article 1 of the 1858 Treaty of Aigun, which had delineated the border and left the Chinese and Manchus under the jurisdiction of Chinese authorities on the other side.[34] As a population whose presence predated the Russian settlement, the Chinese were a constant reminder of the region's former Qing identity. Chinese and Manchu success in the local Russian economy was also a symbol of the fragility and artificial nature of the state-sponsored Russian colonial settlement of the newly occupied Russian Far East, especially in the face of the enormous Russian expenditures to create a viable "Russian" economy in the region, attempts that were ultimately unsuccessful. Finally, the Chinese and Manchu communities were a tiny portion of the greater "yellow" population just over the Qing border, a population for whom the recently established border was little more than a national abstraction, demonstrated by the fact that the region's native populations on both sides of the border were in constant economic, social, and familial contact.

The Boxer Uprising would be the moment when these Russian colonial anxieties manifested themselves in the decimation of Blagoveshchensk's Asian population and the complete physical destruction of the community. In July 1900, following what the Russian authorities claimed was a "Boxer" (i.e., Chinese) bombardment from the Chinese settlement of Aigun on the other side of the river, the local police rounded up the Chinese and Manchu population and forced the people to march toward the border at the Amur River. Those unable to complete the thirty-five-mile journey were killed in their tracks, and the survivors were taken to the narrowest point of the river and forced to swim toward Qing territory. Of the 4,000 Chinese and Manchu men, women, and children involved, it is estimated that only 10 percent survived the ordeal.[35]

The striking absence of any significant mention of the event in both Russian and Chinese sources before the 1920s was an acknowledgment of the tenuously peaceful settlement among the region's multi-ethnic and multinational residents – a settlement that demanded the "forgetting" of the Blagoveshchensk incident in the name of inter-ethnic harmony.[36] Guides to Harbin's municipal government of the 1920s, for example, focused on the need for the new Chinese-controlled administration to maintain good relations between the Russian and Chinese populations. The Chinese provincial and regional governments were also negotiating in this period with the new Soviet administration – negotiations, it was hoped, that would solve the longstanding problems of mutual ownership of the region's shared natural resources and industry. Finally, the Blagoveshchensk victims, as poor Manchu and Chinese farmers and trades people, did not fit into a narrative of modernity and development that was self-consciously adopted by the Manchurian Chinese elite in the 1920s. The victims, as subjects of the former Qing Dynasty and majority ethnic Manchus, did not fit into the agenda of the regional elite, in much the same way that the memory of the 1937 Nanjing Massacre victims did not fit into the agenda of the Communist government. As James Flath points out in this volume, these memories resurfaced as "public" only within the changing context of domestic politics and Sino-Japanese relations in the 1980s. Remembering the Blagoveshchensk Massacre also did not serve the interests of the local representatives of Soviet power, who did not wish to draw attention to the legitimate presence of a large Asian population in their territory, so recently acquired from the Qing. Furthermore, local Russian interests relied on trade, foodstuffs, and labour from the Chinese side. As a result, the elimination of the event from the region's collective memory served the interests of both of the region's populations, on either side of the border, during the 1920s. As for contemporary China and Russia, Victor Zatsepine's chapter shows that whereas the massacre is still an uneasy topic for the Russians, who avoid any mention or commemoration of the topic, the Chinese, with a powerful, post-1949 national identity and a Chinese Northeast cleared of its alternate histories, commemorate the act as Russian genocide against the region's Chinese population, their Manchu ethnicity forgotten.

Icons express holiness and the links between heaven and earth, and they can also act as national symbols or expressions of an ideal world. Ma was an icon of the Boxer Uprising in the Northeast and of the eventual seizure of a Chinese administrative victory from the jaws of the Boxer defeat. In his fierce patriotic nature, his bilingual and bicultural skills, and his blend of the region's two dominant cultures, Ma was a symbol of Chinese renewal following the Boxer Uprising. He was also a symbol of the reassertion of a Chinese, not Manchu, administrative identity in the Chinese Northeast following the Boxer Uprising and thus, in the 1920s, was an icon of eventual Chinese victory, not defeat.

The memory and the icon of the 220 Holy Chinese Martyrs of the Boxer Rebellion was first a symbol of Russian anxiety and chauvinism in northern China. Before 1917, as Albazinians, descendants of Russians captured by the Chinese government, the martyrs were representatives of the extension of Russian religion and culture into China. Yet, like the Russian presence in the Far East and in the Chinese Northeast itself, the memory and image of the martyrs was unstable. Following the 1917 Revolution, when the Russian Orthodox Church in China was forced to depend on its congregation and on the benevolence of the Chinese government, the 220 martyrs became the symbol of a new relationship between the Orthodox Church, the Chinese, and the Chinese state representatives who were increasingly patronizing and protecting the church. As a representative of a former colonial power in a new postcolonial context, the church needed to reinvent itself as an institution with links to the Chinese and to China. The icon, and the changed memory of the 220 martyrs, was part of this social and religious adjustment. As for the thousands of Chinese and Manchus murdered on the Sino-Russian frontier, the memory itself was too raw for any official commemoration that might tear apart the uneasy consensus in the Chinese Northeast. Only after 1949, when the region was cleansed of its alternate pasts, identities, and settlers, was the memory of the Blagoveshchensk Massacre allowed to emerge and stand alongside the newly reformed proto-nationalist and proto-socialist Boxer patriots.

The different ways that the Chinese and Russians commemorated, or did not commemorate, the shared experience of the Boxer Uprising, which so transformed the administrative landscape of the contested region, known to some as Manchuria, speaks to many conclusions. First, in a region with many identities and many histories, one memory and one commemoration is both impossible and undesirable, for in the naming of one memory as *the* memory, one risks effacing other histories in an attempt to impose a unitary identity on a multi-ethnic region. Second, memories and commemoration are subject to change – change in meaning and change in form – as the political and social context of those creating the memory changes and opens subjects (often by force) to new interpretations that fit their changed situation. Finally, some events are perhaps too painful to remember, for in doing so, one risks rending a fragile society or accommodation asunder. Perhaps what stands out most, in the end, from the memories of the holy martyrs, of brave General Ma, and of the forgotten victims of the Blagoveshchensk Massacre is the mutability and changeability of acts of memory and commemoration, acts that we often hold as solid and unchanging inasmuch as actions can be solid and unchanging, such is our reliance on these acts to define us in our national, religious, or ethnic identities.

Chapter 10: Chinese Savages and Chinese Saints

1 Paul A. Cohen, *History in Three Keys: The Boxers as Event, Experience, and Myth* (New York: Columbia University Press, 1997).

2 Xin Peilin, "Ma Zhongjun shensheng" [A biographical sketch of Mr. Ma Zhongjun], *Harbin wenshi ziliao* [Harbin Cultural and Historical Materials] 6 (1985): 1-22.

3 The siege of Harbin was a relatively unimportant event, and at no point was the Russian community seriously threatened. Russian soldiers in the concession numbered close to 5,000. Isolated Chinese attacks did result in the cutting of the Chinese Eastern Railway and the delay of the line's completion. See R. Polchanikov, "A Short History of Harbin" (n.d.), unpublished manuscript, in the Loukaskin Papers, Hoover Institute, reel 12, folder 2.

4 Dongchui shangbao [Northern Frontier Business Association], "Waiguo guanxi: Zhongdong tielu de qiyuan" [Foreign relations: The origins of the CER], in *Haerbin zhinan* [Guide to Harbin], ed. Northern Frontier Business Association (Harbin, 1922), vol. 2, ch. 3, sec. 1.
5 Lewis Siegelbaum, "Another 'Yellow Peril': Chinese Migrants to the Russian Far East and the Russian Reaction before 1917," *Modern Asian Studies* 12, 2 (April 1978): 307-29.
6 Sergei Yulievich Witte, *The Memoirs of Count Witte* (New York: Doubleday, Page, 1921).
7 For more, see Andrew Malozemoff, *Russian Far Eastern Policy, 1881-1904* (Berkeley: University of California Press, 1958); S.C.M. Paine, *Imperial Rivals: China, Russia and Their Disputed Frontier* (New York: M.E. Sharpe, 1996); and David Schimmelpenninck van der Oye, *Towards the Rising Sun: Russian Ideologies of Empire and the Path to War with Japan* (DeKalb, IL: Northern Illinois University Press, 2001).
8 David Schimmelpenninck van der Oye, "Russia's Ambivalent Reaction to the Boxers," *Cahiers du Monde Russe* 41, 1 (January-March 2000): 57-78. For further discussion of Imperial Russia's perception of the Russo-Chinese relationship, see Paine, *Imperial Rivals*; Schimmelpenninck van der Oye, *Toward the Rising Sun;* and R.K.I. Quested, *"Matey" Imperialists: The Tsarist Russians in Manchuria, 1895-1917* (Hong Kong: Centre for Asian Studies, University of Hong Kong, 1982).
9 See Dmitrii Pozdneev, *56 dnei pekinskogo sideniia v sviazi s blizhaishimi k nemu sobytiiami pekinskoi zhizni* [56 Peking Days in Connection to the Latest Events in Peking Life] (St. Petersburg: V.F. Kirshbaum, 1901); V.V. Korsakov, *Pekinskaia sobytiia* [Events in Peking] (St. Petersburg: A.S. Suvorin, 1901); Pavel Stepanovich Popov, "Dva mesiatsa osady v Pekine" [The two-month siege in Peking], *Viestnik Evropy* 36, 2 (1901): 517-36.
10 Howard Spendelow, "Conflict of Authority in South Manchuria: The Early Years of the Russian Leasehold, 1898-1900" (PhD diss., Department of History, Harvard University, 1982), 210-17.
11 Paine, *Imperial Rivals,* 217.
12 Tsar Nicholas II, "Russian Imperial Order Regarding Imperial Lieutenancy of the Far East. 12 August 1903. Article One," in *Treaties and Agreements with and Concerning China, 1894-1919,* ed. John V.A. MacMurray (New York: Oxford University Press, 1921), 122.
13 *Administrativnoe ustroistvo Severnoi Man'chzhurii* [Administrative Structure of Northern Manchuria] (Harbin, 1926), Shkurkin Archive, San Pablo, California.
14 After the Chinese Communist Revolution, the property belonging to the Spiritual Mission of the Russian Orthodox Church in Beijing was given, over the protests of the church, to the Soviet Union, which found itself in possession of the largest foreign compound in Beijing. The Soviet government demolished most of the churches, including the church that housed the icon of the 220 martyrs, in order to erect the Soviet embassy. In recent years, the Russian Orthodox Church and others have lobbied the Russian government to rebuild some of these buildings, and a monument to the mission has been built on the site.
15 The icon has been reproduced in a calendar published by the Russian Youth Committee for Enlightenment and Welfare, affiliated with the Astoria, New York, branch of the Russian Orthodox Church in America. The calendar's front page depicts the icon of the 220 Holy Martyrs of the Boxer Rebellion. See Russian Youth Committee for Enlightenment and Welfare under the Protection of his Eminence Most Rev. Metropolitan Vitaly, *Calendar 1998: Orthodoxy in the Far East* (Astoria, NY: Russian Youth Committee for Enlightenment and Welfare, 1998).
16 All Saints of North America Orthodox Church, Hamilton, Ontario, Akathist to the Chinese Martyr Saints of the Boxer Rebellion, http://www.asna.ca/resources/akathist-chinese-martyrs-1900.pdf.

17 Metropolitan Anthony Bloom, "The Russian Church Abroad," in *The Other Russia: The Experience of Exile,* ed. Michael Glenny and Norman Stone, 182-95 (London: Faber and Faber, 1990); *Russkaia paraslavnaia tser'kov za granitseif* [The Russian Orthodox Church Abroad] (Jerusalem: Russian Orthodox Mission, 1968).

18 Georg Seide, *Verantwortung in der diaspora: Die Russische Orthodoxe Kirche im ausland* [Responsibility in the Diaspora: The Russian Orthodox Church Abroad] (Munich: Kyril and Method Verlag, 1989).

19 *Bio-guan': Kpatkaia ictoriia pocciikoi duhovhoi missii v kitae* [Bay-Guon: A Short History of the Russian Spirtual Mission in China] (Moscow: Al'ianc-Arheo, 2006), 130-35.

20 In Harbin the Orthodox Church was given tax-exempt status and in addition received subsidies from the municipal and provincial governments; see "The Harbin Temporary Self-Government Committee Meetings: Minutes," *Haerbin tiebieshi bagao* [Harbin Special City Report] (Harbin, 1931), 88. See also Seide, *Verantwortung in der diaspora,* 213.

21 After 1925, when the newly installed Soviet co-managers of the Chinese Eastern Railway demanded that the Republic of China in the Northeast lose its railway subsidy, provincial and municipal governments stepped in to help maintain the institution. Zhang Zuolin also refused to turn over church property to the Soviets, contrary to the Soviet-Chinese agreement on the CER. See United States National Archives, RG 59, roll 154 861.77/3974, 22 January 1926.

22 Russian Youth Committee for Enlightenment and Welfare, 1998 Calendar, 2.

23 Xin, "Ma Zhongjun shensheng," 12.

24 See Cohen, *History in Three Keys.*

25 Dongchui shangbao [Northern Frontier Business Association], "Introduction," in *Haerbin zhinan* [Guide to Harbin], ed. Northern Frontier Business Association (Harbin, 1922), vol. 1, ch. 1, sec. 3.

26 H.S. Brunnert and V.V. Hagelstrom, *Present Day Political Organization of China* (Peking, 1913), 386.

27 Ironically, the CER, built as an instrument of Russian economic and demographic colonization, served as the means by which the Chinese settled the area and rapidly outnumbered the Russians.

28 Chinese Government Bureau of Economic Information, Shanghai, "Colonization in North Manchuria," *Chinese Economic Bulletin,* 15 March 1926; Brunnert and Hagelstrom, *Present Day Political Organization,* 386.

29 Dongchui shangbao [Northern Frontier Business Association], "Negotiation Bureaus," in *Haerbin zhinan* [Guide to Harbin], ed. Northern Frontier Business Association (Harbin, 1922), vol. 2, ch. 2, sec. 3.

30 Quested, *"Matey" Imperialists,* 181.

31 Ibid., 185.

32 Xin, "Ma Zhongjun shensheng," 6. All translations of quotations from non-English sources are mine.

33 Ibid., 15.

34 Paine, *Imperial Rivals,* 213.

35 Ibid., 214.

36 Only one source, dated 1926 and from the Soviet Union, mentioned the killing of Chinese during the Boxer Uprising in retaliation for the Chinese bombardment of Blagoveshchensk. See A.L. Popov, "Bokserskoe vosstanie" [The Boxer Uprising], *Kprachyi arhiv* [Red Archive] 14 (1926): 1-49.

11

Setting Moon and Rising Nationalism: Lugou Bridge as Monument and Memory

James Flath

On a summer's day in 1985 one last bus trundled over the elegant arches of Beijing's Lugou (Marco Polo) Bridge, and after 793 years of service the span was sealed off to begin a new career as a national monument. This act of bureaucratic finesse did not create the monument, nor did it create the concept of monumentality by which concrete objects are given extraordinary historical significance. The process of designation, however, does mark an important development in China of how historical artifacts are treated by the state.

Lugou Bridge has long been appreciated for its beauty and antiquity, but in the twentieth century it was destined to play a strikingly different role in China's grim struggle against Japan in the war of 1937-45, thus creating an alternate nationalist identity as a modern symbol of anti-imperialism. The combination of explicit narratives of heritage and nationalism in one site thus offers an opportunity to study how the two interact in the production of the modern historical site. Nonetheless, it must be recognized that concepts like "heritage," "nation," and "nationalism" are problematic and widely contested. Publications such as *Chinese Nationalism,* edited by Jonathan Unger, and *Exploring Nationalisms of China,* edited by C.X. George Wei and Xiaoyuan Liu, have begun to untangle some of the many complexities of Chinese nationalism, but they have also made it clear that with its constantly evolving dimensions, Chinese nationalism can never be reduced to a simple or standard definition.[1]

Some generalizations about Chinese nationalism, however, are relatively useful. In particular, the "culturalism-nationalism" thesis has been influencing discussions of Chinese nationalism ever since it was revised and published by Joseph Levenson in the late 1950s. Levenson's idea, greatly simplified, was that China's traditional polity operated under a system in which the elite owed its allegiance not to a particular territory but to a more abstract belief in the superiority of Chinese culture – that is, "culturalism." In the late nineteenth and early twentieth centuries this worldview came into conflict with the emerging system of nation-states and its imperative of territorial sovereignty. The response, Levenson argued, was for the Chinese elite to adopt nationalism, through which territorial claims could be asserted. The cultural past was not exactly abandoned in the process, but it was reduced to the function of traditionalism.[2]

This thesis, with its overtones of modernization theory, does contain problematic assumptions about the dichotomy between culture and nation and about the absence of any sense of nationalism in premodern China. The culturalism-nationalism thesis, however, remains a useful starting point for the discussion of changing concepts of monumentalism since, as the following discussion argues, premodern Chinese regimes essentially treated their monuments as culturalist artifacts. That is to say, monuments were used by cultural/political elites to legitimate authority not over a geographic space but over a universal culture. This began to change in the twentieth century when monuments and other cultural artifacts began to reflect the heightened concerns over the territorial integrity of the nation. Where this discussion departs from the culturalism-nationalism thesis, however, is in the observation that those artifacts never ceased to represent culturalism and now serve to legitimate authority over both culture *and* national space. Situating the historical monument within nationalist discourse shows that culturalism, or more specifically the cultural monument, is thoroughly embedded in what Wang Gungwu has referred to as "restoration nationalism."[3] The monument, in other words, is not a remnant of sentimental traditionalism but a concrete structure of authority.

In the post-Mao era, the People's Republic of China (PRC) has had to deal with multiple challenges to its identity, ranging from the loss of its primary icon (Chairman Mao Zedong) to rapid modernization, the end of the Cold War, and the 1989 Tiananmen Square Uprising. In response, Wang Gungwu suggests, China has become engaged in a soul-searching form of nationalism that "combines elements of both preservation and renewal, but ties in the faith in a glorious past more directly with a vision of a great future."[4] In this sense, the monumental conception of the nation too is built on the appropriation of earlier forms of monumental narratives that themselves were constructed in the interests of power. In this way, the monument becomes part of a structure of power that follows the logic of genealogy, depending on the selection and superscription of authoritative and monumental inscriptions of the past, to create authority in the present. The construction of a modern monument or the reconstitution of an ancient monument does not invalidate past inscriptions as negative examples but rather manipulates them as positive tools of legitimacy. Successful use now depends, as it always has, on channelling representations into specific forms of memory that support the interests of those having authority over the site. The glorious past, like the glorious future, has its primary application in supporting authority in the present.

Despite this focus on the nation as an expression of monumentality, it is also important to note the diversity of monuments in China and the fact that many are only problematically connected with this national metanarrative. I have elsewhere argued that provincial museums and monuments show significantly more scope for alternative narratives and thus work at cross-purposes to the establishment of a monolithic national-heritage structure.[5] But in turning attention to Beijing, one cannot help but recognize the powerful impression that the Chinese state has made on the public spaces under the jurisdiction of its capital city. This impression has appeared in other studies of Beijing monuments and museums, including Wu Hung's examination of Tiananmen Square in the wake of the 1989 Tiananmen Square Massacre, which focuses on the process of destruction and construction by which the Chinese Communist Party (CCP) remoulded the space in its own image.[6] Rubie Watson's expanded view of Beijing considers how the city has been spatially organized to reflect a national narrative, and in a more focused evaluation of a single site, Tamara Hamlish argues that the Palace Museum has become an ideal venue for the assertion of state hegemony.[7]

Although Lugou Bridge has much in common with each of these sites, it is also a unique historical experience. The structure is not as awesome as the Great Wall, nor does it possess the grandeur of the Palace Museum or the architecture of Tiananmen Square. But few heritage sites can match Lugou Bridge in its ability to draw the visitor into an imaginary teleology or evolutionary chronology that begins over eight centuries in the past and progresses inexorably toward the modern nation-state. It is the power to literally bridge past and present that makes this site so emotive of the continuing relevance of monumentalism.

Lugou Bridge in Imperial China

Lugou Bridge was completed in 1192 under the direction of the Jin, a dynasty founded by the Jurchen people of Manchuria who conquered north China and established their capital on the site of Yanjing, where Beijing stands today.[8] With eleven spans stretching 266 metres over the Lugou River, and its virtually countless stone lions,[9] the bridge immediately attracted admirers, including the Zhangzong emperor (r. 1190-1208). Although the Jurchen had once been culturally distinct, the Jin is widely cited in Chinese history as a model case of sinicization – a foreign dynasty that gave up its militaristic traditions and adopted settled Chinese ways.[10] The Zhangzong emperor in particular is remembered as one of the emperors who presided over this cultural transition, and it seems fitting that it was he who gave up the practice of hunting and began to seek the finer points of nature in the hills outside the capital. The best vistas he summarized as Yanshan bajing (The Eight Scenes of Mount Yan), and among them he included the vision of a full moon setting over the Lugou River.[11] This view, along with the bridge that defined it, would become the most enduring part of the Jin cultural legacy, and whereas other sights were forgotten or altered over the subsequent dynasties, Lugou xiaoyue (The Moon over the Lugou at Dawn) has persisted into the present as a widely celebrated vista.

The Jin had only a few years to enjoy the view over the Lugou before their capital fell to Genghis Khan in 1215. The bridge, however, stood firm, and when Kublai Khan returned to establish the Yuan Dynasty in 1279, it continued to serve as an inspiration to those who crossed it, including Marco Polo, who described it in his memoir as "a very handsome bridge of stone, perhaps unequalled by another in the world," thus lending the bridge his name in later Western accounts.[12] More relevant to the Chinese conception of the bridge are the poets and artists who captured the structure in word and image not as a singular monolith but as a complement to nature.

This understanding of the place of Lugou Bridge within the grandeur of nature continued to develop throughout the Yuan Dynasty[13] but was carried forward with greater articulation in the subsequent Ming Dynasty when the bridge and its environs were again grouped together with other scenic wonders as Yanjing bajing (The Eight Scenes of Yanjing). As Susan Naquin suggests, the artistic development of the Eight Scenes should not be taken merely as a flight of artistic enterprise but also as a concentrated effort to lend scenic and historic legitimacy to the region as it prepared to accept its renewed designation as capital of the Ming Dynasty.[14]

Liu Tong's descriptive Ming Dynasty text *Dijing jingwu lue (Brief Account of the Scenery of the Imperial City)* (1635), in addition to outlining the history of the bridge, devotes considerable space to transcribing poems that pay homage to it. Certainly, the most eminent of those poets was Hu Guang (1370-1418), a scholar who rose in the early Ming to obtain, among other appointments, the position of chancellor of Hanlin Academy and the highest court position of grand secretary of Wenyuan Hall. Unofficially, Hu Guang was also a close confidant of the third Ming emperor, Yongle, under whose authority the capital would be officially moved from Nanjing to Beijing in 1420.[15] Hu accompanied the emperor on a number of his journeys to and from his home base in Beijing, and it may have been on one of those occasions that he stopped at Lugou Bridge to author the following lines:

Lugou Bridge
Broken cloud, a tilted pale moon,
The waters of the Sanggan [Lugou] River shine yellow.

A man in a thatched cottage dreams peacefully,
The travellers on the stone bridge alert to the twilight.
The distant city is illuminated flame-red,
Frost on the plain as far as the eye can see.
Attendants to the emperor stationed upon the bridge,
The flags are soughing; the horses neighing long.[16]

Wang Fu (1362-1416) was both a contemporary and colleague of Hu Guang, and it was owing to his skill as a calligrapher that Wang found an official position as a draftsman. Beyond the confines of his day job, however, Wang was recognized as perhaps the finest painter and calligrapher of the early Ming Dynasty. Following in the style of the great Yuan Dynasty master Ni Zan, Wang Fu was described by his contemporaries as "particularly skilled in painting landscapes, bamboos, and stones. Whenever he got drunk he used to put on a yellow hat and robe and took on a haughty mien. He spread out some paper, rolled up his sleeves, waved the brush and went on splashing and scattering, doing the strangest things which are quite impossible to describe."[17] In 1413 and 1414 Wang also accompanied the emperor on his journeys to Beijing, and it was on the second trip in 1414 that he composed the hand scroll "Picture of Eight Scenes."[18] This imagined landscape included, naturally, "A Picture of the Moon over the Lugou at Dawn," which he also described in an associated poem, "Crossing Lugou Bridge in the Emperor's Retinue":

The emperor's retinue dons its morning clothes,
Cock's crow; setting moon; trees in mist.
Clouds cast shadows across the expanse of mountain peaks,
A light shimmers across the horizon.
Whispers are heard from the lonely garrison fire,
Horse hooves clatter across the frost-covered bridge.
The landscape inspires the imagination,
And the towers are the hometown of the emperor.[19]

Although it is notable that individuals as powerful as Hu Guang or as talented as Wang Fu chose Lugou Bridge as their artistic subject, it is more important to our understanding of their concept of monumentality that in doing so, they produced descriptions that diminish or even ignore the physical structure of the bridge itself. This is best explained through reference to contemporary artistic values, where the mastery of landscape painting, poetry, and calligraphy was recognized as the peak of civility. In the pursuit of an art form that could give full rein to the individual's emotional expression, there was little call for the technical accuracy or frank description that the manufactured object demanded. For this reason, objects such as bridges were seldom included as more than a supporting text to the soaring mountains, stately trees, or in this case, setting moon that could represent the spirit of the artist. In the context of the Ming Dynasty, therefore, an object such as Lugou Bridge is best understood not as a singular monument but as a prop to a grander and more abstract form of monument found in the natural surroundings and authorized by celebrity recognition in past and present. It was also this impression that would be retained in the text-based memory.

With the fall of the Ming Dynasty in 1644, Lugou Bridge once again passed into the hands of an alien dynasty, one that perceived itself to be heir to the earlier Jin.[20] As the sole physical reminder of the earlier dynasty, Lugou Bridge was a living statement of Manchu legitimacy. Repairs to the bridge were conducted repeatedly throughout the dynasty, beginning with the reign of the Kangxi emperor (r. 1662-1722), who was a frequent visitor to the site. In 1698 he renamed the river Yongding (Ever Stable) in the apparent hope that the new nomenclature would help to control the river's unpredictable behaviour. Three years later, he marked the occasion with a poem and stele bearing the title "Perusing the Yongding River."[21] The real boost to the bridge's image, however, came when the Qianlong emperor (r. 1736-95) renewed its status as one of The Eight Scenes of Beijing and offered his own views of the vista Moon over the Lugou at Dawn in 1751.[22] The Qianlong emperor, however, bettered his predecessors by having his calligraphic interpretation of the Zhangzong emperor's 550-year-old words inscribed on a 3.6-metre tablet mounted on a granite tortoise at the eastern approach to the bridge.[23] Given the perceived lineage of the Manchu, and the real lineage of the bridge, the Qianlong emperor's attention to the structure might be interpreted as an act of piety toward his alleged ancestors and a potent claim for Manchu legitimacy.

What the Qianlong emperor had accomplished in the process was not simply to stake a claim to territory but also to legitimate this claim by appropriating the literary authority of the past and delivering this idea into the common realm by fixing it in stone. Whether or not most people understood the reference to the Jin Dynasty, the idea of the vista Moon over the Lugou at Dawn was no longer just a poetic allusion by which an educated elite could contextualize the past; it was now on public display as a physical link to the past for all who crossed the bridge. This display, however, was not for the purpose of honouring the past or of being remembered in the future; it was about sustaining political legitimacy in the present. The Qianlong emperor had created and patronized a concrete link to past authority as an element of political authority in his present – the bridge had become a monument.

Lugou Bridge in the Age of Nationalism

The reputation of Lugou Bridge as a venerable antique and object of beauty began to undergo a radical transformation in the twentieth century. Travel guides to Beijing from the late-Qing and early Republican years continued to portray the bridge as an interesting artifact, although the construction of a railway bridge several hundred metres from the original meant that the original was no longer the primary passage in the south-western approach to Beijing.[24] The bridge continued to serve local traffic, but for long-distance travellers the structure had become an object more likely to be observed in passage from the speeding train. In any case, the deteriorating international situation and the growing threat of war with Japan increasingly overshadowed preoccupations such as tourism. Far from being forgotten amid the turmoil, however, Lugou Bridge was to become one of the greatest symbols of anti-Japanese resistance.

The emergence of a strong Japanese military in the late nineteenth century posed a continuing threat to China, beginning with defeat and the loss of territory in the First Sino-Japanese War (1894-95) and continuing through Japan's ever-increasing encroachments on Chinese sovereignty as spelled out by the infamous Twenty-One Demands of 1915 and by the 1919 Treaty of Versailles, which gave Japan control over former German holdings in Shandong province. Tensions had been heightened in the 1930s with the occupation of Manchuria by the Japanese Kwantung army and the establishment of the puppet-state Manchukuo.

According to treaty, Japan had also obtained the right to exercise troops in the vicinity of Lugou Bridge and the neighbouring railway bridge, which now appeared as strategically important to the control of rail traffic throughout the region. It was during one such manoeuvre on 7 July 1937 that a Chinese military detachment on the opposite side of the river lobbed a shell into the Japanese camp, and although this produced no casualties, the failure of one Japanese soldier to appear for roll call prompted an abortive attack on the Chinese position in the town of Wanping. From that point, the diplomatic and military situation deteriorated, and by the end of the month Japan had occupied the entire Beijing-Tianjin region in what was effectively the first offensive of the Second World War, better known in China as Kang-Ri zhanzheng (the Anti-Japanese War).[25]

The recognition of Lugou Bridge as a symbol of resistance was immediate. It took only three days for a collective of Shanghai dramatists to write a three-act play titled *Protect Lugou Bridge*.[26] Within weeks, other poems and memorials began to appear with titles such as "Lugouqiao zhange" ("Battle Anthem of Lugou Bridge"), by Huo Songlin, and "Qiqi shibian" ("July Seventh Incident"), by Tang Runmin.[27] Popular songs also emerged and were taken up as marching tunes by the Chinese military, including the following, known simply as "Lugou Bridge":

> Lugou Bridge, Lugou Bridge,
> Where our men laid down their lives,
> We will avenge their sacrifice.
> No fear when planes and tanks attack,
> We lift our swords and drive them back.
> Lugou Bridge, Lugou Bridge,
> This is where our nation lives or dies.[28]

The battle also coincides with the early development of Chinese journalistic correspondence, and it was largely through the medium of the newspaper that Lugou Bridge began to develop its status as an icon of resistance. The leading Tianjin newspaper, *Dagongbao (l'Impartial),* for example, began to cover the story on 9 July and continued to do so in subsequent days as the details unfolded. In the heat of war, the reports naturally focused on problems of immediate importance rather than on any sentimentality about the history or scenic beauty of Lugou Bridge. Many of these reports, however, did carry with them a visual reminder, as photographs began to juxtapose the arches and stone lions of Lugou Bridge with the headlines of Japanese aggression.[29] These were supplemented after 23 July by the stirring editorials of Fan Changjiang, one of China's more celebrated correspondents, who illustrated the first instalment of his three-piece series on the Lugou Bridge Incident with a photograph of the Qianlong emperor's setting-moon stele.[30] Another contemporary newspaper, *Shibao (The Times),* took a more traditional approach to Lugou Bridge, on 9 July 1937 reproducing ancient poetry to commemorate the situation and on 13 July printing an ode to the stone lions that had borne witness to the battle a week earlier.[31] Although the bridge never again figured prominently in battle, the media had played its role in securing the place of the bridge as a definitive symbol of the war.

Popular as the bridge was as a symbol of resistance, it nonetheless took a remarkably long time for it to acquire official recognition. The tenth anniversary of the July Seventh Incident might have been an appropriate moment to commemorate the site, and indeed *Dagongbao*'s Wang Lingqi did return to the scene on 8 July 1947, where he reported that the stele "Moon over the Lugou" still stood erect – its lettering now coloured red as though to symbolize "the bloodbath of the Anti-Japanese War."[32] When the Communists came to power in 1949, Lugou Bridge continued to appear in newspapers on important anniversaries, including 7 July 1957, when it was acknowledged in *Renmin ribao (People's Daily),* the official voice of the CCP, with an article titled "Remembering This Day

Twenty Years Ago."[33] The tone of the article, however, was set by its opening phrase, "9/18," referring not to the Lugou Bridge Incident but to the Mukden Incident of 18 September 1931 – a date that is regarded in PRC historiography as the real beginning of the Japanese invasion, which Chiang Kai-shek had supposedly declined to resist until that fateful day in 1937. The recognition of the event was thus not without its political implications, and these had to be handled with care lest the authors appear to sanction a rival that still posed a significant threat from Taiwan. The appropriation of Guomindang glory, therefore, required that the incident be framed within the wider "people's war," which the People's Liberation Army (PLA) had patronized. A following article in the same newspaper, using the prevailing tone of socialist romanticism, squeezed further significance out of the anniversary by contrasting the violence of twenty years past with the present peaceful scenery and promised to return in twenty more years to report on how things had turned out.[34]

In terms of physical protection and preservation, it was not until 1961 that the National Representative Committee designated the bridge and adjacent walled town of Wanping as national historic sites.[35] This in itself should be regarded as a departure from policy in a state where what little had been done to preserve historical artifacts had been left to local and provincial authorities.[36] The timing of 1961 corresponds to the more significant, although temporary, political departure of Mao Zedong from the apex of power and his replacement by Liu Shaoqi and Deng Xiaoping. The creation of a state-sponsored program of heritage conservation under this rival administration suggests the intent to diversify state iconography and draw attention away from Mao himself. But even with that level of recognition, there was no attempt to physically interpret the bridge as a symbol of nationalism or antimilitarism through any form of public facility.

Whatever intentions the Deng/Liu administration may have had for developing a system of state-protected historical artifacts, all such policies went into abeyance with the return of Mao and the beginning of the Cultural Revolution in 1966, when far beyond simply ignoring objects of antiquity, the state and its radical adherents actively demolished them. Although Lugou Bridge survived this period, *Renmin ribao* of 7 July 1967 demonstrates its diminished reputation. As in previous decennial anniversaries, the editorial returned to the subject of the Anti-Japanese War but not to Lugou Bridge, focusing exclusively on the evils of Japanese imperialism and the brilliance of Mao Zedong's thought.[37] Likewise, in 1977, if anyone had actually been lured back by the promise of twenty years earlier, they would have been disappointed to find that the issue of *Renmin ribao* to mark the fortieth anniversary of the Anti-Japanese War contained not a single reference to either the war or the bridge.[38]

China is by no means the only country to have neglected its memories of the Second World War during this timeframe, but it is worth considering why the memory of Lugou Bridge and other notable battle sites were languishing after four decades. An obvious reason, relating especially to Lugou Bridge, is that the bridge had originally been defended not by the Communist-run People's Liberation Army but by the Guomindang military, with which the Communists had engaged in a long and bloody civil war. A more subtle reason concerning wartime memories in general may be, as Diana Lary and Stephen MacKinnon suggest,[39] that the society had simply been too traumatized by continual warfare to have any desire to preserve it in memory.

A less emotional but equally relevant factor in the underdevelopment of monuments and museums of all sorts concerns the nature of recreation under the PRC. There is little question that the development of tourism has had a profound effect on the development of museums and monuments elsewhere in the world, and a consideration of this dynamic in China also helps to explain why they were slow to develop there before the 1980s. China had always upheld a tradition of pilgrimage to well-known temples and scenic mountains, and although this was curtailed under Communist rule, it was in part replaced by pilgrimages to sites of political interest, such as Chairman Mao's hometown of Shaoshan, the revolutionary base of Yan'an, and the model commune of Dazhai. Mao personally inspired the first real wave of popular interest in the Great Wall with his statement "He who has not been to the Great Wall is not a real man." And as the place where one could most likely catch a glimpse of Mao himself, Beijing's Tiananmen Square attracted enormous crowds, especially during the high tide of the Cultural Revolution. It was also at Tiananmen that the new National Museum of History and the central Monument to the People's Martyrs had been constructed in the late 1950s.[40] Outside of this small selection of mass-tourist destinations, however, there was little encouragement for people to travel to historic sites such as battlefields and nothing for them to do or see should they make the effort. The nature of Mao-era tourism, however, also highlights the primary reason why Lugou Bridge and past wars in general were largely overlooked in Maoist China – that being the monolithic nature of Mao himself. From the mid-1950s through to the mid-1970s, it was the Great Leader alone who stood as the symbol of the nation, and virtually all other developments were explicitly designed to support his further aggrandizement.

The Awakening Lion and the War of Memory

The passing of the Mao era following his death in 1976 and the final return of Deng Xiaoping ushered in the so-called Reform Era in the late 1970s, bringing about a gradual diversification in the previously monolithic national culture.

Official attitudes toward Lugou Bridge began to change in 1979 when the Beijing Planning Committee announced its intention to establish Lugouqiao wenwu baoguan suo (Lugou Bridge Artifact Preservation Institute), inaugurating it on 7 July 1981 – the forty-fourth anniversary of the Lugou Bridge Incident. Accompanying this institute was a small exhibit hall near the eastern approach to the bridge. This was initially divided into two sections – the first being a general history of the bridge and town of Wanping, the second dealing with the struggle against Japan.[41]

This shift in policy can be attributed to several factors. First, the 1980s saw the maturity of the first modern generation to have grown up without protracted war and consequently the first generation in need of concrete reminders that the Chinese Communist Party had been forged during the Anti-Japanese War and that the People's Liberation Army had "liberated" the country from its enemies. More significant, this same period marks the final rise to power of Deng Xiaoping and the implementation of his policy of economic development and opening to the outside world. Tourism, both domestic and international, was to become a key element in promoting China's economic growth and international stature, and as part of this promotion the country would begin to develop its battlefields as potential tourist sites.

The commemoration of the Anti-Japanese War must also be read in connection with continuing anti-Japanese sentiments, which have been piqued repeatedly since the re-establishment of official ties in the 1970s. Foremost among these issues is the question of Japanese war responsibility. With some justification, China regularly charges Japan with distorting the circumstances of the war, especially through high school textbooks that ignore such incidents as the 1937 Nanjing Massacre, which Chinese historians believe to have claimed some 300,000 civilian lives.[42] Although Japan and China re-established diplomatic ties in 1972 and signed a friendship pact in 1978, relations continue to be tainted by China's demand for formal apology and by Japan's reluctance to comply. High-level diplomatic visits from Japan to China tend to be prefaced by a recapitulation of the Chinese evaluation of Japanese atrocities and the call for apology and tend to conclude with Japan's expression of "regret" for any mistakes it may have made in the past. It may be an exaggeration to say that the Anti-Japanese War Memorial Hall of the Chinese People functions as a branch of foreign affairs,[43] but because of the nature of Sino-Japanese relations, edifices such as the Anti-Japanese War Memorial Hall are international in scope and must be evaluated in those terms.

It was on the tenth anniversary of the normalization of relations between China and Japan that the two countries became embroiled in the "textbook" controversy. In June 1982 the Japanese Ministry of Education publicized the results of its recent textbook-screening process, and by the end of the month the Japanese press had begun to describe textbook language as having reverted to an aggressive "prewar" tone.[44] These reports were quickly picked up by the Chinese press, which began a media campaign that marked the 15 August anniversary of the Japanese surrender with the *Renmin ribao* headline "Past experience, if not forgotten, is a guide to the future."[45] Before the year was out, it had been determined that there would be an Anti-Japanese War Memorial Hall, and in December 1982 the Cultural Artefact Division of the Department of Culture ratified the decision to repair the city walls of Wanping town and to establish the memorial hall.[46]

The Anti-Japanese War Memorial Hall Committee was established in 1985 under the direction of the Departments of Propaganda and Culture and was chaired by Minister of Culture Zhu Muzhi. At the opening meeting in 1985, it was determined that the hall would be under the jurisdiction of the City of Beijing, and exhibits were to be managed by the Political Department of the PLA and by the Chinese People's Military Revolution Museum.[47] The National People's Congress joined the effort in April 1986 by confirming that the Anti-Japanese War Memorial Hall was to be a key construction item of the 7th Five-Year Plan. Shortly thereafter, the Beijing People's Government established the Lugou Bridge Historical Renovation Committee and a Bridge Repair Steering Department staffed by a who's who of high-end political leaders, such as Beijing vice-mayors Bai Jiefu and Chen Haosu.[48] In 1987 the Anti-Japanese War Memorial Hall was finally opened with due ceremony, and the curtain was raised by General Yang Shangkun on 7 July – the fiftieth anniversary of the Lugou Bridge Incident.[49]

The Anti-Japanese War Memorial Hall, described in detail elsewhere by Rana Mitter, is defined largely by its architecture.[50] The emphasis throughout is on creating a monument, but in spite of the grandiosity of its implementation, the hall itself is certainly less than monumental. In lieu of that, organizers have made every effort to connect the site to the true national monuments, myths, and myths in the making. Standing a short distance from Lugou Bridge in Wanping town, the hall is enclosed by a traditional courtyard that both blocks any outside view of the interior and preserves the historical appearance of the town. On entering the courtyard, the visitor is greeted by *The Awakening Lion,* a massive sculpture that ties the museum to the historical site by invoking the bridge's most famous attribute while also giving expression to the popular idea that the modern Chinese "sleeping giant" is becoming a world power. When interviewed in 1995, Cheng Yunxian, one of three collaborators on the project, indicated that the sculpture had also been designed to incorporate elements of the Great Wall in order to create the "sense of a historic remnant" and that it included gunshot marks "to let the people feel the history."[51] A less obvious reference is to a form of the festive "lion dance" in which the term "Awakening Lion" refers to General Guan Yu (d. 220), regarded throughout East Asia as one of China's greatest military heroes, ultimate model of honour and loyalty, and God of War to the Qing Dynasty. Inside the main entrance, which is itself decorated by the calligraphic inscription of Deng Xiaoping, a second sculpture provides an equally resounding statement of the museum's message through reference to another of China's proudest representatives. Standing some twenty feet high and a hundred feet across, the sculpture presents row on row of stolid soldiers and citizens as living stone – the title is borrowed from a verse of China's militaristic national anthem (which is itself inscribed on an adjacent wall) and makes the intent of the piece apparent to all: "Build a New Great Wall with Our Flesh and Blood."

One of the key functions of the Anti-Japanese War Memorial Hall has been to wage the war of memory and hold Japan to historical account. Following the hall's opening in 1987, Lugou Bridge and the hall stood again at the frontlines when China and the world marked the fiftieth anniversary of Japan's unconditional surrender and the conclusion of the Second World War. To mark the occasion, Japan's prime minister, Tomiichi Murayama, chose this time to pay an official state visit to China and on 4 May 1995 toured the memorial hall and the bridge, where *Renmin ribao* photographed him beside the Qianlong emperor's memorial to the setting moon. The editorial board of *Renmin ribao* returned again the following 22 June with another article, "Gunshots Awaken the Ferocious Lion: A Sketch of the Resistance War Memorial of the Chinese People," and again on 7 July to mark the fifty-eighth anniversary of the Lugou Bridge Incident. A final editorial appeared on the armistice anniversary of 15 August, when Jiang Zemin visited the memorial hall and the bridge, where he repeated the now-familiar line "the past, if not forgotten, can be a guide to the future."[52]

If Chinese authorities had felt they were making progress in negotiating the memory of the Anti-Japanese War, they received affirmation six years later, on 8 October 2001, when Prime Minister Junichiro Koizumi raised the political stakes set by his predecessor by placing a wreath at the sculpture *Build a New Great Wall of Our Bones and Flesh*. But if anyone had thought this constituted the long-sought apology, they were sorely disappointed when Koizumi negated the good will after seven months by visiting the controversial Yasukuni Shrine to Japan's war dead on 21 April 2002 and again on 14 January 2003. Fulfilling its role as critic, the Anti-Japanese War Memorial Hall rose to the occasion two days later by hosting a historical seminar to reiterate the Chinese position on the war, condemn the Japanese prime minister's actions as "absurd" and "notorious," and remind Koizumi that he "cannot change historical facts."[53]

There may not be a direct causation between politics and the production of monuments in modern China, but an overview of the connection between Anti-Japanese War memorials and the development of Sino-Japanese relations makes it clear that the two are intimately connected. The development of Lugou Bridge and the Anti-Japanese War Memorial Hall had been conceived as part of China's response to the 1982 textbook crisis, and the museum has ever since played the role as arbiter of truth from the Chinese perspective. But in terms of diplomacy, truth and memory are not the only issues on the table. Indeed, with the high-stakes negotiation of trade and investment, truth and memory may not even be the key issues. But the negotiation of memory is nonetheless the one issue that precedes and contextualizes all else. By extension, Lugou Bridge and the Anti-Japanese War Memorial Hall are the venues of political theatre in which the rituals of Sino-Japanese relations are increasingly performed.

Conclusion

Nothing seems to represent the past as concretely as the concrete object itself. Armed with a little information and imagination, any visitor to a historic monument can perceive the venerable physical construction not merely as the arrangement of brick, stone, or concrete that it technically is but also as a profound statement on the past that it was made in or was made to represent. The logic of the monument is simple, and it is the ease of association between the tangible object and the abstract past that makes the monument so compelling as a concrete historical text and so inviting as a venue for partisan historical interpretation. Of course, the problem is seldom as simple as it appears, and the historian might point out that the relationship between the object and the past is infinitely more complicated or perhaps depressingly more mundane than it first appears. Such opinions, however, are peripheral to the process of monumentality, which is less about examining the complications of actual history than it is about creating social memory by which the object is reduced to a simple and effective monumental identity.

Prasenjit Duara has argued that historical narratives create a linear history that supports a "self-same, national subject evolving through time."[54] I agree with this observation, at least in respect to Lugou Bridge, but would add that historicizing monuments such as Lugou Bridge involves an ongoing process of legitimating their present through reference to the past. The constitution of present legitimacy (i.e., the "national subject") depends not just on contemporary authorization but also on the continuing appropriation of the authoritative lineage. In other words, the monument and museum have a strong potential to encode past authorizations in the present not through pure imagination but through recognition of the patterns of authority that have always been present in the authoritative texts that form the basis for the modern museum or ancient monument.

Although the Zhangzong emperor staked his own political/cultural claim to Lugou Bridge by coining the poetic phrase "Moon over the Lugou at Dawn," this stake was appropriated by later generations of literati who wished to establish the bridge as a symbol of antiquity by which their present, and the political structure that employed them, gained relevance. During the Qing Dynasty, the Qianlong emperor took that same textual fragment but fixed it in concrete form and made it the defining element of the bridge for all to see. The Zhangzong emperor's setting moon, as appropriated by the Qianlong emperor's stele, still makes up a dominant component of the bridge's identity, such that photographing a Japanese prime minister standing beside that stele in 1995 still had the effect of invoking the past 800 years of history. But in much the same way as the Qianlong emperor inscribed his interpretation on the bridge in 1751, present-day political leaders draw on past legitimacy while selecting other historical fragments to be monumentalized under the weight of their own authority. The subtle forms of the past are now embedded in the modern and expanded historical site and serve to authorize the modern message of nationalism and internationalism that is delivered through the interpretation of the modern museum.

Acknowledgment

An earlier version of this chapter was published with the same title in *International Journal of Heritage Studies* 10, 2 (2004): 175-92, http://www.informaworld.com.

Notes

1 Jonathan Unger, ed., *Chinese Nationalism* (Armonk, NY: M.E. Sharpe, 1996); Liu Xiaoyuan and C.X. George Wei, eds., *Exploring Nationalisms of China: Themes and Conflicts* (Westport, CT: Greenwood Press, 2002).

2 Arthur Levenson, *Confucian China and Its Modern Fate Trilogy* (Berkeley: University of California Press, 1958), 95-108.

3 Wang Gungwu, quoted in Zheng Yongnian, *Discovering Chinese Nationalisms in China* (Cambridge, UK: Cambridge University Press 1999), 15.

4 Ibid.

5 James Flath, "Managing Historical Capital in Shandong," *Public Historian* 24, 2 (2002): 41-59.

6 Wu Hung, "Tiananmen Square: A Political History of Monuments," *Representations* 35 (Summer 1991): 84-117.

7 Rubie Watson, "Palaces, Museums, and Squares: Chinese National Spaces," *Museum Anthropology* 19, 2 (1995): 7-19; Tamara Hamlish, "Global Culture, Modern Heritage:

Re-membering the Chinese Imperial Collections," in *Museums and Memory,* ed. Susan E. Crane, 137-58 (Palo Alto, CA: Stanford University Press, 2000).

8 The original name used by the Jin was "Guangli." The name "Lugou" [Reed Ditch] was adopted in the Yuan Dynasty. See Beijing Bowuguan Xuehui, *Beijing bolan* [Beijing Exhibits] (Beijing: Beijing Bowuguan Xuehui, 1987), 146-47.

9 Technically, there are 485 stone lions on the bridge, but folklore holds them to be defiant of attempts at enumeration. See Luo Zhewen et al., eds., *Lugou qiao wenji* [Collected Writings on Lugou Bridge] (Beijing, 1987), 44-45.

10 See in particular the discussion by Tao Jing-shen, *The Jurchen in Twelfth-Century China: A Study of Sinicization* (Seattle: University of Washington Press, 1976).

11 Luo et al., eds., *Lugou qiao wenji,* 16.

12 Thomas Wright, ed., *The Travels of Marco Polo,* trans. William Marsden (London: Henry G. Bohn, 1854), 238.

13 For examples of relevant Yuan Dynasty poetry, see Liu Tong, *Dijing jingwu lue* [A Record of the Scenery of the Capital] (1635; reprint, Beijing: Beijing guji chubanshe, 2000), 144. For samples of relevant Yuan Dynasty graphic art, see Luo et al., eds., *Lugou qiao wenji,* n.p.

14 Susan Naquin, *Peking: Temples and City Life, 1400-1900* (Berkeley: University of California Press, 2000), 112.

15 Carrington Goodrich, ed., *Dictionary of Ming Biography* (New York: Columbia University Press, 1976), vol. 2, 627.

16 Hu Guang, reproduced in Liu, *Dijing jingwu lue,* 145, as translated by Jianmeng He of the University of Western Ontario.

17 Jiang Shaoshu (fl. 1642-79), *Wusheng shishi* [History of Silent Poetry], quoted in Osvald Siren, *A History of Later Chinese Painting* (London: Medici, 1938), vol. 1, 31-32.

18 Goodrich, ed., *Dictionary of Ming Biography,* vol. 2, 1374.

19 Wang Fu, reproduced in Liu, *Dijing jingwu lue,* 145, as translated by Jianmeng He of the University of Western Ontario.

20 On the topic of Jin heritage, see Evelyn Rawski, *The Last Emperors: A Social History of Qing Imperial Institutions* (Berkeley: University of California Press, 1998), 295.

21 Luo et al., eds., *Lugou qiao wenji,* 59. The name of the river had earlier been changed from "Lugou" to "Wuding" [Never Stable]. Repairs were conducted in 1662, 1668, 1752, 1785, and 1787; see ibid., 36.

22 The other sites were Layered Shades of Green at Juyong Pass, Cascading Rainbow at Jade Spring Hill, Crystal Clear Waves on Taiye Pond, Spring Clouds on Jasper Flower Island, Misty Trees at the Gate of Jizhou, Clearing Snow in the Western Hills, and Sunset at the Golden Terrace. See Sun Chengze, *Tianfu guangji* [Extensive Records on the Celestial Capital] (Beijing: Beijing guji chubanshe, 2000), 564; translations based on Naquin, *Peking,* 111-12.

23 Luo et al., eds., *Lugou qiao wenji,* 70.

24 See, for example, *Beiping zhinan* [Guide to Beiping] (Beijing: Beiping Minshi, 1929), 61.

25 For a full account of this stage of the war, see Marvin Williamsen, "The Military Dimension, 1937-1941," in *China's Bitter Victory: The War with Japan, 1937-1945,* ed. James C. Hsiung and Steven Levine, 135-56 (Armonk, NY: M.E. Sharpe, 1992).

26 Leo Ou-fan Lee, "Literary Trends in the Road to Revolution," in *Cambridge History of China,* ed. Denis Twitchett and John King Fairbank (Cambridge, UK: Cambridge University Press, 1985), vol. 13, pt. 2, 470.

27 Xiong Xianyu et al., eds., *Lugou qiao kangzhan shici xuan* [Collected Poems Concerning the War of Resistance and Lugou Bridge] (Beijing: Yanshan chubanshe, 1997), 8, 11.

28 Ibid., 15, my translation.
29 See *Dagongbao* [l'Impartial], 9 July 1937, 10 July 1937, 15 July 1937.
30 See Fan Changjiang's reports in *Dagongbao,* 23 July 1937, 24 July 1937, 25 July 1937.
31 *Shibao* [The Times], 9 July 1937, 13 July 1937.
32 *Dagongbao,* 8 July 1947.
33 *Renmin ribao* [People's Daily], 7 July 1957.
34 *Renmin ribao,* 7 July 1957.
35 Beijing bowuguan xuehui [Beijing Museum Studies Association], eds., *Beijing bowuguan nianjian, 1912-1987* [Yearbook of Beijing Museums, 1912-1987] (Beijing: Yanshan chubanshe, 1987), 255. The City of Beijing government had extended protected status to these sites in the late 1950s.
36 On provincial artifact-preservation policies during the 1950s, see Flath, "Managing Historical Capital."
37 *Renmin ribao,* 7 July 1967.
38 *Renmin ribao,* 7 July 1977.
39 Diana Lary and Stephen MacKinnon, eds., *Scars of War: The Impact of Warfare on Modern China* (Vancouver: UBC Press, 2001), 4.
40 On the modern development of tourism at the Great Wall, see Arthur Waldron, *The Great Wall of China* (Cambridge, UK: Cambridge University Press, 1990), 194-226. On the construction of Tiananmen Square, see Wu, "Tiananmen Square."
41 Beijing bowuguan xuehui, eds., *Beijing bowuguan nianjian, 1912-1987,* 255.
42 Recent protests have focused on the textbook by Nishio Kanji et al., *Atarashii rekishi kyokasho* [New History Textbook] (Tokyo: Fushosha, 2001), which was approved for school distribution in 2002; see report by the Center for Research and Documentation on Japan's War Responsibility at http://www.jca.apc.org. Chinese high school textbooks, on the other hand, use increasingly strong language to portray the Nanjing Massacre as "hell on earth," explaining variously that Chinese citizens were "buried alive," were "burnt to death," "had their intestines removed," and were "killed after being raped." Students are also reminded that "the debt of blood caused by the Japanese aggressors will never be forgotten by the Chinese people." See Chang Jui-te, "The Politics of Commemoration," in *Scars of War: The Impact of Warfare on Modern China,* ed. Diana Lary and Stephen MacKinnon (Vancouver: UBC Press, 2001), 152.
43 "Zhongguo kang-Ri zhanzheng jinianguan" has been variously translated as "Memorial Museum of the Chinese People's War of Resistance against Japan," "Museum of the War of Chinese People's Resistance against Japan," and "Memorial Hall of the War of Resistance against Japan." In light of the inconsistencies, I use my own translation, "Anti-Japanese War Memorial Hall of the Chinese People."
44 Caroline Rose, *Interpreting History in Sino-Japanese Relations: A Case Study in Political Decision-Making* (New York: Routledge, 1998), 80-82.
45 *Renmin ribao,* 15 August 1982, my translation.
46 Beijing bowuguan xuehui, eds., *Beijing bowuguan nianjian, 1912-1987,* 255.
47 Beijing bowuguan xuehui, eds., *Beijing bowuguan nianjian, 1988-1991* [Yearbook of Beijing Museums, 1988-1991] (Beijing: Yanshan Chubanshe, 1991), 75.
48 Beijing bowuguan xuehui, eds., *Beijing bowuguan nianjian, 1912-1987,* 255-57.
49 Ibid., 105-8.
50 Rana Mitter, "Behind the Scenes at the Museum: Nationalism, History, and Memory in the Beijing War of Resistance Museum, 1987-1997," *China Quarterly* 161 (March 2000): 279-93.

51 John T. Young, *Contemporary Public Art in China* (Seattle: University of Washington Press, 1999), 32.
52 *Renmin ribao,* 4 May 1995, 22 June 1995, 7 July 1995, 15 August 1995, my translations.
53 *Renmin ribao,* 16 January 2003, my translation.
54 Prasenjit Duara, *Rescuing History from the Nation* (Chicago: University of Chicago Press, 1995), 4.

12

War and Remembering: Memories of China at War

Diana Lary

> *China is sometimes called the land of disasters. During an ordinary flood along the Yangze [Yangzi], the surplus waters are carried off by the lakes, tributaries and swamps along its course, and this results in no serious damage to the fields. The same is true with the social structure of the country. For a calamity of ordinary dimensions, the social system in China is able to absorb the resultant shock with little strain. But in an unprecedented disaster such as is now confronting China, as a result of the Japanese invasion and the extension of hostilities over no less than ten provinces, the system has neared breaking point.*
>
> – *China at War*, January 1939

The Resistance War was one of the most traumatic periods of China's long history. It was a protracted, painful, and universal experience; very few parts of China and very few Chinese families or individuals escaped its impact. The war was an even more invasive experience for China than the First and Second World Wars were for the West. The periodic outpourings of rage and anger in China over Japanese attitudes to the war, whether politically inspired or not, are a reminder of the ways that the immense and lasting upheaval caused by the war lives on in memory.

The scale of the suffering in China, expressed in numerical terms, is vast and almost numbing; in a population so huge, the numbers are bound to be enormous, hard to grasp. The danger is that the sense of numbness is transmuted into a feeling of impersonal indifference, a reaction that belittles and diminishes the suffering.

The war affected almost every aspect of life in China. Some of these effects are well known. In the political sphere, the war brought the gradual decline of the Guomindang (GMD) and the ascendancy of the Chinese Communist Party (CCP). To the modern economy, the war brought disruption and collapse; China's currency went into freefall, and much of the country's infrastructure was destroyed. Beyond these calamities, most of which can be documented, are the devastating social effects. They are difficult to document, almost impossible to quantify, and therefore much less well known, at least in print. There was little contemporary survey research. Although there were Western-trained sociologists and psychologists in China by the start of the war, there was very little opportunity to conduct survey work. Without such data, however, rich evidence can be found. Journalists provided great insights; fiction written in the war painted grim pictures of a society in turmoil. And the memories and the memoirs of those who lived through the war show what the war did to Chinese society.[1]

The social effects were direct and indirect; what they had in common was that most were sad and sombre. Almost all Chinese shared the insecurity and tension that the war brought; the country and its people were robbed of any sense of security – personal, economic, or physical – for the eight years of war. Few people were able to detach themselves from the prevailing climate of fear and anxiety or from the sense of interminable confusion and chaos. At the end of the war, few Chinese looked back on the past eight years with much sense of excitement or triumph, nor did they feel, to use an English expression, that they had "had a good war."

For a long time, individual Chinese who survived the war found the memories of this time of chaos and endurance too painful to talk about; they were buried, submerged, pushed into *oubliettes*. The closing-down of memory was a way to erase pain – and with the silence, a tacit recognition that the memories themselves were of pain, not of glory or triumph, seldom uplifting, not memories that people would be eager to recall.

The events of the war were followed by further upheavals, including the Civil War, the Land Reform, the Great Leap Forward, and the Cultural Revolution, with each upheaval generating more painful memories. The burying of memories by survivors became almost habitual. Memories of the Resistance War were especially sensitive. In the political campaigns of the first two decades of the Communist period, it was essential to bury memories of the war, which could only have been dangerous since they stemmed from the GMD era and the Japanese occupation. But burying memories does not mean destroying them; they are there to be unearthed. Over the past two decades, a number of personal shifts and political changes have come together to bring wartime memories back to the surface:

1 As the people who lived through the war come close to the end of their lives, there is a need to bring their memories out into the open. This need may be prompted by the survivors themselves or by relatives who want to know about their own family history. Professional historians see the elderly as eyewitnesses to events that are not recorded in written form and interview them for oral-history projects.
2 The government's "policy of restitution" *(luoshi zhengze)* in the 1980s, after the Cultural Revolution, was aimed at compensating people for the material

losses they had suffered during the "ten years of turbulence." The process required people to describe in detail what they or their forebears had lost in order to make claims for restitution. In the process, memories of losses from earlier periods, including the war, were revived.

3 Tortuous international relations have fostered the revival of memories of the war. China's rocky relationship with Japan has been made manifest at the commemorations of anniversaries of the war. There are so many major anniversaries that any one of them can be used as the focus for a major protest if the Chinese government decides to do so.[2] Promoting anti-Japanese sentiment is useful not only as a domestic issue but also as a link to other Asian countries that were occupied by Japan during the war. Commemoration is a potent diplomatic tool, as well as a practical one. Animosity to Japan also separates Taiwan independentists from Beijing, some of whom look back on the colonial period as a better time than the GMD rule after 1945. Nothing could be more infuriating to nationalist Beijing.

4 The revival of regional and local history over the past two decades and the compilation of regional and local gazetteers has brought attention to all periods of regional history, including the war. The focus tends to be on the major events in a given region; when a region showed particular courage or suffered particular atrocities during the war, the event is now commemorated with a monument or a museum. The Qisanyao [Unit 731] Museum near Haerbin details Japanese wartime biological experiments. The memorial to the Kunlunguan Battle (1939) in Guangxi has been refurbished as a tourist destination and as a site for patriotic education.

5 There are practical reasons for tapping into memory, such as the identification of sites where chemical and biological materials were hidden at the end of the war. Work on the sites of chemical and biological warfare in Manchuria has involved practical retrieval of oral history and memory.[3]

6 The writings of foreigners and overseas Chinese, most notably Iris Chang, have had major impacts in China, spurring people there to conduct their own research in order to bring other events to light and to reveal other hidden memories.

Since the retrieval of memory began, the sufferings of the war have been remembered and commemorated with passion and anguish by the state, by regions and communities, and by families. The term used to describe the pain and suffering inflicted on China is *wangji buliao* (they can never be forgotten) – as though the memories had not been in cold storage for decades.

Memories have a life of their own. They can be suppressed, but suppression cannot guarantee their destruction. They may die with the person in whose mind they first lodged, but they may live on, passed on to later generations, dormant but ready to be revived when there is a trigger. Memories are not passed on in the formal way that historical documents are, lodged in archives, subject to scrutiny. They are transmitted along unsystematic, sometimes mysterious paths. They may be brought to light by the desire of younger generations to understand their elders. They may also be used by older people to make younger ones feel grateful for what they have.[4] In an atavistic society such as China has been, there is a constraint to cherish and embellish family and clan memories in order to keep the connections to the ancestors. Public memory is intimately connected to personal memory, it is a source of pride or sorrow for a whole community, and it reflects the desire of a society to know where it comes from. Public memories are told in folk stories, expressed in the work of creative artists, carried in "proverbs" *(chengyu).*

There is a temptation to doubt memories, to categorize them as "true" or "false." Memories can be presented as inaccurate or partial, unlike hard, written facts. There was a vogue in the 1990s to dismiss memories of abuse, for which there was no evidence, as the product of "false-memory syndrome." This kind of dismissal does little to touch the power of memory. Memories are bound to be subjective, bound to be partial, because they are what people chose to remember, to select from a vast repertoire of happenings. The story that is told is "what you make it mean in the present."[5]

The capriciousness and unpredictability of memory, of what is remembered and what forgotten, gives rise to irritation and annoyance in those who are committed to rational, document-based approaches to the past; they prefer a history stripped of emotion and sentiment. The past is something to analyze and understand, not to wallow in. Phrases like "dwelling in the past," "harbouring grievances," and "refusing to move on" criticize those who want to remember too much.

These critiques appear to be based on rationality and hard-headedness, to give precedence to the objective over the subjective. This rationality fails to recognize the force or the role of memory. Nowhere is this clearer than in looking at the Resistance War. Remembering the war has not been a straightforward process, nor has it been continuous or linear. Two ways to look at memory, and to understand its power and its emotive force, are to look at the locus of memory and at the content of memory.

The Locus of Memory

Looking at the locus of memory is an entrée to understanding the complexity of memory and the variety of forms it takes. The locus has much to do with the form of memory. The Chinese state, whether led by the GMD or the CCP, has tended to be cautious, controlling, and even contradictory in remembering and commemorating the war. In the popular media, now freer to choose its topics than they were in the era of Mao Zedong, the war has been given considerable coverage, much of it in the form of memories. In the regions and localities of China, remembering the war varies greatly, complicated by the nature of the experience of the war, which was glorious for some areas, horrible for others, and shameful for yet others. For the family and the individual, experiences that are direct and personal comprise the dominant aspects of memory.

The State and the Memory of War

For the state, historical memory is mutable and often self-serving. Governments choose what events they want to remember, what events and people they want to commemorate. Paul Cohen's masterful study *History in Three Keys* shows how events can be given mythical dimensions, far removed from what actually happened, when the state promotes a particular interpretation – in this case, its view of the Boxers as class heroes.[6]

A graphic illustration of the state's commemoration of the war is the portrayal of the victory ceremony at the end of the war, held on 19 September 1945, in the hall of the Central Military Academy in Nanjing. A contemporary photograph shows a small-scale ceremony taking place in a shabby hall that is furnished with a makeshift collection of tables and chairs. A Japanese general leans forward to hand the document of surrender to a Chinese general; neither is easy to identify. The photograph suggests the sombre historical mood. The Chinese government had not yet returned to the capital, and the wartime leader of the government, Chiang Kai-shek, was not present. The victory was not glorious. China had paid an awful price for the war; the victory had been bought at a terrible cost. The low-key ceremony conveyed the sadness that accompanied the victory.

Almost sixty years later, in 2004, when the state had decided to view the end of the war as a glorious, nationalist victory, it staged a national painting contest in search of appropriate images, awarding first prize to a huge oil painting that was displayed in the place of honour in the Meishuguan in Beijing. The six-by-three-metre painting is by Chen Jian, a celebrated painter of epic battle scenes who serves with the People's Liberation Army. It shows a grandiloquent scene played out in a soaring, pillared hall; the painting could be an homage to Jacques-Louis David's *Coronation of Napoleon*. A tall, handsome Chinese general is taking the surrender from a Japanese commander who is bowing low in abject surrender. Phalanxes of Chinese and foreign soldiers look on.

The painting is less a representation of what actually happened than an indication of how the Government of China in 2004 wanted to commemorate the war and set the stage for the sixtieth anniversary of Japan's surrender the following year. China is triumphant, standing in full equality with her allies; the Japanese are almost effaced by defeat.[7] Anything negative, anything sad, is missing from the picture. There is no sense of the costs of the war, the losses and the pain. The glorious celebration of victory makes the war itself glorious. In the cause of the nation, even former villains are transformed. General He Yingqin, the general who took the surrender, was in real life a short, squat, unassuming figure; he was portrayed in Mainland China only in the most invidious terms after he fled to Taiwan with the GMD in 1949. In Chen Jian's picture, he makes his reappearance on the historical stage not as himself but as someone drawn from the ranks of film actors who play the heroes of the victorious Chinese race.

The Chinese state, like other authoritarian states, has the power to change and manipulate official historical memory. The 2004 picture is in a long tradition of commemoration of victories; it is a linear descendant of the portrayals of the Qianlong emperor's campaigns, all glorious victories (although in fact several were failures). This is the convention of war art in most victorious states – a memory is honed and polished to the point of fabrication in order to meet the contemporary ends of the state. State memories tell one as much about the current political situation as they do about what actually happened.

Official commemoration of the war is directly related to the political climate.[8] On the Mainland, the war, for a long time ignored, is now highlighted in ways that are not always predictable. Some of the many anniversaries of the wartime period are commemorated, and some are not.[9] There is no single day and time for the commemoration of the war dead; the eleventh hour of the eleventh day of the eleventh month is the moment of remembrance in the West. But 9 September may some day be given such status in China; the surrender was taken at 9 a.m. on 9 September 1945, the ninth hour of the ninth day of the ninth month. The seventieth anniversary of the Nanjing Massacre in 2007 was expected to be the focus of massive commemoration. A huge new museum, almost four times the size of the previous museum, had been opened to mark the anniversary in Nanjing, at a cost of almost US$60 million.[10] In actuality, the anniversary was muted and was not used as a pretext for renewed attacks on Japan, a lacuna that was a relief to the Japanese government, although not a permanent relief because there are always other anniversaries to come.

In Taiwan commemoration of the war was out of style for some time, the change in interest driven by the dominant views of the independentist Democratic Progressive Party (DPP). The prevailing mood was to forget the war. The Martyrs' Memorial in Taibei, the most formal memorial to the military dead of the war in the Chinese world, had a brief revival in visitors between 2007 and early 2009 when the spectacular changing of the guard was cancelled at Chiang Kai-shek Memorial Hall in downtown Taibei. The only convenient place to see the guards was at the Martyrs' Memorial. Now that the changing of the guard has been reinstated at the memorial hall (renamed National Taiwan Democracy Memorial Hall), the number of visitors to the Martyrs' Memorial may diminish.[11]

Under the DPP, the event to be commemorated in Taiwan was not the war but the GMD repression of native Taiwanese, which started on Ererba (28 February 1947). The focus was not on remembering what happened in Taiwan *during* the war but on the events after the Japanese defeat. The commemoration of the war was diminished by the feeling of Taiwanese that the colonial period was not as bad as the period of GMD rule that followed it – and by the hope that Japanese interest in the "model colony" would translate into diplomatic and material help in Taiwan's struggle with the Mainland.

The memory of war in Hong Kong is complicated by the fact that Hong Kong went into the war as a British colony and emerged from the war still a colony, which it remained for another half-century. Before the Japanese occupation at the end of 1941, Hong Kong had been a refuge for many people from the Mainland. Once the defending forces, British and Canadian, were defeated, and British and Commonwealth citizens interned, Hong Kong emptied out; much of the Chinese population fled to the Mainland, leaving the rump to endure a miserable period of occupation. It is a time best forgotten, with only a discreet physical reminder or two of the Japanese presence, such as the tower on Government House.

State memories and commemorations are detached from other levels of memory. They are the creations of the political world and often manipulated. There is no guarantee that they will intersect with community and personal memories or bear much resemblance to them.

This view of state memory suggests that the state is mainly concerned with self-glorification and has little interest in the damage that the war did to communities and individuals. This would be misleading in one major respect: given that the People's Republic of China controls whether and how individuals can seek compensation from Japan for what they suffered in the war, the state is the key actor in enabling claims for compensation.

The Popular Media and Memory

One of the main arenas for fostering and creating popular memory is the popular media. The Chinese media used to be indistinguishable from the state, managed under tight censorship, but the past two decades of marketization have seen the flourishing of popular media, with a vast increase in the coverage of almost any issue, except democracy or human rights. There has been an outpouring of books, films, television, and online media about the war.[12] Historical works, novels, television series, and exhibitions pour out in an inexhaustible torrent. Films have been one of the key creators, or liberators, of memory, and some of the finest recent films deal with the war: *Hong Gaoliang (Red Sorghum;* director Zhang Yimou, 1987), *Guizi laile (Devils on the Doorstep;* director Jiang Wen, 2000), and *Sejie (Lust Caution;* director Ang Lee, 2007).

Overseas Chinese writers have played a major role in remembering the war and in some cases have stimulated it. In the 1980s North American Chinese started to research the contributions of their communities to the war. They looked at the transformative effect the war had on them, and they did this by using oral history to revive memory. Iris Chang's book on the Nanjing Massacre sparked an enormous response and some often bitter recriminations from Japan.[13] Foreign scholars have questioned the accuracy of the details she provides and have worried about the emotive tone of the book, but Chang's book arrived at just the right time to release a pent-up torrent of memory. She speaks of the need to recover the memory of awful things that happened in her parents' home town – a need that turned out to be widely shared.

The media and the creative arts, whether free or controlled, have a tremendous ability to create and to channel memory. The recent discovery and publication of Irene Nemirovsky's unfinished novel *Suite française* has triggered a rush of memories of the fall of France in 1940.[14] The honesty of her portrayals of both French and German behaviour has moved the remembering of a terrible phase of French history away from simplistic right or wrong, good or evil, and has allowed for the emergence of memories that are probably truer to what actually happened than are more detached historical accounts.

In China certain periods are still off-limits for any kind of commemoration, most notably the Tiananmen Square Massacre of 1989. But the fact that they cannot be talked about publicly does not annihilate them. On the contrary, it encourages creativity in finding ways of sparking memory indirectly, as in Dai Sijie's novel and film *Balzac and the Little Chinese Seamstress* (2002). The film starts and ends with a middle-age man driving through ultramodern China. He has been away from China for a long time for no stated reason – but one that any Chinese could supply: 4 June 1989.

The Region and War Memory

At the level of the region and the locality, memories of the war are less subject to political manipulation. They are more varied, depending on where the community lies. The experience of the war differed so much from region to region that memories have to differ too.

Some regions were directly involved in fighting; others were not. Some were bombed; others were not. Some were totally dislocated, even devastated; others were hardly damaged. Much of China was occupied; other parts were free, being under Chinese government or Communist control.

The regions most directly affected are the ones most likely to have organized their own museums, memorials, and commemorations. The most comprehensive commemorations are in Nanjing, the city most tragically affected by the war. The museum, heavily subsidized by the city government and open free to the hundreds of thousands of visitors who go there each year, is the most prominent commemoration, but close behind it come monumental book series, major research projects, and collections of oral histories.[15]

Other regions were indirectly affected by what did not happen in them during the war. Prosperous cities, on an economic upswing in the 1930s, such as Xiamen and Quanzhou (Fujian) or Yantai (Shandong) languished in unhappy stagnation for the duration of the war. They look back on the war not as an awful time, since there was little bloodshed or direct damage, but as a time of decline and lost opportunities, a period to be recovered from rather than to be glorified.

For some regions, remembering the war could be only embarrassing or shaming. The cities of north China (i.e., Beijing and Tianjin) and of Manchuria passed through the war with very little direct damage. The Japanese occupation was civil, and there was little hardship beyond a slow economic decline. There was also little overt resistance and quite a lot of fairly active collaboration. Manchuria and its cities had been under Japanese control for so long by the time that all-out war started in 1937 that there was no expectation of a shift toward resistance, and very little occurred. Regions where Japanese rule was accepted, however unwillingly, tend to draw a veil over the period. The occasional anodyne publication about what happened in the war sheds very little light on what actually happened.[16]

The Family and the Individual

The war had a profound effect on families, and the depth of this effect is reflected in memory. The war killed many millions and forced even more into flight and exile. Many people fought in the war or were active in the wartime resistance; others were passive or were blown about by the winds of war. The war brought for many people the necessity to function without their family, to act as individuals. Being cut off from their community and family took them on new and unexpected trajectories.

The new, individualist life could be exciting and liberating, but it was shot through with feelings of loss and anxiety over family members with whom there was no contact. The war was hard on those separated from their families, especially the young. The psychiatrist Leslie Cheng, writing from Chengdu in 1944, reported cases of withdrawal, poor appetite, headaches, insomnia, and depression in students from the occupied areas. "They seldom hear from their families and each new battle on the war front of China starts an epidemic of worry, and all its resultant ailments."[17]

These experiences of upheaval and dissociation were replicated in the lives of myriad individuals in the uprooted population of China. The replication did not make the experience easier since each experience was critical to one person or one family.

Six decades later, the impact of wartime separations has not disappeared. The memories of lost family members, and of members permanently separated, are still there. They may be overlaid with the memories of deaths and separations that came later, in the Civil War and the social upheavals of the Mao era, but there is a common recognition that the bad times started in the chaos of the war, that the war broke down the old social structures, forcing people to rely only on themselves in the battle for survival. The war created the preconditions for the fragmented society in which Mao's ideology flourished.

The Content of Memory

Memory is not a neat, uniform phenomenon. People cherish memories of special events in their lives, although often in variant versions (as in Maurice Chevalier's famous song "Oh Yes I Remember It Well"). Some events produce memories that are usually happy (weddings, the birth of a new baby); others occasion memories that are usually sad (a death, a quarrel). For an experience as total as war, the range of memory is huge. What is remembered may be moments of glory and triumph but also the costs of war and the losses it brought. These are some of the major contents of memory, which are not exclusive to each other but usually occur in juxtaposition.

Finest Moments

The new official interpretations of the war have made it possible for memories of events that were long suppressed to be revived, memories that were anathema to the controlling political forces in the Mao era because they were the memories of people who were then on the political outs. These revived memories came flooding out in the 1980s in the nationwide collection and publication of *wenshi ziliao* (materials on history and literature); a major category within these publications was personal memories of wartime.

One example of a memory that must have been long-suppressed is a vivid memoir written by Xia Lumin of an event that was one of the most important in his life; it appeared in print only fifty years afterward. In August 1945 he was appointed, with six days' lead time, to arrange the formal surrender of Japanese forces in China. One of his keenest memories was of standing over a Japanese labour detail as he made the men clean up the hall of the military academy, where the ceremony was to take place. It had been severely damaged during the occupation; the labour detail even had to deal with eleven stinking corpses. Xia recalled every name of those who attended the ceremony and the seating order, with the senior Chinese symbolically facing south, the allies east and west, and the Japanese north. Xia remembered weeping hot tears in reflecting on what this day meant for China. He was still indignant, given what the war had meant for China, that He Yingqin stood to receive the document of surrender, instead of receiving it sitting down.[18]

During the Mao era, memories of proud and heroic moments in the Resistance War were permitted only for those who had fought in the guerrilla warfare led by the CCP. All memories of other heroes and heroic deeds were suppressed, expunged from public memory. The only foreigner who could be commemorated was Norman Bethune, a worthy hero, but his contributions were minor compared to those of the many other foreigners, missionaries, journalists, and diplomats who worked in the anti-Japanese cause. Suddenly, memories of non-Communist heroes started to see the light of day in the 1980s. "New" heroes were discovered, such as Zhang Zizhong, the most senior commander to be killed during the war, who came back from ignominy in the failed defence of Beijing to die heroically in a later battle.[19] Zhang has been commemorated at numerous sites, and almost anyone who ever knew him has written about him.

The flood of retrieved memories of the war has not yet stopped, although it is more and more difficult to find those who actually lived through the war. Some of the memories are now secondhand, as children recount what their parents told them.

Memories of the Dead

The death of young men in the armed forces and the disappearance of many others into the interior left holes in families and communities that could not be filled. These losses meant the loss of a future, the loss of security that people would be looked after in old age. The number of war-related deaths, whether 10 million or 20 million, will never be accurately established given the dearth of accurate records. The lack of accuracy matters less than that the dead were not mere numbers but were people who belonged to communities and families, and these people remember those who were lost – even if they never knew them. And if they died without their death being properly recognized, their loss is amplified by the nagging uncertainty about what happened to them. The GMD general Fang Zhenwu, the grandfather of Anson Chan, was an early leader of resistance against Japan; he was later exiled by the GMD and disappeared in flight from Hong Kong in 1941. The exact circumstances of his death have never been established, although there are many theories as to who killed him.

Political events get in the way of social memory. Many communities and families were unable for decades to commemorate their dead, especially those who died under the flag of the GMD and who were therefore deemed to have been fighting for the wrong side – as defined by the Civil War, not the Resistance War. A miniature obelisk put up in 1941 in Yongningzhen (Quanzhou) to commemorate the local people killed in a Japanese raid the year before now stands forlornly by the side of a new highway.[20] This modest monument is all that the community was able to put up to commemorate the dead of a terrifying attack, but at least it is there. It is more commemoration than exists at the moment for many of the dead of the war, civilians or soldiers. In Xuzhou the grand monument commemorating a battle is not for the victory over the Japanese in 1938, the only Chinese victory in the early stages of the war, in which Chinese forces expunged the shame of 1937, but for the Civil War campaign a decade later, in which forces of the People's Liberation Army defeated the GMD.[21] And the Martyrs' Memorial in Tiananmen Square commemorates the dead of the Civil War; there is no parallel memorial for those who fought against the Japanese.

Sixty years after the end of the war, there are still people who remember their losses and far more of their descendants who have inherited these memories. Some of them want to commemorate their dead, even after such a long stretch of time. This is not surprising; memory keeps its own conventions about the passage of time. It is erroneous to adhere to the rather simplistic and banal idea that once the last person who experienced a certain event is dead, so is the memory. In the West the memories of those who died in the First World War have been strongly revived in the past few decades. More people than ever, now the grandchildren and great-grandchildren of the dead, visit the war graves in France.[22] The sadness over the loss of so many men has been enhanced rather than reduced by time. As interest has waned in who was to blame for the war or what its political outcomes were, the sense of loss and waste has deepened.

The Memory of Separation

The war produced myriad separations; communities and families were divided by the war. The most common separations were physical; some people in a community left their homes and joined the huge refugee flows; others stayed put or fled only short distances and then returned. These separations started out as short-term ones, but many became permanent, some never to be resolved.

Paul Ho (He Jibu), whose school was evacuated from Nanchang in 1938, was one of the hundreds of thousands of students who were cut off from their families for most of the war. Ho went first to Yongxin, at the foot of the Jinggangshan Mountains, less than a hundred miles from home, then to Guizhou. The wartime separation was followed by a much longer one, when he migrated first to Taiwan and then to America, but it was the first one that set him on his life course. Almost seventy years later, he still felt the pain of that separation, one that had made him resourceful and resilient but had deprived him of his native home and family.[23]

Separation from home could be exhilarating, depending on the age and adaptability of the individual and on the strength of the ties to home and the locality. Some people thrived on it. My teacher Jerome Ch'en, as a young student, went off from Chengdu to Kunming and there benefited from one of the best educations that any student has ever had, taught by the leading intellectuals of the time in Xinan Lianda (Southwest United University). He greatly valued his education, but he did not know then that he would never return home, except for brief visits, most of them almost fifty years later. The memory of the benefit of his education is qualified by the loss of family and community that it involved.

The great raft of separations from home and family started early in the war and often did not cease with the end of the war. In the short run, the Civil War made reunions and reconciliation impossible; the subsequent accession of the Communist Party to power made the separations permanent. Many of the soldiers who fought the Japanese never went back to their homes. There was very little leave during the war, even for men whose homes were in "Free China." The looming Civil War prevented them from going home in 1945, and in 1949 many of those in GMD units were evacuated to Taiwan. Only in the 1980s were members of the lower ranks of the Republic of China army able to go home and see their families, fifty years after they had gone off to fight. The reunions were often sad; many of those closest to them, particularly parents, were dead; and family members who had suffered from having relatives in Taiwan were not as ecstatic to see them as the returnees might have hoped. The reunifications were only partial. Issues of the monthly journal *Guangxi wenxian (Guangxi Documents)*, published in Taiwan, continue to print advertisements from people in Guangxi who are looking for their absent relatives, almost sixty years after they were taken to Taiwan.

These soldiers were more fortunate than the great number of Guangxi GMD soldiers who were taken prisoner at the end of the Civil War; many of them were sent to labour camps or to the borderlands, notably to the *bingtuan* (army-run agricultural settlements). Their memories of the war, published in articles in many *wenshi ziliao* from different parts of Guangxi, describe their wartime experiences but give no details of what happened to them after the end of the Civil War, beyond a terse mention of their arrest and banishment.

The war brought political as well as physical separations. These separations occurred when some members of a community or family decided to resist, either by leaving home or by covertly supporting the resistance, while others decided or, more commonly, had no option but to live with the enemy.[24] These separations are hard to remember; most are painful. Those who lived with the enemy have not wanted to retrieve what turned out to be shameful memories. Those who left at the start of the war and came back at the end had no time or energy to settle accounts on their return; they blocked out their memories of their family members and friends who had lived with the Japanese. These subterranean memories have festered. China has yet to go through the kind of process generated in France by *Le chagrin et la pitie (The Sorrow and the Pity)*, Marcel Ophul's film that stimulated a flood of shock and recrimination in 1970 at the scale of French collaboration with the Germans. Given that Chinese culture has not been forgiving of those who failed their country (see the continued vilification of Qin Gui, the Song Dynasty official who betrayed Yue Fei a thousand years ago), there is no guarantee that what is still forgotten at the moment will not be remembered later on. Qin Gui still kneels abjectly at the entrance to the Yue Fei Temple in Hangzhou, although the public is no longer allowed to spit on the statue for reasons of hygiene.

Sometimes, the blocking of memory has gone beyond the individual and family to encompass a whole society. In places that were occupied for a long time, so many people were compromised that there was a tacit decision not to go too much into what had happened during the occupation. This is the case with Beijing and Tianjin, but it was common in all the occupied cities. In Xiamen much of the population, including the university, left the city just before Japanese troops arrived in 1938. Those who stayed on lived with the Japanese, and a few actively collaborated. Very few people were punished at the end of the war. Some of the collaborators had gone; the Taiwanese who had worked for the Japanese during the occupation returned to Taiwan at the end of the war and were not punished. The man who had served as mayor under the Japanese, Li Enxian, who was anyhow from Guangdong, was sentenced to fifteen years in jail.[25] This was the stiffest punishment. For the rest, Xiamen kept a discreet silence about what had gone on, a silence that is replicated in most places that were occupied in the war.

Memory of Material Loss

The material losses to China of the war were staggering and incalculable; there was no counting of losses, nor was there any stable currency to measure them in. The most obvious form of loss was bomb damage, but there were many other forms. One was the loss of property by abandonment, as people fled inland, leaving their property to the tender mercies of relatives or friends. Then there was the loss of land and property due to military engagements or to confiscation of land for military purposes. In 1942 Japanese forces cleared 42,000 square kilometres of land in north China to create a security zone and a "no-man's land" *(wurenqu)*.[26] And then there were the losses due to general turbulence and to the activities of people who flourished in such times – bandits, robbers, and speculators.

Few of the material losses could be documented since the records needed to do so – written titles to property, inventories and photographs of valuables – did not exist. But the sense of dispossession, of the injustice of material loss, pays little attention to whether a loss can be documented or not. If anything, the inability to prove loss may exacerbate the feeling of loss.

One particular cascade of losses was well documented on the orders of the man responsible for it, Zhang Zhizhong. This was the damage caused by the Great Fire of Changsha in October 1938. The firing of the city by defending forces, convinced that the Japanese forces were about to arrive (they did not), led to the almost total destruction of a wealthy trading centre and of an ancient centre of culture and learning. In the conflagration, only 34 percent of the city's structures survived.[27]

At least for Changsha, there was an official report to document the damage, although the global figures probably meant little to individual owners. For other wartime catastrophes, whether the product of enemy action, usually bombing, or of scorched-earth tactics by Chinese forces, there was almost no detail on the enormous losses.

Cultural losses, the destruction of historic buildings or of artifacts, were less personal than national, the loss of cultural patrimony. The issue of lost, looted, and stolen art, books, and antiquities is as bitter in China as it is in Europe, where the search for treasures stolen by the Nazis still continues.[28] Sometimes, the losses were both cultural and personal. In 1938 Feng Zikai, at the height of his career as a cartoonist, had just built himself a house and studio in his hometown, Shimenwan, near Hangzhou; the bulk of his work was stored there. The

TABLE 12.1

Property losses in the Great Fire of Changsha, 1938

Property type	Original stock	Destroyed	Half-destroyed
Stores	–	10,336	85
Residences	–	10,198	169
Schools	–	55	16
Government offices	–	62	13
Banks	–	11	2
Hospitals	–	13	–
Temples	–	108	4
Factories	–	10	3
Foreign property	–	55	7
Total	31,884	20,848	299

Source: State Historical Archives, Zhang Zhizhong, "Hunan sheng zhengfu chenbao: Changsha dahuo caiqing" [Report of the Hunan provincial government: Damage from the Great Fire of Changsha], January 1939.

bombing of the town forced him to leave in panic, with his entire family of sixteen people. When he returned eight years later, the house he had built had been destroyed and with it much of his work. He could not bring himself to live there again.[29] His memories of his home and his art, and the feeling of loss, were too powerful to let him return to what had become a haunted place.

Some of the material losses of the war involved not personal property but businesses. The Chinese economy was looking up in the 1930s; industry, international trade, and cash crops were all on the upswing. This growth was stopped in its tracks by the war. Industry declined as plants were destroyed by bombs or were relocated to the interior; markets were interrupted or lost. The Yangzi ports (excluding Shanghai) were devastated by the fighting in the lower reaches of the river and by the barrage put across the river by government forces to prevent the enemy from moving upriver. Customs revenues on imports for 1938 were under 10 percent of 1937's total, and exports fell to about 5 percent of the previous year.[30] In the occupied areas, Chinese merchants and entrepreneurs were at the mercy of Japanese companies and were often ruined by the completely unequal competition.

The wartime losses wiped out large parts of the mercantile community. The war reduced the modern business community on the Lower Yangzi River, in Tianjin, Guangdong, and Fujian, from its positive position before the war to a shadow of itself, a shadow then attacked in the Mao era. A few business families escaped and prospered in Hong Kong.[31] The business world in China did not grow again until the post-Mao era, a gap of fifty years – and one initiated by the invasion of 1937. Xiamen took more than fifty years to come back to the trading levels of just before the war. The economic revival, when it came, was centred in the places that had grown before the war. Location is one answer for the rapid retrieval of a lost position, but the stimulus of memories of past business acumen may be another.

Memories of material loss are easy to recall and just as easy to magnify. In China they are also the source of especially deep bitterness since the losses were usually absolute. Few property owners had insurance coverage; China had only a tiny insurance industry in the 1930s and 1940s (in any case, acts of war are seldom covered by insurance policies). Nor was there any compensation for material loss after the war. Few efforts were made to hold Japan responsible for the damages caused in China; the Japanese government has not had to pay restitution and reparations, unlike the German government, whose payments to individual Jewish victims of Nazi persecution and to the state of Israel have amounted to billions of dollars.[32] The issue of (non)compensation was decided by treaty and by subsequent political agreements between China and Japan, in which the actual victims have had no say.

Payments from Japan would not have been appropriate to compensate many of the victims of war. Japan was not responsible for what happened in Changsha, nor for the losses caused when the Yellow River dyke was breached in 1938. Japan could not be held responsible for the collapse of Japanese "puppet" currencies at the end of the war or for the nonpayment of pensions to people who had worked for the Japanese during the war. The last two losses have a particularly bitter twist because they can be documented. People still hold bank books and pension records from the time.

There was an attempt after the war to put right some of the key infrastructural losses in China through United Nations Relief and Rehabilitation Administration (UNRRA) programs (1945-47). Almost US$700 million was spent in China; the largest single project was the closing of the Yellow River dyke at Huayuankou in Henan and the redirection of the river.[33] But the UNRRA itself was short-lived, and the funds it could provide were miniscule in proportion to the needs.

The absence of compensation for material losses might seem to be the end of the matter, but it cannot be, for lack of compensation did not eliminate the sense of loss; losses stayed on in memory, often inflated in value and size, as the memories of past prosperity, a prosperity that came to an end with the war. Much more was lost in the Land Reform of the late 1940s and the early 1950s and in the forced requisition of urban property. But the wartime losses were the first of many and therefore often the most bitter.

The material losses produced two kinds of memory: one was quiet nostalgia for the glory days before the war, for lost prosperity; the other was deep bitterness that individuals and families had been the victims of robbery, that all their efforts to succeed had been nullified by the war. The bitter memories, transposed to younger generations, have helped to fuel a fierce desire to recoup the losses, to make China and Chinese individuals rich again, as some of them were in the 1930s. Much of the present-day pride in China's economic boom is premised on the conviction that China is finally finding her rightful place in the global economic system, one that was denied to her for many decades – a denial that started with the war.

Memories of the Abuse of Rituals

One of the most painful memories of the war, in a society that valued traditional social rituals, was of the inability to perform the proper rites for family members. The disruption of the war meant that failure to perform family rituals became a dismal reality for many people. For eight years, many people could not get home for the New Year to celebrate the strength of their commitment to their families. Marriages were difficult to arrange in separated families. The proper burial of the dead in their native places was often impossible; people who died far from home were separated in perpetuity from their homes.

The inability to perform the proper rites and rituals during the war left people with a sense of inadequacy and grief – and guilt that they had somehow let down their family members. The inability was exacerbated in the Mao era: parents were forbidden to arrange marriages, leaving young people to make their own choices; earth burials were banned in favour of cremation; and celebration of the ancestors was outlawed.

In the new climate of the 1980s, many of the old social rituals (except for arranged marriage) were revived. The revival was in the hands of families and communities, with the tacit support of the state. With the revival, memories of those once denied proper ceremonies were retrieved. The revival did much to make up for the ritual failures that had gone before: the proper rites were performed decades after they should have been, the remains of dead forebears reburied, shrines built to commemorate them, and family records and genealogies reconstructed. A new class of ritual specialists emerged. In Fujian a spate of building – of clan temples, shrines, and graves – replaced what was lost in the Cultural Revolution and in the periods that preceded it, especially the eight years of war.

Memories of Abuse: Prisoners of War, Forced Labour, and Comfort Women

Memory is a prelude for the recognition of wrongs and then for the pursuit of compensation. The cases have required the retrieval of individual memories of victims because it is these memories that become the basis for financial claims for wartime abuse in circumstances where there is little written evidence. Litigants also require state sanction to proceed with cases outside China (i.e., in Japan). One of the first cases was heard in 2004. The Hiroshima High Court awarded five Chinese who had worked as slave labourers for Nishimatsu Construction 27.5 million yen (US$250,000).[34] These cases will be limited to the actual victims. Most will fail, and descendants will not be able to apply for posthumous compensation.

The process of getting elderly people to remember past abuse, to relate the horrors that they went through as sex slaves or as slave labourers, is painful, and it is hard to work out whether the pain is worth the possibility of compensation. But there are precedents. The process fits within two patterns. One is the Chinese tradition of "speaking bitterness," of speaking out in passionate, almost histrionic terms about wrongs suffered, a tradition continued in the class struggles and denunciation meetings of the Mao era. The second is the global movement of truth and reconciliation started in South Africa, which requires that people speak publicly about what has happened to them in the hope that their tormentors can recognize their guilt.

Memories of a Lost World

The old world was already on the way out when the war started, experiencing a gradual process of change that had begun in the late Qing Dynasty and that continued in the early Republic, rippling out from the treaty ports and the new cities. In the war the process accelerated to breakneck speed. The old extended family broke down under the pressures of division and of economic collapse. New social forms emerged by necessity, such as the nuclear family looking after only its few members. With this diminution of the family came a permanent loss of a larger social security and a loss of trust in any but one's closest relatives.

The conflicted feelings of the time produced equally conflicted memories later on, sometimes relief at the loss of a claustrophobic society but sometimes rose-coloured memories of an ideal time before the war, in which the old world is recalled in nostalgic memories that are often stereotyped and border on the pleasant fantasies of costume dramas – memories of beautiful houses, sunlit courtyards, deferential servants, and charming men and women, all wrapped up in sanitized visions such as that of "Old Beijing." Much of the demise of the old society can be put down to the revolutionary process after 1949, but the start of the process came with the start of the war.

Memories of the Birth of a New Society

What has been discussed so far may seem an unrelieved catalogue of loss. But there were positive sides to the social experience of the war, and these too are remembered. The war brought new roles for women in Free China, especially young women. There were women's army units and women's support groups for the troops. Women went out to work. Young women away from home were able to find their own husbands; the accounts of life in Free China are full of stories of love matches and the exhilaration of romance.

Women left behind in the occupied areas when their husbands went to war or were killed were forced to become more self-sufficient. This was not easy, and for many of them the war brought awful burdens and insecurity, but it did represent a move toward greater freedom and initiative, something that might not have come without the war. These women, now very elderly, look back at the war as a time when they came into their own, an involuntary liberation, but one to be very proud of.

The war also produced some effects that were deeply resented at first but turned out to be salutary. In the *qiaoxiang* (emigrant communities) in Guangdong and Fujian, the flow of remittance from overseas Chinese dried up in the early years of the war. The relatives at home who had become accustomed to living easy lives were suddenly forced to manage on their own and had to get jobs or to find some other way of surviving without the lubrication of remittances from abroad. These people have mixed memories about the war, a combination of anger toward the Japanese for having messed up their comfortable worlds and pride that they survived it.[35]

The impact of the war was greater at the North American ends of the overseas Chinese networks. There, the war forced a change in identity and the acceptance that those born abroad belonged first to the nation they lived in (Canada or the United States) and were anxious to serve in the armies that were fighting the enemy of China, Japan.[36] From the start of the war until the 1980s, connections with China were almost severed.

Memories of Survival and Self-Sufficiency

The war generated a make-do-and-mend approach to life, an involuntary self-sufficiency in which many took pride. During the Second World War the British took pride in getting by, from enjoying the Woolton Pie (carrots instead of meat) to pretending that Camp Coffee (100 percent ground chicory) was the real thing. These experiences have been made into myth, the belief in a simpler, united world of shortages, of a social ability to cope with adversity, to carry on through bombs and destruction.[37]

British experience of shortage was nothing compared to the shortages that China faced in the war or to the bombing of unoccupied cities. The once wealthy were reduced to destitution; material security was a thing of the past. In Free China the shortages often seemed to outsiders to bring out the worst in the population, encouraging every form of hoarding and selfishness.[38] This view is probably as biased as the glowing portrayals of the celebration of poverty in the Communist-controlled areas, a celebration that became ingrained during the Mao era, when materialism was held in contempt; there was a pride in simplicity and austerity, and this pride has lived on as a nostalgia for a cleaner, leaner time. Now, in an era of boisterous materialism, looking back on shortage and destitution arouses not only pride in memories of scarcity but also indirect criticism of those who are immersed in materialism.

The survival techniques learned in the occupied areas did not produce positive memories. The long-term experience of living under occupation taught self-preservation techniques, the forerunners of the techniques necessary for survival during the Mao era. The Kempeitai (Japanese secret police) ran extensive networks for collecting intelligence and information, which forced people to inform on each other. Taking hostages and using paid informers made it impossible for members of a community to trust each other; they could look after only themselves and their closest relatives. The memories of wartime compromises and betrayals had to be suppressed, although the survival techniques for getting through a dreadful period were not.

Memories to Be Kept Buried

The many Chinese who lived out the war under Japanese rule have not been able, nor have wanted, to bring their memories out into the open. Most of the people who continued with their "normal" lives, perhaps half of the population, were without the resources to flee or were too old and frail to do so. Others made conscious decisions at the beginning of the war against heroic resistance, resolving to stay on and live, however unhappily, under occupation; these decisions were often made on the basis of practicality, as it was impossible to leave with a raft of children and elderly dependants and impossible to leave without money. Some more cynical people saw a Japanese victory as inevitable and decided to throw their hand in with the new rulers. In the short run, this seemed to be a sensible course of action, and the adaptations and compromises involved were regarded as annoying but unavoidable. But they were dealing with the unknown. The situation was never stable – or rather, there were long periods of stability punctuated by sickening lurches downward. What was supposed to be resignation became gloom and despondency.

Some people just made the wrong decision when the point came to leave – or stay. The most famous of those who made mistakes was Zhou Zuoren, at the time the more famous brother of Lu Xun (Zhou Shuren). His decision not to leave was prompted by his anxiety at taking his Japanese wife into Free China. So instead of abandoning her, he stayed in Beijing and later paid the high price of being imprisoned as a traitor.

Very few people paid such high prices, although making the wrong decision could in the end mean permanent shame. When his colleagues left Beijing, the palaeontologist Pei Wenzhong, the discoverer of Peking Man, stayed behind to work on Peking Man with Pierre Teilhard de Chardin. But they were unable to continue their work; no more excavation was possible because the area around Zhoukoudian, where the Peking Man cave lay, was unsafe, filled with guerrillas. Teilhard used his unexpected leisure to return to his philosophical work on the nature of man, in what turned out to be one of the most productive phases of his intellectual life, but Pei had little to do. After 1941, when Japanese experts arrived in Beijing to collect the fossil bones of Peking Man, they immediately recognized that the ones left at the Peking Union Medical College were copies. In their fury, they turned on Pei and accused him of being involved in the disappearance of the real fossils. He was then cast into a long period of inactivity and isolation, which continued after the end of the war. His connections to most of his colleagues were lost forever, at the same time that his pretext for staying on had been nullified.[39] None of the biographies of Pei mention the wartime period of his life; this part of his life is mentioned only in an account by Dominique Wang, who was, like Teilhard, a French national, not an enemy alien, and who had no compunction about staying in occupied Beijing, given that the Vichy government accepted the Japanese occupation.

Wang is one of a small number of foreigners who have written about their life under Japanese occupation, a life beset by suspicion, anxiety, shortages, and boredom.[40] Few of the millions of people who lived under the Japanese have ever tried to discuss, let alone to justify, what they did or did not do during the war. Their reticence is understandable and not culpable, but it is based on a sense of shame. The memories of the elderly people who survive from this period are best kept under cover and passed over in silence. These may be memories that will never be recovered; the people who hold them will not bring them to light or pass them on to the next generations.

Why Remember?

With all the sadness of the Resistance War, isn't it better to forget about this painful period of history, to look forward, to recognize the length of time that has passed since the war and to draw a line across it? Or perhaps it is better to be selective with memory, to block out the sad parts of the war and the period that preceded it and to look at the happy and glorious aspects only. At a talk I gave in Shanghai, a young graduate student asked me why I wanted to look at a topic as sad as the social suffering engendered by the war. She herself was working on Shanghai's nightlife in the 1930s, an exotic and racy topic that she loved and one that aroused great enthusiasm in other people. She had chosen to remember an exciting, vibrant past, not a bitter period of suffering and shame. This is not indifference to the past but a positive choice, one shared by the many people caught up in the vogue for Shanghai nostalgia.

But the past is not easy to order or control. Memory and commemoration take different paths. The emotive expression *wangji buliao,* mentioned above, haunts China. It conveys the weight of sadness occasioned by the memories of separation and death that are always there in any country that has gone through a brutal war. It is an expression of the grief and loss that linger in the shadows of the grandiloquent official commemoration of the glories of China's past.

The official memories are all about contemporary political legitimacy. A particularly vivid example is literally carved in stone in the form of the Museum of the History of Beijing. In the museum there is no mention of war, poverty, or suffering and no mention of the Japanese occupation.[41] The museum is only one of a great range of official-history projects, all designed to boost the status of the present government. Another is the new history of the Qing Dynasty, which is expected to prove conclusively, among other key issues, that various outlying regions have always been part of China.

In the academic world, officially sanctioned history is no longer de rigeur. Professional historians in China struggled in the 1950s and 1960s to prove a Marxist version of history. The new generation of historians work on objective history. Those who work on the war see it not simply as the key historical process that brought the Communist Party to power but also as a period of great complexity and confusion that abruptly brought to an end the old order and was the prologue to the disasters of the Mao era.

Mao Zedong did simplify the war when he "thanked" the Japanese prime minister, Tanaka Kakuei, in September 1972. "We must express our gratitude to Japan. If Japan didn't invade China, we could have never achieved the co-operation between the GMD (Guomindang) and the Communist Party. We could have never developed and eventually taken political power for ourselves. It is due to Japan's help that we are able to meet here in Beijing."[42]

The past is tied to the present by bloodlines, by powerful sinews of connectedness and belonging, and by a past – one that is both very long and quite short. The recent past has been restored over the past two decades, the old forward-looking Marxism discredited or quietly abandoned. Every region and community in China has, over the past two decades, rewritten its history and brought its own past back to life. The same concern with recreating the past is shown by families and individuals. "Lineage histories" *(zupu, jiapu)* have been recreated. Families have reasserted their own histories and brought the previously "forgotten" back into the light. Once it was a real danger to be connected to the famous of the past if the Communist Party had designated them as enemies; now it is a huge advantage. The relatives of GMD leaders are valued guests on the Mainland, especially in their native places. The descendants of General Bai Chongxi, a man once considered a public enemy, are welcomed with open arms in Guangxi, where he is now one of the local heroes.

Delving into the past, recalling memories, runs the risk of finding out about the bad times as well as the good times – and this means coming to know and having to come to terms with the Resistance War, the first of a cascade of tragic events that fell on China, to be followed by the Civil War, the Land Reform, the Great Leap Forward, the Hunger Years, and the Cultural Revolution. Some of this knowledge is objective and impersonal. But given the nature and extent of the war, and the number of people it affected, the knowledge is also deeply personal, and it is based on the memories of communities, families, and individuals whose lives were distorted, blighted, destroyed by the war – or transformed and glorified.

Notes

Epigraph: China at War 2, 1 (January 1939): 52-53.

1 For a longer discussion of the war and society, see Diana Lary, *The Chinese People at War* (New York: Cambridge University Press, 2010).

2 For example, 2001 was the seventieth anniversary of Jiuyiba 9-1-8, the loss of Manchuria; 2005 was the sixtieth anniversary of the end of the war; 2007 was the seventieth anniversary of Lugouqiao, which marked the start of all-out war, and of the Nanjing Massacre; and 2011 will be the eightieth anniversary of Jiuyiba and the seventieth anniversary of Pearl Harbor.

3 Bu Ping, *A Research Report on Japanese Use of Chemical Weapons during World War II* (Beijing: Institute of Modern History, Chinese Academy of Social Sciences, 2004).

4 One of my daughter Tanya's earliest memories is of her Russian grandmother forcing her to eat her vegetables by relating, with great drama, her own childhood memories of starvation in the Soviet Union.

5 Dr. Gabor Maté, talk in Vancouver, 27 March 2008. Dr. Maté was talking about the therapeutic adaptation and retelling of painful stories as a means to allow for healing.

6 Paul A. Cohen, *History in Three Keys: The Boxers as Event, Experience, and Myth* (New York: Columbia University Press, 1997).

7 There is one serious anachronism in this picture. The Maple Leaf flag shown in the picture was not used as the flag of Canada for another twenty years.

8 Chang Jui-te, "War and Commemoration," in *The Scars of War*, ed. Diana Lary and Stephen MacKinnon, 136-61 (Vancouver: UBC Press, 2001).

9 In 1985 there was a flurry of "approved" anti-Japanese demonstrations for the fortieth anniversary of the end of the war, but in 1987 the fiftieth anniversary of the start of the all-out invasion passed without notice. With a group of foreign diplomats and journalists, I spent part of 7 July 1987 at Lugouqiao to see what would happen. Nothing did.

10 *China Daily*, 27 September 2006.

11 *Taipei Times*, 25 January 2009, 3.

12 Rana Mitter, "China's Good War: Voices, Locations and Generations in the Interpretation of the War of Resistance to Japan," in *Ruptured Histories*, ed. Sheila Jaeger and Rana Mitter, 172-91 (Cambridge: Harvard University Press, 2007).

13 Iris Chang, *The Rape of Nanking: The Forgotten Holocaust of World War II* (New York: Basic Books, 1997).

14 Irene Nemirovsky, *Suite française* (New York: Knopf, 2006).

15 One massive project is Zhang Xianwen, *Nanjing da tusha* [The Nanjing Massacre], 30 vols. (Nanjing: Jiangsu renmin chubanshe, 2006).

16 See, for example, Zhongyang Beijingshi weiyuanhui, *Beijing kangzhan tushi* [An Illustrated History of Beijing during the Resistance War] (Beijing: Beijing chubanshe, 2005). This collection of pictures has almost nothing to do with the war. Nor does the collection of press photographs from the Mainichi Archives, which purport to picture Hong Kong during the war; see "The Battle for Hong Kong – Hong Kong under the Camera of the Japanese Army," Hong Kong Museum of History, 2002.

17 Leslie Cheng, quoted in *China at War* 13, 3 (September 1944): 34.

18 Xia Lumin, "Nanjing shouxiang muji jilu" [An eyewitness account of the surrender in Nanjing], in *Zhonghua wenshi ziliao wenku zhengzhi junshi pian* [Political and Military Section, China Materials on Literature and History] (Beijing: Zhonghua wenshi chubanshe, 1996), vol. 5, 926-27.

19 Arthur Waldron, "China's New Remembering of World War II: The Case of Zhang Zizhong," *Modern Asian Studies* 30, 4 (1996): 945-78.

20 Visit to Yongningzhen, Quanzhou, 16 May 2005, with Xing Tianying, local historian.

21 One of Chen Jian's most famous paintings before he painted the surrender ceremony was of the Communist victory in the Xuzhou Campaign of 1949.

22 My family was told about the increase in visitors to graves by the staff of the Commonwealth War Graves Commission when we went to visit my grandfather's grave near Arras. Howard Symmes was killed on Easter Monday, 1917, along with nearly 2,500 Canadians.

23 Paul Ho, interview by author, Los Angeles, 1 August 2006. Paul Ho is the father of David Ho, the virologist whose work on the AIDS virus and on the avian flu has made him world-celebrated.

24 I prefer the phrase "live with" to the word "collaboration," which is usually used in English to describe people who work with an army of occupation. There are Chinese terms to translate the active end of "collaboration," *tongdi* (consorting with the enemy) or *hanjian* (traitor), but neither of these is useful in talking about the large number of people who continued their lives under enemy occupation.

25 Wang Fangwen, *Xiamen KangRi zhanzheng dangan ziliao* [Archival Materials from Wartime Xiamen] (Xiamen: Xiamen daxue chubanshe, 1997), 598, 610-14.

26 Chen Jianhui, *Wurenqu* [Places Without People] (Beijing: Zhongyang biance chubanshe, 2005).

27 State Historical Archives, Zhang Zhizhong, "Hunan sheng zhengfu chenbao: Changsha dahuo caiqing" [Report of the Hunan provincial government: Damage from the Great Fire of Changsha], January 1939.

28 Some of the greatest wartime losses were of artifacts originally purloined from China in the late nineteenth and early twentieth centuries: frescoes from Dunhuang taken to Berlin and destroyed there in bombing raids; and the great collection of Yue drums, housed in the Museum für Ostasiatische Kunst and not seen since the war, although there are suggestions they may have made their way to the Soviet Union.

29 Geremie Barme, *An Artistic Exile: The Life of Feng Zikai (1898-1975)* (Berkeley: University of California Press, 2002).

30 *China Year Book, 1939* (Shanghai: Kelly and Walsh), 612-13.

31 Wong Siu-lun, *Emigrant Entrepreneurs: Shanghai Capitalists in Hong Kong* (Hong Kong: Oxford University Press, 1988).

32 According to an article published in 1998, Germany had by then paid almost US$62 billion in restitution to victims of Nazism and in reparations to Israel. See J. Kummer, "Wird die Wiedergutmachung ein Fass ohne Boden?" [Will reparations be a bottomless pit?], *Die Welt am Sonntag* [The World on Sunday], 4 October 1998, 54.

33 The dyke had been opened in 1938 to prevent the westward movement of Japanese armies, with terrible casualties. On the closing of the breach, see George Woodbridge, *UNRRA: The History of the United Nations Relief and Rehabilitation Administration* (New York: Columbia University Press, 1950), vol. 3, 371.

34 *China Daily,* 10 July 2004.

35 Interviews by author, Quanzhou, April 2006.

36 Wing Chung Ng, *The Chinese in Vancouver* (Vancouver: UBC Press, 1989).

37 Angus Calder, *The Myth of the Blitz* (London: Cape, 1969).

38 Robert Payne, *Chungking Diary* (London: Heinemann, 1945), 99.

39 Pierre Teilhard de Chardin, *Letters from a Traveller* (London: Collins, 1962); Dominique Wang, *Á Pékin avec Teilhard de Chardin* (Paris: Robert Lafont, 1981).

40 See also Wolfgang Franke, *Im Banne Chinas* [In the Jurisdiction of China] (Dortmund, Germany: Edition Cathay, 1997).

41 Diana Lary, "The Uses of the Past: History and Legitimacy," in *The Chinese Party State in the 21st Century,* ed. André Laliberté and Marc Lanteigne, 130-44 (London: Routledge, 2008).

42 Mao Zedong, quoted in Geremie Barme, "Mirrors of History: On a Sino-Japanese Moment and Some Antecedents," *Japan Focus,* 16 May 2005.

Glossary

Abe Tomoji	阿部知二	
An le dong	安乐洞	"Shelters of Well-being and Happiness"
An Lushan	安祿山	
Anson Chan	陳方安生	
Ba bu	八不	"The Eight Abstentions"
Bai Chongxi	白崇禧	
Bai Jiefu	白介夫	
baolu zhenshi	暴露真实	"expose reality"
baoyuyuan	保育院	"welfare-education-institution" or "children's home"
Baptist Church of Guangdong-Guangxi	兩廣浸信會總會	
bingbian	兵變	"troop mutinies"
bingtuan	兵团	"army-run agricultural settlements"
Cai E	蔡锷	
Cai Songpo	蔡松坡	
Cao Kun	曹錕	
Chang Shun	长顺	
Chen Haosu	陈昊苏	
Chen Heqin	陈鶴琴	
Chen Jian	陈坚	
Chen Lifu	陈立夫	
Cheng Dequan	承德全	
Cheng Yunxian	程允贤	
Chuanqian	川黔	
Chung Chi College	崇基書院	
Dai Sijie	戴思杰	
Daya Bay	大亞灣	
Deng Wenyi	邓文仪	

diyu de renjian	地狱的人间	"a hell on earth"
Dongchuan	东川	
Donglin	东林	
Dongshan	东山	
Du Mu	杜牧	
Duan Qirui	段祺瑞	
East River Guerrillas	東江游擊隊	
Ererba	二二八	"28 February 1947"
Fan Changjiang	范长江	
Fang Zhenwu	方振武	
fawei maqi	发威馬齐	"forward march"
fubing	府兵	"garrison militia"
Gu Ding	古丁	
Gu Hongming	辜鸿铭	
Guangdong Shengli Zhongqu Linshi Zhongxue	廣東省立中區臨時中學	"Guangdong Provincial Interim Middle School for the Central District"
Guangzhou Daxue	廣州大學	
Guangzhouwan (Zhanjiang)	廣州灣 (湛江)	
Guilin	桂林	
Guningtou	古宁头	
guojia de ertong	国家的儿童	"the nation's children"
guojia guke	过价孤客	"priceless orphan guest"
Guomin Daxue	國民大學	
hanjian	汉奸	"traitor"
He Peirong	何佩鎔	
He Yingqin	何应钦	
Ho Paul (He Jibu)	何基步	
Hon Chi-fun (Han Zhixun)	韓志勳	
Hong Kong Baptist College	香港浸會書院	
Hu Guang	胡广	
Hu Linyi	胡林翼	
Huang Zongxi	黄宗羲	
Huizhou	惠州	
Hung, K.W. (Hong Gaohuang)	洪高煌	

Jiang Baili	将百里	
jiaoyangyuan	教养院	"teach-nurture-institution" or "children's home"
jiapu	家谱	"lineage histories"
jiating jiaoyu	家庭教育	"family education"
Jin Chang	晋昌	
jin zhong bao guo	尽忠报国	"repay the nation with absolute loyalty"
Jinchuan	金川	
jingji baoguo	经济报国	"Dedicated Service to the National Economy"
Jinmen fangwei silingbu	金门防卫司令部	"Jinmen Defence Headquarters"
Jun Hui	君慧	
Kangle	康樂	
Kangsheng yuan	康生院	"Healthy Life Institutes"
Kengsheng yuan	坑生院	"Cheating Life Institutes"
Kishida Kunio	岸田國士	
Kitamura Kenjiro	北村谦三郎	
Kobayashi Hideo	小林秀雄	
Kunlunguan	昆仑关	
Kwan, Stanley (Guan Shiguang)	關士光	
Lam See-chai (Lin Siqi, David S.C. Lam)	林思齊	
Lam Tse-fung (Lin Zifeng)	林子豐	
Lan Ling	蓝苓	
Lao She	老舍	
Lee, W.L. (Li Yinglin)	李應林	
Li Hongzhang	李鸿章	
Li Xianglan	李香兰	
Li Yuanhong	黎元洪	
Li Zhiming	李志明	
Li Zonghuang	李宗黄	
Liang Qichao	梁启超	
Lin Zexu	林则徐	
Ling Ying (Lingying)	嶺英	
Lingnan University	嶺南大學	
Liu Cheng'en	劉承恩	

Liu Chi	刘峙	
Liu Yongyao	刘咏尧	
Liu Zuolong	劉佐龍	
Lo Sheung-fu (Lu Xiangfu)	盧湘父	
Lo Wai-luen (Lu Weiluan)	盧瑋鑾	
Lugou qiao	卢沟桥	"Marco Polo Bridge"
luoshi zhengze	落实政策	"policy of restitution"
Ma Shucheng	马书成	
Ma Zhongjun	马忠骏	
mafei gui	吗啡鬼	"morphine ghosts"
Manzhou wenyijia xiehui	满洲文艺家协会	"Manchukuo Writers and Artists Concordia"
Mei Niang	梅娘	
Meishuguan	美术馆	
Meixian	梅縣	
miaoxie zhenshi	描写真实	"describe reality"
minzu de ertong	民族的儿童	"children of the *minzu*"
minzu yishi	民族意识	"consciousness of the *minzu*"
mizui	迷醉	"intoxication"
Muto Tomio	武滕富男	
Nakamura Kōjirō	中村廣治郎	
Nanji	南极	
nantong	难童	"refugee child"
naoxiang	鬧餉	"clamour over troop pay"
New Asia College	新亞書院	
Pingle	平樂	
Pui Ching (Peizheng)	培正	
Pui To (Peidao)	培道	
Pui Ying (Peiying)	培英	
pumie anxing	扑灭暗行	"exterminate dark behaviour"
Qi Jiguang	戚继光	
Qian Dajun	钱大钧	
Qian Mu	錢穆	
Qianlong	乾隆	
qiaoxiang	侨乡	"emigrant communities"
Qingmuguan	青木关	
Qisanyao	七三一	"Unit 731"
quan ya	犬牙	"dog's teeth"

Qujiang (Shaoguan)	曲江 (韶關)	
Rikugun Shikan Gakkō	陸軍士官学校	"[Japanese] Imperial Army Officer Academy"
San Lang	三郎	
seishin kyōiku	精神教育	"[Japanese] spiritual education"
Shamshuipo	深水埗	
shang wu jingshen	尚武精神	"martial spirit"
Shangqingsi	上清寺	
Shantou	汕頭	
Shanxi	山西	
shehui youzhi rencai	社会优质人才	"socially high-quality people of talent"
Shen Zijiu	沈兹九	
Shengkang yuan	生抗院	"Raising Resistance Institutes"
Shijie Hongshizihui Beiquan Ciyouyuan	世界红十字会北泉慈幼院	"International Red Cross Beiquan Loving Children's Home"
Shou Shan	寿山	
si de qi suo	死得其所	"died a proper death"
Sin Yuk-ching (Xian Yuqing)	冼玉清	
sishu	私塾	"privately established schools"
Sun Chuanfang	孫傳芳	
Suzhou	苏州	
Szeto Wah (Situ Hua)	司徒華	
Tang Junyi	唐君毅	
Tang Yingwei	唐英伟	
Tao Xingzhi	陶行知	
tongdi	通敌	"consorting with the enemy"
Tongliang	铜梁	
United College of Hong Kong	香港聯合書院	
Valtorta, Henry	恩主教	
Vitasoy	維他奶	
Wah Yan College	華仁書院	
Wang Chang	王昶	
Wang Fu	王绂	
Wang Qiuying	王秋萤	

Wang Zhanyuan	王占元	
wangguo	亡国	"lost country"
wangji buliao	忘记不了	"they can never be forgotten"
Wanping	宛平	
weisuo	衛所	"guards"
Wen Tianxiang	文天祥	
Weng Mingzhi	翁明志	
Whampoa Military Academy	黄埔军校	
Wu Guangxin	吳光新	
Wu Guozhen	吴国桢	
Wu Peifu	吳佩孚	
Wuhan Chorus	武漢合唱團	
wurenqu	无人区	"no-man's land"
Wuzhou	梧州	
Xia Shoukang	夏壽康	
xianqi liangmu	贤妻良母	"good wife, wise mother"
Xiao Yaonan	蕭耀南	
Xiaosantong	小三通	"The Three Small Links"
Xinan Lianda	西南聯大	"Southwest United University"
Xingwu she	醒吾社	"I Awake Society"
Xiao Jun	萧军	
Xiquan	西泉	
xiu xi	休息	"rest from toil"
yan ji	烟妓	"opium prostitute"
yan ji	烟季	"smoke season"
yan ke	烟客	"opium addicts"
Yanjing bajing	燕京八景	"The Eight Scenes of Yanjing"
Yanshan bajing	燕山八景	"The Eight Scenes of Mount Yan"
Yao Nai	姚鼐	
yaoming de yanyin	要命的烟瘾	"life-killing addiction"
Ye Li	也丽	
yi bi dai jian	以笔代剑	"wielding pens as swords"
Yoshiko Yamaguchi	山口淑子	
youxia	游侠	"knight errant"
Yu Hanmou	余漢謀	
Yuan Shikai	袁世凱	
Yue Fei	岳飞	
Zeng Guofan	曾国藩	
Zeng Qi	增棋	

Zengjiayan	曾家岩	
Zhandi zhengwu	战地政务	"War Zone Administration"
zhandoucun	战斗村	"combat village"
Zhang Guochen	张国臣	
Zhang Henshui	张恨水	
Zhang Jingtang	張敬湯	
Zhang Jingyao	張敬堯	
Zhang Jiyou	张继有	
Zhang Juzheng	张居正	
Zhang Lizhun	张李准	
Zhang Zhidong	张之洞	
Zhang Zizhong	张自忠	
Zhangzong	张宗	
Zhao Hengdi	趙恆惕	
Zhao Shihui	赵师惠	
Zhaoping	昭平	
Zhenguang	真光	"True Light"
zhi bing	治兵	"governing soldiers"
zhidaoyuan	指导员	"commissar"
Zhoukoudian	周口店	
Zhu Muzhi	朱穆之	
Zhu Zhixin	朱执信	
zongbing yangmin	縱兵殃民	"condoned troops in their harm of the people"
zongfa shehui	宗法社会	"patriarchal society"
zuguo de haizimen	祖国的孩子们	"children of the ancestral homeland"
zupu	族谱	"lineage histories"

Selected Bibliography

Accinelli, Robert. *Crisis and Commitment: United States Policy toward Taiwan, 1950-1955*. Chapel Hill, NC: University of North Carolina Press, 1996.

Barnhart, Michael A. *Japan Prepares for Total War: The Search for Economic Security, 1919-41*. Ithaca, NY: Cornell University Press, 1987.

Baumler, Alan. *The Chinese and Opium under the Republic: Worse Than Floods and Wild Beasts*. New York: State University of New York Press, 2007.

Brook, Timothy, and Bob Tadashi Wakabayashi, eds. *Opium Regimes: China, Britain, and Japan, 1839-1952*. Berkeley: University of California Press, 2000.

Bu Ping. *A Research Report on Japanese Use of Chemical Weapons during World War II*. Beijing: Institute of Modern History, Chinese Academy of Social Sciences, 2004.

Chang, Gordon. *Friends and Enemies: The United States, China, and the Soviet Union, 1948-1972*. Stanford, CA: Stanford University Press, 1990.

Chang, Iris. *The Rape of Nanking: The Forgotten Holocaust of World War II*. New York: Basic Books, 1997.

Chen Jian. *Mao's China and the Cold War*. Chapel Hill, NC: University of North Carolina Press, 2001.

Chen Jiying. "Chongqing da hongzha" [The great bombing of Chongqing]. *Zhuanji wenxue* [Biographical Literature] 24, 4 (April 1974): 60-65.

Chiu, T.N. *The Port of Hong Kong*. Hong Kong: Hong Kong University Press, 1973.

Christensen, Thomas. *Useful Adversaries: Grand Strategy, Domestic Mobilization, and Sino-American Conflict, 1947-1958*. Princeton, NJ: Princeton University Press, 1996.

Cohen, Paul A. *History in Three Keys: The Boxers as Event, Experience, and Myth*. New York: Columbia University Press, 1997.

Datsyshen, V.G. *Russko-Kitaiskaya Voina: Manchzhuria, 1900* [Russo-Chinese War: Manchuria, 1900]. St. Petersburg: Tsytadel, 1996.

Duara, Prasenjit. *Rescuing History from the Nation*. Chicago: University of Chicago Press, 1995.

Fung, Edmund. *The Military Dimension of the Chinese Revolution*. Vancouver: UBC Press, 1980.

He Changling, comp. *Huangchao jingshi wenbian* [Statecraft Essays of the Imperial Court]. 1826. Reprint, Taibei: Wenhai chubanshe, 1972.

He Ziquan. *Aiguo yi shusheng: Bashiwu zishu* [A Patriotic Literatus: An Account of Myself at the Age of Eighty-Five]. Shanghai: Huadong shifan daxue chubanshe, 1997.

Hsiung Ping-Chen. *A Tender Voyage: Children and Childhood in Late Imperial China*. Stanford, CA: Stanford University Press, 2005.

Huang Zhenliang. *Huangpu Junxiao zhi Chengli ji qi Chuqi Fazhan* [The Founding of the Whampoa Military Academy and its Early Development]. Taibei: Zhengzhong Books, 1993.

Huang Zongxi quanji [Complete Works of Huang Zongxi]. 12 vols. Hangzhou: Zhejiang guji chubanshe, 1985.

Jennings, John M. *The Opium Empire: Japanese Imperialism and Drug Trafficking in Asia, 1895-1945*. London: Praeger, 1997.
Jiao Runming. *Jindai Dongbei shehui zhu wenti yanjiu* [Research on Various Questions in Modern Northeast Society]. Beijing: Zhongguo shehui kexue chubanshe, 2004.
Kinney, Anne Behnke, ed. *Chinese Views of Childhood*. Honolulu: University of Hawai'i Press, 1995.
Kuropatkin, A.N. *Russko-Yaponskaya Voina, 1904-1905: Itogi voiny* [Russo-Japanese War, 1904-1905: Results of war]. 1906. Reprint, St. Petersburg: Poligon, 2002.
Laliberté, André, and Marc Lanteigne, eds. *The Chinese Party State in the 21st Century*. London: Routledge, 2008.
Lary, Diana. *Warlord Soldier: Chinese Common Soldiers, 1911-1937*. Cambridge, UK: Cambridge University Press, 1985.
Lary, Diana, and Stephen MacKinnon, eds. *Scars of War: The Impact of Warfare on Modern China*. Vancouver: UBC Press, 2001.
Lattimore, Owen. *China Memoirs: Chiang Kai-shek and the War against Japan*. Tokyo: University of Tokyo Press, 1990.
Levenson, Arthur. *Confucian China and Its Modern Fate Trilogy*. Berkeley: University of California Press, 1958.
Li Ruiming. *Lingnan Daxue* [Lingnan University]. Hong Kong: Choumu Fazhan Weiyuanhui, 1997.
Lin Rusi. *Zhanshi Chongqing Fengguang* [The wartime Chongqing Scene]. Chongqing: Chongqing chubanshe, 1986.
Liu Xiaoyuan and C.X. George Wei, eds. *Exploring Nationalisms of China: Themes and Conflicts*. Westport, CT: Greenwood Press, 2002.
Lu Hongji. *Cong Rongshuxia dao Diannaoqian: Xianggang Jiaoyu de Gushi* [From under the Banyan Tree to in Front of the Computer: The Story of Hong Kong Education]. Hong Kong: Step Forward Press, 2003.
Lu Weiluan. *Xianggang de Youyu* [The Melancholy of Hong Kong]. Hong Kong: Wide Angle Press, 1985.
Luo Taiqi. *Chongqing da hongzha jishi* [A Record of the Great Bombing of Chongqing]. Huhehaote: Neimenggu renmin chubanshe, 1998.
Maeda Tetsuo. *Chongqing da hongzha* [The Great Bombing of Chongqing]. Trans. Li Hong and Huang Ying. Chengdu: Chengdu keji daxue chubanshe, 1990.
McCord, Edward A. *The Power of the Gun: The Emergence of Modern Chinese Warlordism*. Berkeley: University of California Press, 1993.
Miasnikov, V.S. *Russko-Kitaiskie dogovorno-pravovye akty (1689-1916)* [Sino-Russian Treaties and Legal Acts (1689-1916)]. Moscow: Pamyatniki Istoricheskoi Mysli, 2004.
Mitter, Rana. "Behind the Scenes at the Museum: Nationalism, History, and Memory in the Beijing War of Resistance Museum, 1987-1997." *China Quarterly* 161 (March 2000): 279-93.
Naquin, Susan. *Peking: Temples and City Life, 1400-1900*. Berkeley: University of California Press, 2000.
Ni Zhongwen, ed. *Beiyang junfa tongzhi Hubei shi* [History of Beiyang Warlord Rule of Hubei]. Wuhan: Hubei renmin chubanshe, 1989.
Paine, S.C.M. *Imperial Rivals: China, Russia and Their Disputed Frontier*. Armonk, NY: M.E. Sharpe, 1996.
Quested, R.K.I. *"Matey" Imperialists: The Tsarist Russians in Manchuria, 1895-1917*. Hong Kong: Centre of Asian Studies, University of Hong Kong, 1982.

Rose, Caroline. *Interpreting History in Sino-Japanese Relations: A Case Study in Political Decision-Making.* New York: Routledge, 1998.

Ross, Robert, and Jiang Changbin, eds. *Re-examining the Cold War: US-China Diplomacy, 1954-1973.* Cambridge, MA: Harvard University Asia Center, 2001.

Suleski, Ronald. *Civil Government in Warlord China: Tradition, Modernization, and Manchuria.* New York: Peter Lang, 2002.

Tong, Hollington K., ed. *The China Handbook, 1937-1945: A Comprehensive Survey of Major Developments in China in Eight Years of War.* New York: MacMillan, 1947.

Unger, Jonathan, ed. *Chinese Nationalism.* Armonk, NY: M.E. Sharpe, 1996.

Wang Lianbin. *Zhonghua wude tongshi* [A Comprehensive History of Chinese Military Virtue]. Beijing: Jiefangjun chubanshe, 1999.

Wei Rulin. *Zhongguo Junshi Sixiang Shi* [A History of Chinese Military Thought]. Taibei: HuaGang Chubanshe, 1979.

White, Theodore H., and Annalee Jacoby. *Thunder out of China.* New York: Sloane, 1961.

Williamsen, Marvin. "The Military Dimension, 1937-1941." In *China's Bitter Victory: The War with Japan, 1937-1945,* ed. James C. Hsiung and Steven Levine, 135-56. Armonk, NY: M.E. Sharpe, 1992.

Witte, Sergei Yulievich. *The Memoirs of Count Witte.* New York: Doubleday, Page, 1921.

Xie Benshu. *Cai E Zhuan* [The Biography of Cai E]. Tianjin: Tianjin renmin chubanshe, 1983.

Xu Naixiang and Huang Wanhua. *Zhongguo kangzhan shiqi lunxianqu wenxue shi* [History of the Literature of the Enemy-Occupied Territories during China's War of Resistance]. Fuzhou: Fujian jiaoyu chubanshe, 1995.

Yamamuro Shin'ichi, Joshua Fogel, ed. *Manchuria under Japanese Dominion.* Philadelphia: University of Pennsylvania Press, 2006.

Zhai Qiang. *The Dragon, the Lion and the Eagle: Chinese/British/American Relations, 1949-1958.* Kent, OH: Kent State University Press, 1994.

Zhang Xianwen. *Nanjing da tusha* [The Nanjing Massacre]. Nanjing: Jiangsu renmin chubanshe, 2006.

Zhang Zonghai. *Yuandong diqu shiji zhijiao de Zhong-E guanxi* [Sino-Russian Relations in the Far East at the Turn of the Century]. Haerbin: Heilongjiang renmin chubanshe, 2000.

Zheng Yangwen. *The Social Life of Opium.* Cambridge, UK: Cambridge University Press, 2006.

Zheng Yongnian. *Discovering Chinese Nationalisms in China.* Cambridge, UK: Cambridge University Press, 1999.

Zhongguo shehui kexueyuan jindai shi yanjiusuo, ed. *Sha-E qin Hua shi* [The History of Imperial Russian Aggression in China]. Vol. 4, pt. 1. Beijing: Renmin chubanshe, 1987.

Contributors

Timothy Brook is a professor of Chinese history at the University of British Columbia. He is the author of, among other books, *Collaboration: Japanese Agents and Local Elites in Wartime China* (2006).

Chang Jui-te is a professor in the History Department at Chinese Culture University and an adjunct researcher at Academia Sinica, Taiwan.

Blaine Chiasson is an associate professor of modern Chinese history and Sino-Russian relations at Wilfrid Laurier University. He is the author of *Administering the Colonizer: Manchuria's Russians under Chinese Rule, 1918-29* (2010).

James Flath is an associate professor of history at the University of Western Ontario. He is the author of *The Cult of Happiness: Nianhua, Art and History in Rural North China* (2004) and is currently completing a book on the architectural and monumental history of Confucius (Kong) Temple in Qufu, Shandong.

Colin Green is a faculty member of the History Department at Kwantlen Polytechnic University in Vancouver. His research interests include Chinese military history and comparative martial/warrior cultures. His current research focuses on the role of the military and militarization in modern China.

Bernard Hung-kay Luk (MA, PhD, MSEd) is an associate professor in the History Department of York University.

Diana Lary is a professor emerita of Chinese history at the University of British Columbia. She works on war and society and on migration.

Edward A. McCord is an associate professor of history and international affairs at George Washington University. He is the author of *The Power of the Gun: The Emergence of Modern Chinese Warlordism* (1993).

M. Colette Plum is an assistant professor in the History Department at Widener University. Her work focuses on Chinese orphans during the Anti-Japanese War, the history of children and childhood, and war and nationalism.

Norman Smith is an associate professor in the History Department at the University of Guelph. He is the author of *Resisting Manchukuo: Chinese Women Writers and the Japanese Occupation* (2008).

Michael Szonyi is a professor of Chinese history at Harvard University. His most recent book is *Cold War Island: Quemoy on the Front Line* (2008), and he is currently working on a social history of the military in the Ming Dynasty.

Alexander Woodside has taught modern Chinese and Southeast Asian history at Harvard University and at the University of British Columbia. His most recent book is *Lost Modernities: China, Vietnam, Korea and the Hazards of World History* (2006).

Victor Zatsepine is a research assistant professor in the History Department at the University of Hong Kong. A graduate of the University of British Columbia, he is preparing a manuscript on the history of the Sino-Russian frontier.

Index

Note: "(f)" after a page number indicates a figure